HONOLULU & O'AHU

KEVIN WHITTON

O'AHU

Kahuku Point

Kuilima Point

TURTLE BAY RESORT

Turtle Bay

Sunset Beach

'Ehukai Beach
BONZAI PIPELINE

Waimea

Waimea Bay

Waimea Beach

Pupukea-Paumalu Forest Reserve

WAIMEA VALLEY AUDUBON CENTER

Pu'u Ka'inapua'a 2,360ft

Kaua'i Channel

Hale'iwa Beach County Park

83

Mokule'ia Beach County Park

Hale'iwa

Waialua

99

Ka'ena Point

Pu'u Pueo ▲ 768ft

DILLINGHAM AIRFIELD

930

FARRINGTON HWY

KAMEHAMEHA

803

Whitmore Village

Ka'ena Point State Park

Kuaokala Forest Reserve

KAUKONAHUA HWY

KAMEHAMEHA HWY

Yokohama Bay

Wai'anae Range

Mokuleia Forest Reserve

Mt Ka'ala 4,020ft ▲

KUKANILOKO BIRTHING STONES ★

Wahiawa
★ WAHIAWA BOTANICAL GARDEN

93

Makua Keaau Forest Reserve

Schofield Barracks

Kea'au Beach County Park

▲ Puu Kalena 3,504ft

KANE'AKI HEIAU ★

Waianae Kai Forest Reserve

WHEELER AIR FORCE BASE

Makaha Beach

Makaha

Wai'anae Harbor

Wai'anae

LUALUALEI NAVAL RESERVATION

750

KUNIA RD

Mililani

H2

Poka'i Bay Beach County Park

Ma'ili

99

Lualualei

▲ Palikea 3,098ft

Patsy T. Mink Central Oahu Regional Park

Pearl City

PACIFIC

93

Nanakuli Forest Reserve

Waipahu

Nanakuli

Nanakuli Beach County Park

OCEAN

Makakilo

H1

Pearl Harbor

Kahe Point Beach County Park

FARRINGTON HWY

FORT WEAVER RD

USS MISSOURI ▲

KO'OLINA RESORT

Kapolei

'Ewa

US NAVAL RESERVATION

'Ewa Beach

BARBERS POINT NAVAL AIR STATION

Barbers Point

Mamala Bay

0   5 mi

0   5 km

JAMES CAMPBELL
WILDLIFE REFUGE

Kahuku

La'ie Bay

Malaekahana State
Recreation Area

La'ie

MORMON
TEMPLE   POLYNESIAN
CULTURAL CENTER

Hau'ula Beach
County Park

Hau'ula

Kaliuwa'a
Sacred Falls

Ko'olau Range

Punalu'u

Kaipapa'u
Forest
Reserve

Kahana Bay

Swanzy Beach
County Park

Ka'a'awa

Pu'u Pauao
2,565ft

Kahana Valley
State Park

83

Ewa Forest
Reserve

Kualoa
Park

Waikane

Pu'u Ka'aumakua
2,681ft

Waiahole

Waiahole
Forest
Reserve

Kahalu'u

He'eia Kea
Harbor

830

KANE'OHE MARINE
CORPS AIR STATION

Mokapu Point

Ewa Forest
Reserve

83

BYODO-IN
TEMPLE

Kane'ohe
Bay

Mokolea Rock

Keaiwa Heiau
State Recreation Area

KANE'KU HWY

Kailua
Bay

H3

Kane'ohe

HO'OMALUHIA
BOTANICAL
GARDEN

KAWAINUI
MARSH

'Aiea

H3

ULUPO
HEIAU

Kailua Beach
County Park

Kailua

Mokulua
Islands

ALOHA
STADIUM

Honolulu
Forest Reserve

63

KALUA RD

USS ARIZONA MEMORIAL

78

Ko'olau Range

PALI
TUNNELS

IKELIKE HWY

Lanikai
Beach

Bellows Field Beach
County Park

FORT
SHAFTER

Manoa
Falls

72

HICKAM
AFB

BISHOP
MUSEUM

PALI
LOOKOUT

PALI HWY

Waimanalo

Waimanalo Beach
County Park

H1

Round Top
Forest Reserve

Waimanalo
Beach

KALANIANA'OLE HWY

Makapu'u Beach
County Park

HONOLULU INT'L
AIRPORT

61

HONOLULU

UNIVERSITY OF
HAWAII AT MANOA

Koko
Crater

Makapu'u
Point

Sand Island State
Recreation Area

'IOLANI PALACE/
STATE CAPITOL

H1

'Aina
Haina

Hawaii
Kai

Sandy Beach
County Park

Waikiki

Le'ahi
761ft

Maunalua
Bay

72

Hanauma
Bay

Kaiwi Channel

Diamond
Head

Diamond Head
State Monument

Koko Head
642ft

PACIFIC

OCEAN

Kaua'i

Ni'ihau   O'ahu

Moloka'i

Lana'i   Maui

Kaho'olawe

Hawai'i

Contents

Honolulu & O'ahu

A ptly named the Gathering Place, Oʻahu is the heartbeat of the Hawaiian Islands. The island is home to one million residents, about 72 percent of the state's total population, and is, by far, the most culturally and socially diverse of the eight main Hawaiian Islands. It is a unique destination, where you can experience the comforts and convenience of city life alongside Hawaiʻi's natural beauty.

Oʻahu is home to Honolulu, the state's capital, main marine port, and its economic and political center. By Hawaiʻi standards, Oʻahu is a big city. You might be surprised to encounter rush-hour traffic, skyscrapers, and suburban sprawl on a small island in the middle of the Pacific. Pull back the curtain of Oʻahu's urban landscape and there is a natural backdrop that informs the ebb and flow of island style and tropical living.

Thanks to 112 miles of coastline, ocean activities are the cornerstone of daily life here. For pastimes from fishing and diving to surfing and kayaking, there are myriad beaches and locales that are just right for the day's activity and weather conditions. The powerful waves of the North Shore draw the world's best surfers.

Clockwise from top left: The leeward side is arid but beautiful; Iconic Diamond Head overlooks Waikiki; Lyon Arboretum; canoes on Magic Island; launching a kayak; view of Kaneʻohe.

The ledges off the leeward coast attract big game fish. Waikiki's calm water is the ultimate playground for the outrigger canoe. Kailua's fine, white sand rivals the most beautiful beaches in the world. Two mountain ranges span the island from north to south, with valleys, ridges, and cliffs offering lush open space and ample hiking.

From the Polynesian roots of its first settlers, the gift of surfing and the spirit of aloha to O'ahu's strategic role for the United States during World War II and its importance as an international agricultural hub, the breadth of the island's history and evolution is tangible from the leeward to the windward side. With no ethnic majority, O'ahu best exemplifies the state's east-meets-west, melting-pot culture through its exceptional regional cuisine. In Honolulu, historic buildings and art museums pepper the city's historic district, while Kaka'ako and Chinatown are the epicenter of O'ahu's local urban and fine art scene.

For every budget and every taste, for every tourist, visitor, backpacker, traveler, and globe-trotter seeking adventure or leisure, town or country, fine dining or food truck, mountains or beaches—O'ahu has it all.

Clockwise from top left: surfboards on Waikiki beach; plumeria flowers; Waikiki beach from rooftop; popular Hawaiian souvenirs.

Planning Your Trip

Where to Go

Waikiki

The quintessential O'ahu destination, Waikiki has beaches with **gentle surf** and **warm water,** great weather year-round, ocean activities, shopping, and dining, and is home to the majority of the hotels on the island. Waikiki's 2.5-mile strip of coastline is the stuff of legends. Not too far away is iconic landmark **Diamond Head.** The **Honolulu Zoo** and the **Waikiki Aquarium** exhibit local flora and fauna, while **Kapi'olani Park** is a beautiful green space in the city. Waikiki's bars and restaurants offer cuisine from around the world and a **lively bar scene** once the sun sets.

Honolulu

The **economic and political center** of the state, Honolulu is also the capital of Hawai'i. Best

known for its **historic district** and Chinatown, Honolulu stretches from Honolulu International Airport to the ridges and valleys of the Ko'olau Mountains. Here you'll find **stately government buildings** like the **Hawaii State Capitol** and historic sites such as **Washington Place** and **'Iolani Palace.** For museum enthusiasts, there's the **Hawai'i State Art Museum** and the **Honolulu Museum of Art.** Chinatown offers both **fine art galleries** and **Pacific Rim cuisine. Just west of Honolulu,** the **Pearl Harbor Historic Sites** are a must-see to grasp the history of Hawai'i and O'ahu and their role during World War II.

North Shore

O'ahu's rural North Shore is all about **beautiful beaches, diving, surfing,** and

plumeria in bloom at the Koko Crater Botanical Garden

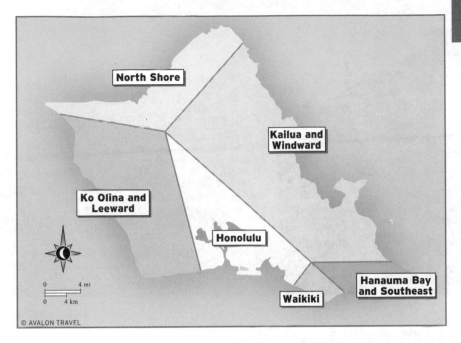

North Shore

Kailua and Windward

Ko Olina and Leeward

Honolulu

0   4 mi
0   4 km

Hanauma Bay and Southeast

Waikiki

© AVALON TRAVEL

snorkeling. The coastline is natural and unspoiled, and the beaches are the hallmark of **tropical bliss.** During winter, the North Shore attracts surfers from around the world to ride the **powerful, barreling waves** that break all along the coast. During summer, the ocean surface remains calm and flat, the perfect conditions for diving and snorkeling at **Three Tables** and **Sharks Cove.** Relax at **Waimea Bay,** take a walk through a botanical garden and historic cultural site at **Waimea Valley,** or drive up to Pupukea to visit the **Pu'u O Mahuka Heiau,** an ancient Hawaiian temple site.

Hanauma Bay and Southeast

The southeast shore spans affluent Kahala to Makapu'u. **Maunalua Bay** offers a variety of **water activities,** from Jet Skiing and wakeboarding to surfing and diving. **Sandy Beach** is the best bodysurfing beach on the island and **Hanauma Bay,** a protected marine preserve, offers the **best snorkeling** on the south shore.

Kailua and Windward

From Makapu'u north to La'ie is the windward coast, hugging the spectacular **verdant cliffs** of the Ko'olau Mountains. The windward side is known for its numerous **white-sand beaches. Kailua** has a beautiful crescent beach with fine sand and calm water, and the town is full of boutiques and restaurants. Hike up to **Maunawili Falls** or along the **Kawainui Marsh** to see **native Hawaiian waterfowl.** Take the leisurely drive up the coast to the quiet town of La'ie, home of the **Polynesian Cultural Center.**

Ko Olina and Leeward

The arid leeward side runs from the **Ko Olina Resort** to **Yokohama Bay** and **Ka'ena Point.** Ko Olina has fine dining, a golf course, and four artificial **seaside lagoons.** The predominantly calm conditions of the leeward beaches mean there is **great visibility** for snorkeling and diving. Hike out to **Ka'ena Point State Park,** the westernmost tip of the island, and look for **Hawaiian monk seals, spinner dolphins,** and **seabirds** nesting in the **sand dunes.**

Kaiwi Coast

Know Before You Go

When to Go

While the weather and water temperature remain comfortable all year long, O'ahu does experience a **high tourist season early December-late April.** There is another busy time, **June-August,** mirroring North America's summer. If you're planning on traveling in the high season, it's absolutely necessary to make reservations in advance. Don't stop making reservations once you arrive either—it's best to book ahead for outrigger canoe rides, catamaran trips, tours, spa services, nightly meals, and lu'au shows several days beforehand. If you can make it to O'ahu during the **off-season,** you'll find a little more room to breathe, and rates will be lower.

O'ahu experiences slight changes in temperature during summer and winter. **Summer temperatures** reach into the low 80s and the air is more humid, while **winter temperatures** dip down into the mid-70s, with slightly higher rainfall. Remember that weather here is localized; it can be pouring rain on the windward side and sunny in Waikiki. Be prepared for passing showers anytime.

The south shore sees waves during the summer, May-September, though they rarely exceed six feet on the face. If you're keen on catching the famous **winter surf** on the North Shore, you'll find that swells start arriving in October, with the peak of the big wave action happening November-February. The North Shore continues to have surf through April. If you plan on **swimming** in Waimea Bay or **snorkeling and diving** Sharks Cove and Turtle Bay, you'll want to visit the North Shore during the summer, when the ocean is flat and conditions are prime. North Pacific **humpback whales** visit nearshore waters December-April.

Transportation

Honolulu International Airport is the main airport for the island as well as the state. It has two terminals: one for interisland carriers and the other for national and international carriers. The easiest way to get from the airport to your hotel and around the island during your vacation is to rent a car. Prebook so that your vehicle is ready to go when you arrive. While certain areas might be a bit confusing to navigate at first—like downtown Honolulu or Waikiki—because of one-way streets or limited freeway on- and off-ramps, getting around on your own is straightforward. There are only two interstate freeways and a handful of highways. If you're heading in one direction, you'll inevitably get to the coast at some point. Be aware that if you stop for directions, people will most likely switch out compass directions for towns on that side of the island. For example, if you're in Honolulu and trying to get to the west side, people will say, "Go Ewa," referring to the Ewa plain, where many people reside, instead of, "Go west."

If you prefer to forgo reserving a **rental car** in advance, you can always pick one up at any point during your stay. There are a few rental kiosks in Waikiki. From the airport, taxis, limousines, and private shuttles offer flat rates from the airport to Waikiki hotels. You can pick up a taxi or limousine at any time, but private shuttles should be booked in advance. Many activities in other regions will offer free transportation to and from Waikiki, just be prepared to spend the day with a small tour group. **TheBus** is currently O'ahu's main form of public transportation (check out the TheBus' mobile app **DaBus**). It's not a viable means of getting from the airport to your hotel, there are luggage restrictions, but if you're traveling light, you'll find it doable to get from Waikiki to just about anywhere on the island, including Pearl Harbor, Hanauma Bay, and the North Shore. What you save in money, you'll definitely give up in time, however. **Uber** and **Lyft** ride-hailing services are also available on O'ahu.

Biking is not recommended as a mode of transportation. The roads are narrow, traffic is heavy, and bike lanes are almost nonexistent. Some areas are better suited for getting around by bike, like Kailua, but unless you're staying in Kailua, you'll need to drive to the locale anyway.

state flag

Best of O'ahu in Seven Days

The average stay on O'ahu is about seven days. With sights and activities on all sides of the island, planning your days will help you take full advantage of your holiday. Let this suggested itinerary to the must-see locales and establishments be a jumping-off point for your travels. If you need more beach days during your stay, by all means, pencil yourself in for all you can handle.

Day 1

For most visitors, Waikiki will be home base. Spend the first day getting acclimated to the weather and acquainted with the surroundings right outside your hotel. Follow the **Historic Waikiki Trail** around town, a self-guided tour describing the history of the area.

Walk the beach path, stop at **Waikiki Beach** for a swim, stroll down **Kalakaua Avenue** and enjoy *pau hana* (happy hour) at **The Shore Bird, The Beach Bar** at the Moana Surfrider, or on the upstairs deck at **Tiki's.**

After freshening up back at the hotel, head out for dinner at the **Hau Tree Lanai, Sansei Seafood,** or **Top of Waikiki.**

Day 2

Have breakfast in Waikiki at **Kai Market** while rush-hour traffic subsides, then head to **Honolulu's historic district.** Start at the **Hawai'i State Capitol,** then go next door and tour **'Iolani Palace.** Visit the **Kamehameha I Statue, Kawaiha'o Church,** and the **Mission Houses Museum.**

Next, head to **Ala Moana Center** for lunch and shopping. Finish up the day in **Chinatown.** Stroll through fine art galleries like **The ARTS at Marks Garage** and the **Pegge Hopper** gallery. For Chinatown s premier Chinese restaurant, visit **Little Village Noodle House.** If you're looking for a sampling of Pacific Rim cuisine, stop by the **Maunakea Marketplace Food Court.** For amazing ramen try **Lucky Belly.**

If you want to keep the party rolling, head into an Irish pub like **J.J. Dolan's** or **Murphy's.**

Explore Chinatown.

'Iolani Palace

If your vacation coincides with the first Friday of the month, save Honolulu for that day and be a part of Chinatown's lively **First Friday** celebration.

Day 3

Head to the southeast and windward shores, where there are a lot of ocean-related activities to consider. Start out by snorkeling **Hanauma Bay.** You'll need to get there before 9am to find a parking spot. If you prefer adventure sports, dive, Jet Ski, wakeboard, parasail, or deep-sea fish in **Maunalua Bay.**

If you prefer hiking, spend the morning on the 1,000-plus steps of the **Koko Crater Trail,** walking through the **Koko Crater Botanical Garden,** or making your way to the lighthouse at **Makapuʻu Point,** a great vantage point for whale-watching.

Next, check out the pounding shore break at **Sandy Beach,** then drive up to **Kailua** for a relaxing afternoon. Have lunch at **Kalapawai Market** or **Buzz's,** then retreat to the beach. Bask on the fine white sand or rent a kayak and paddle out to **Flat Island** or all the way to the North Shore

Mokulua Islands. Alternatively, you can head north to paddle in **Kahana Bay** and visit the ancient fishponds.

If you have any steam left, take the meandering drive up **Kamehameha Highway** to the town of **Laʻie.** You can grab dinner and a show at the **Polynesian Cultural Center** or choose one of the small local eateries along the coast. For the brave of heart, beeline for the **Laʻie Point State Wayside** for cliff-jumping and magnificent views of the windward coast.

Day 4

Strike out early and be at the front of the line to see the **Pearl Harbor Historic Sites.** There are several memorials, museums, and sites to visit, so you can tailor your experience to your liking.

Golfers should head to the ʻEwa Plain to play one of several challenging courses. Or continue past ʻEwa out to **Ko Olina,** where you can play golf, relax in the seaside lagoons, and eat at one of the restaurants famous for Hawaiʻi regional cuisine like **Roy's** or **Monkey Pod Kitchen.**

If hiking is more your style, get up early and drive out to **Yokohama Bay** on the leeward side.

Take a catamaran cruise off the Waikiki coast.

Known as the **Ka'ena Point State Park,** the natural reserve at the western tip of the island can't be missed for its rugged beauty and wildlife. On your way back, surf or relax at **Makaha Beach,** have dinner in Ko Olina, and watch the sunset from **Paradise Cove.**

Day 5

After being out and about for a few days, recalibrate by staying near home and take in the sights around Waikiki. Go up Diamond Head first thing in the morning and then have lunch at **Bogart's** or **Diamond Head Cove Health Bar.** Check out the **Diamond Head** beaches or head back across **Kapi'olani Park** to the **Honolulu Zoo** or the **Waikiki Aquarium.**

For live music during happy hour, head to **Duke's Waikiki** and hang out in the **Barefoot Bar.** Put in your reservation for dinner and enjoy a beachside meal watching the sunset over Waikiki Beach. If you're there on a Sunday, be a part of the festivities of **Duke's on Sunday** on the lanai.

Day 6

It's time to be North Shore bound. For shopping, sightseeing, and dining, stop in **Historic Hale'iwa Town.** Visit the art galleries and get shave ice at **Matsumoto's.**

Kayak or stand-up paddle the **'Anahulu River,** then head north and explore **Waimea Bay, Pipeline,** and **Sunset Beach** for snorkeling in the summertime and wave-watching in the winter. During summer, snorkeling and diving at **Three Tables** and **Sharks Cove** are a must.

Continue north to **Turtle Bay Resort** for sunset drinks at the outdoor, oceanside **Hang Ten Bar & Grill,** then venture over to **Lei Lei's** for dinner on one of Turtle Bay's famous greens. If you're operating on a budget, skip Turtle Bay and drive to **Kahuku Superette** for some of the best *poke* on the island.

To add some adventure, **shark dive** from Hale'iwa Harbor, or take a glider ride or skydive in **Mokule'ia.** Catch a seaside polo match at **Hawai'i Polo** on Sunday afternoons during the summer. If your plans allow for dinner in Hale'iwa, don't miss **Hale'iwa Joe's.**

Day 7

Soak up the sun and take advantage of all the ocean activities Waikiki has to offer. Stop by and chat with one of the **beachboys** about surfing or stand-up paddle lessons and surf iconic Waikiki surf breaks **Queen's** and **Canoes**. Take a ride and surf an outrigger canoe, snorkel in the **Waikiki Marine Life Conservation District**, hydrate under an umbrella on the beach, and take a **catamaran cruise** off the Waikiki coast for a fresh perspective. If there's still daylight left, paddle back out for a second session.

Best Beaches

Tropical island destinations are often defined by the quality of their beaches. Luckily for Oʻahu, the beaches are beautiful and varied from coast to coast. Different beaches have different types of sand, and combined with what's on the ocean floor, the water color glistens from deep blue to sparkling turquoise. Whether you're looking for recreation, isolation, or convenience, there's a beach that's just right for you.

Waikiki Beach and Kuhio Beach Park (page 40 and 41)

Side by side in the middle of Waikiki's legendary shoreline, these two beaches present the essence of Waikiki: white sand framed by Diamond Head, historic hotels, and the sparkling blue Pacific. Queen's and Canoes surf breaks are just off the shore, catamarans and outrigger canoes line the beach, and sunbathers stretch out in all directions.

Waimea Bay Beach Park (page 122)

This marine protected area framed by rocks and boulders on both sides sees pods of spinner dolphins gracing the bay in the summer when the water is calm and perfect for swimming and snorkeling. Don't forget to leap off Jump Rock.

Makapu'u Beach Park

Lyon Arboretum trail

Just as O'ahu shelters an underwater paradise, the majestic mountains and forests hold treasures, too, and these are best seen by getting out and hiking the ridges and valleys. As you gain elevation, you'll see more of O'ahu's endangered and native trees and shrubs, and hear the calls of the forest birds.

Diamond Head Summit Trail (page 50) This hike inside a volcanic cinder cone offers a unique perspective of O'ahu's geology and its military past. The summit offers sweeping views of the south shore.

Lyon Arboretum Trails (page 91) Shaded, damp, and devoid of the crowds that flock to nearby Manoa Falls Trail, the vast network of trails at Lyon Arboretum introduces hikers to hundreds of different tropical plants and trees.

Wa'ahila Ridge Trail (page 92) With views of Manoa Valley, Palolo Valley, and the south shore, this ridge trail terminates at a massive peak at the back of Manoa Valley, Mount Olympus. At nearly 2,500 feet in elevation, you'll find native vegetation, including the slow-growing *hapu'u* fern.

Ka'ena Point (page 132) This hot and dry hike to Ka'ena Point takes you along a rocky and rutted dirt road skirting a rugged and volcanic coastline

with surf pummeling the cliffs. This natural preserve, home to nesting seabirds, native plants, and Hawaiian monk seals, will wow you.

Kuli'ou'ou Ridge and Valley Trails (page 160) These valley and ridge trails reach a summit just above 2,000 feet and offer stunning views of Waimanalo and the windward coast, panning all the way to Diamond Head across Maunalua Bay.

Koko Crater Trail (page 160) Far from a typical hike through the woods, this trail follows an old military railroad bed straight up the southern flank of a volcano to its precipice. With over 1,000 stairs hewn from railroad ties, this hike offers breathtaking summit views, a great workout, and a bit of military history.

Kawainui Marsh (page 190) A paved walking and bike trail that traverses Kawainui Marsh provides a great opportunity to see native Hawaiian waterfowl in one of the few remaining wetland habitats on O'ahu.

Maunawili Falls (page 190) A popular, short hike just outside of Kailua in the shadow of Olomana, the trail follows Maunawili Stream to cascading Maunawili Falls, where there's a deep swimming pool.

Sunset Beach (page 124)

This is the quintessential North Shore beach. The coarse sand made of tiny bits of coral and shells stretches out in both directions and is thick with tropical vegetation along the dune. Walk north to the point for an unspoiled view of the Wai'anae Mountains.

Sandy Beach Park (page 154)

Set along the dramatic volcanic southeast coast next to Halona Blowhole, Sandy Beach is a popular sunbathing locale with an infamous pounding shore break and the best bodysurfing on the island.

Makapu'u Beach Park (page 155)

On the southeastern tip of the island, Makapu'u offers a fine white-sand beach and amazing views of the predominant headland, Ko'olau cliffs, and offshore islands. There is great snorkeling along the headland, tidepools, and whale-watching during the winter.

Kailua Beach Park (page 179)

Fine white sand gently arcing up the coast for four miles; crystalline water with a sandy bottom that's perfect for swimming, stand-up paddling, and kayaking; a grassy and shady park; rental outfitters and dining across the street—what isn't to love about Kailua Beach Park?

Kahana Bay Beach Park (page 183)

Set in a deep bay, the natural scenery here is breathtaking, the water is shallow and calm, and the peace and tranquility are tangible. It's perfect for families looking to escape the crowds.

Moku Nui, Mokulua Islands (page 187)

Sometimes it's not about size, but perspective. This small sandy beach is on the leeward side of Moku Nui, the larger of the Mokulua Islands, just a quick kayak jaunt off the Lanikai shoreline. Witness amazing views of mainland O'ahu, spanning Makapu'u to Kane'ohe, from a vantage point not many others will see.

Sandy Beach Park draws body surfers and sun bathers.

Makaha Beach Park (page 212)

A classic venue on the leeward coast for taking in the sunset, Makaha has a wide beach, great waves, and is soaked in sun. When the water is calm, the area has a reef for snorkelers to explore and is great for swimming.

Best Snorkeling and Diving

Head to the right locales and you'll find that O'ahu's reefs teem with marine life: reef fish, green sea turtles, corals, rays, sharks, octopus, and many other endangered and endemic sea creatures only found in Hawaiian waters. Diving the wrecks, ledges, lava tubes, and deepwater rock formations only adds to the diversity of ocean life. Remember, snorkeling and diving are contingent on the right ocean conditions—namely calm, clear water. If one side of the island has waves or is windy, the other side might be calm and flat, just right to get in the water and explore.

Waikiki Marine Life Conservation District (page 41)

This marine protected area located along Queens Surf Beach offers the best snorkeling in Waikiki. Because the reef-covered area is protected, sealife thrives there, so you're sure to see an abundance of fish. It's also a favorite area for the famed *humuhumunukunukuapua'a*, so keep an eye out.

Three Tables (page 122)

Part of the Pupukea-Waimea Marine Life Conservation District, this area consists of three flat reef outcroppings that barely break the water's surface just 50 feet off the beach, and is a destination that snorkelers delight in exploring. The area teems with endemic marine life like puffer fish and reef squid.

Sharks Cove (page 129)

The premier shore diving area on the North

China Walls

Hanauma Bay has the best snorkeling on the South Shore.

Waimanalo has crystal clear water.

Shore, Sharks Cove has interesting underwater topography like lava tubes, caverns, and walls. Since it is part of the Pupukea-Waimea Marine Life Conservation District, marine life is abundant here, and you're sure to see creatures like the spotted eagle ray, wrasse, and unicorn fish.

Waimea Bay (page 129)

During summer when the waves are flat, Waimea Bay has perfect conditions for snorkeling. Rock outcroppings at both ends of the bay attract marine life and pods of spinner dolphins frequent these waters.

Hanauma Bay Nature Preserve Park (page 150)

This popular marine conservation area on the southeastern corner of the island is set in an arid cinder cone, creating a protected environment where hundreds of marine species thrive. Snorkel beyond the inner fingers of reef to escape the crowd.

China Walls (page 159)

A vertical wall dropping 75 feet off the southern side of Koko Head offers caves and ledges for divers to explore, and is a favorite area for endangered Hawaiian monk seals. During whale season, whale song can be heard echoing off the wall.

Waimanalo Beach Park (page 179)

With a mix of sand, rock, and reef bottom as a great backdrop for marine life, the shallow and beautiful waters along windward Waimanalo beckon snorkelers to simply pull off the road and get in the water.

Best Surfing

The sport of surfing was born in Hawai'i. Legendary Olympic gold-medal swimmer, original beachboy, and ambassador of aloha Duke Kahanamoku introduced surfing to the world on the sands of Waikiki and through traveling exhibitions in California and Australia. Be a part of that legacy and get on a board during your stay on O'ahu. Whether it's your first time or you're a lifelong surfer, there is year-round surf and the perfect wave to suit your skill level.

Beginners

POPULARS AND PARADISE (PAGE 43)

Once you're comfortable with your feet in the wax, paddle out to Populars and Paradise for longer rides on Waikiki's outer reefs.

CANOES (PAGE 44)

No stay in Waikiki is complete without surfing famous Canoes surf break. A slow rolling wave, it's fun whether it's your first time or you can hang ten. Surfing Canoes is being part of the history of Waikiki.

CHUN'S REEF (PAGE 126)

A beautiful right breaking point on the North Shore, the slow-breaking wave is perfect for beginners and even has small waves occasionally during the summertime.

TURTLE BAY (PAGE 127)

Slow, rolling white-water breaks along the rugged point at Turtle Bay. With board rental and surf instructors on-site, it's a great place to give surfing a try and have your friends or family snap some pictures from the cliff.

Experts

ALA MOANA BOWLS (PAGE 43)

Some of the best waves on the south shore are along a strip of reef in front of the Ala Moana Small Boat Harbor. Ala Moana Bowls is a long,

The Banzai Pipeline is for experts only.

Learn about the culture and history of O'ahu to understand its people and place in the modern world. O'ahu's relatively short history has been tumultuous and prosperous, war-torn yet rich, as evident in its museums, historic places, and artifacts, each with a compelling story to tell.

'Iolani Palace: The only royal residence in the United States, this grand and regal palace was the official home of the monarch of the Hawaiian kingdom (page 74).

Hawaii State Art Museum: Located in the No. 1 Capitol Building In the historic district of Honolulu, this fine art museum has four galleries featuring the finest collection of works by Hawaiian artists, including sculpture (page 76).

Hawaii State Art Museum

Mission Houses Museum: This National Historic Landmark was the first wooden structure on O'ahu. The museum includes two main structures as well as the first printing house in the islands (page 77).

Historic Chinatown: With their vibrant mix of cuisine, culture, art, coffee galleries, and nightclubs, Chinatown's historic buildings are home to a curious mix of food and wares (page 77).

Honolulu Museum of Art: O'ahu's premier fine art museum has amassed a collection including 50,000 pieces spanning 5,000 years, featuring Asian, African, American, European, and Oceanic artifacts. There is also a theater, and its sister museum, Spalding House in Makiki Heights, holds a modern art collection (page 78).

Bishop Museum: the foremost natural history museum in the Pacific and the largest museum in the state of Hawai'I, it has seasonal rotating exhibits and an extensive collection of Hawaiian artifacts and cultural artifacts from peoples across the Pacific (page 83).

Pearl Harbor Historic Sites: One of the most heavily visited areas in Hawai'i, the Pearl Harbor Historic Sites has free tours of the USS *Arizona* Memorial and paid tours of the USS *Bowfin* Submarine Museum and Park, the Battleship *Missouri,* and the Pacific Aviation Museum. The historic sites are part of the World War II Valor in the Pacific National Monument (page 84).

Pu'u O Mahuka Heiau: Overlooking Waimea Bay, this is the largest *heiau* on the island. The two-acre site has three- to six-foot stacked stone walls for three original enclosures and was connected to the thriving community that once inhabited Waimea Valley (page 119).

OUTDOOR ADVENTURES

Celebrate your nuptials outdoors with a **horse-back trail ride** (page 133), a visit to the most raw and beautiful natural preserve on the island at **Ka'ena Point State Park** (page 207), and sunset **catamaran cruise** (page 49).

SCENIC STROLLS

Walk the beautiful **Kailua Beach Park** (page 179) at sunrise and surround yourself with colorful blossoms at the **Koko Crater Botanical Garden** (page 151).

COUPLES MASSAGE

Share the experience of pampering and deep relaxation spa treatments for two at the **Kahala Spa** (page 163), the pinnacle of luxury or at **Spa Luana** (page 135), in a romantic outdoor cabana.

beautiful Kailua Beach Park

SUNSET COCKTAILS AND FINE DINING

Watching the sun escape below the horizon at the **Hang Ten Bar & Grill** (page 137). Enjoy the romantic view at **Hau Tree Lanai** (page 59). Soak up the elegant atmosphere at Waikiki's **Nobu** (page 61). Feast on exquisite seafood at **Azure** in Waikiki's Royal Hawaiian (page 60).

---

fast left that local surfers keep under lock and key, coveting every barrel.

LANIAKEA (PAGE 125)

Just past Hale'iwa town on the North Shore, Laniakea is a long, right point break. On the right swell, fast, perfect waves grind down the point. Lani's, as it's often called, is surfable up to 20 feet on the face.

BANZAI PIPELINE (PAGE 126)

One of the most dangerous and deadliest waves on the planet, the Banzai Pipeline is a heavy, barreling left that detonates over shallow reefs and offers some of the best and biggest barrels in the world.

SUNSET BEACH (PAGE 127)

This powerful and unforgiving wave, no matter what size, is famous for separating the experts from the herd. The right boards, the right frame of mind, and stamina are a must to paddle out and surf the heaving walls of water that break along Sunset Beach.

MAKAHA (PAGE 213)

Makaha is a predominant right-hand point break, famous for its powerful surf, the characters in the lineup, and its backwash close to shore. Makaha breaks nearly all year long, on south, west, and north swells, and sees gigantic waves during the winter; it's the biggest surfable break on the leeward side.

Family Fun

It takes activities of a more hands-on, interactive nature to keep the kids excited and entertained. When traveling with the family, consider these sights and establishments to create the best experience for everyone of every age.

Honolulu Zoo (page 35)

With plants and animals emphasizing tropical ecosystems and the African Savannah, the Honolulu Zoo is a must do for families. From large mammals to small reptiles and a host of birds, the zoo also offers a children's interactive petting zoo and a massive jungle gym.

Waikiki Aquarium (page 36)

Grab the family and escape the sun and heat at the Waikiki Aquarium. Get up close and personal with marine life that calls the Pacific region home. Get to know what's swimming around Oʻahu, visit the monk seals, and get your hands wet petting some of the reef's smaller sea creatures.

Sans Souci Beach (page 42)

Just outside of Waikiki proper, this swath of sandy beach is perfect for families with small children. An outer reef blocks waves from reaching the shore, and the water is clear, calm, and shallow, with the best conditions for kids at low tide.

Sea Life Park (page 152)

By Makapuʻu, Sea Life Park is an aquatic park specializing in education and interaction with sea life. At the park you can swim with dolphins and even take a dorsal fin ride. Guests can also swim with sharks, sea lions, or rays. There are even child-oriented animal encounters.

residents of the Honolulu Zoo

the Waikiki Aquarium

Kualoa Ranch (page 177)

A real outdoor adventure, this working 4,000-acre ranch offers horseback rides, ATV rides, Jeep tours, kayak tours, and tours of rainforests and fishponds. It also has educational experiences like hula instruction.

Aston Hotels (page 224)

Aston Hotels & Resorts has several hotels and condominiums in Waikiki that are perfect for families, like the Aston at the Waikiki Banyan and the Aston Waikiki Beach Tower. They offer multiple-bedroom condominiums with full kitchens at reasonable rates.

Waikiki

Look for ★ to find recommended
sights, activities, dining, and lodging.

Highlights

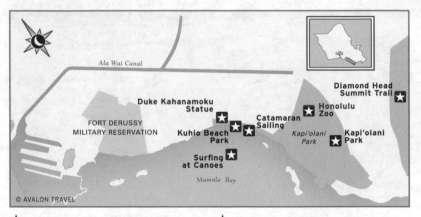

© AVALON TRAVEL

★ **Honolulu Zoo:** The Honolulu Zoo showcases the African savannah, the Asian and American tropical forests, and the Pacific Islands in a great family outing (page 35).

★ **Kapi'olani Park:** It's Waikiki's outdoor gym. Play tennis, go for a run, stretch out with beachside yoga, or just throw down a blanket and enjoy lunch under flowering canopy trees (page 37).

★ **Duke Kahanamoku Statue:** Pay homage to the original ambassador of aloha, the man who grew up in Waikiki and brought the sport of surfing to the world (page 38).

★ **Kuhio Beach Park:** Relax under a palm tree, lay out on the beach, rent a surfboard, or take a canoe or catamaran ride (page 41).

★ **Surfing at Canoes:** No stay in Waikiki is complete without surfing, whether it's your first time getting your feet on the wax or you've been surfing your entire life. Become a part of the legacy (page 44).

★ **Catamaran Sailing:** Take a break from the crowds on the beach and get out on the open water. The sunset sails on the bigger boats offer a particularly good time (page 49).

★ **Diamond Head Summit Trail:** Combine O'ahu's unique volcanic geography, military history, and a short hike that will get your heart pumping. It's also home to the best views in Waikiki (page 50).

W hite-sand beaches, swaying palm trees, surfers, stand-up paddle surfers, and outrigger canoes share the lineup at the famous Canoes and Queen's surfing breaks.

Swimmers and sunbathers grace the shoreline for a refreshing dip—with an average daytime high temperature in the low 80s and water temperatures in the mid-70s. It's no wonder Waikiki has long been a coveted destination for world travelers seeking the enchantment of a tropical oasis. But make no mistake, while the surf and sun rarely disappoint, you'll be hard pressed to find peace, solitude, or tranquility on Waikiki's narrow beaches, busy avenues, or in its packed restaurants.

A scant 2.5 miles of shoreline on the South Shore between Diamond Head and the Ala Wai Small Boat Harbor, Waikiki pulses year-round, with the footsteps of visitors from all over the world marching up and down Kalakaua and Kuhio Avenues and sinking their toes in the sand. Lined with high-rise hotels, condominiums, and apartment buildings, Waikiki is a complete destination, a beach-side hamlet with all the amenities of city life within its mesmerizing embrace: shopping, dining, nightlife, health, fitness, spas, and,

of course, ocean sports and activities. The Honolulu Zoo and the Waikiki Aquarium are a must for families. Kapi'olani Park is a runner's delight, and tai chi and yoga are commonplace under the park's flowering canopy trees.

As cliché as it might sound, make sure to take a surf lesson or go on a canoe ride with a beachboy to become a part of a Waikiki tradition that harks back a century to the father of modern-day surfing and the original ambassador of aloha, Duke Kahanamoku. Across Waikiki, *pau hana* (happy hour) is celebrated every day with food and drink specials, and live music, to welcome the sunset. Once the sun goes down, Waikiki takes on a whole new tempo. The sidewalks of Kalakaua Avenue teem with street performers and swell with curious onlookers, and the clubs and bars welcome patrons till four in the morning.

Waikiki is not without its blemishes, and the town can get rough and rowdy in the cool hours of early morning. Prostitution is illegal, but tolerated on Kuhio Avenue; homelessness

Waikiki Northwest

To H-1

McCULLY ST

KALAKAUA AVE

KAPI'OLANI BLVD

ATKINSON DR

HAWAIIAN
CONVENTION
CENTER

HIDEAWAY
BAR

IRISH ROSE
SALOON

ENA RD

NIU ST

PAU ST

DOUBLETREE
ALANA

ALA MOANA
HOTEL

FORT

YMCA CENTRAL
BRANCH

DERUSSY

P

HOBRON LN

AQUA PALMS

ALA MOANA BLVD

KALIA RD

AQUA
MARINA

RAMADA
PLAZA

EQUUS

DISCOVERY BAY

GRAND
WAIKIKIAN

RAINBOW DR

HAWAII
PRINCE

HOLOMOANA

MODERN HONOLULU
ADDICTIONS

ILIKAI

SARENTO'S

KAHANAMOKU ST

PAOA PL

HALE KOA

Ala Wai

HILTON
HAWAIIAN
VILLAGE

Yacht

Duke
Kahanamoku
Lagoon

Harbor

Duke
Kahanamoku
Beach

0   200 yds

0   200 m

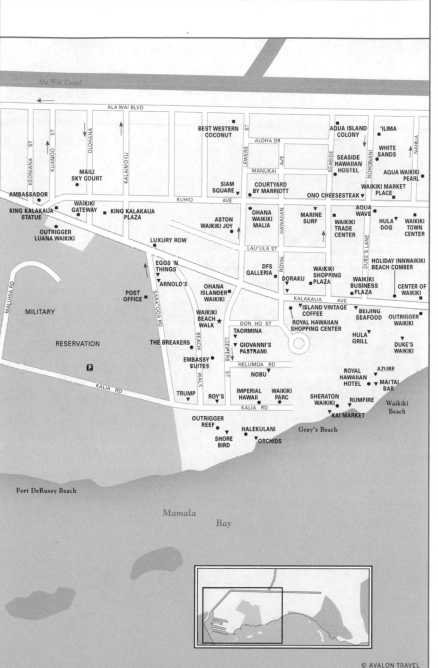

Ala Wai Canal

ALA WAI BLVD

KEONIANA ST
KUAMOO ST
OLOHANA
KALAIMOKU
AMBASSADOR
MAILI SKY COURT
BEST WESTERN COCONUT
ALOHA DR
LEWERS ST
MANUKAI
AVE
SIAM SQUARE
COURTYARD BY MARRIOTT
KUHIO AVE
AQUA ISLAND COLONY
SEASIDE ST
'ILIMA
WHITE SANDS
NOHONANI
NAHUA
SEASIDE HAWAIIAN HOSTEL
AQUA WAIKIKI PEARL
WAIKIKI MARKET PLACE
ONO CHEESESTEAK

KING KALAKAUA STATUE
WAIKIKI GATEWAY
KING KALAKAUA PLAZA
ASTON WAIKIKI JOY
OHANA WAIKIKI MALIA
HAWAIIAN
MARINE SURF
AQUA WAVE
WAIKIKI TRADE CENTER
HULA DOG
WAIKIKI TOWN CENTER
OUTRIGGER LUANA WAIKIKI
LUXURY ROW
LAU'ULA ST
ROYAL
DUKE'S LANE

EGGS 'N THINGS
DFS GALLERIA
DORAKU
WAIKIKI SHOPPING PLAZA
HOLIDAY INN WAIKIKI BEACH COMBER
ARNOLD'S
POST OFFICE
SARATOGA RD
OHANA ISLANDER WAIKIKI
WAIKIKI BUSINESS PLAZA
CENTER OF WAIKIKI

MALUHIA RD
KALAKAUA AVE
ISLAND VINTAGE COFFEE
BEIJING SEAFOOD
OUTRIGGER WAIKIKI
MILITARY
WAIKIKI BEACH WALK
DON HO ST
ROYAL HAWAIIAN SHOPPING CENTER
HULA GRILL
RESERVATION
TAORMINA
BEACH WALK
LEEWERS ST
GIOVANNI'S PASTRAMI
DUKE'S WAIKIKI
THE BREAKERS
HELUMOA RD
NOBU
AZURE
EMBASSY SUITES
ROYAL HAWAIIAN HOTEL
MAI TAI BAR
P
KALIA RD
TRUMP
ROY'S
IMPERIAL HAWAII
WAIKIKI PARC
SHERATON WAIKIKI
RUMFIRE
Waikiki Beach
KALIA RD
KAI MARKET
OUTRIGGER REEF
HALEKULANI
Gray's Beach
SHORE BIRD
ORCHIDS

Fort DeRussy Beach

Mamala   Bay

© AVALON TRAVEL

Waikiki Southeast

© AVALON TRAVEL

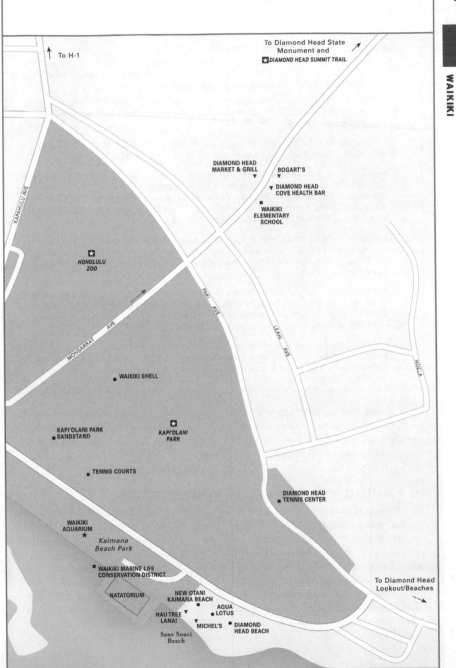

To Diamond Head State
Monument and
⭐ *DIAMOND HEAD SUMMIT TRAIL*

↑ To H-1

KAPAHULU AVE

DIAMOND HEAD
MARKET & GRILL
▼

BOGART'S
▼

DIAMOND HEAD
COVE HEALTH BAR
■

WAIKIKI
ELEMENTARY
SCHOOL

⭐
HONOLULU
ZOO

PAKI AVE

LEAHI AVE

NOELA

MONSARRAT AVE

■ WAIKIKI SHELL

KAPI'OLANI PARK
■ BANDSTAND

⭐
KAPI'OLANI
PARK

■ TENNIS COURTS

DIAMOND HEAD
■ TENNIS CENTER

WAIKIKI
AQUARIUM
★

*Kaimana
Beach Park*

■ WAIKIKI MARINE LIFE
CONSERVATION DISTRICT

To Diamond Head
Lookout/Beaches

NATATORIUM

NEW OTANI
KAIMANA BEACH
▼ ● AQUA
● LOTUS

HAU TREE
LANAI
▼
● DIAMOND
MICHEL'S ● HEAD BEACH

*Sans Souci
Beach*

Your Best Day in Waikiki

There is so much to do in Waikiki, from outdoor activities like surfing, stand-up paddling, snorkeling, and hiking to shopping, dining, or simply relaxing on the beach under an umbrella. Of all the activities on offer, some tap into the history and character of Waikiki, which have evolved to make Waikiki the iconic and unique place that it is today.

- Wake up early and walk, run, bike, taxi, or bus to the **Diamond Head State Monument.** Hike through the extinct Diamond Head crater to the summit and take in the entire south shore from your morning perch.

- On your way back to Waikiki proper, stop at **Diamond Head Cove Health Bar** for a delicious acai bowl. If you'd rather have eggs or a bagel, try **Bogart's** next door.

- After refueling, you'll want to head back to the beach and partake in Waikiki's ample ocean activities. If you snorkel, post up at **Queen's Surf Beach** and check out the fish and reef in the marine protected area. If you surf or stand-up paddle, head straight to **Kuhio Beach Park** or **Waikiki Beach,** where you can rent a board and paddle out into the legendary Waikiki surf at **Canoes** or **Queen's.**

- As afternoon rolls around, freshen up back at the hotel and head back outside and cruise the shops on Kalakaua Avenue while being entertained by the street performers. Stop by the **Royal Hawaiian Center** to pick up all sorts of Hawaiian goodies for your friends and loved ones back home.

- Is it five yet? Happy hour, better known as *pau hana* in the islands, beckons you into one of Waikiki's many dining establishments. Your best bet is to choose one with an **ocean view**—think oceanfront hotel. If you'd rather be on the water for sunset, hop on one of the **catamaran cruises** along the beach for a 1.5-hour sail.

- For dinner, immerse yourself in the beach culture of Waikiki and head to **Duke's Waikiki** for an amazing beachfront steak and seafood meal with the best sunset views. Make sure to order a Hula Pie after dinner. If sushi is your game, try **Doraku** in the Royal Hawaiian Center.

is ever present; theft and muggings occur; and bar fights spill out onto the sidewalks after hours. But if you keep your eyes focused on the surf and sun, it's easy to find the paradise Waikiki is famous for.

PLANNING YOUR TIME

For first-time O'ahu travelers and many returning visitors, Waikiki is the perfect home base. The majority of the hotel and resort accommodations are found here and it's easy to take a day trip anywhere around the island and make it back in time for dinner. With high-end shopping, myriad restaurants, and plenty of sights and activities, you could spend your entire vacation in Waikiki and leave satisfied. It's the ideal locale to relax at the water's edge in very close proximity to your accommodations. To experience the gamut of Waikiki's sights and activities, set aside a day to spend in the Diamond Head area in addition to the time you plan for beach activities and shopping in Waikiki proper.

ORIENTATION

Waikiki is framed by the Ala Wai Canal to the north and west, Diamond Head to the east, and the beautiful Pacific Ocean to the south. Most streets in Waikiki are one-way thoroughfares: **Kalakaua Avenue,** the main drag, runs east to Diamond Head, **Ala Wai Boulevard** runs west, and in between them, **Kuhio Avenue** has two-way traffic east and west. Residents generally define directionality in relation to towns or major landmarks.

Art on the Zoo Fence

Fancy yourself an art aficionado? Maybe you'd like to take home a piece of art to remember Hawai'i. **Art on the Zoo Fence** (www.artonthezoofence.com, Sat.-Sun. 9am-4pm) is a great outdoor venue where you can check out a range of art, from photography to postcards to paintings, and speak with the artists, as well. A tradition in Waikiki for over 50 years, artists hang their works from the exterior of the zoo fence along Monsarrat Avenue. Stroll under the towering banyan trees, peruse the art, and engage the artists. It's not uncommon for the artists to be painting on-site.

Sights

★ Honolulu Zoo

Only a mere 2,392 miles from the nearest zoo, the **Honolulu Zoo** (151 Kapahulu Ave., 808/971-7171, www.honoluluzoo.org, 9am-4:30pm daily, $14 adults, $8 military adults, $6 children 3-12 with an adult, $4 military children with an adult, children 2 and under free) is a must-see in Waikiki. The plant and animal collections emphasize Pacific tropical

flamingos at the Honolulu Zoo

ecosystems and are organized into three ecological zones: the African savannah, the Asian and American tropical forests, and the Pacific Islands. Mammals and birds are the spotlight here, with just a few reptiles on display, including a handful of Galapagos tortoises, a Komodo dragon, and dangerous-looking gharials. There's an expanded Indian elephant enclosure, opened in 2012 for the two playful inhabitants; the orangutans, Rusti and Violet, sleep mostly during the day; and the zebras, giraffes, hippos, and rhinoceroses on the savannah are a major draw. The baboons are quite interactive as well. The kids will love the massive jungle gym by the snack bar and the Sumatran tiger area. Right next door is the Keiki Zoo, with a crawl-through circular koi fish tank, lizards, farm animals, and a goat-petting area.

There are several after-hours events at the zoo, as well. Twilight Tours are held Friday and Saturday evenings. The guided, two-hour walk is a great chance to see who wakes up after everyone has left, and the Dinner Safari is a buffet and a two-hour guided night tour. Every Wednesday during the summer, the Wildest Show Summer Concert Series is a fun family event featuring local musicians. Check the website for the schedule. If you plan on returning to the zoo more than once during your stay or visit O'ahu several times a year, consider an annual pass. There are several levels of membership, but the average family can take advantage of the Chimpanzee Family membership: unlimited entrance and benefits for one year for two adults and up to four children under 18 ($55). There is a pay parking lot for the zoo on Kapahulu Avenue, $1 per hour and the kiosks accept credit cards or coins only, no bills. Free parking is located at the Waikiki Shell parking lots across Monsarrat Avenue on the *makai* side (ocean side) of the zoo.

WAIKIKI AQUARIUM

Situated on 2.35 acres right on the shoreline in Kapiʻolani Park, the **Waikiki Aquarium** (2777 Kalakaua Ave., 808/923-9741, www.waikikiaquarium.org, 9am-4:30pm daily, $12 adults, $8 military, $5 junior ages 4-12 and seniors, children 3 and under free) has a number of beautiful collections focusing on the South Pacific and Hawaiian marine communities. With your paid admission you receive a free audio tour wand, which gives insight and information on all the different collections. The aquarium has both indoor and outdoor viewing areas. Inside you'll find displays showcasing the marine life around the different islands and the creatures living in various marine ecosystems, from the intertidal zone to the open ocean. Corals, giant clams, colorful reef-dwelling fish, predators like sharks, trevally, and groupers, jellyfish, chambered nautilus, and even a gold American lobster (only one in 30 million American lobsters show this genetic disposition) are some of the curious residents at the aquarium. Outside you'll find the monk seal, a tidal pool with fish that reflect the marine life around Waikiki, an interactive area where people can hold hermit crabs and other little creatures, and a serene grassy open space under palm trees right next to the ocean for the kids to run around on and burn some energy or to sit and enjoy a snack.

The Waikiki Aquarium also has a signature summer concert series on the lawn that draws a more mature crowd than the zoo's summer concert series. Ke Kani O Ke Kai: The Sound of the Ocean runs June-August. Check the website for the latest schedule and information. Parking at the aquarium is limited. Park along Kalakaua Avenue, the ocean side is free and the mountain side is metered parking, $0.25 per half hour.

Kapiʻolani Park stretches all the way to the slopes of Diamond Head.

The Legacy of Duke

Born Duke Paoa Kahinu Mokoe Hulikohola Kahanamoku on August 24, 1890, Duke grew up in Waikiki near what is now the Hilton Hawaiian Village. In the course of his childhood on the beach, Duke quickly became a skilled waterman, mastering surfing, outrigger canoe paddling, and swimming. As one of the original Waikiki beachboys, Duke shared his passions with wealthy, upper-class tourists from the U.S. mainland, and by doing so saved the sport of surfing from near extinction. A champion swimmer, Duke won his first gold medal at the 1912 Olympics in Stockholm, Sweden. That same year he also traveled to Southern California to give swimming and surfing exhibitions, introducing surfing to America. In 1914, he traveled to Sydney, Australia, for more exhibitions and turned the Aussies on to surfing as well. In the 1920 Olympics in Antwerp, Belgium, he won two more gold medals in swimming. Duke's success and early relationships as a beachboy opened doors for him in the Hollywood film industry, where he played in nearly 20 films from 1925 until 1967. He also served as the sheriff of Honolulu from 1932 to 1961. Known as the original ambassador of aloha, Duke is immortalized in Hawai'i for sharing the sport of surfing with the world and embodying the aloha spirit throughout his life.

★ KAPI'OLANI PARK

Kapi'olani Park (intersection of Kapahulu and Kalakaua Avenues, www.kapiolanipark. net) is the oldest public park in Hawai'i, established in 1877 by King David Kalakaua, monarch of Hawai'i. What was once marshland and lagoons is now a 300-acre expanse of grass, sports fields, canopy trees, and a running trail. The park attracts all types of sports, from rugby and cricket to soccer and softball and has four lit tennis courts. It's a hub for picnics, birthdays, large family gatherings, and barbecues. The park also draws runners and walkers, who circle it on the 3-mile running path. The park is the best spot for birdwatching on the South Shore, and birders set up binoculars and cameras to spy on the avian park goers in the mature shower trees, mesquite, and banyans.

The Waikiki Shell, an outdoor concert venue, and the Victorian-style Kapi'olani Bandstand, built in the late 1890s, are in close proximity, just across from the zoo. The park hosts festivals all year long to celebrate culture, food, and community, such as the Korean Festival and the Ukulele Festival. The park extends across Kalakaua Avenue, all the way to the beach. There is free parking along Monsarrat Avenue by the Waikiki Shell and the bandstand, along Paki Avenue, and on the ocean side of Kalakaua Avenue. There are parking meters (10am-6pm daily, $0.25/30 min., 4-hour limit) on the mountain side of Kalakaua Avenue.

DIAMOND HEAD LOOKOUT

Where Kalakaua Avenue and Paki Avenue meet at the east end of Kapi'olani Park, Diamond Head Road begins its easy climb to the Diamond Head Lookout. At the apex, there are two designated areas to pull off the road and park right at the edge of the cliff for spectacular views up and down the coast. Keep in mind that the Waikiki Trolley and tour buses of all sizes also stop at the lookouts, so sometimes they are tranquil and uncrowded, while at other times they are infiltrated by mobs of visitors, taking pictures shoulder to shoulder. The tour buses will block any parked cars from leaving, but on the bright side, they usually don't stay long. From the lookout you can see the waves crashing on shallow reefs to the west, the surfers at Diamond Head's popular surf spots, and Black Point to the east, its rugged coastline fringed by palm trees and mansions.

Just before the first parking area on the ocean side of Diamond Head Road, coming from Waikiki, is the Diamond Head Lighthouse (3399 Diamond Head Rd.). First constructed in 1899, then rebuilt in 1917, the lighthouse still uses its original Fresnel lens, and its beacon can be seen more than 18 miles out to sea. The lighthouse keeper's dwelling, where the lighthouse is situated, is a private residence, the quarters of the commander of the Fourteenth Coast Guard district. A gate restricts access to the lighthouse, but its close proximity to the gate, approximately 30 feet, still makes for a Kodak moment.

★ DUKE KAHANAMOKU STATUE

"The Father of Modern Surfing," **Duke Paoa Kahanamoku**, is immortalized in a larger-than-life bronze statue on the sidewalk fronting Kuhio Beach. Hang lei from his outstretched arms, pose with a loved one in front of Duke, and have someone snap a picture—a stop at the **Duke statue** is a must in Waikiki. Duke is the embodiment of Waikiki, of ocean recreation, and of aloha. Visit in the morning to avoid crowds and to catch the sunlight illuminating the statue. Duke grew up near the Hilton Hawaiian Village and was an accomplished surfer, canoe paddler, and Olympic gold-medalist swimmer. As Hawai'i's first ambassador of aloha, Duke spread the sport of surfing around the world, traveling to the U.S. mainland and Australia for surfing exhibitions. Later in life he became a Hollywood star and held elected office in Honolulu for 29 years.

U.S. ARMY MUSEUM OF HAWAI'I

Located on Fort DeRussy Beach, the **U.S. Army Museum of Hawai'i** (808/955-9552, http://hiarmymuseumsoc.org, 9am-4:15pm Tues.-Sat., free) highlights O'ahu's military history. The museum is actually inside Battery Randolph, a massive concrete coastal defense structure with reinforced walls up to 12 feet thick. The battery was constructed in 1911 to house two 14-inch guns, part of a system set up to protect Honolulu Harbor

The U.S. Army Museum of Hawai'i showcases O'ahu's military history.

from invasion. The battery was rendered obsolete by the rise of the aircraft carrier in World War II. Audio tours are available for $5. The museum validates parking tickets for the Fort DeRussy Parking Facility directly across the street.

DAMIEN MUSEUM

Across from Kuhio Beach is St. Augustine Catholic Church, a David among the high-rise Goliaths. Look for its angular, oxidized green roof resembling a series of A-frames. The **Damien Museum** (130 Ohua Ave., 808/923-2690, 9am-3pm Mon.-Fri., free) is housed in a separate building to the rear, displaying photos and other artifacts of Father Damien, the Belgian priest who humanely cared for the lepers of Kalaupapa, Moloka'i, until his own death from complications of leprosy. Although entrance is free, donations are gratefully accepted and are the museum's only source of revenue.

Beaches

Waikiki's narrow beaches are generally packed shoulder to shoulder with people, or umbrella to umbrella, for most of the day. In the heart of Waikiki, the towering hotels have been built right to the water's edge, leaving anywhere from 20 to 50 feet of beach for public use. If a leisurely walk along the beach is your fancy, the feat is best accomplished during the first few hours after sunrise or after 6pm, when most people have made their way back to their hotels to prepare for dinner. It's not uncommon for the moon to rise over Diamond Head while the sun is still setting in the west. To get away from the crowds altogether, find a patch of sand along Diamond Head's seaside cliffs and revel in the fact that a short, steep walk down a gravelly path will deter most visitors.

DUKE KAHANAMOKU BEACH

At the west end, or 'Ewa (EH-va) side of Waikiki, is **Duke Kahanamoku Beach,** one of the wider beaches in Waikiki. Fronting the Hilton Hawaiian Village and Beach Resort, it stretches from the Ala Wai Small Boat Harbor to Hilton's catamaran pier. A shallow outer reef with great waves keeps the inner waters calm and very kid friendly. There's even an artificial ocean-fed lagoon between the beach and the hotel, the perfect spot to try out stand-up paddle surfing without having to worry about ocean chop or currents. The lagoon does have a synthetic feel to it, though, especially apparent in its coarse compacted shoreline that makes sand play an all-out construction job.

There is a beach path that runs the length of Waikiki, but if you're coming from Kalakaua Avenue, you'll have to trek down Lewers Street, Beach Walk, or Saratoga Road to reach the sand. There is public beach access on the west side of the Outrigger Reef. Once you hit the beach path, keep walking west till you pass the catamaran pier. If you're coming by car, there is free parking in the Ala Wai Small Boat Harbor.

Duke Kahanamoku Beach

FORT DERUSSY BEACH

Just east of the catamaran pier, **Fort DeRussy Beach** runs all the way to the Outrigger Reef. Now a clean and tidy public beach and manicured park shaded by canopy trees, this military reservation was one of several shore batteries on O'ahu during World War II and served as an R&R locale for soldiers during the Vietnam War. The beach fronts the Hale Koa hotel, which caters strictly to armed forces personnel and their families, and the U.S. Army Museum, and has a distinct military presence and vibe. It's also known for its calm inner waters perfect for swimming or snorkeling and volleyball courts. An open-air parking lot across from Fort DeRussy Beach Park on Kalia Road is a relatively safe place to park for access to the beach. The rates are average for Waikiki standards at $3 per half hour, and it offers military discounts.

GRAY'S BEACH

Continuing east, the beach ends, and a raised cement walking path on top of the armored shoreline provides transport to **Gray's Beach,** a nook of coarse imported sand in between the Halekulani and Sheraton Waikiki Hotel. There is also beach access from Kalia Road between the two hotels.

WAIKIKI BEACH

Widened in the spring of 2012, **Waikiki Beach** is half of the heart of Waikiki. Stretching from the Royal Hawaiian to the Moana Surfrider, the first two hotels in Waikiki, this is prime real estate for visitors and the sand fills up quickly with beachgoers. This strip is lined with beach service providers and beachside bars and dining. Because of the sand bottom off Waikiki Beach, the water is a translucent aqua-green and perfect for swimming, stand-up paddling, or just floating on a fluorescent blow-up mat. There is a sandbar just offshore from the Royal Hawaiian that people wade or float out to in order to play in the knee-deep water and small surf. For snorkeling, there's not much to see in the way of marine life, save for the occasional green sea turtle. The famous surf spot Canoes breaks quite a way offshore, and while this part of the beach does have a small shore break—quite exciting for the kids—the inner waters are calm and sheltered from the prevailing trade winds.

The easiest way to get to Waikiki Beach is to walk down the shore from Kuhio Beach to the east. Otherwise, make your way through one of the big hotels on the beach to access the world-famous sand, sparkling waters,

Waikiki Beach in the early morning

and iconic view of Diamond Head. Parking in Waikiki is very expensive, whether you valet or self-park at one of the hotel parking garages. Your best bet is to park in the Waikiki Shell parking lot, which is free, and walk down Kalakaua Avenue. There is also free parking on the *makai* side (ocean side) of Kalakaua Avenue from Kapahulu Avenue all the way down to Diamond Head. Since landing one of the coveted free parking spots is hard to do, there is also metered parking on the *mauka* side (mountain side) of Kalakaua Avenue along Kapiʻolani Park for a reasonable $0.25 per half hour.

★ KUHIO BEACH PARK

Stretching from the east side of the Moana Surfrider to the concrete pier where Kapahulu Avenue intersects Kalakaua Avenue, **Kuhio Beach Park** is the other half to the thumping heart of Waikiki. It has a snack bar, restrooms, and showers at the west end, two lagoons for sheltered swimming, grassy knolls for relaxing in the shade under a palm tree, ample beach services, and one of the best waves in Waikiki—Queen's. Just as on Waikiki Beach, you'll want to arrive early to stake a claim in the sand with a beach towel or chair.

Kuhio Beach Park is the hub of surfing in Waikiki, with the forgiving waves of Queen's and Canoes breaking fairly close to shore by Hawaiʻi standards. You'll find a host of beachboys in red shorts stoked to rent surfboards, stand-up paddleboards, bodyboards, and floating mats. They also offer surf lessons and outrigger canoe rides. Along the beach park you'll also find the iconic lei-adorned statue of Duke Kahanamoku and the statue of Prince Kuhio, as well. Once again, it's best to find parking around Kapiʻolani Park and walk to Kuhio Beach Park. The beach park is closed 2am-5am.

QUEEN'S SURF BEACH

On the east side of the concrete pier, **Queen's Surf Beach** offers two things you won't find anywhere else in Waikiki: a "No Surfboard" zone and the **Waikiki Marine Life Conservation District**. Demarcated by buoys on the east side of the concrete pier, just off the shoreline, the No Surfboard zone sees small waves roll across the shallow waters and up the beach. While action of the water would be great for bodyboarding, the ocean floor is sharp, flat reef with the odd coral head, so swimming and bodysurfing are not good ideas.

On the east side of the jetty, the Waikiki

Kuhio Beach Park, the heart of Waikiki

Marine Life Conservation District stretches to the Waikiki War Memorial Natatorium's crumbling western wall. With fishing forbidden in this 76-acre marine conservation area and calm, shallow inner waters, this healthy reef ecosystem offers the best snorkeling in Waikiki.

Kapi'olani Park, with its wide-stretching banyan trees, runs the length of the beach. There are restrooms, showers, and a hip shoreline café open for breakfast, lunch, and dinner. The Waikiki Aquarium is at the Diamond Head end of the park. Publics is the main surfing wave along the beach, a dangerous left that breaks along a shallow reef of odd-shaped coral heads that rise above sea level on an extremely low tide. The beach and park area at Publics, where the beach ends, is a favorite for LGBT visitors. The park is also home to many of Waikiki's homeless population. Parking is available along Kalakaua Avenue and around Kapi'olani Park.

SANS SOUCI BEACH PARK

A small patch of sand between the eroding Waikiki War Memorial Natatorium and the New Otani Kaimana Beach Hotel, Sans Souci Beach Park, also known as Kaimana Beach, is a favorite spot for residents seeking easy access to a family-friendly beach and park without the hassle of getting in and out of Waikiki. There's limited free parking, restrooms, an outdoor shower at the beach, and indoor showers at the natatorium. In front of the natatorium is great for snorkeling, and swimmers take advantage of a wide, deep channel through the reef and out to a wind sock fixed on its outer corner. Four laps from the beach to the wind sock is roughly a mile. The water is very calm, making it the perfect locale for children of all ages.

MAKALEI BEACH PARK

If you're in the mood to escape Waikiki and find solace on your own slice of beach, Makalei Beach Park is the best option within Waikiki. Only the quaint park is visible from Diamond Head Road. Tucked back behind some houses in the southwest corner of the park, the beach is a quiet, small strip of sand no more than 100 feet long that is favored by residents and surfers attracted to the Suicides surf break. It's best to visit on a low tide, when more sand is exposed. Once you are in the water, the seafloor is entirely reef, so ocean life abounds, but choppy conditions

Sans Souci Beach Park, also known as Kaimana Beach

and strong currents are prevalent in this area. There are no lifeguards, so exercise caution when snorkeling and swimming off the beach. There are a shower and picnic tables in the beach park. To get there, park around Kapi'olani Park and walk east up Diamond Head Road. The entrance to the beach park is signed.

DIAMOND HEAD BEACH PARK

At the base of Diamond Head's seaside cliffs are some of the best beaches on the South Shore for escaping the crowds and enjoying the island's natural scenery. There's parking on both sides of Diamond Head Road and a paved footpath that cuts down the cliff. At the bottom of the path, **Diamond Head Beach Park** stretches out in both directions. The shoreline is lined with shells and sea glass, and there are tidepools on the west end of the beach. There are several surf breaks along the reef, but the pervasive trade winds, strong ocean currents, wind chop, and extremely shallow patches of reef make snorkeling and swimming dangerous. The beach below Diamond Head is a great spot for a romantic winter-season stroll as the sun sets straight off Waikiki. Diamond Head Beach Park is closed 10pm-5am.

Water Sports

SURFING

Surfing is synonymous with Waikiki. Not only did Hawaiians invent the sport of surfing, but the legendary Duke Kahanamoku—original beachboy, Olympic gold-medal swimmer, and the father of modern-day surfing, who hailed from Waikiki—introduced the fluid sport to the world. The surf breaks that Duke made famous riding on heavy wooden boards are the same spots that surfers seek out today. While the waves are biggest, best, and most consistent during summer, June-September, Waikiki has the potential to see surf at any time during the year. Whether you are a longboarder, a shortboarder, experienced, a novice, or a first-timer, Waikiki has a number of breaks that suit all abilities. Just remember that proper surfing etiquette applies at all breaks, and with so many people in the water, safety and respect for others are of the utmost importance. When in doubt, don't go out.

Ala Moana Bowls to Kaiser's

Ala Moana Bowls is a fast, hollow left that is heavily guarded by a seasoned crew of local surfers. The wave breaks into the mouth of the Ala Wai Small Boat Harbor and is best viewed from across the channel on Magic Island. **Kaiser's** is a predominant right that breaks over a very shallow reef shelf. With a tight takeoff zone and a pack of hungry locals, it's also best left to the residents. If you plan on surfing in this area, it's best to surf the stretch of reef between the two spots, known as **Rockpile.** Good for both shortboarding and longboarding, the fast lefts break over sharp, shallow reef and allow for a quick cover-up if you're lucky. Paddle out from the small swatch of beach fronting the parking lot (with designated free and paid parking), but avoid the areas of very shallow reef straight out from the beach. There are some slow whitewater rollers on the inside perfect for beginner surfers.

Fours to Populars

Straight out from the U.S. Army Museum, on the east side of a deep channel, is **Fours,** a wave that only comes alive when the surf gets big. Just to the east of Fours, way out over the outer reef, is **Threes,** a perfect right that breaks best on a low tide and holds its shape at all sizes. Threes is a favorite with local surfers and gets very crowded. To the east of Threes is **Paradise,** a surf zone with big, rolling, shifty peaks. It's a favorite for longboarders and stand-up paddle surfers. Continuing east, the next break is a favorite for all board riders—**Populars.** Locally referred to as Pops, this long right breaks over a sand-covered reef and can handle big surf. When the trade winds are stiff, Pops does get choppy.

★ Canoes

Canoes is straight out from the west end of Kuhio Beach Park. It breaks both right and left and has several takeoff zones. A slow, rolling longboard wave, Canoes is perfect for beginners. Start off slowly on the inside, catching the whitewater till you learn to stand up and balance on the board. Once you're more confident and comfortable, sit out the back with a mix of locals, beachboys, and people from all around the world sharing in this Hawaiian tradition. Canoes is very crowded with all types of watercraft, from 12-foot longboards to canoes and catamarans. Stay aware and, by all means, if something large is coming your way, don't be a deer in the headlights; paddle out of the way.

Queen's

Queen's, also called **Queen's Surf,** is one of the best waves in Waikiki. Straight off the beach from the east end of Kuhio Beach Park,

before the lagoon, it's best for longboarding. Professional and amateur contests are often held here. The perfect turquoise rights draw a host of the best longboarders in Hawai'i, who hang ten down the line with style and ease. Queen's is usually very crowded, and if there's any swell in the water, Queen's is breaking. Because of the tight takeoff zone and thick crowd, beginners should stick to Canoes.

Publics to Tongg's

Just on the east side of the rock jetty off Queen's Surf Beach, way off the beach on the outer reef, **Publics** is a long left that breaks over shallow, sharp, and irregular-shaped coral heads. Sound inviting? For longboarders, the long, sloping wave offers a chance to get out of the thick crowds in the heart of Waikiki. The wave is best ridden at high tide, when the coral heads are submerged. On low tide, the coral heads go dry and the wave breaks right over them. The break can get choppy from its exposure to the trade winds, and on big south swells, the waves can get quite big and the currents very strong. A lifeguard in the tower on the beach can assist you with ocean conditions.

To the east of Kaimana are two breaks best

Canoe surfing is definitely a team sport.

Waikiki Beachboys

If there's something about Waikiki that sets it apart from other tropical sea destinations, it's the **Waikiki beachboys.** Hailing back a century, the beachboy culture has evolved with the changing face of tourism in Hawai'i, but the gentlemen in the red shorts still practice the same core values of sharing the sports of surfing, outrigger canoeing, and aloha with visitors.

After Calvinist missionaries decimated the Hawaiian culture in the 19th century, the sport of surfing, a purely Hawaiian endeavor, was nearly extinguished. It was seen as sinful because of how much skin was shown while surfing. Only a few surfers remained at the end of the century, namely legendary waterman and three-time Olympic gold medalist Duke Kahanamoku and a few of his friends. As the first wave of wealthy American tourists arrived on steamers in the early decades of the 20th century, these few surfers took it upon themselves to entertain the visitors, teaching them how to surf, ride canoes, and relax and have a good time in general. In essence, they created a way to earn a living surfing year-round on the beach at Waikiki. These first visitors came to Hawai'i for extended stays and were able to develop relationships with the beachboys, who became their tour guides and a bridge to the Hawaiian culture and a different lifestyle. After giving surfing lessons during the day, the beachboys entertained their guests with ukulele, song, and libations at night, a hedonistic lifestyle by all accounts.

The fun was curtailed by World War II, and as travel and tourism have changed since then, so too have the beachboys. With the ease and affordability of flying across the Pacific, a vacation to Waikiki is accessible for so many more people, not just the wealthy elite. Today, with thousands of visitors flocking to the beach daily, the beachboys focus on surfing and outrigger canoe surfing and have shifted roles from entertainers and tour guides to beach services. While only a few of Waikiki's beachboys can still trace their ties back to the original beachboys, any beachboy can still show you how to have the time of your life in Waikiki's gentle surf.

for longboarding on the outer reef: **Old Man's** is on the left side of the channel and **Tongg's** just up the reef. These soft, sloping waves offer respite from the Waikiki crowds, but keep an eye peeled for coral heads.

Diamond Head

On the west end of **Diamond Head,** off Makalei Beach Park, is **Suicides,** a left for experts only. It's windy, quite a ways offshore, and subject to strong currents. Below the Diamond Head Lookout parking lots are several good breaks, the two most popular being **Lighthouse** and **Cliffs.** At the bottom of the trail down the cliff is a deep channel through the reef. From the beach, to the right of the channel is Lighthouse, a fast and powerful right for experts only. On the left of the channel is Cliffs, several peaks along the reef that break both right and left and are suited for all types of board riders. Diamond Head can get very windy as the trade winds blow right across the break, and is a favorite for

kiteboarders and sailboarders during the extreme conditions.

Outfitters

Koa Board Sports (2420 Koa Ave., 808/923-0189, www.koaboardsports.com, 10am-6pm daily) has a huge selection of longboards and shortboards available for rent. Rates go from $20 for a half day, $25 for one day (overnight), to $50 for two days. You can also switch the board anytime the shop is open. **Hans Hedemann Surf Adventures** (2586 Kalakaua Ave., 808/924-7778, www.hhsurf. com, 8am-5pm daily) is located in the Park Shore Hotel, between Starbucks and the hotel lobby. The surf school specializes in surf lessons out at Publics. You will have to carry a soft-top longboard from the retail outlet to the break, about a 10-minute walk. It also offers stand-up paddle lessons, guided surf adventures, and surfboard rentals.

If you prefer to rent your board right on the beach, or take a lesson with one of Waikiki's famous beachboys, then you'll want to check out some of Waikiki's vetted beach services. **Faith Surf School** (www.faithsurfschool. com), operated by the legendary Moniz family, offers its expertise at several beach locations: the Outrigger Reef (2169 Kalia Rd., 808/924-6084), the Outrigger Waikiki (2335 Kalakaua Ave., 808/926-9889), and the Sheraton (2255 Kalakaua Ave., 808/922-4422). Faith rents longboards starting at $20 per hour and offers 1.5-hour group lessons for $60 and private lessons for $125.

Aloha Beach Services (808/922-3111, http://alohabeachservices.com, 8am-4pm daily), serving guests since 1932, has a small palapa but a lot of boards, in between the Outrigger Waikiki and the Moana Surfrider. It rents longboards for $15 per hour and $5 each additional hour and offers one-hour group lessons for $40 and private lessons for $80. A photo package is included with the group lesson. Aloha rents beach umbrellas, chairs, air mats, and rings and accepts cash only.

You'll find **Star Beachboys** (808/699-3750, www.starbeachboys.com, 8am-4pm daily) at the west end of Kuhio Beach Park, by the concession stand and the bathrooms. Star rents 8- to 10-foot longboards for $10 per hour and 11- to 12-foot boards for $15 per hour, with a $5 charge for each additional hour. It also offers one-hour group lessons for $40 and private lessons for $75. On the sand just to the east of the Duke Kahanamoku Statue and at the far eastern end of Kuhio Beach Park are the **Hawaiian Oceans Waikiki** (808/306-4586, http://hawaiianoceanswaikiki.com/) beachboys. They have one-hour group lessons for $40 and two-hour private lessons for $100. They also rent longboards starting at $10 per hour and shortboards for $15 per hour, with $5 each additional hour or $35 for a half day. Beach chairs and umbrellas also are available to rent.

SNORKELING

The **snorkeling** in Waikiki is decent at best any time of year. Overuse and overfishing for decades have led to the decline in the number of species and fish in the nearshore waters, and all that fine white sand over the reef, which gives the water its clear, light blue color, leaves little shelter for reef dwellers. Patience, and the luck of being in the right place at the right time, can yield some great underwater exploring.

Duke Kahanamoku Beach and Fort DeRussy Beach

Since the nearshore waters off **Duke Kahanamoku Beach** and **Fort DeRussy Beach** are not heavily used, the potential to encounter marine life is definitely heightened. The water is shallow, waist to chest deep, all the way out to the waves breaking at Threes and Fours, and the bottom is a mix of reef and sand. As an added bonus, you won't have to keep your eye out for surfers, swimmers, canoes, or catamarans, so you can stay focused on what fish you can find.

Waikiki Marine Life Conservation District

The **Waikiki Marine Life Conservation District,** located along Queen's Surf Beach from the jetty to the Waikiki War Memorial Natatorium's western wall, is hands down the best snorkeling in Waikiki. The 76-acre marine conservation area is a regulated and patrolled no-take zone, where fishing or removing of any sea creature is illegal. The protection has allowed a plethora of reef-dwelling vertebrates and invertebrates to thrive. The shallow inner waters are generally calm, but heavy trade winds can texture the surface. Look for bonefish, funny face fish, wrasse, puffer fish, eel, and yellow tang. Chances are you'll even catch a glimpse of the sleek *humuhumunukunukuapua'a.*

Diamond Head

The nearshore waters off the beaches of Diamond Head are great for snorkeling but more suited for experienced snorkelers and swimmers. The reefs at Diamond Head attract all sorts of marine life, including sharks and the endangered Hawaiian monk seal.

Shallow water and lots of nooks and crannies in the sharp reef make for great habitat, but beware of extremely shallow areas of reef, strong currents, and wind chop. Snorkeling is best in winter, when the waves are small to nonexistent.

Outfitters

Whether you purchase your own snorkel gear or rent equipment is for you to decide. Renting allows you to travel without lugging around cumbersome snorkel gear, while owning gives you the luxury of a custom fit only your mouth knows. **Aqua Zone Scuba Diving & Snorkeling** (2552 Kalakaua Ave., 866/923-3483, www.aquazonescuba.com, 8am-5pm daily), in the Waikiki Beach Marriott, rents and sells gear and is a short walk from the Waikiki Marine Life Conservation District. It rents complete snorkel sets starting at $10 for 24 hours, $20 for three days, and $25 for five days.

Snorkel Bob's (702 Kapahulu Ave., 808/735-7944, www.snorkelbob.com, 8am-5pm daily), just outside of Waikiki, sells equipment and rents complete snorkeling sets, individual snorkels, fins, flotation devices, and wetsuits. The most basic equipment starts at $2.50 per day and $9 per week.

Nearly all the beach services at the beachfront hotels rent and sell snorkel gear, and most **ABC Stores** sell complete sets as well.

SCUBA DIVING

Once you get offshore from Waikiki, the seafloor slowly sinks away and the water becomes a rich, deep blue. At these greater depths are a few great dive sites, from reefs to shipwrecks. Offshore, the water teems with life, and turtles, eels, triggerfish, octopus, and a host of other reef fish abound. Diving off Waikiki is a year-round pursuit, weather and wave permitting.

In the heart of Waikiki you'll find two Professional Association of Diving Instructors (PADI) centers. **Waikiki Diving Center** (424 Nahua St., 808/922-2121, www.waikikidiving.com) dives two wrecks and

10 different sites right off Waikiki. With 32 years of experience, the center offers dives for every type of diver, rents and sells equipment, and offers PADI certification. Two-tank beginner dives start at $109, wreck dives start at $125, night dives start at $135, and PADI certification courses start at $250. **Aqua Zone Scuba Diving & Snorkeling** (2552 Kalakaua Ave., 866/923-3483, www.aquazonescuba.com) is in the Waikiki Beach Marriott. It includes free in-pool lessons for beginners and rusty divers and daily boat dives for all levels. It offers two levels of PADI certification and provides daily snorkel tours and equipment rental and sales. Two-tank boat dives with rental equipment start at $129. Both Waikiki Diving Center and Aqua Zone dive numerous locations outside of Waikiki as well.

STAND-UP PADDLING

Long before stand-up paddling became a full-fledged sport, a few of the Waikiki beachboys were known to cruise around the lineups kneeling or standing up on longboards and paddling with their canoe paddles. Now the equipment has been refined and stand-up paddling is popular both for surfing and flat-water paddling (also known as stand-up paddleboarding), both of which are full-body workouts. **Paradise, Populars, and Canoes** are the go-to surf breaks for stand-up paddle surfing in Waikiki. If you prefer to just paddle and check out the water from a different perspective, get away from the crowds by paddling out beyond Canoes and **Queen's** and explore. Make your way to **Publics** and paddle in with the wind at your back. You'll be amazed that even at 10-15 feet deep, you'll still be able to see the bottom.

Faith Surf School (www.faithsurfschool.com) rents stand-up paddleboards from the Outrigger Reef (2169 Kalia Rd., 808/924-6084), Outrigger Waikiki (2335 Kalakaua Ave., 808/926-9889), and Sheraton (2255 Kalakaua Ave., 808/922-4422) starting at $25 for one hour and going up to $70 for all day. The school also offers stand-up paddle lessons

Stand-Up Paddling vs. Stand-Up Paddle Surfing

Stand-up paddle surfing, also known as **SUP,** is popular in the surfing world. Originally used by Waikiki beachboys who would rest on their knees on their big longboards and use a canoe paddle to get around, today's stand-up paddleboards are high-tech, light, and very stable. Stand-up paddleboards range 9-12 feet long, are thick and wide, and made from epoxy resin. Surfers stand with their feet parallel, like a skier, in the center of the board and use a long paddle to accelerate forward. With a little practice, it's easy to pick up the technique rather quickly. Stand-up paddleboards are great for flat-water paddling (distance paddling) and for surfing. Stand-up paddle surfing is a great workout for your core, legs, and arms, and it affords a great perspective looking down over the reef. Because the boards are so big, though, only experienced stand-up paddlers should try surfing waves, as the boards are hard to maneuver and can be very dangerous for others in the water.

starting at $65 up to $125 for a 1.5-hour private lesson.

Aloha Beach Services (808/922-3111, http://alohabeachservices.com, 8am-4pm daily), between the Outrigger Waikiki and the Moana Surfrider, rents stand-up paddleboards for $30 for the first hour and $10 each additional hour. Lessons start at $60 and go to $80 for a private one-hour session. In Kuhio Beach Park, **Star Beachboys** (808/699-3750, www.starbeachboys.com, 6am-6pm daily) rent boards for $20 for the first hour and $10 for the second. Nearby, **Hawaiian Oceans Waikiki** (808/721-5443, 6am-6pm daily) rents stand-up paddleboards for $25 for the first hour and $10 for each additional hour.

BODYBOARDING

While you can bodyboard any of the waves around Waikiki, there are two areas where bodyboarders tend to congregate. Just off the cement pier at the east end of Kuhio Beach Park is a break called **Walls,** where warbly waves break over very shallow reef and wash over the lagoon wall. To the east of the pier, along Queen's Surf Beach, is a specially marked No Surfboard zone. The waves here break over some shallow coral heads along the fringe reef and roll all the way to the shore.

Aloha Beach Services (808/922-3111, http://alohabeachservices.com, 8am-4pm

daily), **Star Beachboys** (Kuhio Beach Park, 808/699-3750, www.starbeachboys.com, 6am-6pm daily), and **Hawaiian Oceans Waikiki** (Kuhio Beach Park, 808/721-5443, 6am-6pm daily) rents bodyboards for $5 per hour or $20 per day.

OUTRIGGER CANOEING

The outrigger canoe is one of the defining facets of Hawaiian culture. After all, it is how early Polynesian voyagers first arrived in these islands. Before surfboards came along, native Hawaiian fishers would stand up and "surf" their canoes back to shore. Outrigger canoe paddling and surfing have remained popular in Hawai'i to this day, and Waikiki offers the only place on O'ahu you'll be able to hop into a real six-person outrigger canoe with a professional rudder operator to guide you through the surf.

Faith Surf School (www.faithsurfschool. com) runs six-person canoes at $25 each for three waves, with locations at the Outrigger Reef (2169 Kalia Rd., 808/924-6084, 8am-5:30pm), the Outrigger Waikiki (2335 Kalakaua Ave., 808/926-9889, 8am-5:30pm), and the Sheraton (2255 Kalakaua Ave., 808/922-4422, 8am-5:30pm). Note that their last surfboard rental is at 4:30pm. **Aloha Beach Services** (808/922-3111, http:// alohabeachservices.com, 8am-4pm daily) runs eight-person canoes for $15 each for two a sunset sail for $55, a fireworks sail for $50 and a snorkeling sail for $60. Book online or at the beach.

Waikiki Rigger (808/922-2210, www.waikikirigger.com, $30 pp), a championship racing catamaran, also launches from the beach fronting the Outrigger Reef. The High Speed Tradewind Sail departs at 11am, 1pm, and 3pm on Tuesday, Thursday, Saturday, and Sunday, and 1pm and 3pm on Monday, Wednesday, and Friday. Nonalcoholic beverages are $1, cocktails are $3. The daily Sunset Sail ($42 pp) departs at 5pm and offers complimentary beverages. Waikiki Rigger also has a 2.5-hour Aquatic Eco Tour ($51 pp) combining sailing and snorkeling. The 44-foot *Maita'i Catamaran* (808/922-5665, www.leahi.com) seats 47 people comfortably and departs from the beach between the Sheraton Waikiki and the Halekulani hotels. The 90-minute Tradewind Sail ($28 adults, $14 children) leaves the beach at 11am, 1pm, and 3pm. Beverages start at $3. There is a two-hour Underwater Adventure Sail ($45 adults, $27 children) at 10:30am on Monday, Wednesday, and Friday. The Sunset Mai Tai Sail ($39 adults, $19 children) is aptly named for its stocked bar and free beverages. It departs at 5pm. On selected nights the Maita'i offers a Mahina Moonlight Sail ($39 adults, $19 children); times may vary. Children three and under are free on all trips.

On Waikiki Beach you'll find three catamaran operators. In front of the Royal Hawaiian is the *Kepoikai II* (808/224-9775, www.kepoikai.com), a 42-foot cat operating in Waikiki for more than 35 years. Its one-hour sail begins at 10:30am daily for $20 per person. Last sail is at 6pm during the summer. On board are sold $1 mai tais, $2 beer, juice, soda, and water. You'll need to make reservations or bookings from the beach.

The *Manu Kai* (808/792-1572, https://manukaicatamaran.com) beaches in front of the Outrigger Waikiki and offers one-hour trips ($25 pp with alcoholic beverages,

If you'd like to sail on the *Manu Kai,* it's best to make reservations.

waves. In Kuhio Beach Park **Star Beachboys** (808/699-3750, www.starbeachboys.com, 6am-6pm daily) canoe rides are $15 per person for three waves, and **Hawaiian Oceans Waikiki** (808/721-5443, 6am-6pm daily) runs a four-person canoe at $15 each for two waves.

★ CATAMARAN SAILING

There are seven catamaran cruises that launch from the beach and sail the waters off Waikiki almost every day, weather dependent, from Ala Moana to Diamond Head. The boats are different sizes and cater to different interests (some of the catamaran tours are known locally as the "booze cruise"), but the tours all offer a beautiful perspective of Waikiki, the city skyline, and the Ko'olau Mountains from out at sea. *Holokai Catamaran* (808/922-2210, https://sailholokai.com, 8am-7pm) is Waikiki's first new catamaran in almost two decades and launches from the beach fronting the Outrigger Reef. The company offers a tradewind sail for $35,

$20 pp without). The 43-foot catamaran's last sail ($30 pp) is at 5:30pm and is a 1.5-hour trip. Right next to the Manu Kai you'll find the famous yellow and red *Na Hoku II* (808/554-5990, www.nahokuii.com, $30 pp with alcoholic beverages, $25 pp without). It offers 1.5-hour trips, and the first leaves the beach at 11:30am. A sunset sail departs at 5:30pm. Both of these boats have a 49-person maximum capacity and fill up quickly. If you're planning a weekend sunset sail, it's best to make a reservation at least a few days in advance.

At Kuhio Beach Park you'll find the *Mana Kai* (844/626-2524, http://waikikisailing.com, $20 pp), which holds up to 27 passengers, but will sail with just 6. The crew does not serve any beverages, but you are welcome to bring your own. The first one-hour sail departs at 9:30am, and the last sail is around 6pm, depending on the season.

PARASAILING

Parasailing offers the thrill of hang gliding while affixed by a prescribed length of line to a boat motoring across the warm Pacific Ocean. The parachute can soar up to 1,000 feet above the ocean, and as you can imagine, it really is a bird's-eye view. **Hawaiian Parasail** (1651 Ala Moana Blvd., slip 600B, 808/591-8884, http://hawaiianparasail.com, 8am-5pm) is located in the Ala Wai Small Boat Harbor. The slip is in between the two main free-parking areas and visible from the street. Rates start at $50 for 300 feet of line and three minutes in the air. Observers ride for $30. **Hawaii Active** (808/871-8884 or 866/766-6284, www.hawaiiactive.com) is an easy way to book a parasailing trip. There are four options for line length and time in the air, starting with the 300-foot line for 5-7 minutes for $44 per person, up to a 1,000-foot line for 10-12 minutes for $77.

Hiking, Biking, and Bird-Watching

HIKING

You won't need a pair of hiking boots during your stay in Waikiki, even if you do plan on trekking the two "trails" on offer: the Diamond Head Summit Trail or the Waikiki Historic Trail that encircles the region.

★ Diamond Head Summit Trail

The **Diamond Head Summit Trail** is inside the Diamond Head crater, an extinct tuff cone volcano that erupted about 300,000 years ago, and is part of the **Diamond Head State Monument** (www.hawaiistateparks.org, 6am-6pm daily, $5 per vehicle, $1 walk-in visitor). The historic trail, built in 1908, climbs 560 feet from the crater floor to the summit in just 0.8 miles. The steep trail up the inner southwestern rim of the crater is a combination of concrete walkway, switchbacks, stairs, uneven natural terrain, and lighted tunnels. Inside the semiarid crater it's hot and rather dry, so bring plenty of water and sun protection. Along the hike you'll see remnants of O'ahu's natural and military history, punctuated by the breathtaking views of the entire South Shore from the observation station at the summit. Plan on 1.5-2 hours round-trip. The entrance to the Diamond Head State Monument is off Diamond Head Road between Makapu'u Avenue and 18th Avenue. The last entrance to hike the trail is 4:30pm. Visitors must exit the park by 6pm. To get there by bus, use routes 22, 23, or 24.

Waikiki Historic Trail

The self-guided **Waikiki Historic Trail** (www.waikikihistorictrail.com) takes you throughout Waikiki, covering fascinating historical, geological, and cultural sights with tidbits about Waikiki past and present.

Look for these surfboard markers along the Waikiki Historic Trail.

Informative surfboard markers at viewing areas correspond to a prescribed map and program available online. Print out a copy of the map and guide to take with you or use a personal electronic device while on the go. You can follow the order of sights in the program or just visit those areas you prefer. The trail begins at Queen's Surf Beach, hugs the coast to the west (the most scenic section of the trail), rounds up to the Ala Wai Canal and follows Kalakaua Avenue back into the heart of Waikiki. At a normal walking pace, the trail takes about two hours to complete.

BIKING

Since bicycles are prohibited on Waikiki sidewalks and the busy avenues of Waikiki, sans bike lanes, are not exactly bike friendly for those wishing to get around on two wheels, biking is best suited to near and around **Diamond Head,** where traffic is lighter and moves a bit slower. Biking to the Diamond Head lookout and beaches will also alleviate the task of finding parking and allow more time for exploring and enjoying your surroundings. You can circumnavigate Diamond Head easily by traveling from Diamond Head Road to Monsarrat Avenue (a great place to stop for a beverage and a bite to eat) to Paki Avenue and then back to Diamond Head Road.

Hawaiian Style Rentals (2556 Lemon Rd., 808/946-6733, www.hawaiianstylerentals.com, 8:30am-5:30pm daily) rents bicycles with helmet, lock, map, front pouch, and rear rack starting at $15 for four hours, $20 per day, and $15 per day for three days or more. You'll also find bicycle rentals at **Adventure Rentals** (159 Kaiulani Ave., 808/924-2700, 8am-5:30pm daily) and **Big Kahuna Motorcycle Tours and Rentals** (407 Seaside Ave., 808/924-2736 or 888/451-5544, www.bigkahunarentals.com, 8am-5pm daily), which rents mountain bikes for $10 for four hours, $15 for 10 hours, and $100 weekly.

BIRD-WATCHING

On the east end of Waikiki, on the Diamond Head side of where Kapahulu and Kalakaua Avenues intersect, **Kapi'olani Park** (www.kapiolanipark.net) is the place to spot birds in Waikiki. Look up in the trees for green parrots, several types of waxbills, northern and red-crested cardinals, spotted and zebra doves, and the yellow-fronted canary. Look in the grass for the cute Java sparrow, Pacific golden plovers, cattle egrets, and the sassy common myna.

A Day at Diamond Head

Diamond Head, named Le'ahi in Hawaiian, is the tuff cone of an extinct volcano that erupted approximately 300,000 years ago. Today, the profile of Diamond Head as seen from Waikiki has become an iconic image that conjures up all the beauty and lore of Hawai'i. However, there's more to do at this natural wonder than just take a picture for prosperity's sake. Here are a few great ways to explore Diamond Head:

- The **Diamond Head Summit Trail** is the most heart-pumping trail in Waikiki. The summit hike climbs 560 feet inside the volcano, from the crater floor to the rim. It is as much a walk through a natural museum as it is a window to O'ahu's military role in the 20th century: Diamond Head's panoramic view made it the perfect site for coastal defense; five artillery batteries were installed in the crater. The views at the summit lookout are breathtaking and span the entire South Shore.

Black Point from the Daimond Head Lookout

- Whether you walk, run, or drive to the **Diamond Head Lookout** on Diamond Head Road, it's a great place to relax for a spell and take in the scenery. Mansions line the beach to the east out to rugged Black Point, surfers and windsurfers ride the waves below and sailboats and barges cruise the Pacific in the distance. From December through May, humpback whales can be seen breaching, spouting, and playing off the coast from this vantage point. There's even a working lighthouse on the edge of the cliff.

- Located on Diamond Head Road in between the lookout and Kapi'olani Park, **Le'ahi Beach Park** is a quiet, seaside spot that is a great retreat for a picnic or simply to unwind and gaze out at the ocean. There is no beach at this park, as the surf rushes up against a rock wall protecting the oceanside estates, but there is a nice shaded area, and the park is seldom used.

- To experience Diamond Head in its entirety, take the short paved path down the cliff and take a walk on the beach. There are tidepools at both ends of the beach and straight out from lookout up above is the surf spot called **Cliffs.** It's a great wave for longboarding, and the view from the water, looking back up at magnificent Diamond Head, is something most people don't get to see.

- The **Diamond Head Tennis Center,** a 10-court tennis complex, is nestled up against the west side of the outer crater wall. There's nothing like hitting the ball back and forth with the ever-present Diamond Head as your spectator.

Running and Tennis

RUNNING

Kapi'olani Park (intersection of Kapahulu and Kalakaua Avenues) and **Diamond Head** are a runner's delight, and the area is host to myriad walking events and marathons throughout the year, the most famous being the Honolulu Marathon, held annually in December. Kapi'olani Park has a paved path circling the perimeter of the park, a two-mile circumference. Run under the bright and colorful white, yellow, and sherbet-colored flowers of the shower trees, and through the aerial

Kapi'olani Park runner's path

Park back to the sidewalk on Kalakaua Avenue and follow it to Diamond Head Road. From here you can access Kapi'olani Park or run up Diamond Head Road to the lookout.

Running Room (819 Kapahulu Ave., 808/737-2422, www.runningroom.com, 10am-7pm Mon.-Fri., 10am-5pm Sat.-Sun.) has a wide selection of footwear, apparel, accessories, and info about what's new in O'ahu's running and racing community.

TENNIS

The **Diamond Head Tennis Center** (3908 Paki Ave.) is on the east end of Kapi'olani Park. This 10-court public complex is a favorite for local and visiting players. Because of the demand for court time, games are limited to 45 minutes if others are waiting. There are restrooms, shaded benches, and clocks for each court to keep track of playing time. The public courts are free but unlit, so playing time is subject to daylight hours. The parking lot for the courts is open from 6am-7pm daily.

Across the park on Kalakaua Avenue, at the east end of Queen's Surf Beach, are the **Kapi'olani Park Tennis Courts** (5am-midnight daily). These four public courts light up once the sun goes down. The courts are open during park hours, and the same rules of court etiquette as at Diamond Head Tennis Center apply.

roots and trunks of a banyan tree. There is also an exercise station near the Kapi'olani Park Tennis Courts.

If you would like to get a little closer to the ocean during your jog, there is a seaside paved trail stretching from Queen's Surf Beach to the natatorium. Cut through Kaimana Beach

Yoga and Spas

YOGA

Two key aspects of island life are physical activity and relaxing, two pastimes that seem at odds until you consider yoga. There are several yoga studios, indoors and out, for centering yourself through stretching and breathing.

Open Space Yoga (3106 Monsarrat Ave., 808/232-8851, www.yogaopenspace.com) offers hot yoga in its second-floor Diamond Head Studio. Opened in 2011, Open Space Yoga offers visitors one-week unlimited yoga

for $50 and single classes for $18. You can even book classes online.

Another option for yoga in Waikiki proper is **Chocolate Pineapple Sports-Yoga Studio** (2345 Kuhio Ave., 808/277-9935, www.waikikihotyoga.com), which offers daily beach yoga at 7am, park yoga at 9:30am and sunset yoga in the park at 5:30pm. Meet at the entrance to Kapiolani Park, across the street from the zoo at the standing surfer boy statue, near Queen's Surf Beach. One class is $20, and a three-class pass is $45.

If you're keen to practice yoga out of doors in Kapi'olani Park just steps from Queen's Surf Beach, check out **Yoga with Christine** (808/927-7335, www.yogachristine.com, 9am-10am Mon.-Fri.). What you give up in privacy you'll get back in scenery. Certified instructor Christine Okamoto leads classes, conducted in English and Japanese, under a tree near lifeguard tower 2F.

SPAS

Several high-end hotels offer spa services. **SpaHalekulani** (2199 Kalia Rd., 808/931-5322, www.halekulani.com/living/spahalekulani, 9am-8pm daily), in the luxurious Halekulani hotel, incorporates Polynesian therapeutic rituals into its award-winning services. The spa's professional salon staff offers a full range of custom massage treatments. Fifty-minute experiences start at $175; facials start at $185. Special spa offerings are for women, men, and for couples. Complete packages start at $295.

The **Abhasa Waikiki Spa** (2259 Kalakaua Ave., 808/922-8200, www.abhasa.com, 9am-9pm daily) offers private garden cabanas nestled in the secluded Royal Grove Courtyard of the Royal Hawaiian. The outdoor tropical garden setting is a one-of-a-kind spa experience in Waikiki. Massages and facials start at $145 for 50 minutes, and packages begin at $280.

Next door at the Outrigger Waikiki on the Beach you'll find the **Waikiki Plantation Spa** (2335 Kalakaua Ave., 808/926-2880, www.waikikiplantationspa.com, 9am-7pm daily) in the hotel's penthouse on the 17th floor, offering a different, expansive perspective, with views of Waikiki Beach and the Pacific Ocean. Stylized with elements of a traditional Zen rock garden, the full-service spa also offers private fitness programs to highlight the spa experience. Massages start at $115 for 50 minutes, facials begin at $120 for 50 minutes, packages start at $250, and the spa also features a host of body polishes and wraps, like the popular Papa'ala, which uses cooling aids to help heal sunburns—$100 for the 50-minute treatment.

Set in the historic Moana Surfrider, Waikiki's first hotel, **Moanalani Spa** (2365 Kalakaua Ave., 808/237-2543, www.moanalanispa.com, 8am-8pm daily) combines traditional Hawaiian healing with steam rooms, dry saunas, and water therapy areas with ocean views, along with all the other standard spa services. Moanalani also caters to couples treatments, with two private oceanfront lanai. Massages and facials start at $145 for 50-minute sessions, and spa packages begin at $245.

The **Na Ho'ola Spa** (2424 Kalakaua Ave., 808/923-1234, www.nahoolaspawaikiki.com, 7:30am-9pm daily) is located on the fifth floor of the Hyatt Regency Waikiki. The two-story, 10,000-square-foot spa has 16 treatment rooms that evoke the sense of Waikiki, a dry sauna, and steam showers. Massages and body treatments start at $155 for 50 minutes, 50-minute facials begin at $150, body treatments start at $150 and the spa also offers couples treatments.

Shopping

ROYAL HAWAIIAN CENTER

The **Royal Hawaiian Center** (2201 Kalakaua Ave., 808/922-2299, www.royalhawaiiancenter.com, 10am-10pm daily), in the heart of Waikiki on Kalakaua Avenue, stretches from Lewers Street to the Outrigger Waikiki hotel. Here you'll find a mix of high-end retailers—clothing, accessories, and jewelry—surf shops and aloha wear, boutiques, beauty products, and food and drink from coffee to cocktails. If you're looking for a few comfortable T-shirts with some personality, check out **Crazy Shirts** (808/971-6024) on the second floor of building B. For women's swimwear, **Allure Swimwear** (808/926-1174) is located on the first level of building C. For those visiting Waikiki for romance, visit **Princesse Tam-Tam Lingerie** (808/922-3330) on the third level of building A for fine to moderate French lingerie. For all things leather, find **Pipeline Leather** (808/926-2288) on the first level of building C. The center has more than 110 shops and restaurants, including an **Apple Store** (808/931-2480) for your tech needs. Big-name stores front Kalakaua Avenue, but there is a parallel walkway through the mall with a host of other stores, a great way to get out of the sun. A small outdoor performance area with hewn stone seats under a banyan tree leads to a beautifully landscaped Hawaiian botanical garden and into the Royal Hawaiian hotel courtyard.

T GALLERIA

Just to the west of the Royal Hawaiian Center on Kalakaua Avenue, on the mountain side of the street, is **T Galleria by DFS** (330 Kalakaua Ave., 808/931-2700, www.dfs.com, 9am-10:30pm daily). The mall features the world's luxury brands and highly personalized service. International travelers can show their passport and purchase goods duty free, or with no tax added to the retail price. A word

of caution, the mall is designed so that once you enter, it's hard to find the exit in order to keep you shopping.

LUXURY ROW

A few blocks west of T Galleria on Kalakaua Avenue, on the same side of the street, is **Luxury Row** (2100 Kalakaua Ave., 808/541-5136, www.luxuryrow.com, 10am-10pm daily). The name says it all. At Luxury Row you'll find high-end international brands like **Coach** (808/924-1677), **Chanel** (808/971-9011), **Tiffany & Co.** (808/926-2600), **Yves Saint Laurent** (808/924-6900), **Bottega Veneta** (808/923-0800), and **Gucci** (808/921-1000).

ART GALLERIES

Art abounds in Waikiki, with Hawaiian, ocean, and nature themes being the most prevalent. **Wyland Galleries Waikiki** (270 Lewers St., 808/924-1322, www.wyland.com, 10am-10pm daily) features Wyland's signature ocean art and is the most comprehensive Wyland source in Hawai'i. Also on Lewers Street in the Waikiki Beach Walk shops is the **Peter Lik Gallery** (226 Lewers St., 808/926-5656, www.lik.com/galleries/waikiki.html, 10am-11pm daily), featuring bold prints from landscape photographer Peter Lik. Inside the **Sheraton Princess Kaiulani Hotel** (2352 Kalakaua Ave.) you'll find **Tabora Gallery** (808/922-5400, https://taboragallery.com, 9am-10:30pm daily), with originals from seascape painter Roy Tabora.

FARMERS MARKETS

There are two farmers markets in the heart of Waikiki operated by **Mahiku Farmers Markets** (808/225-4002, www.mahikufarmersmarket.com): every Thursday 4pm-8pm in the Hyatt Regency (2424 Kalakaua Ave.), and at King's Village (131 Kaiulani Ave.) every Mon., Wed., Fri., and Sat. from 4pm-9pm.

Entertainment and Events

NIGHTLIFE

Lu Lu's (2270 Kalakaua Ave., 808/979-7590, www.luluswaikiki.com, 7am-2am daily) serves breakfast, lunch, and dinner, but is more widely known as a place to hang out, have a beer, and enjoy its second-story view. Right on the corner of Kalakaua and Kapahulu Avenues, it's the spot for people-watching.

Sky Waikiki (2330 Kalakaua Ave., 808/921-9978, www.skywaikiki.com, 5pm-midnight Sun.-Thurs., 5pm-close Fri.-Sat.) is an upscale club, which offers amazing views, tapas, signature cocktails, and all the things nightclubs are known for. Expect a line to get in after 9pm and a cover charge at the door. You must get bottle service and a table if you'd like to order food.

The Hideaway Bar (1913 Dudoit Ln., 808/949-9885, 6am-2am daily) is a famous little dive that prides itself on being the first establishment in Waikiki to start serving alcohol fresh and early, at 6am. It's also notorious for interesting characters.

For a more upscale bar experience check out Rum Fire (2255 Kalakaua Ave., 808/922-4422, www.rumfirewaikiki.com, 11am-12:30am Fri.-Sat., 11am-midnight Sun.-Thurs.) in the Sheraton Waikiki. Set by the infinity pool, the food is globally influenced to complement the cocktails.

Next door at the Royal Hawaiian is the Mai Tai Bar (2259 Kalakaua Ave., 866/716-8109, www.royal-hawaiian.com/dining/maitaibar, 10am-midnight daily). Right on the beach, the views are exquisite, and there are a couple of cabanas to lounge under. The food and drink are on the expensive side.

The Irish Rose Saloon (478 Ena Rd., 808/947-3414, www.irishrosesaloon.com, 6am-2am daily) is a great Irish pub with live and loud rock and roll and a great selection of Irish whiskey, of course. Smoking is still allowed in the Irish Rose, which you'll either love or hate.

Arnold's Beach Bar & Grill (339 Saratoga Rd., 808/924-6887, 10am-2am daily) is a kitschy throwback to the 1950s. It's warm and cozy, the service is friendly, and the drinks are priced just right.

One of the only true nightclubs in Waikiki, Addiction Nightclub (1775 Ala Moana Blvd., 808/943-5800, http://addictionnightclub.com, 10:30pm-3am Thurs.-Sat.) is in the chic Modern Honolulu hotel. DJs, dancing, bottle service—check the website for who's spinning while you're in town.

On the second floor of the Waikiki Grand hotel, Hula's Bar & Lei Stand (134 Kapahulu Ave., 808/923-0669, www.hulas.com, 10am-2am daily) is Waikiki's premier gay and lesbian bar. Famous for its open-air lanai and beautiful views from the rail, Hula's has DJs and dancing, daily drink specials, and a limited menu of entrées and appetizers. Check its website for a complete monthly events calendar.

LU'AU AND REVUES

There are two traditional lu'au in Waikiki. The Waikiki Starlight Luau at the Hilton Hawaiian Village (2005 Kalia Rd., 808/949-4321, www.hiltonhawaiianvillage.com) is an outdoor event featuring traditional Hawaiian, Tahitian, and Samoan live music and dance, as well as traditional lu'au fare, with accompanying dishes for the less adventurous like huli huli chicken and Hawaiian fried rice. Held Sunday-Thursday (weather permitting) on the rooftop of the Mid-Pacific Conference Center, the two-hour show begins at 5:30pm, with general seating at $99 for adults, $49.50 for children 4-11, and premier seating at $125 for adults, $62.50 for children 4-11. Children under 3 are free. The premier seating includes a fresh orchid lei greeting, preferred table seating closest to the stage, and first dibs at the buffet. All prices include two complimentary beverages. The Sheraton Princess Kaiulani (120 Kaiulani Ave., 808/922-5811, www.princess-kaiulani.com) hosts Creation: A Polynesian Journey,

Street Performers

Once the sun sets over Waikiki, the streets teem with people shopping, walking to dinner (or just waiting for a table), and strolling the main drag, simply enjoying the warm tropical night. Taking advantage of this makeshift nightly audience, Waikiki's **street performers** line the mountain side of the 2300 block of Kalakaua Avenue, wrapping around Kaiulani Avenue and up to King's Village. Break-dancers, spray-paint artists, portrait artists, musicians, and gold- and silver-painted mimes entertain for a drop in the hat. Some of the acts draw quite a crowd, so if you're on the move and don't want to get caught up in the melee, it's best to walk on the other side of the street.

a lavish and dramatic lu'au and show featuring Hawaiian legend, Samoan and New Zealand dance, and modern hula. Creation shows five nights a week (closed Monday and Wednesday) starting at $110 for adults, $82.50 for children 5-12, for the basic dinner show package. There is also a deluxe dinner show package for a higher rate, as well as a cocktail show package for $65 for adults and $48.75 for children 5-12.

The **Royal Hawaiian** (2259 Kalakaua Ave., 808/923-7311, www.royal-hawaiian.com) has a plated lu'au dinner and show held on the Ocean Lawn called **'Aha'aina**, a cultural journey through time. The special dinner is served Monday evenings 5:30pm-9pm for $175 for adults, $97 for children 5-12. There is a nominal charge for children under 5.

If you're in the mood for an evening with Elvis, check out **Burn'n Love Waikiki** (2300 Kalakaua Ave., 808/971-4321, www. burnnlove.com) at the Magic of Polynesia Theatre. The show relives Elvis's time in Hawai'i and the influence it had on his life, his movies, and his music, including *Blue Hawaii* and the Aloha from Hawaii live concert broadcast.

LIVE MUSIC AND CONCERT VENUES

The **Waikiki Shell** (2805 Monsarrat Ave., www.blaisdellcenter.com/venues/waikikishell.html) in Kapi'olani Park is Waikiki's premier concert venue and draws all sorts of performers and musicians. The outdoor, shell-shaped amphitheater has an acoustically sophisticated stage to help amplify music and sound, which reaches all the way to the Pacific Ocean with remarkable clarity. With seating and an expansive lawn area, the Shell is the perfect venue for twilight concerts. There is a free parking lot at the Shell and ample free and paid parking around the park. An events schedule is posted online.

A good portion of the restaurants and bars in Waikiki, especially the oceanfront establishments, have live music during *pau hana* and at night, usually a solo guitarist and singer or duo playing a mix of island-style classic rock peppered with a few island lounge classics. By far, the most popular free concert in Waikiki is **Duke's on Sunday.** From 4pm-6pm every Sunday at Duke's Waikiki (2335 Kalakaua Ave., 808/922-2268, www. dukeswaikiki.com) in the Outrigger Waikiki hotel, Hawaiian rock legend Henry Kapono plays a lively 2-hour rock-and-roll set of his own hits and classic rock covers done in his own style. Known as the "Wild Hawaiian," he draws residents and visitors alike to Duke's lower lanai, right on the sand, to catch the show, dance, and enjoy a few beverages in the afternoon sun. Kapono plays every Sunday unless he's on tour, in which case there are several other noteworthy bands in the lineup that put on a great show.

FESTIVALS AND EVENTS

There is no shortage of cultural events, festivals, and parades throughout the year that close down Kalakaua Avenue to vehicular traffic and bring out the live music and food vendors to invoke a celebratory atmosphere.

Spring

The **Waikiki Spam Jam** (www.spamjamha-waii.com) goes off at the end of April, with two stages on Kalakaua Avenue and featuring live music, food vendors, and a party till 10pm celebrating local Hawaiian culture. On May 1 **Lei Day** is celebrated with a colorful parade of flowers.

Summer

June is packed full of festivals: the **Honolulu Pride Parade and Celebration** (http://honolulupradeparade.blogspot.com) is in early June, the **Pan-Pacific Festival** (www.pan-pacific-festival.com) is a three-day event celebrating Pacific Rim culture with performances, food, events, and a parade, and the **Kamehameha Day Floral Parade** should not be missed if you're in Waikiki on June 11. In late July, the **Ukulele Festival** (www.ukulelefestivalhawaii.org) is a local favorite, when local and international ukulele talents entertain at the Kapi'olani Bandstand. **Duke's Oceanfest** (http://dukesoceanfest.com) is a weeklong series of ocean events in late August celebrating ocean sports and the legacy of Duke Kahanamoku. Competitions in longboarding, paddleboarding, swimming, tandem surfing, surf polo, beach volleyball, and other events go down from sunrise to sunset along Kuhio Beach Park.

Food

COFFEE

Honolulu Coffee Company (2365 Kalakaua Ave., 808/533-1500, ext. 4, www.honolulucoffee.com, 6am-10:30pm daily) can be found at the Moana Surfrider, but right on the sidewalk of Kalakaua Avenue, so you don't need to enter the hotel to find it. It has a wide variety of bagels, breads and pastries, and several tables, even sidewalk window seats.

Upstairs in the Royal Hawaiian Shopping Center, on the second floor, you'll find **Island Vintage Coffee** (2201 Kalakaua Ave., 808/922-2299, www.islandvintagecoffee.com, 6am-11pm daily), serving 100 percent Kona coffee, prepared foods, bakery treats, and acai bowls. It also has a nice lanai, where you can enjoy your coffee and snack.

QUICK BITES AND CAFÉS

Giovanni's Pastrami (227 Lewers St., 808/923-2100, www.giovannipastrami.com, 7am-midnight daily, $9-23) is a great New York-style deli and sports bar. With choice ingredients to nosh, 17 TVs, breakfast served till midnight, and a weekday happy hour 3pm-6pm, it's a great place to watch the game and have a sandwich and beer in style.

A toasted hole in the bun, tropical relishes, and one-of-a-kind garlic-lemon sauces on a polish sausage make **Hula Dog** (2301 Kuhio Ave., 808/924-7887, www.huladog.com, 10am-9pm daily, $7) a snack, or meal, to experience. Doubling as a sports bar, during football season it opens at 6am.

Mac 24/7 (2500 Kuhio Ave., 808/921-5564, www.mac247waikiki.com, open 24 hours daily, $14-28) serves so many different purposes in Waikiki. It's a bar, it's a club, it's a restaurant, and it's a breakfast joint. Find it inside the Hilton Waikiki Beach Hotel and see if you're up to the pancake challenge—eat three, 14-inch pancakes topped with a slew of fixings in under 90 minutes for free breakfast, prizes, and bragging rights.

What's the perfect meal in Waikiki? How about an afternoon surf at Publics and then dinner at **Barefoot Beach Cafe** (2701 Kalakaua Ave., 808/924-2233, https://barefootbeachcafe.wordpress.com, 7am-8:30pm daily, $9-15), overlooking Queen's Surf Beach and the beautiful waves that peel along the reef. Open-air seating right on the beach and good food—what could be better? Live music daily and beach barbecue Friday and Saturday starting at 5:30pm—that's what.

Bogart's Café (3045 Monsarrat Ave., 808/739-0999, http://bogartscafe.webs.com, 6am-6:30pm Mon.-Fri., 6am-6pm Sat.-Sun., $6-21) is a great little breakfast spot for escaping the bustle of Waikiki proper. The eggs, bagels, pancakes, waffles, and coffee are the perfect breakfast options after a walk or run across Kapi'olani Park.

From homemade cakes, salads, and dips to cold sandwiches, local food, and burgers right off the grill, **Diamond Head Market & Grill** (3158 Monsarrat Ave., 808/732-0077, www.diamondheadmarket.com, 6:30am-9pm daily, $5-17) has a little bit of everything on offer. The grill has a walk-up window on the exterior of the building. Be prepared for a bit of a wait at lunch, as the food is popular with locals and visitors alike. And check out all the bakery delights inside. The scones are beyond delicious, if there are any left.

BREAKFAST

Eggs 'n Things (343 Saratoga Rd., 808/923-3447, www.eggsnthings.com, 6am-2pm, 4pm-10pm daily, $8-17) is an extremely popular breakfast joint serving American-style breakfast with a few local variations. Meat, eggs, pancakes, waffles, and even crepes are the crux of the menu. Dinner is served as well. There is also a location on Kalakaua Avenue, called the **Waikiki Beach Eggspress** (2464 Kalakaua Ave., 808/926-3447, 6am-2pm, 4pm-10pm daily, $8-17), which has an interesting seating method. First you wait in line to order, then you wait in line to get seated, and then sometimes you have to wait a little longer for your food to arrive. With an average wait of 30-40 minutes from the moment it opens, it's apparent Eggs 'n Things has developed quite a following.

STEAK AND SEAFOOD

The **Hau Tree Lanai** (2863 Kalakaua Ave., 808/921-7066, http://kaimana.com/hautreelanai.htm, 7am-2pm, 5:30pm-9pm daily, $30-52) is a quaint open-air restaurant right on Sans Souci Beach, nestled under the canopy of a distinctive hau tree growing on the property for more than a century. In fact, Scottish author Robert Louis Stevenson enjoyed its shade in the early 1900s as a place where he could relax and put pen to paper. Serving breakfast, lunch, and dinner, the restaurant offers traditional American and Asian-influenced cuisine.

Eggs 'n Things is the "in" breakfast joint, so be prepared to wait at least 30 minutes for a stack of pancakes.

Azure (2259 Kalakaua Ave., 808/923-7311, www.azurewaikiki.com, 5:30pm-9pm daily, $26-52) is the pinnacle of fine seafood dining. Set inside the Royal Hawaiian, it serves the freshest seafood there is, hand selected from the Honolulu fish auction every morning. The focus is on high-heat, aromatic, herb-roasted Hawai'i regional preparations with bright tropical flavors. Sommeliers can assist in selecting the perfect wine for your dinner. Azure has beachfront dining cabanas in addition to the dining room and a traditional six-course degustation menu, with samplings of the chef's signature dishes and wine pairings.

Tired of ordering a steak and finding it not done to your liking? Then the **Shore Bird** (2169 Kalia Rd., 808/922-2887, http://shorebirdwaikiki.com, 7am-2am daily, $16-30), a beachfront restaurant in the Outrigger Reef, is your calling. At the Shore Bird's Famous Grill, you can cook your own steak, chicken, or fish. It also serves breakfast and lunch, and has a late-night menu with classic bar food.

Roy's (226 Lewers St., 808/923-7697, http://royshawaii.com, 11am-9:30pm Mon.-Thurs., 11am-10pm Fri.-Sun., $15-45) has Hawaiian fusion wired, and the quality of ingredients, consistency, and service are exceptional. It is open for appetizer service 11am-5pm and offers a prix fixe menu with a sampling of favorites, a well-balanced offering of meat and fish entrées, and sushi.

Orchids (2199 Kalia Rd., 808/923-2311, www.halekulani.com/living/dining/orchids, 7:30am-10pm daily, $28-60) is located inside the Halekulani hotel. As the name suggests, colorful orchids abound, and the restaurant opens out to a breathtaking view of the Pacific Ocean unencumbered by beach umbrellas or sunbathers. The Sunday brunch is punctuated by a three-meat carving station, something you won't find at most Waikiki breakfast buffets, and the signature dinner entrée is a light *onaga* (snapper) Orchids style, with sesame oil, shoyu, and ginger. It also offers a lunch menu.

★ **Kai Market** (2255 Kalakaua Ave., 808/921-4600, www.sheraton-waikiki.com/dining/kai, 6am-11am, 5:30pm-9:30pm daily, breakfast $22-29, dinner $55-58) prides itself on locally sourcing all its products and ingredients, from the baked goods to the meat and produce. Kai Market is inside the Sheraton Waikiki, and both breakfast and dinner are buffet style. Kids 5 and under eat free anytime, and children 6-12 eat for half price.

Top of Waikiki (2270 Kalakaua Ave., 808/923-3877, http://topofwaikiki.com, 4:30pm-11pm daily, starting at $37) is truly a unique dining experience. On the top floor of the Waikiki Business Plaza, the three-tiered round restaurant slowly revolves 360 degrees per hour, offering guests a complete view of O'ahu's glowing South Shore. An open sit-down bar provides an additional level for viewing the sights. Great Pacific Rim cuisine and nightly happy hour specials—5pm-7pm and 9pm-11pm—complete the experience. Dinner is served until 9:30pm.

★ **Duke's Waikiki** (2335 Kalakaua Ave., 808/922-2268, www.dukeswaikiki.com, 7am-midnight daily, $15-33) is a must, whether it's for the breakfast buffet, lunch, dinner, or just cruising in the **Barefoot Bar** and watching the surfers out at Canoes and Queen's. Decorated with historic and recent pictures of the Waikiki beachboys and surf nostalgia, the relaxed, beachside atmosphere complements the excellent food and service Duke's has live music Monday-Thursday in the bar 4pm-6pm, and Friday-Sunday the show moves out to the lower lanai under the sun, the highlight being Duke's on Sunday, featuring Henry Kapono (unless he's on tour). For dinner, make reservations or be prepared to wait up to an hour during busy times, which isn't that bad if you retire to the bar and relax till your table is ready.

Hula Grill (2335 Kalakaua Ave., 808/923-4852, www.hulagrillwaikiki.com, 6:30am-10pm daily, $20-34), in the Outrigger Waikiki and just upstairs from Duke's, is a great steak and seafood option if you don't have the time to wait for a table downstairs. With comfortable, Hawaiian home decor and live music nightly, 7pm-9pm, Hula Grill provides a comfortable ambience in which to savor several fish specialties, including the popular Macadamia Nut Crusted as well as the succulent Filet Steak Kiana, a take on the steak Diane. Hula Grill has a great Aloha Hour 4pm-6pm with half-off selected menu and drink items.

Chuck's Cellar (150 Kaiulani Ave., 808/923-4488, www.chuckshawaii.com/cellar.html, 5:30pm-10pm daily, starting at $20) offers an all-you-can-eat salad bar with every entrée, but the real draw for Chuck's Cellar is live jazz Thursday-Sunday. The decor, and a little jazz flute, will take you back in time.

In the Aston Waikiki Beach Hotel, on the second floor overlooking Kuhio Beach Park, **Tiki's Grill & Bar** (2570 Kalakaua Ave., 808/923-8454, http://tikisgrill.com, 10:30am-2am daily, $24-29) is a locally owned and operated establishment with tasty lunch and dinner menus serving regional and Pacific Rim cuisine. Its ingredients are locally sourced, and it partners with local farmers for the freshest produce, as well as following a Green Program in all aspects of its business. Catch Hawaiian Hula Nights every Thursday 5pm-11pm, featuring traditional and contemporary Hawaiian music, hula, and food and drink specials on the open lanai.

Michel's (2895 Kalakaua Ave., 808/923-6552, http://michelshawaii.com, 5:30pm-9pm Sun.-Thurs., 5:30pm-10pm Fri.-Sat., $40-75) is the pinnacle of French haute cuisine in Waikiki and has been recognized as the "Best Restaurant for Romance" by *Honolulu Magazine* since 1985. Overlooking a beautiful stretch of reef and ocean closer to Diamond Head and away from the Waikiki crowds, the stunning setting, live music, and delectable menu are worth the price for a truly special occasion. Michel's also offers a chef's choice six-course tasting menu.

MEXICAN

Buho Cocina Y Cantina (2250 Kalakaua Ave., 808/922-2846, http://buhocantina.com, 11am-1am Sun.-Thurs., 11am-2am Fri.-Sat., $10-29) is a great change of pace for your palate. The rooftop restaurant has mostly outdoor seating and a warm, festive atmosphere. Start with the guacamole appetizer and then dive into the many delicious entrées. You can't go wrong with the smoked brisket tacos and a signature margarita. From the sidewalk on Kalakaua, take the elevator from the street level directly to the restaurant.

ITALIAN

Perched at the top of the Ilikai hotel, **Sarento's** (1777 Ala Moana Blvd., 808/955-5559, www.sarentoswaikiki.com, 5pm-10:30pm Sun.-Thurs., 5pm-midnight Fri.-Sat., $24-42) has magnificent views of Waikiki and Honolulu's skyline. Fine Italian dining is accompanied with live piano music and great service.

Taormina (227 Lewers St., 808/926-5050, http://taorminarestaurant.com, 11am-10pm Sun.-Thurs., 11am-11pm Fri.-Sat., $17-49) serves Sicilian cuisine in a fine-dining setting. With fresh fish and homemade breads and pastas as specials, it offers over 125 wines for the perfect pairing. A favorite is the Fresh Pasta Nero "Frutti Di Mare."

JAPANESE

No detail has been left unexplored at **Nobu** (2233 Helumoa Rd., 808/237-6999, www.noburestaurants.com, 5:30pm-10pm Mon.-Thurs. and Sun., 5:30pm-10:30pm Fri.-Sat., $3-48), where the architecture and interior help create an intimate and elegant setting, and the innovative and award-winning "New Style" Japanese cuisine is unmatched. Located in the Waikiki Parc Hotel, the sophisticated seafood-centric menu covers a range of hot and cold dishes, sushi and sashimi, complete dinners, and kushiyaki and tempura. The happy hour (5pm-7pm Sun.-Thurs.) has drink and food specials that could suffice for a meal by themselves, though it's only available in the bar and lounge area.

Serving contemporary, inventive sushi and Asian-influenced dishes, ★ **Sansei Seafood Restaurant and Sushi Bar** (2552 Kalakaua Ave., 808/931-6286, www.sanseihawaii.com, 5:30pm-10pm Mon.-Thurs. and Sun., 5:30pm-1am Fri.-Sat., starting at $8) is one of the most popular sushi restaurants in Waikiki. With its handful of award-winning sushi creations, the à la carte menu is perfect for sampling the gamut. Sansei has a popular early bird special 5:30pm-6pm Sunday and Monday, with half off most of the menu (people line up early at the door) and half-off drink specials 10pm-1am Friday and Saturday.

Odoriko (2400 Koa Ave., 808/923-7368, http://odorikohawaii.com, noon-midnight Mon.-Sat., $4-50) serves up traditional Japanese cuisine for lunch and dinner, as well as offering an assortment of fresh seafood and sushi—even live Maine lobster. If you're not feeling like fish, it also serves hot pot entrées like shabu-shabu or sukiyaki. Odoriko has private party and karaoke rooms for rent by the hour starting at $30.

Tanaka of Tokyo (150 Kaiulani Ave., 808/922-4233, www.tanakaoftokyo.com, 5:30pm-11pm daily, $19-95) is a Japanese seafood and steak house *teppanyaki* restaurant, where the food is prepared by master chefs on tabletop grills. It's a fun and relaxed atmosphere with excellent food and service. The Shogun Special, with tenderloin, lobster tail, and sea scallops, is a house favorite. Find Tanaka on the ground floor of the Ohana Waikiki East hotel, with access from Kaiulani Avenue.

Doraku Sushi (2233 Kalakaua Ave., 808/922-3323, http://dorakusushi.com, 11:30am-11pm Mon.-Thurs., 11:30am-2am Fri.-Sat., 11:30-midnight Sun., $4-44) features *izakaya* dining, where dishes are brought to the table throughout the meal to share. On the menu you'll find hot and cold dishes as well as a beautiful assortment of specialty sushi rolls, sashimi, and soups and salads. A relaxing and enjoyable experience.

CHINESE

For fine Chinese seafood dining check out **Beijing Chinese Seafood Restaurant** (2301 Kalakaua Ave., 808/971-8833, www.beijinghawaii.com, 11:30am-2:30pm, 5pm-9:30pm daily, $35-92). Specializing in set dinner menus with a variety of delectable seafood creations paired with entrées including duck, chicken, and beef, this place won't let you leave hungry. The lunch menu features a range of steamed dumplings.

HEALTH FOOD

★ **Diamond Head Cove Health Bar** (3045 Monsarrat Ave., 808/732-8744, www.diamondheadcove.com, 9am-8pm Mon. and Fri.-Sat., 9am-11pm Tues.-Thurs. and Sun., $5-13) is a small juice and kava bar that also serves fresh omelets, hummus, salads, and is famous for its hearty and healthy *aiai* bowls. The staff is friendly, the food is fresh and delicious, and surf art, posters, and decorations fill every space on the walls and ceiling, creating a cool hangout to beat the midday heat. The Cove, as it's known by local patrons, stays open late for Kava Nights, Tuesday through Thursday, when it turns the lights low and lets the live musicians set the mood.

One of the few places in Waikiki that caters to vegetarians and vegans, **Ruffage Natural Foods** (2443 Kuhio Ave., 808/922-2042, 9am-9pm daily, $5-10) has simple but great sandwiches, salads, burritos, and other prepared foods (it does have meat options, too). It also sells health foods and blends great smoothies.

MARKETS

Food Pantry (2370 Kuhio Ave., 808/923-9831, 6am-1am daily) is the closest thing to a proper grocery store in Waikiki. It's also notorious for being ridiculously expensive, which can also be called the price of convenience.

Information and Services

MAIL

While most of the hotels offer outgoing mail service, Waikiki does have a **post office** (330 Saratoga Rd., 808/973-7517, 9am-4:30pm Mon.-Fri., 9am-1pm Sat.). There is an Automated Postal Center for after-hours business or if you want to avoid the line.

MEDICAL

Should you be in need of medical service, there are several options for care: **Straub Doctors on Call** (808/971-6000 or 808/923-9966 for Japanese-speaking doctors) for emergencies and "house calls" to your hotel, 24 hours a day; **Kuhio Walk-in Medical Clinic** (2310 Kuhio Ave., Ste. 223, 808/924-6688, 9am-4pm Mon.-Fri., 9am-1pm Sat.) at the corner of Nahua in Waikiki; **Urgent Care Clinic of Waikiki** (2155 Kalakaua Ave., Ste. 308, 808/924-3399, www.waikikiclinic.org, 8:30am-6:30pm Mon.-Fri., till 5pm Sat.-Sun.) in the ANA Kalakaua Building, with lab and x-ray capabilities; **The Medical Corner** (1860 Ala Moana Blvd., #101, 808/943-1111, www.themedicalcorner.com, 8am-4:30pm Mon.-Fri., 9am-noon Sat.) for minor emergencies; and **Waikiki Health Center** (277 Ohua Ave., 808/922-4787, www.waikikihc. org, 8:30am-7pm Mon. and Wed., 8:30am-6:30pm Tues., Thurs.-Fri., 8:30am-12:30pm Sat.), for low-cost care.

LIBRARY

Internet access is available at the **Waikiki-Kapahulu Public Library** (400 Kapahulu Ave., 808/733-8488, http://hawaii.sdp.sirsi.net/custom/web, 10am-5pm Tues., Wed., Fri., Sat., noon-7pm Thurs.) on the outskirts of Waikiki at the corner of Kapahulu Avenue and Ala Wai Boulevard. Visitors need a valid Hawai'i State Public Library System (HSPLS) card to use an Internet computer Three-month visitor cards are available for $10. You can reserve Internet computer time online or in person. You can also find printed bus schedules and browse titles online for availability. Closed Monday and Tuesday.

GAS

There is one gas station in Waikiki proper, **Aloha Island Mart** (2025 Kalakaua Ave., 808/942-0075). The convenience store and the pumps are open 24 hours a day. You can also fill up near the Diamond Head businesses at the **Aloha Island Mart** (3203 Monsarrat Ave., 808/735-5333).

Getting There and Around

CAR

If you didn't pick up a rental car at the airport and find you would like to make use of a vehicle during your stay, there are national big-brand companies in Waikiki as well as several smaller independent firms that rent vehicles, including sedans, four-wheel drives, SUVs, and convertibles. Thrifty (2002 Kalakaua Ave., 808/971-2660, www.thrifty.com, 7am-8pm daily) and Dollar (2002 Kalakaua Ave., 808/952-4264, www.dollar.com, 7am-8pm daily) share a lot at the west end of Waikiki. Among the independent companies are VIP (Very Inexpensive Prices) Car Rentals (234 Beach Walk, 808/922-4605, www.vip-carrentalhawaii.com, 7am-5pm daily) and Paradise Rent-A-Car (1837 Ala Moana Blvd., 808/946-7777; 151 Uluniu Ave., 808/926-7777; http://paradiserentacarhawaii.com, 8am-5pm daily).

The most distinctive cars in Waikiki are the sports cars and luxury imports available from Hawaii Luxury Car Rentals (2025 Kalakaua Ave., 808/222-2277, www.hiluxurycarrentals.com, 8am-5pm daily). This company has a fleet of American and European classic cars, like the Viper, Corvette, Porsche, Cadillac Escalade, Hummer H2, BMW, and the only Prowler for rent in Hawai'i, all at the Aloha Gas Station. Rates start at $250 per day for the Prowler. The company offers multiple-day discounts and welcomes customers 21 and over.

BUS

Many popular island destinations and attractions are reachable via the Honolulu public bus system, called TheBus (www.thebus.org), either directly from Waikiki or from the Ala Moana Shopping Center bus depot after a short ride from Waikiki. Routes 19 and 20 will get travelers to the airport in Honolulu; Diamond Head can be reached via buses running on Routes 22, 23, and 24.

Check out DaBus (http://www.honolulu.gov/mobile/dabus.html), the O'ahu Bus app, which is available for Apple and Android phones. Using near real-time arrival information, it estimates when the next bus will arrive, you can search for bus stops by street name or stop number, find bus routes and even track the location of the bus you're interested in.

TAXI AND LIMOUSINE

There are several taxicab companies that service Waikiki. Star Discount Taxi Service (808/942-7827, www.startaxihawaii.com) offers a $30-or-less flat rate to or from the Honolulu International Airport from any Waikiki hotel and has discount flat-rate fares for a variety of O'ahu destinations; TheCAB (808/422-2222, www.thecabhawaii.com) operates 24 hours a day, 365 days a year; Honolulu Taxi Service (808/699-9999, http://honolulu-taxi.com) has door-to-door service; and for Honolulu Taxi Cab (808/741-7545), call one hour ahead for best service.

Limos are a great way to get around in style and are popular for wedding parties and transfers to and from the airport. Duke's Limousine (808/738-1878, www.dukes-limo.com) has a fleet of limos with varying carrying capacities and rates starting at $75 per hour, with a two-hour minimum. Royal Hawaiian Limousine (808/275-6030, www.royalhawaiianlimousine.com) offers car and limousine service, airport transportation, private charters and tours. Platinum Limousine Hawaii (808/739-0007, http://platinumlimohawaii.com) operates 24 hours a day, seven days a week, and with award-winning service and high-end, showy luxurious vehicles, Platinum has built quite a star-studded clientele. Rates start at $85 per hour for the eight-passenger Lincoln Towncar limo, with a two-hour minimum, or a three-hour minimum on Sunday.

Uber and Lyft ride-hailing options are also available in Waikiki.

MOTORCYCLE, MOPED, AND BICYCLE

For rentals, try Big Kahuna Motorcycle Tours and Rentals (407 Seaside Ave., 808/924-2736 or 888/451-5544, www.bigkahunarentals.com, 8am-5pm daily), where motorcycle rentals run $50-180 for four hours, with full-day and weekly rentals available. It also rents mopeds and bicycles, with mountain bikes starting at $10 for four hours. Cruzin Hawaii (1980 Kalakaua Ave., 808/945-9595 or 877/945-9595, www.cruzinhawaii.com, 8am-6pm daily) rents Harley-Davidsons at its shop near the Ambassador Hotel, $79-99 for three hours, $99-149 all day, with 24-hour, three-day, and weekly rates available. Paradise Rent-A-Car (1837 Ala Moana Blvd., 808/946-7777; 151 Uluniu Ave., 808/926-7777; http://paradiserentacarhawaii.com, 8am-5pm daily) also rents Harleys and scooters. And Chase Hawaii Rentals (355 Royal Hawaiian Ave., 808/942-4273, www.chasehawaiirentals.com; 138 Uluniu Ave., 808/348-6070; 8am-6pm daily) has over 30 models of Harley-Davidsons for rent, as well as sport bikes and cruisers.

Mopeds and motor scooters are common across the island and are a great way to get around, but accident statistics prove they are quite dangerous. Even though there is no helmet law in Hawai'i, motorcycle and moped riders should always wear one for safety purposes. Big Kahuna Motorcycle Tours and Rentals (407 Seaside Ave., 808/924-2736 or 888/451-5544, www.bigkahunarentals.com, 8am-5pm daily) rents mopeds starting at $25 for four hours and larger scooters starting at $65 for four hours, with full-day and weekly rentals available. Chase Hawaii Rentals (355 Royal Hawaiian Ave., 808/942-4273; 138 Uluniu Ave., 808/348-6070; www.chasehawaiirentals.com, 8am-6pm daily) rents Vespas starting at $79 for 10 hours and $99 for 24 hours. Paradise Cruisers (2413 Kuhio Ave., 808/926-2847, http://paradisecruisershawaii.com, 8am-8pm daily) rents mopeds and scoot cars (two-passenger vehicles with two wheels in the front and one in the back; the car is open to the elements), and you can also find mopeds and scooters at Adventure on 2 Wheels (1946 Ala Moana Ave., 808/944-3131, 8am-4pm daily; 2552 Lemon Rd., 808/921-8111, 8am-5pm daily).

Honolulu

The capital of the Hawaiian Islands since 1845, Honolulu means "sheltered bay" in the Hawaiian language.

Honolulu is the political, cultural, and economic center of O'ahu and the state of Hawai'i, thanks largely to Honolulu Harbor's commercial port and the Honolulu International Airport. Its more than 400 high-rises create a skyline in stark contrast to the verdant backdrop of forested ridges and valleys. Honolulu combines the hustle, convenience, and abundance of a major city and an ethnically diverse population of 350,000 people with a history made unique by its architecture and thriving neighborhoods.

Just east of Pearl Harbor, Honolulu is defined by its city center, the economic heart of the county and state. Containing the Hawai'i state capitol building that neighbors 'Iolani Palace, the only royal residence in the United States, the historic district is beset by towering skyscrapers. It gives way to Chinatown, a relic of O'ahu's whaling, migrant worker, and war-torn past. Today, Chinatown is chock-full of art galleries, nightclubs, bars, and some of O'ahu's best restaurants.

Honolulu's neighborhoods spread out in all directions and are as dynamic as the rainbows that hang over the mountains. Manoa Valley is home to the University of Hawai'i and Lyon Arboretum at the back of the valley. Kaimuki is known for its shopping and restaurants. Kaka'ako's industrial spaces have become the bastion for a burgeoning urban art scene, and Ala Moana Beach Park affords expansive grassy space, great waves, and a calm swimming area on the inside of the reef.

PLANNING YOUR TIME

Many of the activities in Honolulu, whether sightseeing in the historic district or hiking in the Ko'olau Mountains, require at least a half day's time. Mix in a meal or two and you have a packed schedule.

When heading downtown to see the historic district, leave early to beat the hot midday sun, since the best option is walking to the different buildings and museums. Downtown metered street parking has a two-hour time limit, so when it's time to get back to the car, head over to Chinatown, park in one of the municipal lots, and explore the small, historic city blocks. Plan on saving your appetite for eating in Chinatown, as the diversity of cuisine here will make your head spin.

Previous: downtown Honolulu; 'Iolani Palace. **Above:** the Pearl Harbor Historic Sites.

Look for ★ to find recommended
sights, activities, dining, and lodging.

Highlights

★ **'Iolani Palace:** The only royal residence in the United States, this grand and stately palace sits on 11 grassy acres with beautiful shade trees (page 74).

★ **Historic Chinatown:** Chinatown is a hub for international dining, art, nightlife—and for Chinese food and goods, of course (page 77).

★ **Honolulu Museum of Art:** Hawai'i's most prestigious art museum, with over 50,000 pieces spanning 5,000 years, was established in 1927. The museum's holdings include Asian, European, American, and African works of art (page 78).

★ **Foster Botanical Garden:** Century-old trees, palms, orchids, and cycads—curious leafy plants that date back to prehistoric times—can all be found in this majestic spot (page 79).

★ **Nu'uanu Pali State Wayside:** The Pali Lookout is a beautiful spot to take in the grandeur of the Ko'olau Mountains and the tropical splendor of Kane'ohe Bay. (page 80).

★ **Tantalus-Round Top Drive:** This leisurely scenic drive winds up the Tantalus Crater to beautiful Pu'u 'Ualaka'a Park at the top of the volcano's cinder cone. The view scans Diamond Head, Punchbowl Crater, and greater Honolulu (page 81).

★ **Bishop Museum:** The premier museum in the Pacific explores Hawaiian culture and history, the other Polynesian and Pacific cultures, and the natural history of the islands. It also features a planetarium and interactive Science Adventure Center (page 83).

★ **Pearl Harbor Historic Sites:** Pay homage to the lives lost during the Pearl Harbor attack on December 7, 1941 (page 84).

★ **Magic Island:** Paths wind beneath the branches of beautiful trees. There's a protected beach and lagoon where *keiki* can safely play. Beautiful views along the coast make it perfect for a seaside picnic (page 86).

For an art day, start out at the Honolulu Museum of Art. With your paid admission you'll also get entry at the Honolulu Museum of Art Spalding House in Makiki Heights, featuring contemporary art and a botanical garden. Stop by the Hawaii State Art Museum, which is free to the public, to check out the finest work from top local artists, then hop over to Chinatown for a walking tour of art galleries and dinner on Bethel Street and Nuuanu Avenue.

After a day in the city center, you might enjoy a little peace and quiet. To attain such solace in nature, go for a hike in Manoa Valley or at Wa'ahila Ridge State Park, then grab a bite to eat at one of the casual BYOBs in Kaimuki. If you need to expand your horizons, take the windy drive up Tantalus or Round Top Drives to Pu'u 'Ualaka'a Park and relax with views of Honolulu and Diamond Head. If you feel like walking, there are several trailheads in the vicinity.

Honolulu might be urban, but it still has beaches. Spend the morning swimming, surfing, or stand-up paddling at Ala Moana Beach Park, then head across the street to Ala Moana Center for shopping and dining.

ORIENTATION
Downtown
Downtown is the epicenter of Honolulu and the financial and political center of the island and the state. Within downtown are the historic district, comprised of the state capitol, 'Iolani Palace, government buildings and offices, as well as other historical and cultural buildings. To the immediate west of the historic district is the financial district, where high-rise office buildings perch along one-way streets.

Chinatown
Just west of the financial district is the historic Chinatown neighborhood, which stretches from Vineyard Boulevard to the north, to Aloha Tower along the harbor, with the Nu'uanu Stream as its western border. Chinatown is home to a curious mix of bars, hip ethnic restaurants, Chinese and Pacific Rim cuisine, Chinese grocery stores, small local eateries, art galleries, and chic coffee shops.

Kaka'ako
At the forefront of the urban art scene, much of Kaka'ako is industrial, especially the streets southeast of downtown. Young artists have transformed the area into an explosion of color and art, and drab building walls are now radiant and expressive. In addition to colorful building exteriors, art galleries, coffee shops, and restaurants, Kaka'ako also has a green waterfront park. Kaka'ako stretches toward the mountains all the way to the H-1 freeway.

Ala Moana
Dominated by Ala Moana Beach Park, Magic Island, and Ala Moana Center, the Ala Moana neighborhood straddles the gap between Kaka'ako, Waikiki, and the McCully residential neighborhoods to the east. This central area for shopping encompasses several other malls located to the west, along Ward Avenue.

Greater Honolulu
Honolulu is a sprawling metropolis with many neighborhoods stretching out in all directions from downtown. Some are industrial, others are urban, and some are in the valleys and on the mountains behind the city.

In the mountains directly behind downtown Honolulu, you'll find **Nu'uanu,** defined by residential neighborhoods spreading from the north side of Chinatown and downtown back through Nu'uanu Valley.

To the east of Nu'uanu, on the mountain side of Interstate H-1, is **Punchbowl,** which consists of the old neighborhoods surrounding Punchbowl Crater.

Northeast of Punchbowl is the **Makiki** neighborhood, which snakes up the mountains.

Heading east takes you to the upscale neighborhood of **Manoa,** which stretches from deep in Manoa Valley to the University of Hawai'i at Manoa.

Greater Honolulu

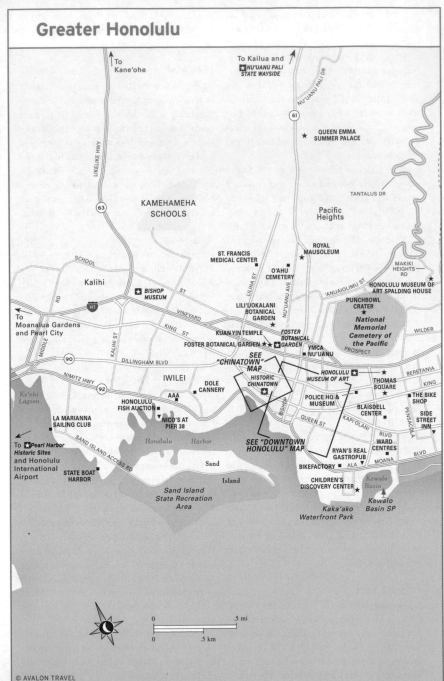

To Kane'ohe

To Kailua and
⊞ NU'UANU PALI
STATE WAYSIDE

NU'UANU PALI DR

61

QUEEN EMMA
★ SUMMER PALACE

LIKELIKE HWY

TANTALUS DR

KAMEHAMEHA
SCHOOLS

Pacific
Heights

63

ROYAL
MAUSOLEUM
★

MAKIKI
HEIGHTS
RD

ST. FRANCIS
MEDICAL CENTER
■

O'AHU
CEMETERY

HONOLULU MUSEUM OF
ART SPALDING HOUSE

SCHOOL

Kalihi

⊞ BISHOP
MUSEUM

'ANUAIOLIMU ST

LILI'UOKALANI
BOTANICAL
GARDEN

PUNCHBOWL
CRATER
★

BISHOP
ST

VINEYARD

National
Memorial
Cemetery of
the Pacific

WILDER

RD

H1

To
Moanalua Gardens
and Pearl City

KING
ST

KALIHI ST

KUAN YIN TEMPLE

FOSTER
BOTANICAL
★★ ⊞ GARDEN

FOSTER BOTANICAL GARDEN

YMCA
■ NU'UANU

PROSPECT

LILIHA ST

NU'UANU AVE

90

DILLINGHAM BLVD

SEE
"CHINATOWN"
MAP

HONOLULU ⊞
MUSEUM OF ART
★

THOMAS
SQUARE
★

BERETANIA

NIMITZ HWY

IWILEI

DOLE
CANNERY

HISTORIC
CHINATOWN
⊞

KING

THE BIKE
SHOP
★

92

Ke'ehi
Lagoon

HONOLULU
FISH AUCTION

AAA
■

■

POLICE HQ &
MUSEUM

QUEEN ST

BLAISDELL
CENTER
■

KAPI'OLANI

PENSACOLA

SIDE
STREET
INN
▼

BISHOP

NICO'S AT
PIER 38

LA MARIANNA
SAILING CLUB

SAND ISLAND ACCESS RD

Honolulu   Harbor

SEE "DOWNTOWN
HONOLULU" MAP

BLVD

RYAN'S REAL
GASTROPUB

WARD
CENTRES
▼

MOANA

BLVD

To ⊞ Pearl Harbor
Historic Sites
and Honolulu
International
Airport

STATE BOAT
HARBOR

Sand

Island

BIKEFACTORY ■ ALA ▼

CHILDREN'S
DISCOVERY CENTER ★

Kewalo
Basin

Sand Island
State Recreation
Area

Kaka'ako
Waterfront Park

Kewalo
Basin SP

0   .5 mi

0   .5 km

© AVALON TRAVEL

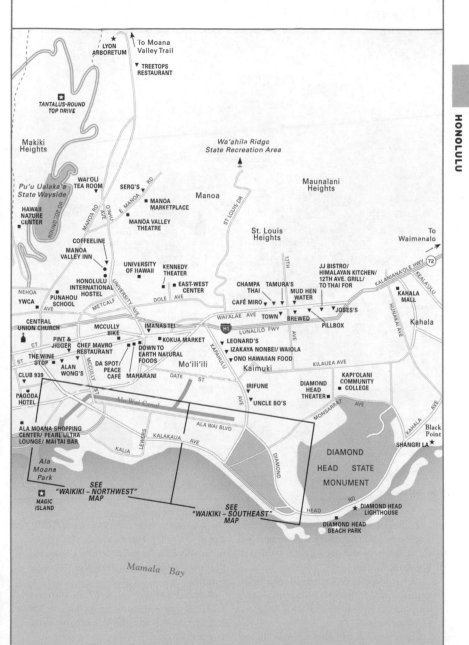

★ LYON ARBORETUM

To Moana Valley Trail

▼ TREETOPS RESTAURANT

✪ TANTALUS-ROUND TOP DRIVE

Makiki Heights

Wa'ahila Ridge State Recreation Area

Maunalani Heights

Pu'u Ualaka'a State Wayside

WAI'OLI TEA ROOM
SERG'S

MANOA RD
O'AHU AVE
E. MANOA RD

Manoa

St. Louis Heights

To Waimanalo

HAWAII NATURE CENTER

■ MANOA MARKETPLACE

MANOA VALLEY THEATRE

ROUND TOP DR

ST LOUIS DR

12TH

JJ BISTRO/ HIMALAYAN KITCHEN/ 12TH AVE. GRILL/ TO THAI FOR

KALANIANA'OLE HWY

72

KEALA'OLU

COFFEELINE

MANOA VALLEY INN ▼

UNIVERSITY OF HAWAII

KENNEDY THEATER

UNIVERSITY AVE

CHAMPA THAI
TAMURA'S

CAFÉ MIRO

MUD HEN WATER

KAHALA MALL

HONOLULU INTERNATIONAL HOSTEL

■ EAST-WEST CENTER

NEHOA

YWCA

PUNAHOU SCHOOL

AVE

CENTRAL UNION CHURCH

ST

DOLE AVE

METCALF

MCCULLY BIKE

IMANAS TEI

WAI'ALAE AVE

TOWN

BREWED

JOSES'S

PILLBOX

HUNAKAI AVE

Kahala

PINT & JIGGER
CHEF MAVRO RESTAURANT

KOKUA MARKET

LEONARD'S

IZAKAYA NONBEI/ WAIOLA

KAPI'OLANI COMMUNITY COLLEGE

KILAUEA AVE

THE WINE STOP

ALAN WONG'S

DA SPOT/ PEACE CAFÉ

DOWN TO EARTH NATURAL FOODS

MAHARANI

DATE ST

ONO HAWAIIAN FOOD

Kaimuki

Mo'ili'ili

CLUB 939 ▼

PAGODA HOTEL

MCCULLY ST

KAPAHULU AVE

IRIFUNE

UNCLE BO'S

DIAMOND HEAD THEATER ■

MONSARRAT AVE

KAHALA AVE

Black Point

SHANGRI LA ★

ALA MOANA SHOPPING CENTER/ PEARL ULTRA LOUNGE/ MAI TAI BAR

Ala Wai Canal

ALA WAI BLVD

KALIA
LEWERS ST

KALAKAUA AVE

DIAMOND HEAD

DIAMOND HEAD STATE MONUMENT

Ala Moana Park

✪ MAGIC ISLAND

SEE "WAIKIKI – NORTHWEST" MAP

SEE "WAIKIKI – SOUTHEAST" MAP

HEAD RD

★ DIAMOND HEAD LIGHTHOUSE

DIAMOND HEAD BEACH PARK

Mamala Bay

HONOLULU

Downtown Honolulu

KUKUI ST
ALAKEA ST
QUEEN'S MEDICAL CENTER
LAUHALA ST
LISBON ST
FORT ST
PALI
MILLER ST
ST. ANDREW'S CATHEDRAL ★
HONOLULU THEATER FOR YOUTH
WAR MEMORIAL
KAPI'OLANI BLVD
P
WASHINGTON PLACE
BERETANIA ST
MUNICIPAL BUILDING
OUR LADY OF PEACE
HAWAII STATE ART MUSEUM ★
KALANIMOKU HALE STATE OFFICE BUILDING
P
BISHOP ST
HAWAII STATE CAPITOL ★
KOREAN AND VIETNAM WAR MEMORIALS ★
PUNCHBOWL ST
PAUAHI ST
HOTEL ST
CITY HALL ANNEX
SOUTH ST
HAWAII THEATER ★
SOUTH KING ST
BETHEL ST
PAUAHI TOWER
RICHARDS ST
STATE ARCHIVES
HONOLULU HALE (CITY HALL)
MISSION HOUSES MUSEUM
FORT ST MALL
LONGS DRUGS
'IOLANI BARRACKS ★
HAWAII STATE LIBRARY
KAWAIAHA'O ST
YWCA
★ 'IOLANI PALACE
KAWAIAHA'O CHURCH ★
P
MACY'S
TAMARIND PARK
BANDSTAND ★
KAMEHAMEHA STATUE ★
P
KING ST
CENTRAL PACIFIC BANK
TOMB OF KING LUNALILO ★
TERRITORIAL OFFICE BUILDING
KUMA KAHUA THEATER
BANK OF HAWAII
FIRST HAWAIIAN CENTER
HAWAIIAN ELECTRIC COMPANY BUILDING
ALI'IOLANI HALE ★
CEMETERY
MISSION LN
AMERICAN SAVINGS BANK
POST OFFICE
MERCHANT ST
DAVIES PACIFIC CENTER
JUDICIARY BUILDING
QUEEN ST
C. BREWER BUILDING
U.S. CUSTOMS/ COURT HOUSE
P
HARBOR COURT
ALEXANDER AND BALDWIN BUILDING
HALE 'AUHAU
DILLINGHAM TRANSPORTATION BUILDING
GROSVENOR CENTER
MILILANI ST
92
NIMITZ HWY
KE'ELIKOLANI BUILDING
To Airport
HALEKUAWILA ST
P
IRWIN PARK
PRINCE KUHIO FEDERAL BUILDING
ALOHA TOWER DR
KA'AHUMANU HALE
ALOHA TOWER/ CHAI'S ISLAND BISTRO
FALLS OF CLYDE ★
PIER 6
ALA MOANA
P
0   200 yds
Aloha Tower Marketplace
PIER 5
0   200 m
PIER 8
92
RESTAURANT ROW
Honolulu   Harbor
To Waikiki
© AVALON TRAVEL

To the east and south are the old, congested neighborhoods of **Kaimuki,** where you'll find ample shopping and dining on Waialae and Kapahulu Avenues.

Just to the west of Kaimuki is **Mo'ili'ili,** another predominantly residential area with some shops and dining along King and Beretania Streets.

To the west of downtown Honolulu and Nu'uanu lie the local communities of **Kalihi** and Kalihi Valley. There is also a small area to the south of Kalihi called **Iwilei,** known for its seafood restaurants on Pier 38 in Honolulu Harbor.

Sand Island, south of downtown Honolulu and across the harbor, is an industrial port with an oceanfront state recreation area.

Chinatown

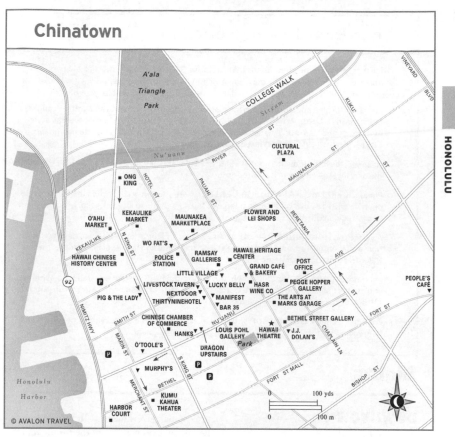

A'ala Triangle Park

COLLEGE WALK

VINEYARD

BLVD

ST

Stream

KUKUI

CULTURAL PLAZA ■

ST

Nuʻuanu RIVER

MAUNAKEA ST

ONG KING ■

HOTEL ST

PAUAHI ST

BERETANIA

O'AHU MARKET ■

KEKAULIKE MARKET ■

MAUNAKEA MARKETPLACE ■

FLOWER AND LEI SHOPS

KEKAULIKE

N KING ST

WO FAT'S ▼

HAWAII CHINESE HISTORY CENTER ■

POLICE STATION ■

RAMSAY GALLERIES ■

HAWAII HERITAGE CENTER ■

AVE

PEOPLE'S CAFÉ ▼

92

NIMITZ HWY

P

LITTLE VILLAGE ▼

GRAND CAFÉ & BAKERY ▼

POST OFFICE ■

PIG & THE LADY ▼

LIVESTOCK TAVERN ▼

NEXTDOOR ▼ THIRTYNINEHOTEL ▼

LUCKY BELLY ▼

MANIFEST ▼

BAR 35 ▼

HASR WINE CO ■

PEGGE HOPPER GALLERY ■

THE ARTS AT MARKS GARAGE ■

ST

FORT ST

SMITH ST

CHINESE CHAMBER OF COMMERCE ■

HANKS ▼ ▼

NUʻUANU

LOUIS POHL GALLERY ▼

Park

HAWAII THEATRE ★

BETHEL STREET GALLERY ■

CHAPLAIN LN

MARIN ST

O'TOOLE'S ▼

P

DRAGON UPSTAIRS

J.J. DOLAN'S ▼

Honolulu Harbor

MERCHANT ST

MURPHY'S ▼

BETHEL

S KING ST

P

FORT ST MALL

BISHOP ST

0   100 yds

HARBOR COURT ■

KUMU KAHUA THEATER

0   100 m

© AVALON TRAVEL

To the west is the airport, and inland from the airport are the **Salt Lake** and **Moanalua** communities.

Southwest of Moanalua is **Pearl Harbor,** a placid, deepwater harbor that still evokes a military presence and sense of reverence for the people who lost their lives during the attack on December 7, 1941. The **World** **War II Valor in the Pacific National Monument** is part of the National Park Service and is comprised of the Pearl Harbor Visitor Center and four historic sites. It is the most heavily visited sight on Oʻahu. The communities of Waipahu, Pearl City, ʻAiea, and Halawa border the harbor from west to east.

Your Best Day in Honolulu

While there are many neighborhoods that comprise Greater Honolulu, most of what appeals to visitors is centrally located in the downtown vicinity. For most visitors based out of Waikiki, plan your Honolulu visit around avoiding the daily rush-hour traffic to maximize your time.

- Instead of rushing immediately into the historic district in the morning and getting caught in traffic, head to **Lyon Arboretum** in Manoa Valley and explore the extensive trail system, bird-watch, and learn about native Hawaiian plants. If you'd like to be closer to downtown, try **Foster Botanical Garden** just outside of Chinatown.

- Next, visit the historic district and take in the **Hawai'i State Capitol** and **'Iolani Palace,** the only royal residence in the United States.

- For lunch, head to the **Ala Moana Center,** where you can grab lunch in the comfortable, open-air **Mai Tai Bar** on the upper lanai of the mall. Or, head into Kaka'ako, where you can find hip and unique shops and restaurants.

- A visit to the **Honolulu Museum of Art** is a must in the afternoon. If you have your own transportation, take advantage of the free same-day admission to the Spalding House in Makiki Heights, a museum of contemporary art.

- For dinner, head back into Chinatown and peruse the many restaurants and bars. Whether you're after Chinese food from **Little Village Noodle House** or pizza from Irish pub **J.J. Dolan's,** Chinatown has you covered.

- For those visiting **Pearl Harbor,** strike out as early as possible to avoid long lines and hours-long waits. Plan for at least a half day at the national monument.

Sights

DOWNTOWN
★ 'Iolani Palace

Set on a grassy 11 acres, shaded by canopy trees in the heart of the Capitol District, **'Iolani Palace** (364 S. King St., 808/522-0822, www.iolanipalace.org, 9am-5pm Mon.-Sat.) is the second royal palace to grace the grounds. The building, with its glass and ironwork imported from San Francisco and its Corinthian columns, is the only true royal palace in America. 'Iolani Palace, begun in late 1879 under orders of King Kalakaua, was completed in December 1882 at a cost of $350,000. It was the first electrified building in Honolulu, having electricity and telephones even before the White House in Washington DC. The palace served as the official residence of the monarch of Hawai'i until the overthrow of the Hawaiian kingdom in 1893. It then became the main executive building for the provisional government, with the House of Representatives meeting in the throne room and the Senate in the dining room, until 1968. It has since been elevated to a state monument and National Historic Landmark.

Through the first floor of this palace runs a broad hallway with a grand stairway that leads to the second story. On the east side of the building is the large and opulent Throne Room, the scene of formal meetings and major royal functions. On the west side are the smaller Blue Room, an informal reception area, and the dining room. The upstairs level was the private residence of the king and his family. It also has a wide hallway, and on each side are bedrooms, sitting rooms, a music room, and office. The basement held servants' quarters, the kitchen, and offices of certain government officials. On the palace grounds you'll find the Coronation Pavilion, which originally stood directly in front of the palace, but was later moved to where it stands today as a bandstand for the Royal Hawaiian Band, and a raised earthen platform, the original site of the royal mausoleum, which was later moved out along the Pali Highway.

'Iolani Palace has docent-guided tours and self-guided tours of the first and second floors, both with self-guided exploration of the basement gallery. One-hour tours enter the palace every 15 minutes. Reservations are required for the **guided tour** (808/522-0832, palacetickets@iolanipalace.org, Tues. and Thurs. 9am-10am, Wed., Fri.-Sat. 9am-11:15am, $21.75 adults, $6 children ages 5-12), but not for the **self-guided audio tour** (9am-4pm Mon., 10:30am-4pm Tues. and Thurs., noon-4pm Wed. and Fri.-Sat., $14.75 adults, $5 children ages 5-12, $1 fee for the audio recording). The **Basement Gallery exhibits** (9:30am-5pm Mon.-Sat., $7 adults, $3 children) are another option for touring. Tickets are also sold at the 'Iolani Barracks (9am-4pm Tues.-Sat.), behind the palace. Also in the barracks is the palace gift shop and bookstore (8:30am-4pm Mon.-Sat.).

There is limited metered parking on the palace grounds. From South King Street, turn left onto Likelike Street, a one-way drive, just before the major Punchbowl Street intersection. Turn left through the decorated gate onto the palace grounds.

Hawaii State Capitol

Directly behind 'Iolani Palace sits the unique **Hawaii State Capitol** (415 S. Beretania St., 808/587 0478, www.capitol.hawaii.gov), built in 1969. The structure is a metaphor for Hawai'i: the pillars surrounding it are palms, the reflecting pool is the sea, and the cone-shaped rooms of the Legislature represent the volcanoes of Hawai'i. The walls are lined with rich *koa* wood from the Big Island and further graced with woven hangings, murals, and two gigantic, four-ton replicas of the State Seal hanging at both entrances. The inner courtyard has a 600,000-tile mosaic and standing at the *mauka* entrance to the building is a poignant sculpture of Saint Damien of Molokai, while the statue *The Spirit of Lili'uokalani* fronts the building on the ocean side. The State Legislature is in session for 60 working days, starting on the third Wednesday in January. The legislative session opens with dancing, music, and festivities, and the public is invited. Peek inside, then take the elevator to the fifth floor for outstanding views of the city. There is also a Korean-Vietnam War

the only royal residence in the United States, 'Iolani Palace

Memorial, paying tribute to those who died in the two wars.

Washington Place

Begun in 1841 by Captain John Dominis, **Washington Place** (320 S. Beretania St., 808/536-8040, www.washingtonplacefoundation.org) is best known as the home of Queen Lili'uokalani and her husband, John Owen Dominis, son of Captain Dominis. The Greek revival mansion was both Queen Lili'uokalani's home and also her prison beginning in 1893, when the Hawaiian kingdom was overthrown. She resided at Washington Place till her death in 1917. In 1918 the home became the official residence of the state governors of Hawai'i. The mansion was converted into a museum in 2001, and a new governor's mansion was built behind it. Washington Place is still used for state dinners and official functions and remains the official residence of the governor. The mansion is on the mountain side of Beretania Street, directly across from the Hawaii State Capitol.

St. Andrew's Cathedral

Just to the west of Washington Place is **St. Andrew's Cathedral** (229 Queen Emma Sq., 808/524-2822, www.thecathedralofstandrew.org). Construction started in 1867 as an Anglican church, but it wasn't really finished until 1958. Many of its stones and ornaments were shipped from England, and its stained-glass windows, especially the large contemporary-style window on the narthex end, the bell tower, and its pipe organ, touted as the largest pipe organ in the Pacific, are of particular interest. Hawai'i's monarchs worshipped here, and the church is still active. There is a free guided tour following the 10:30am Sunday Episcopal service. After the service, simply wait below the pulpit for a docent. There is limited public parking on church grounds during the week.

Hawaii State Art Museum

The **Hawaii State Art Museum** (250 S.

the State Capitol's Father Damien Statue

Hotel St., #2, 808/586-0900, http://hawaii.gov/sfca/HiSAM.html, 10am-4pm Tues.-Sat.) is on the second floor of the No. 1 Capitol District Building and has four galleries: the Diamond Head Gallery, the Ewa Gallery, the Sculpture Lobby, and the Sculpture Garden. The exhibitions highlight the finest collection of work by Hawai'i artists and the gallery displays rotate regularly. The museum gift shop is on the first floor.

King Kamehameha I Statue

The **King Kamehameha I Statue** is centered in a roundabout near the junction of King and Mililani Streets. Running off at an angle is Merchant Street, the oldest thoroughfare in Honolulu. This statue is much more symbolic of Kamehameha's strength as a ruler and unifier of the Hawaiian Islands than as a replica of the man himself. It is one of three. The original, lost at sea near the Falkland Islands en route from Paris, where it was bronzed, was later recovered, but not before the insurance money was used to cast this second one. The original now stands in the tiny town of Kapaʻau, in the Kohala District of the Big Island, not far from where Kamehameha was born. The Honolulu statue was dedicated in 1883, as part of King David Kalakaua's coronation ceremony. Its black and gold colors are striking, but it is most magnificent on June 11, King Kamehameha Day, when 18-foot lei are draped around the neck and the outstretched arms. The third stands in Washington DC, dedicated when Hawaiʻi became a state.

Kawaiahaʻo Church

The **Kawaiahaʻo Church** (957 Punchbowl St., 808/522-1333, www.kawaiahao.org) was built between 1836 and 1842. The first Christian church in Hawaiʻi, its New England-style architecture was crafted from 14,000 coral slabs, quarried by hand from local reefs. King Liholiho and his wife Queen Emma, who bore the last child born to a Hawaiian monarch, wed at the church, and on June 19, 1856, Lunalilo, the first king elected to the throne,

the King Kamehameha I Statue

took his oath of office in the church. Lunalilo is buried in a tomb at the front of the church, along with his father, Charles Kanaʻina, and nearby lies the grave of his mother, Miriam Kekauluohi. In the graveyard at the rear of the church rest many members of the Parker, Green, Brown, and Cooke families, early missionaries to the islands. Most are recognizable as important and influential people in 19th-century Hawaiian history. Hidden away in a corner of the grounds is an unobtrusive adobe building, the remains of a schoolhouse built in 1835 to educate Hawaiian children. Kawaiahaʻo holds beautiful Christmas services with a strong Polynesian and Hawaiian flavor, and Hawaiian-language services are given here every Sunday, along with English-language services.

Mission Houses Museum

The days when tall ships with tattered sails bore in God-fearing missionary families dedicated to Christianizing the savage islands are alive in the halls and buildings of the **Mission Houses Museum** (553 S. King St., 808/447-3910, www.missionhouses. org, Tues.-Sat. 10am-4pm), now a registered National Historic Landmark. Set behind **Kawaiahaʻo Church**, the complex includes two main houses, a printing house annex, a research library, and a gift shop. The printing office was the first in the islands just as the Frame House is the oldest wooden structure in Hawaiʻi. One-hour guided tours are offered every hour 11am-3pm; admission is $10 adults, $6 students.

CHINATOWN
★ Historic Chinatown

Chinese immigrants came to Hawaiʻi in the 1800s as the first contract laborers for the burgeoning sugar industry. They established a vibrant community with herb shops, restaurants, temples, and retail outlets in what is now **historic Chinatown**. Today, Chinatown is a vibrant mix of art galleries, coffeehouses, upscale restaurants, bars and clubs, outdoor markets, and quick and delicious ethnic food restaurants. It also has a seedy side of homeless sleeping in doorways, prostitution, and fights spilling out of dive bars onto the sidewalk, which gives the historic neighborhood depth and character.

The best way to see Chinatown is to park the car and explore the streets on foot. Chinatown is relatively small, and the square grid of streets makes it easy to get around quickly. There are six municipal parking lots across Chinatown, which have the best rates. There is one on River Street, one on Maunakea Street, two on Smith Street, and two on Bethel Street.

On the east side of Chinatown, **Fort Street Mall** is a pedestrian area dominated by take-out restaurants and mingling students from Hawai'i Pacific University as they wait for classes. The art galleries are generally on the east end of Chinatown, on Smith Street, Nu'uanu Avenue, and Bethel Street. The cuisine on offer in Chinatown is truly international, from Irish and Cuban to French and Mediterranean, much of which is found on Bethel Street. But the main draw, traditional Chinese fare, is also readily available. The wealth of Chinese establishments is on Smith and Maunakea Streets. Noodle shops and Chinese restaurants merely complement the variety of Asian food found in the **Maunakea Marketplace Food Court,** on the corner of Maunakea and Hotel Streets. Chinese, Thai, Korean, Vietnamese, and Filipino plates are served from small market stalls with family-style seating available for enjoying the myriad flavors. Just across Beretania Street, on the outskirts of Chinatown, is the **Chinatown Cultural Plaza Center,** a small indoor mall with gift and herb shops, as well as a host of small eateries. There is paid parking at the plaza, as well.

Chinatown has an abundance of historical buildings dating back to the early 20th century, like the **Hawaii Theatre** on Bethel Street, which opened in 1922. The upper-story facades of the buildings along Hotel Street, between Bethel and Maunakea Streets, still retain vestiges from the World War II era.

There is also the **Hawaii Kuan Yin Temple** on the mountain side of Vineyard Boulevard, at the entrance to Foster Botanical Garden. The temple is dedicated to the Chinese deity of compassion.

KAKA'AKO
★ Honolulu Museum of Art

With a rich history dating back to its opening in 1927, the **Honolulu Museum of Art** (900 S. Beretania St., 808/532-8700, http://honolulumuseum.org, 10am-4:30pm Tues.-Sat., 1pm-5pm Sun.) has a collection of 50,000 pieces spanning 5,000 years of Asian art and textiles, American and European painting and decorative art, works on paper, and traditional works from Africa, Oceania, and the Americas. Within its earthy, revival mission-style architecture, the museum also houses a library, an education wing, a contemporary gallery, a café, and a 280-seat theater. Admission is $10 adult, children 17 and under free. The fee also covers the Honolulu Museum of Art Spalding House for same-day entry.

Parking can be a bit tricky. There is metered street parking on the blocks around the museum, but make sure to check for time restrictions. The museum maintains two parking lots: the Honolulu Museum of Art School lot behind the Honolulu Museum of Art School, with entrances on Beretania Street and Young Street ($3 with validation for four hours), and the Kinau Street Lot (1035 Kinau St., 4:30pm-11pm Mon.-Fri., 10am-11pm Sat.-Sun., free). There are five spaces at the museum for visitors with disabilities.

Kaka'ako Waterfront Park and Kewalo Basin Park

Kaka'ako Waterfront Park is a 35-acre expanse of grassy rolling hills that runs to the water's edge on the west side of Kewalo Basin. There are restrooms, picnic tables, and a paved jogging path, but no sandy beach. If you want to jump in the water, there are cement steps that scale down the rocky jetty wall.

Exceptional Trees

In 1975, the Hawai'i state legislature passed Act 105, the **Exceptional Tree Act.** The law recognizes the ecological and cultural significance and value of trees deemed exceptional and establishes the protection of designated trees. What is an exceptional tree? Exceptional trees on O'ahu must have historic or cultural value or meet certain criteria of age, rarity, location, size, aesthetic quality, and endemic status. Exceptional trees are marked with a gold or silver plaque that identifies their scientific and common name and county of origin. There are over 150 exceptional trees on O'ahu. Find the complete list of exceptional trees and their locations at www.honolulu.gov.

Foster Botanical Garden features many of Honolulu's Exceptional Trees.

On the eastern flank of Kewalo Basin is **Kewalo Basin Park,** a small, coastal refuge with shade trees, restrooms, picnic tables, great views of the ocean, and a couple of popular surf breaks. If you've chartered a boat out of Kewalo Basin for diving or fishing, the park is the perfect place to kill some time before or after your tour. There are two small parking lots, which often fill up on the weekends.

Children's Discovery Center
The **Children's Discovery Center** (111 Ohe St., 808/524-5437, www.discoverycenterhawaii.org, 9am-1pm Tues.-Fri., 10am-3pm Sat.-Sun.), at Kaka'ako Waterfront Park, is an interactive, hands-on children's museum and activity center focused on learning and discovering through play. The center has six exhibits, one for visitors five years and younger and five for older children. They can learn about their bodies, role play to discover how a community functions, find out about Hawaiian history and culture as well as cultures beyond Hawaiian shores, and explore and understand the importance of rain forests. Admission is $10 general,

$6 senior citizen, children under one year are free.

NU'UANU
★ Foster Botanical Garden
Wedged between the H-1 freeway and downtown's skyscrapers **Foster Botanical Garden** (50 N. Vineyard Blvd., 808/522-7066, www1.honolulu.gov/parks/hbg/fbg.htm, 9am-4pm daily) finds itself in an unlikely area for abundant greenery. But once you set foot into the garden, you'll be mesmerized by the lush foliage and incredibly tall trees, and all things urban will melt away. Since some of the trees in the collection were planted back in 1853, when the grounds were the residence of German physician and botanist William Hillebrand, the enormity of the trees on the main lawn are a wonder of nature. There are 26 "Exceptional Trees" on the 13.5-acre property, and the garden boasts indoor and outdoor orchid sections, a palm section, as well as a cycad garden. Cycads are curious leafy plants that date back 200 million years, to the Jurassic period. Admission is $5 general, 13 and older, $1 children 6-12, and

children 5 and under are free. The garden has ample parking.

Queen Emma Summer Palace

Hanaiakamalama, today known as the Queen Emma Summer Palace (2913 Pali Hwy., 808/595-3167, http://daughtersofhawaii. org, 9am-4pm daily), was King Kamehameha IV and Queen Emma's summer retreat from 1857 to 1885. Today the historic landmark is a museum set on beautifully landscaped grounds. Admission is $10 per adult and $1 per child. It also offers docent-led tours of the 19th-century home. To get to the palace, take the Pali Highway exit from the H-1 freeway. The palace is on the east side of the highway.

★ Nu'uanu Pali State Wayside

Better known as the Pali Lookout, the Nu'uanu Pali State Wayside is on the Honolulu side of the tunnels on the Pali Highway. The lookout has amazing views of Kane'ohe Bay, Kailua, and the Ko'olau Range. The lookout is often windy. If you're feeling adventurous, take the ramp that leads down to the Old Pali Road, which you can walk along till it is literally swallowed up by vegetation and decay.

PUNCHBOWL
National Memorial Cemetery of the Pacific

The National Memorial Cemetery of the Pacific (2177 Puowaina Dr., 808/532-3720, 8am-6:30pm daily Mar.-Sept., 8am-5:30pm daily Oct.-Feb.) is inside Punchbowl Crater. Established in 1949, the cemetery is a memorial to those who served in the U.S. Armed Forces and is listed on the National Register of Historic Places. Spreading across 112 acres, the beautiful, solemn grounds are a quiet place good for reflection. There is a small office and restrooms located at the entrance open 8am-4:30pm Mon.-Fri., and at the back of the cemetery, behind the main memorial, are restrooms and a pathway that leads to a magnificent viewing area on the crater rim overlooking Honolulu.

There are several ways to reach the cemetery and many signs around the crater indicating the way. From the H-1 freeway eastbound, take the Pali Highway exit, turn right on Iolani Avenue immediately after crossing the bridge, then take the next left onto Lusitana Street. Bear right onto Puowaina Drive and follow the signs. One-lane roads curve through the cemetery.

National Memorial Cemetery of the Pacific

Sailor Jerry

Hawai'i is socially and culturally accepting of tattoos on the whole. After all, tattooing is engrained in Polynesian, and Hawaiian, culture. So it comes as no surprise that the father of the traditional Americana tattoo style, **Sailor Jerry,** practiced his art and gained his international acclaim working from a small shop on Smith Street in Chinatown.

Born Norman Keith Collins in 1911, Sailor Jerry joined the Navy at age 19 and, after his time at sea and abroad, fell in love with the imagery of Southeast Asia and the Hawaiian Islands. He settled in Hawai'i in the 1930s and cemented his reputation as the best tattoo artist in Chinatown during World War II, when sailors docking at Aloha Tower were flocking to Chinatown for booze, hookers, and tattoos. Sailor Jerry established paradigms in tattooing for cleanliness and sterilization, pigments producing bright colors, and a technique and style that is still mimicked to this day.

Sailor Jerry passed away in 1973 and is buried in the National Memorial Cemetery of the Pacific in Punchbowl Crater. Most important, Sailor Jerry passed on an appreciation for the tattoo as a legitimate form of art to be cultivated and collected. And as for his small shop on Smith Street, it's still a tattoo studio to this day.

MAKIKI
★ Tantalus-Round Top Drive

One of only two roadways in Hawai'i listed on the National Register of Historic Places, **Tantalus Drive** and **Round Top Drive** meet at the **Pu'u 'Ualaka'a State Wayside** on top of a cinder cone with amazing views of Honolulu, from Diamond Head to Pearl Harbor, including Manoa Valley. Tantalus Drive approaches the wayside park from the west, while Round Top Drive comes in from the east. A round-trip on the winding roads is about 20 miles. The leisurely drive passes hillside homes, is thick with vegetation, and often quite narrow. If you're easily carsick, this is a drive you'll probably want to avoid. Reach Tantalus Drive from Auwaiolimu Street via Nehoa Street. Reach Round Top Drive from Makiki Street via Nehoa Street. You can also take Makiki Street, to Makiki Heights Drive, to Tantalus Drive. The wayside park is also the trailhead for several forest hiking trails and known for auto thefts, so be sure not to leave any valuables in your vehicle, even if you're just stopping for a few minutes to take in the view.

Honolulu Museum of Art Spalding House

Formerly the Contemporary Museum, the **Honolulu Museum of Art Spalding** **House** (2411 Makiki Heights Dr., 808/526-0232, http://honolulumuseum.org, 10am-4pm Tues.-Sat., noon-4pm Sun., $10 adults, children 17 and under free) was gifted the entire contemporary art collection, covering from the 1940s to present, in 2011. The museum is

Honolulu Museum of Art Spalding House

set on 3.5 acres of terraced, sculpture, and botanical gardens. Admission also covers entry to the Honolulu Museum of Art for same-day entry. There is a one-hour docent-led walking tour at 1:30pm Tuesday through Sunday, and the museum is free to the public the first Wednesday of each month. Parking is also free. From Nehoa Street, turn onto Makiki Street, then take Makiki Heights Drive at the fork.

MANOA
University of Hawai'i at Manoa

On University Avenue, just off the H-1 freeway, the **University of Hawai'i at Manoa (UH Manoa)** is a beautiful, compact campus with mature landscaping and fascinating architecture spanning decades. Founded in 1907, University of Hawai'i at Manoa holds the distinction of being a land-, sea-, and space-grant research institution, with nine colleges rounding out its academic programs. Of particular interest on campus are the trees planted across its 320 acres. Stop by the botany department and pick up the **Campus Plants** pamphlet. It includes a map of the campus and identifies the myriad unique and unusual plants, making for a lovely walk. Also noteworthy is the art department's two free art galleries. The **University of Hawai'i Art Gallery,** off the main foyer, features local and international artists and thematic exhibitions in many different media. The **Commons Gallery,** upstairs, rotates exhibitions on a weekly basis and allows students to experiment with exhibition design and display. And don't miss the giant baobab tree on the west side of the art building—a natural work of art.

To get to UH Manoa, take the University Avenue exit from the H-1 freeway from either direction. There is free parking in the neighborhoods surrounding campus, requiring a bit of a walk, or there is paid meter parking on campus. You can access on-campus parking lots from East West Road, from Dole Street, or on Maile Way from University Avenue. A great time to visit is mid-May to mid-July,

Bishop Museum

when the summer session is in, but the campus is rather empty.

Lyon Arboretum

Nestled in the back of lush and often misty Manoa Valley, **Lyon Arboretum** (3860 Manoa Rd., 808/988-0456, www.hawaii.edu/lyonarboretum, 8am-4pm Mon.-Fri., 9am-3pm Sat.) is a 194-acre botanical garden in a tropical rainforest setting. With over 5,000 tropical plants and a vast network of trails, you'll have the opportunity to see heliconias, gingers, aroids, native Hawaiian plants, and one of the largest collections of palms in Hawai'i. Initially established as a watershed restoration project in 1918, the garden is shaded with a variety of far-reaching canopy trees, their trunks laden with bromeliads, moss, and ferns. With the arboretum receiving an average of 165 inches of precipitation annually, you should be prepared for long periods of rain, mud, and mosquitoes. Bring binoculars for spotting birds. Pick up a trail map at the visitors center and take the time to explore the smaller trails off the main artery that winds back up the valley.

To get to Lyon Arboretum, follow Manoa Road all the way back into the valley, past Paradise Park, and turn left onto the arboretum's private drive before the end of the road. There's a parking lot after a couple switchbacks. The visitors center also has a very nice bookstore focusing on conservation, biology, and botany.

KALIHI
★ Bishop Museum

The premier natural and cultural history institution in the Pacific and the largest museum in the state, **Bishop Museum** (1525 Bernice St., 808/847-3511, www.bishopmuseum.org, 9am–5pm Wed.–Mon.), the Hawaii State Museum of Culture and Natural History, was founded in 1889 by Charles Reed Bishop, in honor of his late wife, Princess Bernice Pauahi Bishop. It was erected as a bastion for her extensive collection of Hawaiian artifacts and royal family heirlooms as the last descendant of the royal Kamehameha family. The museum also has an extensive library and archives for research purposes.

Bishop Museum has both rotating and mainstay exhibits. Hawaiian Hall utilizes its three floors to explore the different realms of Hawaiian culture, from the gods and legends to the customs of daily life. Polynesian Hall, which opened in 2013, represents the peoples of Pacific cultures across Polynesia, Micronesia, and Melanesia. And the Abigail Kinoiki Kekaulike Kahili Room honors the kings of the Hawaiian monarchy and displays their *kahili* (feather standards) and other heirlooms. The Science Adventure Center has interactive exhibits focusing on Hawai'i's volcanic origins and environment. It's a great installation to let the kids get hands-on and explore every nook and cranny. From the amazing collection of Pacific seashells to the planetarium, Bishop Museum explores Hawai'i's culture through many different disciplines.

Admission is $19.95 adult, $14.95 senior and children age 4-12, children 3 and under are free. To get there from the H-1 freeway, take the Likelike Highway and turn right on Bernice Street.

MOANALUA
Moanalua Gardens

A large grassy park shaded by the famous Hitachi Tree and two other monkeypod trees with canopies creating beautiful,

the home of King Kamehameha V at Moanalua Gardens

cooling shade, **Moanalua Gardens** (1352 Pineapple Pl., 808/839-5334, www.moanaluagardens.com, 7:30am-30 minutes prior to sunset daily) is a 24-acre privately owned reserve open to the public during daylight hours. It is also the site of the home of Prince Lot Kapuaiwa, who later became King Kamehameha V. The Prince Lot Hula Festival is held at Moanalua Gardens every summer. Admission is $3 per person; children 12 and under are free. From the Moanalua Freeway H-201, take the Puuloa Road exit toward Tripler Hospital. Turn right immediately after the exit sign into the gardens. The exit is from the off-ramp.

PEARL HARBOR
★ Pearl Harbor Historic Sites

The USS *Arizona* Memorial, USS *Bowfin* Submarine Museum and Park, USS *Oklahoma* Memorial, and the Battleship *Missouri* Memorial comprise the **Pearl Harbor Historic Sites.** Over 1.7 million people visit the USS *Arizona* Memorial and the historic sites each year, making this one of the most heavily toured areas in the state. The four sites

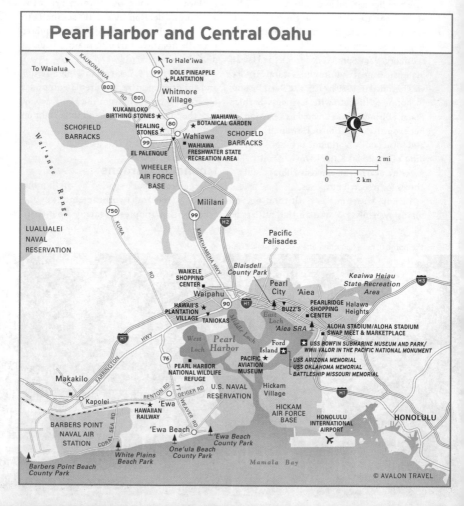

Pearl Harbor and Central Oahu

© AVALON TRAVEL

The Military on O'ahu

O'ahu differs from the other main Hawaiian Islands in that there is a strong military presence here. All four branches of the military have installations on the island, and men and women in uniform are a common sight from the windward to the leeward side.

A few military strategists realized the importance of Hawai'i early in the 19th century, but most didn't recognize the advantages until the Spanish-American War. It was clearly an unsinkable platform in the middle of the Pacific from which the United States could launch military operations. General John M. Schofield first surveyed Pearl Harbor in 1872, and this world-class anchorage was given to the U.S. Navy for its use in 1887 as part of the Sugar Reciprocity Treaty. In August 1898, four days after the United States annexed Hawai'i, U.S. Army troops created Camp McKinley at the foot of Diamond Head, and American troops were stationed there until it became obsolete in 1907. Named in General Schofield's honor, Schofield Barracks in central O'ahu became (and remains) the largest military installation in the state. It first housed the U.S. 5th Cavalry in 1909 and was heavily bombed by the Japanese at the outset of World War II. Pearl Harbor, first dredged in 1908, was officially opened on December 11, 1911. The first warship to enter was the cruiser *California*.

The Japanese navy attacked Pearl Harbor and other military installations on December 7, 1941. The flames of Pearl Harbor ignited World War II's Pacific theater operations, and there has been no looking back. Ever since that war, the military has been a mainstay of the Island economy. Following the war, the number of men, women, and installations decreased; today there is a force of more than 55,000 active duty personnel, with all branches of the military represented.

together tell the story of Hawai'i's and U.S. involvement in World War II, from the surprise attack on Pearl Harbor to the surrender of the Japanese. Pearl Harbor also serves as the central point of the **World War II Valor in the Pacific National Monument.**

Once you arrive and find free parking in one of several designated lots, enter the 17-acre park, where you'll first see the **visitors center** (808/454-1434, www.pearl-harborhistoricsites.org, 7am-5pm daily) and the USS *Bowfin* Submarine Museum. If you're planning on touring any of the historic sites, especially the USS *Arizona*, arrive as early as

the USS *Bowfin* at the World War II Valor in the Pacific National Monument, Pearl Harbor possible and head directly to the visitors center to get in line to receive a stamped ticket for a tour time. Admission to the monument is free and the 1.25-hour program includes a 23-minute documentary and a short boat ride to the memorial. Tickets are issued on a first-come, first-served basis. On a busy day, be prepared to wait several hours for your tour.

A better option is to reserve tickets online at www.recreation.gov. You can select the date, time, tour, or tour package you'd like to take. A separate line at the visitors center awaits those who have reserved tickets.

If you do have a long wait ahead of you, check out the other historical sites, like the USS *Bowfin* Museum, or take the shuttle bus, which departs every 15 minutes, to the Battleship *Missouri* Memorial and the **Pacific Aviation Museum.** Other than the USS *Arizona* Memorial, which is free, all sites charge admission for adults and children ages 4-12. There are also package tours, half-day tours, and one- or two-day passes available.

Alleviate the wait time by taking advantage of the online ticket reservations to streamline your visit to Pearl Harbor.

The Pearl Harbor Historic Sites park is located off Kamehameha Highway, Route 99, just south of Aloha Stadium. There is ample signage coming from both directions. If you're on the H-1 freeway west, take exit 15A and follow the signs. You can also take TheBus, numbers 20 or 42 from Kuhio Avenue in Waikiki, or numbers 20, 42, or 52 from Ala Moana Center or downtown and be dropped off within a minute's walk of the entrance. Depending on stops and traffic, this ride could take over an hour. Also, The Arizona Memorial Bus Shuttle (808/839-0911), a private operation from Waikiki run by VIP Transportation, takes about half an hour and will pick you up at any Waikiki hotel. It charges $11 round-trip; reservations are necessary, so call a day in advance. Because the park is on an active military base, there are no bags allowed inside the area. There is a $3 bag storage fee.

Beaches

Bustling Honolulu Harbor stretches along much of Honolulu's coastline, and only a few beaches fall within its borders. Not to mention, the beach parks in Honolulu are more park than actual sandy beach. The beach parks draw big crowds all summer long when there's surf along the south shore, while the weekends seem to be crowded all year long. The city beaches and parks are also the stomping grounds of many members of Honolulu's pervasive homeless population.

ALA MOANA
★ Magic Island

Magic Island is an artificially constructed peninsula that creates the western flank of the Ala Wai Canal and Small Boat Harbor. This grassy park with shade trees, walking paths, restrooms, and outdoor showers also includes a tranquil *keiki* (child's) beach at the end of the

point. It's blocked from the waves by towering rock jetties and framed in all around by beach, making it a perfect place for the kids to play and swim safely. The jetties are constructed so that fresh ocean water can flow in and out of the lagoon without creating currents or waves. During the summer months, a wave known as Bomburas breaks beyond the jetty at the end of the point.

There is ample parking, but it does fill up during the summer and on weekends, when people turn out en masse with barbecue grills and tents to take advantage of the beautiful weather. To get to Magic Island, turn onto Ala Moana Park Drive from Ala Moana Boulevard where it intersects Atkinson Drive. After you pass the first right bend in the road, the parking lot is on the left, and it's free. The lot and park are closed 10pm-4am daily.

Ala Moana Beach Park

Connected to Magic Island, but on the west side of the peninsula, is **Ala Moana Beach Park.** Ala Moana Beach is a 4,000-foot-long, rather straight strip of sand falling into an artificial channel that runs along the entire beach. Buoys demarcate a swimming lane and one for stand-up paddling. Across the channel is a very shallow reef that stretches way out to the waves washing up on the sharp coral. There are many surf breaks along the outer reef, all the way across the beach park. A rectangular park, with busy Ala Moana Boulevard on one side and the beach on the other, has a tide-fed stream meandering through it, with a pond at each end. There are many shade trees, lots of picnic tables and barbecue areas, facilities, a snack bar, tennis courts, a community center, and lots of parking along Ala Moana Park Drive, which intersects Ala Moana Boulevard at both ends of the park. Parking can get crazy during the summer when the surf is up and on the weekends when the park is packed with families. Be sure to not use one of the designated lifeguard parking spots. Parking is free, but the park is closed 10pm-4am daily.

SAND ISLAND
Sand Island State Recreation Area

Wedged between the Honolulu International Airport's reef runway and Honolulu Harbor sits Sand Island. The expansive, but aesthetically challenged **Sand Island State Recreation Area** (808/832-3781, www.hawaiistateparks.org, sunrise-sunset daily) is on its south shore. There is a camping area, park, picnic areas, restrooms and outdoor showers, and a steep sandy beach that stretches from the island's western point, nearly to the harbor channel entrance. Since the beach and park are in an industrial zone and the park is littered with bits of rubbish, paradise isn't the first thing that comes to mind here. Planes zoom overhead on a regular basis. The large, rectangular sand trappers exposed on both ends of the beach could be a safety hazard for small children. Still, there are a few decent surf breaks off the beach if you're looking to get away from the crowds at Ala Moana Beach, and the area is popular with local families on the weekends. To get to the beach, turn onto Sand Island Access Road from North Nimitz Highway and follow this to the end. Parking is free. The gated parking lot is locked when the recreation area is closed.

HONOLULU BEACHES

Ala Moana Beach Park

Water Sports

SURFING, BODYSURFING, AND STAND-UP PADDLING

The surf breaks in Honolulu come alive during the summer months, when south swells generated by storms in the southern hemisphere travel thousands of miles to Hawaiian waters. And the breaks are usually crowded with bodyboarders, shortboarders, and longboarders.

Bomburas is a predominant left that breaks at the top of Magic Island, with the white water pushing right into the jetty. When the surf is big enough, the waves break far enough out to round the point and swing into the bay on the Ala Moana side. The wave breaks best on a low tide. You'll have to paddle out and in through a gap in the jetty across the *keiki* pool, timing the white water on the way in so you don't get pushed into the rocks.

The reef that stretches across Ala Moana Beach has a handful of waves that break on different conditions. Some of the more shallow breaks are preferred by bodyboarders, and some waves don't start breaking until the surf is above head high. Two of the more popular waves that are easy to pick out from shore are **Concessions** and **Big Rights.** Toward the west side of the beach, in front of the concession stand, there is a sandy path in the reef that leads straight out in between the two breaks. You'll see surfers walking in and out in knee-deep water along the channel. The break to the east is Concessions, a right and left breaking wave that gets pretty shallow if you go right. To the west of the channel in the reef is Big Rights, a predominant right that gets pretty hollow, and surfers will try to nab one of the fast barrels. Park along Ala Moana Park Drive.

There is a channel that runs parallel and spans Ala Moana Beach entirely designated as a swimming and stand-up paddling zone. Buoys demarcate lanes. The water is flat and calm, even when it's windy because the reef protects it from the surf. It's a great place to learn how to paddle or to paddle for exercise.

There are a couple of breaks along Kewalo Basin Park as well, the most popular being a left and right peak called **Kewalo's.** The left breaks into the Kewalo Basin channel that the boats use to access the harbor. The right breaks into shallow and sharp reef. Kewalo's is often crowded since it's a favorite break for school-age kids when class is out. There are a few more breaks along the reef to the east that are usually less crowded. Access the water by carefully climbing down the seawall and paddling out over the reef. Keep in mind you'll have to come in by climbing up the seawall, which can be a challenge when the surf is big and the surges are pushing up and pulling away from it with force.

There are two small parking lots, showers, and restrooms in Kewalo Basin Park. To get to Kewalo Basin, drive east on Ala Moana Boulevard. Once you pass Ward Avenue, take the second right turn into the harbor. If you come to the signal at Ala Moana Park Road, you've missed it. Follow the road past all the boats and tour operators. It bends right at the park, and the two parking lots are just ahead on the right.

Across the Kewalo Basin Harbor channel, fronting Kaka'ako Waterfront Park and the Kewalo Marine Laboratory, is O'ahu's only strictly bodysurfing wave, **Point Panic.** It is against the law and punishable by a fine to surf the break with a board. Point Panic is a beautiful, barreling right off the rocky point. There is no beach in this area. However, there are restrooms, showers, and a small parking lot at the end of Ahui Street.

Flies is a lumpy, soft wave that breaks in front of the seawall along Kaka'ako Waterfront Park. There are several right- and left-breaking peaks that break best on a low tide, as the backwash can be a bit much on a higher tide. It is a good break for novice surfers intimidated by the crowds at other spots. Watch how the local surfers enter and exit the water. To get to the waterfront, park at the end of Ahui Street.

Outfitters

Hawaiian South Shore (320 Ward Ave., #112, 808/597-9055, www.hawaiiansouthshore.com, 10:30am-7pm Mon.-Sat., 11am-6pm Sun.) is a complete surf shop in the Ala Moana/Kaka'ako area, right by Ala Moana Beach. It sells surf-related apparel, accessories, new shortboards and longboards, and rents shortboards and longboards for $25 per day. **Blue Planet** (540 Ward Ave., 808/596-7755, www.blueplanetsurf.com, 10am-6pm daily) is just up the street and still conveniently close to Ala Moana Beach. It sells new and used longboards, shortboards, stand-up paddleboards, and accessories. It also offers long-term surfboard rentals (two or more days) starting at $40, long-term stand-up paddleboard rentals starting at $75, and 90-minute private stand-up paddle lessons for $90.

Surf Garage (2716 S. King St., 808/951-1173, www.surfgarage.com, 10am-7pm Mon.-Sat., 11am-5pm Sun.) and **Aloha Boardshop** (2600 S. King St., 808/955-6030, www.alohaboardshop.com, 10am-6pm Mon.-Sat., 11am-5pm Sun.) are right next to each other at the intersection of University Avenue and King Street. Check out Surf Garage for longboards, stand-up paddleboards, and accessories. Surf Garage rents surfboards starting at $20 and $125 weekly. Aloha Boardshop has a ton of shortboards, new and used, as well as longboards and surf accessories for sale.

Closer to Waikiki and Diamond Head in the Kapahulu area, **RV's Ocean Sport** (3348 Campbell Ave., 808/732-7137, http://rvsocean.com, 11am-5:30pm daily) is the place for used longboards and shortboards. The small shop is wall-to-wall boards, and it also specializes in ding repair. If you're looking to buy a board for your stay and then sell it back when you leave, this is the place to shop.

DIVING

Diving Honolulu waters is all about exploring shipwrecks and finger reefs. The **YO-257** and **San Pedro** wrecks are home to whitetip reef sharks, eels, and green sea turtles with deep water reef fish on the surrounding reefs. The **Sea Tiger** wreck, rumored to be a forcibly retired smuggling vessel, rests in a protected area. Look for white-spotted eagle rays, large puffer fish, and filefish. There is also an area of finger reefs called **Turtle Canyons** that is

Sand Island is popular with locals for fishing, surfing, and weekend camping.

home to a number of eel species, reef fish, and turtles. Most of the dive charters leave from Kewalo Basin.

Kaimana Divers (1051 Ala Moana Blvd., 808/772-1795, www.waikikiscuba.com, 7am-8pm daily) two-tank boat charters start at $109, including tanks and weights. Two-tank shore dives start at $89. Gear rental is $5 per piece or $10 full set. Kaimana also has a 10-dive package with everything included for $595. In addition to charters, it offers intro dive, private, standard, and advanced open-water courses starting at $145.

Dive Oahu (1085 Ala Moana Blvd., 808/922-3483, http://diveoahu.com, 8am-3pm daily) offers two-tank charters with Waikiki hotel pickup and drop-off, gear, tanks, and weights included in the rate: $139 standard, $385 five-day unlimited package. It also offers Professional Association of Diving Instructors (PADI) online scuba courses and has a full dive shop.

Also in Kewalo Basin is **Rainbow Scuba** (1086 Ala Moana Blvd., 808/224-7857, http://rainbowscuba.com, 7am-5pm daily). Rainbow's rates include Waikiki hotel transportation, light snacks, and water on the charter, two tanks, and full gear rental. It offers two-site beginner dives for $100 for first-time divers, certified divers charter to one wreck site and one reef site for $120, and PADI certification courses starting at $420.

Breeze Hawaii Diving Adventures (3014 Kaimuki Ave., 808/735-1857, http://breezehawaiidiving.com, 7am-5pm daily) has a retail shop in the Kapahulu area and offers two-tank boat charters for $115, three-tank charters for $172, one-tank night dives $149, and two-tank sunset/night dives for $200. It also has three levels of PADI beginner dive courses and daily dives in Hanauma Bay.

While **Patrick's Diving Adventures** (85-601 Farrington Hwy., 808/589-2177, http://patricksdiving.com, 8am-2pm daily by appointment) has dive charters available only on the leeward side, it offers shore dives and scuba courses in the Honolulu area. PADI, National Association of Underwater Instructors (NAUI), Technical Diving International (TDI) and Scuba Diving International (SDI) certification starts at $379 group and $479 private.

FISHING

The bulk of the fishing charters are found in Kewalo Basin, where they can easily access the deeper south shore waters. If you're interested in shoreline fishing, you can cast from anywhere along the seawall at Kaka'ako Waterfront Park or from the beach at Sand Island.

Magic Sport Fishing (1125 Ala Moana Blvd., 808/596-2998, www.magicsportfishing.com) runs a 50-foot Pacifica Sportfishing Yacht out of Kewalo Basin and provides everything except lunch and beverages. The captain has over 35 years of experience in commercial fishing in Hawaiian waters, and the company will divvy up a small portion of fish per person on shared trips and larger portions for private charters. With up to six passengers, eight-hour full-day shared trips run $200 per person, private trips $975. There are also half-day private charters for $775.

Operating since 1985, **Tradewind Charters** (1125 Ala Moana Blvd., 808/973-0311, www.tradewindcharters.com) has a variety of vessels for different types of fishing expeditions, from 40-foot sailing yachts to a 65-foot sportfishing yacht, and it offers two different fishing expeditions: catch-and-release reef fishing and deep-sea sportfishing. Its private reef-fishing charter includes snorkeling and sightseeing and for 1-6 people starts at $595 for 3 hours, $795 for 4.5 hours, $995 for 6 hours, and $1,195 for 8 hours. The private deep-sea charters for one to six people start at $895 for 4 hours, $1,095 for 6 hours, and $1,295 for 8 hours.

Aikane Sport Fishing (866/920-0979, www.aikanesportfishing.com) has shallow-water fishing charters for trevally and snappers or deep-sea fishing charters for big game fish like wahoo, mahimahi, blue marlin, and yellowfin tuna. It has a 42-foot Ocean Yacht and 38-foot Bertram Sportfisher. The shallow-water charters start at $500 for 4 hours and go to $625 for 8 hours; the deep-sea big game fishing charters start at $650 for 4 hours and go to $990 for 10 hours.

Established in 1950, **Maggie Joe Sport Fishing** (1025 Ala Moana Blvd., 808/591-8888, www.maggiejoe.com) has a fleet of boats designed to catch big game fish like blue marlin, yellowfin tuna, mahimahi, and skipjack tuna. It has half-day to full-day private and shared trips as well as night shark fishing for $550. The biggest boat, a 53-foot Custom Sport Fishing Yacht, starts at $890 for a three-quarter day and $933 for a private, full-day charter. Full-day shared charters are $179 per person, and half-day shared charters are $150 per person. Bananas are not permitted onboard due to superstition. If the captain deems the catch a successful haul, fishers are eligible to take home up to half of all the fish caught weighing under 100 pounds.

Hiking, Biking, and Bird-Watching

HIKING
Makiki

The **Makiki-Tantalus** hike is an eight-mile loop that circles Tantalus Peak and is a great way to see a few different valleys and Ko'olau peaks up close. The trail is known for songbirds and some native Hawaiian flora. Look for the native white hibiscus and 'ohi'a 'ahihi, with clusters of delicate red flowers. The hike takes advantage of the Kanealole Trail at the trailhead, which then connects in succession to the Makiki Valley Trail, the Nahuina Trail, the Kalawahine Trail, the Pauoa Flats Trail, the Manoa Cliff Trail, the Moleka Trail, and back to the Makiki Valley Trail as it rounds Tantalus. The junctions are marked well. To get to the trailhead, from Makiki Street heading north, bear left on Makiki Heights Drive. As the road switches back to the left, continue straight on an unnamed paved road into the Makiki Forest Recreation Area and past the Hawai'i Nature Center. Park on the side of the road by the gate. There is a native plant identification guide available in the nature center office for a small fee.

Manoa

In the back of rainy **Manoa Valley** are a myriad of trails all within **Lyon Arboretum** (3860 Manoa Rd., 808/988-0456, www.hawaii.edu/lyonarboretum, 8am-4pm Mon.-Fri., 9am-3pm Sat.). These trails are designed to take you through the different sections of the arboretum, so there's a wealth of interesting and colorful exotic, tropical, and native Hawaiian plants and trees everywhere you look. You could hike for a half day and not walk the same trail twice there's so much area to cover. The trails range from wide and dry to narrow, muddy, and graded. They are marked with numbers on wooden stakes that correspond to a trail map, which you can pick up in the visitors center. The main trail through

Manoa Falls

the arboretum terminates at a small waterfall. Be prepared for mud, rain, and mosquitoes. Lyon Arboretum has its own free private parking lot by the visitors center. Follow Manoa Road all the way to the back of the valley, past the houses, past Paradise Park, and turn onto the arboretum's private drive before the end of the road.

Also in the rear of Manoa Valley are several of the 18 trails that comprise the Honolulu *mauka* trail system. **Manoa Falls** is a great introduction to the area, a short 0.8-mile hike with a gradual grade under canopy and through lush foliage, up to a small waterfall and pool. Manoa is famous for its pervasive mist, so the trail can be muddy and crossed with roots in some sections. This is a popular hike, so it is well used, especially on the weekends. To get to the trailhead, either park on Manoa Road just before it narrows at the intersection with Waʻakaua Street, or continue driving on Manoa Road till you reach Paradise Park, where $5 flat-rate parking is available. If you prefer to park for free in the nearby neighborhood, tack on a 0.25-mile walk just to reach the trailhead. From the paid parking lot, continue on foot on the gravel road until it becomes the Manoa Falls

Trail. The trail follows Waihi Stream to the falls and pool.

Kaimuki

At the top of Saint Louis Heights, in **Kaimuki,** you'll find a hike with views of Manoa Valley and Palolo Valley, terminating on top of Mount Olympus, a massive peak at the back of Manoa Valley. The **Waʻahila Ridge Trail** begins in a stand of Cook pines—a misnomer since they are actually columnar araucaria, native to New Caledonia. The hike along the ridgeline is perfect for novices, but once you find the narrow trail that ascends to the summit, the route is more suited for intermediate hikers. At the 2,486-foot summit, in addition to breathtaking views, you'll find a thicket of native vegetation, including slow-growing *hapuʻu* ferns. The hike is six miles roundtrip. To get to the trailhead, park in the **Waʻahila Ridge State Recreation Area** (www.hawaiistateparks.org, 7am-7:45pm daily Apr-early Sept., 7am-6:45pm daily early Sept.-Mar.) by following Saint Louis Drive to nearly the top of the rise and turning left on Ruth Place. There are restrooms, drinking fountains, and picnic tables by the parking

Verdant Lyon Arboretum is a great place to spot forest birds.

lot. Parking is free, but the gate is locked when the recreation area is closed.

MOUNTAIN BIKING

While there is a plethora of trails all around O'ahu, mountain biking is prohibited on most of them. Fortunately for those looking to go off road on two wheels, there are a handful of mountain biking trails on the North Shore and the southeast and windward sides. Mountain biking is prohibited on all Honolulu area trails, but the big name local bicycle shops are all in town.

Outfitters

The Bike Shop (1149 S. King St., 808/596-0588, www.bikeshophawaii.com, 9am-8pm Mon.-Fri., 9am-5pm Sat., 10am-5pm Sun.) is a full-service rental, retail, and repair shop in the Kaka'ako neighborhood. It rents mountain bikes for $85 per day, road bikes starting at $40 per day, and seven-speed city bikes for $20 per day. If you need a rack for your rental car, you will pay $5 per day.

The **BikeFactory** (740 Ala Moana Blvd., 808/596-8844, http://bikefactoryhawaii.com, 10am-7pm Mon.-Fri., 9am-5pm Sat.,

11am-5pm Sun.), also in Kaka'ako, sells bicycles and accessories but does not rent equipment. And in Mo'ili'ili, **McCully Bicycle and Sporting Goods** (2124 S. King Street, 808/955-6329, http://mccullybike.com, 9am-8pm Mon.-Fri., 9am-6pm Sat., 10am-5pm Sun.) sells bicycles of all shapes and sizes, as well as other sporting goods, like fishing gear, tennis rackets, and athletic shoes. McCully does not rent bicycles, however.

BIRD-WATCHING

Bird-watching in Honolulu is all about finding the forest birds along the **Ko'olau Range trails,** including the **Lyon Arboretum trails.** Most of the birds are introduced species, like the shama thrush and the red-billed leiothrix, but beautiful nonetheless. The shama thrush is black on top with a chestnut-colored chest and a long, black and white tail and is able to mimic other birds' songs. There are few native forest birds remaining on O'ahu in accessible places, but this region is a great place to look for the red *'apapane*, which likes to feed on nectar from *'ohi'a lehua* blossoms, and the *'amakihi*, a yellow Hawaiian honeycreeper with a black, curved beak.

Golf and Tennis

GOLF
Kaimuki

The **Ala Wai Golf Course** (404 Kapahulu Ave., 808/296-2000, www.honolulu.gov/des/golf/alawai.htm), on the mountain side of the Ala Wai Canal, is the closest golf course to Waikiki and a local favorite for a quick round of golf. The 18-hole course is flat and has views of Diamond Head and the Ko'olau Range. Greens fees are $55 daily for 18 holes and $27.50 daily for twilight or nine holes. Golf cart fees are $20 for 18 holes, $10 for nine holes.

Moanalua

Even though Hawai'i's oldest golf course,

Moanalua Golf Club (1250 Ala Aolani St., 808/839-2311, www.mgchawaii.com), is a private club with membership benefits, access is open to the public. Built in 1898, the nine-hole course can be played as an 18-hole course by utilizing different sets of tees. The Moanalua Stream winds through the challenging course, set along the slopes of Moanalua, creating natural hazards. There are views of Diamond Head and the Honolulu skyline. Greens fees start at $45.

Greater Honolulu

Overlooking Pearl Harbor, the USS *Arizona* Memorial, and the USS *Missouri*, the **Pearl County Club** (98-535 Kaonohi St.,

808/487-3802, www.pearlcc.com) combines scenery and engaging golf with challenging course conditions and speedy downhill putts. The mature course also has a driving range, practice putting green, and a short game area. Rates for 18 holes are $130, twilight (after 3:30pm) $50.

With views of Pearl Harbor, downtown Honolulu, and Diamond Head, the **Royal Kunia Country Club** (94-1509 Anonui St., 808/688-9222, www.royalkuniacc.com) in Waipahu is a Robin Nelson-designed course situated across an undulating landscape with abundant water features and 101 bunkers. Greens fees for 18 holes are $150, twilight rates (after 2pm) are $80.

TENNIS

Public tennis courts can be found throughout the greater Honolulu area. **Kaimuki Community Park** (3521 Waialae Ave., 808/733-7351) has two courts, but the parking can be a hassle. There is free parking on 10th Avenue, metered parking on Waialae Avenue, or if those options are exhausted, park on 10th on the north side of Waialae. **Makiki District Park** (1527 Keeamoku St., 808/522-7082) has four courts, and **Manoa Valley District Park** (2721 Kaaipu Ave., 808/988-0580, www1.honolulu.gov/parks) has five courts. Both **Ala Moana Park** (1201 Ala Moana Blvd., 808/592-2288) and **Ala Moana Tennis Park** (1135 Hoolai St., 808/524-6626) have 10 courts each.

Yoga and Spas

YOGA
Manoa
In the Manoa Marketplace, **Iyengar Yoga** (2752 Woodlawn Dr., 808/382-3910, www.manoayoga.com) strives to promote physical health and mental poise. This type of yoga makes frequent use of props to adjust the body into the different poses. Single beginner classes are $13, and single intermediate classes are $16. It also offers yoga for kids at $30 for four classes.

Kaimuki
Bikram Yoga Honolulu (1120 12th Ave., 808/737-5519, www.bikramyogahonolulu.com) is no-nonsense hot yoga. Its second-floor studio has showers, locker rooms, and a naturally lit classroom. These are silent classes, so no talking during the session. Single classes are $25.

Also in Kaimuki, **Dahn Yoga** (3569 Harding Ave., #B, 808/738-5522, www.dahn-yoga.com) is a holistic health center offering classes in dahn yoga, a variety of mind and body exercises, tai chi, and meditation. One-hour classes start at $10. There is

another studio in Kaka'ako (401 Kamakee St., 808/596-9642).

Mo'ili'ili
Purple Yoga (2615 S. King St., 808/944-8585, www.purpleyoga.com) specializes in ashtanga yoga, as well as vinyasa, pregnancy, and mom-and-baby yoga. Purple Yoga encourages students to go at their own, comfortable pace. Single classes are $18, five classes are $80, and 10 classes are $135.

SPAS
Downtown
Heaven on Earth Salon & Day Spa (1050 Alakea St., 808/599-5501, www.heavenonearthhawaii.com, 9am-7pm Mon.-Fri., 8am-5pm Sat., 10am-4pm Sun.) is a full-service salon and spa located in the heart of downtown Honolulu. In addition to its complete set of services, it offers signature spa packages of skin and body treatments, or you can create your own. Massages start at $88 for 50 minutes and $118 for 80 minutes, facials start at $80 for 50 minutes, and 50-minute body treatments are $95. The spa

Ice in Honolulu?

A great way to cool off in the Salt Lake area is to lace up some ice skates and glide around O'ahu's only ice-skating venue, **Ice Palace** (4510 Salt Lake Blvd., 808/487-9921, www.icepalacehawaii. com), Complete with DJ and light show, it also has a closed-off section of the rink with special "walkers" that slide on the ice to help beginners get the hang of skating. Check the monthly schedule for public skating days and hours, as these do change for classes and sporting events. Generally, public skating is 9am-3pm, and admission is $8.90.

packages range from 80 minutes to four hours and start at $210. It also has gentlemen's spa services like facials, manicures, pedicures, and waxing.

Ala Moana

On the third floor in the Ala Moana Center is **Ho'ala Salon and Spa** (1450 Ala Moana Blvd., 808/947-6141, http://hoalasalonspa. com, 9am-9pm Mon.-Sat., 10am-7pm Sun.), a full-service salon and spa using natural and eco-sensitive products from Aveda. The award-winning spa is a quiet respite from the bustle of the mall and town. The signature massage care ranges from 25 to 90 minutes; 50-minute therapies start at $100 and 75 minutes start at $150. It has an extensive menu of facials; 25 minutes start at $65 and 60 minutes start at $125. Ho'ala Spa also offers nail, hand and foot care, spa body treatments, and hair care, as well as a 50- or 75-minute pregnancy massage.

Elements Spa and Salon (1726 Kapiolani Blvd., #206, 808/942-0033, http://client.supernaturalmedia.com/ ElementsSpa/beta/index.html, 10am-8pm Mon.-Fri., 9am-6pm Sat., 10am-6pm Sun.) is right across from the Hawai'i Convention Center and specializes in custom offerings, including tea service, foot treatments, mini facials, and scalp massages with its full-service salon and spa treatments. It provides three basic massages and several specialty massages like shiatsu, hot stone, and deep tissue. The basic massages are $50 for 30 minutes, $85 for 60 minutes, and $110 for 90 minutes. The specialty massages start at $100 for 60 minutes. It also has a couples massages starting at $165 for 60 minutes. Facials start at $85 for 60 minutes, and It offers series rates for both facials and massages. Elements provides salon, nail, waxing, and bridal services.

Shopping

ALA MOANA AND KAKA'AKO
Ala Moana Center

Ala Moana Center (1450 Ala Moana Blvd., 808/955-9517, www.alamoanacenter.com, 9:30am-9pm Mon.-Sat., 10am-7pm Sun.) is the world's largest open-air shopping center, with over 290 stores and restaurants. The mall is conveniently located near Waikiki and features high-end international clothiers

and jewelers, alongside popular brand-name stores. Department stores **Macy's** (808/941-2345), **Neiman Marcus** (808/951-8887), and **Nordstrom** (808/953-6100) surround the open-air central mall area. At the heart of the mall is an auditorium with seating on multiple mall levels, where daily hula performances and other shows are put on.

For technical athletic wear for yoga, running, dancing, and other aerobic pursuits, check out **Lululemon Athletica** (808/946-7220, www.lululemon.com/honolulu/alamoanacenter) on the second floor, Nordstrom wing. Also on the second level, right by **Bloomindale's**, is **Na Hoku** (808/946-2100, www.nahoku.com), a local jewelry store featuring island-themed jewelry, stones, and pearls. **Shirokiya** (808/973-9111, www.shirokiya.com), next to Macy's on the second floor, is like a Japanese mall within the mall. There are food and confections, a beer garden, Japanese goods, health-care needs, as well as toys, trinkets, and other wares.

If you're in need of a bikini (or a one-piece), on the first level is **San Lorenzo Bikinis** (808/946-3200, www.sanlorenzobikinis.com), with all the best in Brazilian bikini fashion. For local surfwear, **Hawaiian Island Creations** (808/973-6780, www.hicsurf.com) is on the first floor by Bloomindale's, and **T&C Surf Designs** (808/973-5199, www.tcsurf.com) is on the third floor, Bloomindale's wing. And for authentic Hawaiian quilts and accessories, head up to the Ho'okipa Terrace and check out **Hawaiian Quilt Collection** (808/946-2233, www.hawaiian-quilts.com).

If you're looking for a great used-book store in the Kaka'ako area, check out **Jelly's** (670 Auahi St., 808/587-7001, www.jellyshawaii.com, 10am-7pm Mon.-Sat., 10am-6pm Sun.). Not only does it have a great selection of fiction, nonfiction, and children's books, but it also sells used LPs, CDs, and videos.

Ward Warehouse

Just a couple blocks west of Ala Moana Center is a small, two-story open-air mall called **Ward Warehouse** (1050 Ala Moana Blvd., 808/591-8411, www.wardcenters.com, 10am-9pm Mon.-Sat., 10am-6pm Sun.), part of a conglomerate of five open-air malls in the immediate vicinity.

For the musician on the go in Honolulu, **Island Guitars** (808/591-2910, www.island-guitars.com) is a one-stop shop for new, used, and vintage fretted instruments. **Native Books/Na Mea Hawaii** (808/596-8885,

Ala Moana Center

www.nativebookshawaii.com) has locally made gifts, clothing, food, and art, as well as a complete collection of books about Hawai'i and the Pacific. If you're in the mood for a specialty beer, wine, or liquor, the **Liquor Collection** (808/524-8808, http://liquorcollection.com) is a must.

CHINATOWN

If you're interested in picking up a bottle of wine, stop by **HASR Wine Co.** (31 N. Pauahi St., 808/535-9463, www.hasrwineco.com, 10am-8pm Mon.-Fri., 10am-5pm Sat.-Sun.), which has a very knowledgeable staff and offers wine tastings Tuesday and Friday (5pm-7pm). **Tin Can Mailman** (1026 Nuuanu Ave., 808/524-3009, www.tincanmailman.net, 11am-5pm Mon.-Fri., till 4pm Sat.) is the king of Hawaiiana vintage and kitsch. It sells aloha shirts, collectibles, pin-up art, posters and hula dolls. The tiny store is packed ceiling to floor with treasures. **Hound and Quail** (920 Maunakea St., 808/779-8436,

Farmers Markets

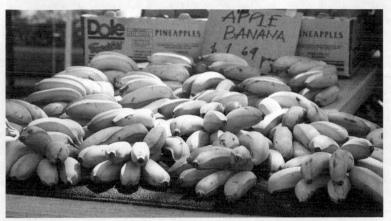

KCC Farmers Market

Honolulu has a rich farm-to-table restaurant culture as restaurants are sourcing their produce directly from local farmers. With the popularity of farmers markets, anyone can get on board and find fresh local produce and prepared foods. Check out these farmers markets in Honolulu:

- **KCC Farmers Market:** 4303 Diamond Head Rd., Kapi'olani Community College Parking Lot C, 4pm-7pm Tuesday, 7:30am-11am Saturday

- **Kaka'ako Farmers Market:** 1240 Ala Moana Blvd., Ward Warehouse parking lot, 8am-noon Saturday

- **Honolulu @ Night:** 777 Ward Ave., Neal Blaisdell Concert Hall, 4pm-7pm Wednesday

- **Manoa Marketplace:** 2752 Woodlawn Dr., 7pm-11pm Sunday, Tuesday, and Thursday

www.houndandquail.com, 1pm-6pm Mon., Wed., and Fri., 11am-4pm Sat.) sells vintage gifts, like old cameras and typewriters, furniture, home décor items and oddities like animal skulls and stuffed birds. For hip clothing and accessories, check out **Homecoming** (12 S. King St., 808/536-6000, 11am-6pm Mon.-Fri., till 5pm Sat.).

KAPAHULU

Kapahulu Avenue is another hub for dining and shopping in Honolulu. The mile-long stretch, running from Leahi Avenue by the fire station nearly up to the H-1 freeway, has plenty of places to grab a quick bite, sit-down restaurants, clothing stores, sporting goods stores, coffee shops, and a supermarket. There are even two tattoo parlors on the strip.

Bailey's Antiques and Aloha Shirts (517 Kapahulu Ave., 808/734-7628, http://alohashirts.com, 10am-9pm daily), next to another gas station up the street, is a score if you're looking for Hawaiiana wear and decoration. Along with over 15,000 aloha shirts in stock—new, used, and vintage—it also sells antiques like figurines, jewelry, postcards, and Hawaiian music LPs. **Island Triathlon & Bike** (569 Kapahulu Ave., 808/732-7227, http://itbhawaii.com, 10am-7pm Mon.-Fri., 10am-5pm Sat., 11am-4pm Sun.) is a one-stop-shop for all things running, swimming, and biking. In addition to equipment rentals and purchases, it carries shoes, clothing, and accessories. Park in the paid parking lot directly across Kapahulu and the shop will reimburse the cost. **Hawaii's Natural High** (465 Kapahulu Ave., 808/926-3000, http://glamrokhawaii. com, 9am-8pm Mon.-Sat., 11am-6pm Sun.) is a head shop with gifts and an abundance of tie-dyed and rock-and-roll T-shirts, as well as concert tickets.

KAIMUKI

If you're crafty, check out **Bead It!** (1152 Koko Head Ave., 808/734-1182, http:// ibeads.com/kaimuki.htm, 10am-6pm Mon.-Sat., noon-4pm Sun.), which has a full range of beads, gemstones, books, chains, tools,

and it also offers beading classes. **Gecko Books & Comics** (1151 12th Ave., 808/732-1292, 11am-7pm Sun.-Tues., 10am-9pm Wed.-Sat.) is right off Waialae Avenue and packed with books and comics. The owner is extremely knowledgeable and helpful. **SurfnHula** (3588 Waialae Ave., 808/428-5518, 11am-5pm Mon.-Fri., till 4pm Sat.) is full of surfing and Hawaiiana kitsch and memorabilia. Vintage collectibles include posters, hula dolls, toys, signs, and jewelry.

MO'ILI'ILI

J & L Trading House (2011 S. Beretania St., 808/941-8887, www.jllei.com, 10am-5pm daily) offers Hawaiiana and hula products.

Entertainment and Events

NIGHTLIFE
Chinatown
On Nuuanu Avenue, **The Dragon Upstairs** (1038 Nuuanu Ave., 808/526-1411, http://the-dragonupstairs.com, 7pm-2am) is a warm and classy jazz club located above Hank's Café that also features world music. For a different beat, check out **O'Toole's Irish Pub** (902 Nuuanu Ave., 808/536-4138, http://otoolesirishpub. com, 10am-2am daily). The pub has live Irish, folk, and reggae music and is also a cigar bar, where smoking is allowed inside.

On Hotel Street, check out **Thirtyninehotel** (39 N. Hotel St., 808/599-2552, www.thirtyninehotel.com, 4pm-2am Tues.-Sat.). This upstairs art gallery and indoor/outdoor bar serves tapas and is a great place to relax outside and listen to live music or DJs. Right next door on the street level is the aptly named **Nextdoor** (43 N. Hotel St., 808/548-6398, http://nextdoorhi.com, 8pm-2am Wed.-Sat.). A two-story combination nightclub and creative arts venue, Nextdoor is as versatile as its acts, ranging from a cinema

house to a dance hall, but it's best known as a music venue. There are full-service bars upstairs and downstairs, with VIP bottle service and table reservations upstairs. Also on the same block is **Bar 35** (35 N. Hotel St., 808/537-3535, www.bar35.com, 4pm-2am Mon.-Fri., 6pm-2am Sat.), a warm and modern spot featuring hundreds of international beers, indoor and patio bars, daily happy hour specials, DJs, and live music. It also has table reservations and bottle service, and serves fusion-gourmet pizzas and simple tapas. **Manifest** (32 N. Hotel St., 808/523-7575, http://manifest-hawaii.com, 8am-2am Mon.-Sat.) also holds valuable real estate on Hotel Street. A coffee shop by day, Manifest is a sophisticated cocktail bar after dark and a venue for artists of all mediums. Live music includes hip-hop, bluegrass, punk, and everything in between. **Downbeat Diner and Lounge** (42 N. Hotel St., 808/533-2328, http://downbeatdiner.com, 4pm-2am Tues.-Sat.) is a full-service bar and music venue hosting punk, bluegrass, reggae and indie music.

Public Art

At first glance, the industrial zone in Kaka'ako, between Ala Moana Boulevard and Kapiolani Boulevard, can be a mind-numbing experience. Auto repair Quonsets, warehouses, and homogeneous industrial edifices appear crushed together with little regard for open space. But young urban artists are gentrifying this industrial zone with imagery and color, free for all to see, sparking a renaissance of cafés, art studios, and galleries.

Artists are taking art outside and have created murals of varying sizes all over the exterior of buildings in parts of Kaka'ako, mostly in the urban graffiti style. Just drive slowly down Queen Street between Cooke Street and Ward Avenue and check out all the public art. Now that you know what to look for, go explore and find more.

Kaka'ako

Kaka'ako has become known for its monthly outdoor street festivals. If your schedule permits, check out Eat the Street and Honolulu Night Market. **Honolulu Night Market** (449 Cooke St., 808/772-3020, www.honolulunightmarket.com, 6pm-11pm, third Sat.) is held monthly on the third Saturday and features pop-up clothing and art vendors, live entertainment and a bevy of food trucks. A full block on Cooke Street is closed to traffic and transformed into a block party atmosphere. **Eat the Street** (1011 Ala Moana Blvd., http://eatthestreethawaii.com, 4pm-9pm) is held the last Friday of the month and showcases Honolulu's eclectic food-truck culture, with over 40 food trucks every month.

Ala Moana

Also on the Ho'okipa Terrace is a lively open-air bar called the **Mai Tai Bar** (1450 Ala Moana Blvd., 808/947-2900, www.maitaibar.com, 11am-1am daily). It offers daily *pau hana* specials (4pm-7pm), nightly happy-hour pricing (9:30pm-12:30am), and beer specials all day long during football season. The appetizers and entrées have local flair, and the restaurant also features island-style live music for happy hour every night (8pm-11pm).

Rumours (410 Atkinson Dr., 808/955-4811, 8pm-midnight Tues., 5pm-2am Fri., 9pm-2am Sat.), located in the Ala Moana Hotel, has a more relaxed atmosphere focusing on the music and dancing. It plays everything from hip-hop to hits of the 1970s, 1980s, and 1990s. Tuesday is Hot Latino Tuesdays, with complimentary dancing lessons from 8:30pm-9pm.

Mo'ili'ili

Pint + Jigger (1936 S. King St., 808/744-9593, www.pintandjigger.com, 4:30pm-midnight Mon.-Wed., 4:30am-2am Thurs., 8am-2pm Fri.-Sat., 8am-midnight Sun.) is a modern public house designed to offer creative pairings of cuisine, beer, and cocktails within a relaxed atmosphere. Along with 21 beers on tap that change regularly, specialty cocktails, and a menu that also teeters to reflect the selection of libations, this bar also takes into account atmosphere, with bar seating, table seating, beer gardens, and shuffleboard.

THE ARTS

Chinatown is the home of Honolulu's art scene, and there are nearly 20 art galleries that support and promote the local artists comprising Honolulu's art community. **The ARTS at Marks Garage** (1159 Nuuanu Ave., 808/521-2903, www.artsatmarks.com, 11am-6pm Tues.-Sat.) is the heartbeat of Chinatown's art scene. With 12 major exhibits and performances, lectures, screenings, and workshops, Marks has transformed the Chinatown community through the arts. **Ong King Art Center** (184 N. King St., http://ongking.com) has carved out a niche for performance art. Whether it be through spoken word, poetry, live music, or visual art, Ong King encourages creative risk taking. **Pegge Hopper** (1164 Nuuanu Ave., 808/524-1160, http://peggehopper.com, 11am-4pm Tues.-Fri., 11am-3pm Sat.) has been a mainstay in Chinatown since the gallery opened in 1983. Famous for Pegge Hopper paintings and drawings of Hawaiian women, the gallery features Hopper's own work, as well as that of guest artists from time to time. **Art Treasures Gallery** (1136 Nuuanu Ave., 808/536-7789, http://arttreasureshawaii.com, 11am-6pm Mon.-Fri.) features world art and jewelry—think Buddha statues, Tibetan Dzi beads, jade jewelry, spiritual art, eastern antiques and artifacts.

THEATER
Downtown
On the grounds of the Honolulu Museum of Art, **Doris Duke Theatre** (900 S. Beretania St., 808/532-8700, http://honolulumuseum.org) screens independent, documentary, and international films, performances, and concerts in a 280-seat venue. For families, the **Honolulu Theatre for Youth** (229 Queen Emma Sq., 808/839-9885, www.htyweb.org) is the perfect introduction to the dramatics for kids aged preschool through high school. The professional company presents a full season of plays every year. Another community theater in downtown Honolulu, **Kumu Kahua Theatre** (46 Merchant St., 808/536-4441, http://kumukahua.org) features Hawaiian playwrights and plays about life in Hawai'i.

Chinatown
The **Hawaii Theatre** (1130 Bethel St., 808/528-0506, www.hawaiitheatre.com) is an old vaudevillian theater dating back more than 90 years and listed on the National Register of Historic Places. Today, the restored multipurpose arts center is a stage for concerts, film, musicals, and ballets. The allure and grandeur of the theater complement any performance.

Kaka'ako
The **Neal S. Blaisdell Concert Hall** (777 Ward Ave., 808/768-5400, www.blaisdell-center.com) is the premier performing arts theater for the Honolulu Symphony and the Hawaii Opera Theatre. With 2,158 seats, a balcony, and a proscenium stage, the theater accommodates many traveling Broadway productions as well.

Manoa
Located on the University of Hawai'i Manoa campus, **Kennedy Theatre** (1770 East-West Rd., 808/956-7655, www.hawaii.edu/kennedy) showcases productions from the university's department of theater and dance. The 620-seat mainstage theater shows Asian productions, Western productions, and contemporary works, including dance performances.

Set back in Manoa Valley, the **Manoa Valley Theatre** (2833 East Manoa Rd., 808/988-6131, www.manoavalleytheatre.com) is Honolulu's Off-Broadway playhouse. The semiprofessional theater showcases mainstream contemporary plays and musicals from Broadway, Off-Broadway, and major regional theaters.

Kaimuki
The oldest performing arts center in Hawai'i, **Diamond Head Theatre** (520 Makapuu Ave., 808/733-0277, www.diamondheadtheatre.com) opened in 1915. The historic venue shows six mainstage theatrical productions each season, including five major musicals. The theater has been dubbed the Broadway of the Pacific.

CINEMA
If you're in the mood for a box office smash, there are two major movie theaters in Honolulu. In Kaka'ako, the **Ward Stadium 16 Cinema** (1044 Auahi St., 808/594-7044, www.consolidatedtheatres.com, $11) may be found in Ward Center. Matinee (before 4pm) showings cost $8.75. Add $4 for 3-D

100 Miles on Two Wheels

The **Honolulu Century Ride** (www.hbl.org, late Sept.) is the largest cycling event on O'ahu. It's not so much a race as an untimed challenging ride to pedal 100 miles from Kapi'olani Park, around Koko Crater, up to Swanzy Beach in Ka'a'awa, then back to Kapi'olani Park. Road closures go into effect for the safety of the thousands of local, national, and international riders who show up to participate.

films. In Iwilei, you've got the **Regal Dole Cannery Stadium 18 and IMAX & RPX** (735 Iwilei Rd., 808/528-3653, www.fandango.com), a participating theater in the **Hawai'i International Film Festival.**

FESTIVALS AND EVENTS

The **Neal S. Blaisdell Center** (777 Ward Ave., 808/768-5400, box office 808/768-5252, www.blaisdellcenter.com) spans a city block and includes a multipurpose circular arena for concerts, shows, and sporting events; a concert hall; and an exhibition hall for expos, fairs, and events.

The **Honolulu Museum of Art** (900 S. Beretania St., 808/532-8700, http://honolulumuseum.org, 10am-4:30pm Tues.-Sat., 1pm-3pm Sun.) hosts **ART after DARK,** a monthly art party exploring different themes on rotating exhibit in the museum, like the art of tattoo or celebrating *Hina matsuri* (Girls' Day in Japan) through elaborate dolls, 6pm-9pm on the last Friday of the month, January through October. Admission is $10.

With myriad bars, nightclubs, restaurants, and art galleries, it's no wonder Chinatown is also the hub of outdoor events. Chinatown hosts annual Chinese New Year, Halloween, St. Patrick's Day, and Cinco De Mayo Festivals, as well as the famous **First Friday.** On the first Friday of every month, people gather in the streets of Chinatown and in the galleries, museums, and art studios to celebrate the vibrant art scene. The festive event includes live music and street entertainment, and bars and restaurants cater to the crowds. Festivities begin around 6pm.

January-March

The **Honolulu Festival** (808/926-2424, http://honolulufestival.com) is a cultural event focusing on Pacific Rim cultures. The three-day festival has educational programs, activities, and performances, like cultural dances and traditional art demonstrations. The finale is a parade down Kalakaua Avenue and a spectacular fireworks display over Waikiki.

The **Hawaii Collectors Expo** (777 Ward Ave., 808/768-5400, box office 808/768-5252, http://hawaiicollectorsexpo.wix.com) in late February features all kinds of art, antiques, and collectibles. With its Hawaiiana, colored glass, handmade aloha shirts, Star Wars figurines, this three-day expo at the Neal S. Blaisdell Exhibition Hall is a favorite of local residents. There is a small entrance fee.

April-June

Memorial Day weekend is celebrated in Honolulu with the annual **Lantern Floating Hawaii** (www.lanternfloatinghawaii.com) festival on Magic Island. On the holiday itself, people from all corners of the world write remembrances and prayers on specially prepared floating lanterns to be placed in the Ala Wai Canal at dusk. The sight of over 3,000 floating lanterns is a powerful and moving experience.

On King Kamehameha Day, June 11, the **King Kamehameha Celebration Floral Parade** (www.kamehamehadaycelebration.

First Friday Gallery Walk

What kicked off in 2003 as a cultural community revival of the art scene in Honolulu has become one of the most attended, and most popular, monthly events on Oʻahu. In doing so, **First Friday** has transformed Chinatown into a community with a hip, vibrant art culture supporting myriad galleries, studios, cafés, and restaurants sponsoring local art and artists as a community. First Friday, a campaign initiated by The **ARTS at Marks Garage**, is a free, self-guided gallery walk 5pm-9pm every first Friday of the month. Chinatown galleries and studios present art exhibits, and live entertainment and refreshments abound for the thousands of art enthusiasts who descend upon the area to celebrate art in all its forms. Visit www.artsatmarks.com, where you'll find a link to a Chinatown gallery map.

org/floral-parade.html) is not to be missed. Beginning at ʻIolani Palace with a lei draping ceremony at the King Kamehameha Statue, the parade marches slowly to Kapiʻolani Park, with a beautiful display of culture, color, and flowers.

The **Islandwide Spring Crafts & Foods Expo** (777 Ward Ave., 808/768-5400, box office 808/768-5252, www.islandwidecraftexpos.com/public/public/index4.htm) is the state's largest craft fair. Over 200 artisans and food vendors come together at the Blaisdell Center to share their handmade goods and cuisine. There is also a larger Christmas show. Entrance fees apply.

July-September

In July, the **Prince Lot Hula Festival** (1352 Pineapple Pl., 808/839-5334, http://moanaluagardensfoundation.org) at Moanalua Gardens is the largest noncompetitive hula event in Hawaiʻi. The daylong display is very popular and honors Prince Lot Kapuaiwa, who helped to revive hula by carrying on the tradition through parties at his home, which is located at the gardens.

The **Hawaii Food & Wine Festival** (www.hawaiifoodandwinefestival.com) is a four-day epicurean delight featuring the specialties of over 50 internationally renowned master chefs and wine and spirit producers. The festival takes place across Honolulu and Koʻolina in September. Check the website for details.

October-December

Every year in early December, over 20,000 runners from around the world flock to Honolulu to participate and compete in the **Honolulu Marathon** (3435 Waialae Ave., Ste. 200, 808/734-7200, www.honolulumarathon.org). Ala Moana Boulevard between Ala Moana Beach Park and Ala Moana Center is transformed into the starting line, where runners begin their 26.2-mile trek to Hawaiʻi Kai and back to finish in Waikiki.

Downtown's historic district, at Honolulu Hale, hosts **Honolulu City Lights** (www.honolulucitylights.org) in December. The Christmas celebration of lights is punctuated by huge statues decorating the exterior of the building, most notably, Shaka Santa.

Food

DOWNTOWN

Hawaiian

On the outskirts of downtown Honolulu is a long-established Hawaiian food joint called the **People's Cafe** (1300 Pali Hwy., 808/536-5789, 10am-8pm Mon.-Sat., 10am-5pm Sun., $6-12). Just *makai* (towards the ocean) of the Pali Long's parking lot, look for the bright red neon sign for this small restaurant serving all the favorite Hawaiian combos plus some extras like salted meat and kimchi.

American

For a delicious burger and seasonal brews overlooking Honolulu Harbor, check out **Gordon Biersch** (1 Aloha Tower Dr., 808/599-4877, www.gordonbiersch.com, 11am-midnight Sun.-Thurs., 11am-1am Fri.-Sat., $12-24). It has a wide variety of beers on tap and live music Wednesday-Saturday.

CHINATOWN

Honolulu's Chinatown is chock-full of restaurants providing regional cuisine from all over the globe. Just about every other storefront is a restaurant or serves food in some fashion.

Tea

For a quaint and quiet afternoon tea, stop in at the unpretentious **Tea at 1024** (1024 Nuuanu Ave., 808/521-9596, www.teaat1024.net, 11am-2pm Tues.-Fri., 11am-3pm Sat.). Relax in the charming teahouse, don a special hat from the hat stand, and choose your china for teatime.

Asian

For a sampling of cuisine from China, Korea, Vietnam, Thailand, and the Philippines, duck inside the **Maunakea Marketplace Food Court** (1120 Maunakea St., 808/524-3409). In the center of the shopping complex that spans the small city block are vendors with stalls lined up shoulder to shoulder and family-style seating in the middle. The air is thick with the sweet smells of seafood and spices from different countries mingling together. Most vendors offer their food bento or plate-lunch style.

Chinese

In historic Chinatown, **Little Village Noodle House** (1113 Smith St., 808/545-3008, http://littlevillagehawaii.com, 10:30am-8pm daily, $13-50) is the quintessential Chinese restaurant for grabbing a bite. With over 100 menu items covering meat, poultry, seafood, rice, and noodle dishes, the family friendly restaurant has every palate covered. For delicious dim sum, check out **The Mandalay** (1055 Alakea St., 808/525-8585, http://themandalayhawaii.com, 10:30am-10:30pm Mon.-Fri., 10:30am-midnight Sat.-Sun., $7-13). It has plenty of entrées, but the dim sum menu is the favorite.

Pacific Rim

For exceptional Pacific Rim cuisine, check out **Lucky Belly** (50 N. Hotel St., 808/531-1888, www.luckybelly.com, 11am-2pm and 5pm-midnigiht Mon.-Sat., $9-23), a very popular eatery in an arty, modern space with exposed brick walls. Seafood and pork are the main proteins in the entrées. Lucky Belly is best known for its ramen, and its slow-cooked brisket is a favorite. **The Pig & the Lady** (83 N. King St., 808/585-8255, http://thepigandthelady.com, 10:30am-2pm and 5:30pm-10pm Mon.-Sat., $14-35) combines Southeast Asian and Pacific Rim cuisine in an eclectic menu of subtle flavors and gourmet ingredients. It serves handcrafted cocktails that pair with specific entrees. For lunch, the pho French dip sandwich is a must.

Irish Pubs

J.J. Dolan's (1147 Bethel St., 808/537-4992, www.jjdolans.com, 11am-2am Mon.-Sat.,

$16-19) is an Irish pub serving delicious New York-style pizza. With a full bar and a selection of Irish whiskey, this small pub can get pretty rowdy when there is a packed house. **Murphy's Bar & Grill** (2 Merchant St., 808/531-0422, http://murphyshawaii. com, 11:30am-2am Mon.-Fri., opens at 4pm Sat.-Sun., $11-19) has a separate bar and dining room under one roof. The menu features a combination of bar food, burgers, and Irish food. The bar favors Irish whiskey and draught beer, with shuffleboard on offer.

American

Check out **Livestock Tavern** (49 N. Hotel St., 808/537-2577, www.livestocktavern.com, 11am-2pm and 5pm-10pm Mon.-Sat., $11-32) for seasonally inspired American plates in a rustic setting. Whether prime rib, burgers, duck, and lamb, Livestock puts a modern twist on comfort food. Reservations are suggested for supper. Across Hotel Street you'll find a diner loved by vegetarians and vegans called **Downbeat Diner & Lounge** (42 N. Hotel St., 808/533-2328, http://downbeatdiner.com, 11am-3pm Mon.-Thurs., 11am-4pm Fri.-Sat., 10am-11pm Sun., $6-15). It serves breakfast, sandwiches, burgers, and has a variety of appetizers and a full bar. Any menu item can be prepared vegetarian or vegan style.

African

Kan Zaman (1028 Nuuanu Ave., 808/554-3847, http://kanzamanhawaii.com, 11am-9:30pm Mon.-Thurs., 11am-10:30pm Fri.-Sat., $12-24) feature dishes from Morocco and Lebanon and is known for its lamb dishes and shwarma entrees. **Ethiopian Love** (1112 Smith St., 808/725-7197, www.ethiopianlovehi.com/, 11am-2pm and 5pm-10pm Mon.-Sat., 5pm-10pm Sun., $11-30) is an eat-with-your-hands restaurant, or rather with injera bread, actually. The dishes are large and meant to be shared. There is indoor and outdoor seating on the back patio.

KAKA'AKO
Quick Bites

For coffee, sandwiches, quick bites, breakfast foods, and Internet access, stop in at **Fresh Café** (831 Queen St., 808/688-8055, http:// freshcafehi.com, 8am-9pm Mon.-Sat., 9am-6pm Sun., $5-9), where the ingredients are locally sourced. Fresh Café is the center of the Kaka'ako urban art scene revival, and hip art decorates the walls of the establishment as well as the walls of the buildings surrounding it. A performance space in the back of the restaurant features live music and art shows. Check the website for the calendar of events. **Pa'ina Café** (1050 Ala Moana Blvd., 808/356-2829, www.painacafe.com, 10am-9pm Mon.-Sat., 10am-6pm Sun., $7-12) is located in Ward Warehouse in the middle of the outdoor mall, on the bottom floor. It offers a variety of fresh and delicious poke bowls, salads, and a few tasty sandwiches. This location also serves delicious acai bowls and smoothies.

On the second floor of Ward Center you'll find a great steak and seafood restaurant. **Ryan's Grill** (1200 Ala Moana Blvd., 808/591-9132, www.ryansgrill.com, 11am-midnight daily, $13-21) has a varied menu with small and big salads, pasta and pizza, sandwiches, and steak and seafood options. It also has a relaxing bar area and beautiful views of Ala Moana Beach Park.

Gastropub

In the Ward Farmers Market, **REAL a gastropub** (1200 Ala Moana Blvd., 808/591-9188, www.realgastropub.com, 2pm-2am Mon.-Sat., $3-12) is spearheading the gastropub trend in Honolulu with smart combinations of flavors in its tapas-style menu items, designed for sampling. You can combine your choice with one of over 200 bottled beers imported from all over the world and 24 rotating taps. It also has a full bar and wine.

Japanese

In Ward Center, **Goma Tei** (1020 Auahi St., 808/596-2526, www.gomatei.com, 11am-9:30pm Mon.-Thurs., till 10pm Fri.-Sat.,

9am-9pm Sun., $3-12) serves the best ramen around. There is limited seating, so be prepared to put your name on the list and wait to be called. Don't forget to try the gyoza as well.

MANOA
Quick Bites
For a coffee, some home-cooked quick bites, and lots of reading material, stop in at **Coffeeline Campus Coffeehouse** (1820 University Ave., 808/778-7909, 8am-2pm Mon.-Fri., 8am-noon Sat.-Sun.). In the back of the YWCA building on University Ave., across from UH Manoa, look for the stairs on the south side of the building leading up to Coffeeline's patio, complete with tables, couches, and more reading material than you can handle. There is free parking behind the building.

Hawaiian
Deep in the valley, by the Manoa Falls trailhead and Lyon Arboretum, is a restaurant set among the trees of Manoa's lush rain forest. **Treetops Restaurant** (3737 Manoa Rd., 808/988-6838, 11am-2pm and 5pm-8pm daily, opens at 10:30am Sat.-Sun., $7-16) serves both a weekday and a weekend buffet lunch, perfect for a post-hike meal.

Mexican
For authentic Mexican food, stop in at **Serg's Mexican Kitchen** (2740 E. Manoa Rd., 808/988-8118, 11am-9pm Mon.-Sat., 8am-8pm Sun., $4-16). With open-air, family-style seating and mariachi music, this BYOB joint is the spot for a quick taco or a sit down meal with a big group.

KAIMUKI
Quick Bites
Rainbow Drive-In (3308 Kanaina Ave., 808/737-0177, www.rainbowdrivein.com, 7am-9pm daily, $6-8) has served choice plate lunches since 1961, always at a reasonable price. Protein, rice, and gravy never tasted so good. **Kaimuki Superette** (3458 Waialae Ave., 808/734-7800, 10am-3pm Mon.-Sat.,

$7-14) serves local and seasonal dishes using locally sourced ingredients. The octopus roll is a favorite, as well the antipasti. It also has great coffee. **Sprout** (1154 Koko Head Ave., 808/737-0177, https://squareup.com/market/sproutwich, 7am-9pm daily, $6-8) is the stop for a fresh, handmade sandwich. Think turkey and bacon with avocado on a fresh ciabatta. Order online if you're on the go.

Steak and Seafood
On Waialae Avenue are a handful of popular restaurants. **Town** (3435 Waialae Ave., 808/735-5900, www.townkaimuki.com, 11am-2:30pm and 5:30-9:30 Mon.-Thurs., 5:30pm-10pm Fri.-Sat., $9-28) serves breakfast, lunch, and dinner. The hip spot, with modern art decor, is a mix between Hawai'i regional and Italian cuisine, all with the focus of serving organic, fresh, and locally sourced ingredients. It has a full bar, or you can BYOB for a corkage fee of $15. Limited street parking is available, but there is a small parking lot behind the restaurant as well.

Café Miro (3446 Waialae Ave., 808/734-2737, www.cafemirohawaii.com, Tues.-Sun. 5:30pm-10:30pm, $43-54) is an exquisite steak and seafood restaurant with mostly French cuisine, serving a three-course prix fixe menu and a four-course Chef's Special menu. Think oysters, lamb, duck, scallops, abalone, and steak, each drizzled with flavorful sauce.

12th Ave Grill (1120 12th Ave., 808/732-9469, www.12thavegrill.com, 5:30pm-10pm Mon.-Thurs., 5:30-11pm Fri.-Sat., 5pm-10pm Sun., $25-36) is just off Waialae Avenue and offers award-winning contemporary American cuisine and a commitment to locally sourced and seasonal ingredients. A well-selected wine list and scratch bar pair nicely with the flavorful fare. The small dining room is intimate, yet comfortable.

On Kapahulu is a popular and often packed **Uncle Bo's** (559 Kapahulu Ave., 808/735-8311, www.unclebosrestaurant.com, 5pm-2am daily, $12-27). Combining American bistro with Pacific Rim cuisine, Uncle Bo's is a small, modern, but casual restaurant. It has an extensive pupu menu, as well as steak, seafood, pasta, and pizza. Be prepared for a bit of a wait on the weekends, and if the bar is full, that means you'll have to stand outside.

Award-winning chef Colin Nishida creates Hawaiian-style comfort food, served as complete meals or pupu style, inside the Prudential Locations building in an offshoot of the famous Side Street Inn in Kaka'ako called **Side Street Inn on Da Strip** (614 Kapahulu Ave., 808/739-3939, http://sidestreetinn.com, 3pm-midnight daily, $12-22). The restaurant has family-style seating with a touch of fine dining, and the portions are quite large and designed to be shared.

Gastropub

Stop in for a pint and poutine at **BREW'd Craft Pub** (3441 Waialae Ave., 808/732-2337, http://brewdcraftpub.com, 4pm-2am Mon.-Sat., $6-13), which has a rotating menu of craft beers on tap and bottled. The small pub is usually packed around 5pm and seating can be hard to find. The menu items are served tapas style and meant to be shared. Truffle deviled eggs and jalapeño candied bacon are house favorites.

Breakfast

Koko Head Café (1145 12th Ave., 808/732-8920, http://kokoheadcafe.com, 7am-2:30pm daily, $6-16) is a very popular island-style brunch house serving Chef Lee Anne Wong's famous dumplings, egg skillets, sweet pancakes, and much more—think Pacific Rim-infused breakfast entrees. Seating is walk-in only and there is almost always a line, but it's worth it. And since it's five o'clock somewhere, you can always order a beer or craft cocktail while you wait.

Hawaiian

For authentic Hawaiian food, check out **Ono Hawaiian Food** (726 Kapahulu Ave., 808/737-2275, www.onohawaiianfoods.com, 11am-8pm Mon.-Sat., $6-22). The family-run

Town restaurant

restaurant is small and cozy, with just a few tables. Be prepared to wait outside during peak hours.

Chinese, Thai, and Vietnamese

In Kaimuki there are three consistent picks for noodles and soup. **Hale Vietnam Restaurant** (140 12th Ave., 808/735-7581, www.champathai.com, 10am-9:45pm daily, $8-14) is best known for its delicious pho. It also has barbecued pork plates and sautéed dishes with your choice of protein. **To Thai For** (3571 Waialae Ave., 808/734-3443, www.itstothaifor.com, 10:30 am-9:30pm Mon. and Wed.-Sat., 5pm-9:30pm Sun., $9-20) has a basic Thai menu through which you can combine the dish with the protein of your liking. **Happy Days** (3553 Waialae Ave., 808/738-8666, 8am-10pm daily, $8-23) is hands down the best Chinese food in the region. It is also known for its selection of dim sum made daily. Don't forget to order the crispy gau gee appetizer.

Japanese

On Kapahulu Avenue are three noteworthy Japanese restaurants. **Irifune** (563 Kapahulu Ave., 808/737-1141, 11:30am-1:30pm and 5:30pm-9:30pm Tues.-Sat., $10-15) is a curious hole-in-the-wall with some of the best ahi on O'ahu. The entire menu consists of some combination of garlic and ahi, served with local-style sides. This restaurant is very popular, and on the weekends you can expect a wait. It does have a bench outside. Park across the street in the pay parking lot, or there is street parking in the neighborhood, behind the restaurant.

Tokkuri Tei (611 Kapahulu Ave., 808/732-6480, www.tokkuritei-hawaii.com, 11am-2pm and 5:30pm-midnight Mon.-Fri., 5:30pm-midnight Sat., 5pm-10:30pm Sun., $4-50) is a popular izakaya restaurant offering traditional Japanese food with a French influence and local uniqueness. With its sushi bar or table seating and an extensive sake and spirits selection, it will take several visits to sample the wealth of food on all 13 pages of the menu. It's located on the second floor of Hee Hing Plaza, and there is free parking under the plaza. Reservations are necessary.

At the opposite end of Kapahulu Avenue, just off the main drag, is another top-notch izakaya establishment offering traditional Japanese fare. **Izakaya Nonbei** (3108 Olu St., 808/734-5573, 5pm-11:30pm Mon.-Sat., 5pm-10:30pm Sun., $6-25) is a small restaurant with a sushi bar and shared and private seating. It has a vast selection of sake and beer but is known for its frozen sake.

Mexican

Jose's Mexican Cafe & Cantina (1134 Koko Head Ave., 808/732-1833, www.joseshonolulu.com, 11am-10pm Mon.-Sat., 11am-9pm Sun., $14-25) serves up simple Mexican food, with seafood, beef and pork specialties, and even a few egg dishes. Jose's has a happy hour weekdays 3pm-6pm and a selection of Mexican beers and different styles of margaritas, mixed either for a glass or a pitcher.

Indian

Himalayan Kitchen (1137 11th Ave., #205, 808/735-1122, 11am-2pm and 5pm-10pm Tues.-Fri., 5pm-10pm Sat.-Mon., $11-22) serves Nepalese and Indian cuisine in a small restaurant with indoor and patio seating. This second story BYOB is a local favorite and often packed with those seeking their variety of vegetarian and meat dishes. The entrance to the restaurant is in an alcove between a gift store, a barbecue joint, an Italian restaurant, and a salon. There is a paid parking lot with ample parking.

Sweets and Treats

You can grab a delicious pastry, dessert, or cup of coffee on Waialae Avenue at **JJ Bistro & French Pastry** (3447 Waialae Ave., 808/739-0993, www.jjfrenchbistro.com, 10am-9pm Mon.-Sat., 11:30am-9pm Sun., $5-19). It also serves pizza, pasta, sandwiches, and à la carte entrées. If you're down for an old-fashioned ice-cream cone, stop by the **Pill Box** (1133 11th Ave., 808/737-4966, 9am-7pm Mon.-Fri., 9am-3pm Sat., 7pm-11pm Sun.). This full-service neighborhood pharmacy has friendly staff, books, and the best ice cream in town. There are a couple spaces out front on 11th Avenue, or you can park in the paid parking lot behind the building. If you're quick and can get your ice cream within the 15-minute grace period, parking is free.

On Kapahulu Avenue, residents and visitors flock to **Leonard's Bakery** (933 Kapahulu Ave., 808/737-5591, www.leonardshawaii.com, 6am-9pm Mon.-Thurs., till 10pm Fri.-Sat.) in record numbers, often backing up traffic on Kapahulu while they wait for a parking stall in the small parking lot out front. Look for the neon sign and the line out the door. Leonard's is famous for its *malasadas* and doughnuts, but it also has delicious pastries, cookies, bread, pies, and wraps. For shave ice, head to **Waiola Shave Ice** (2135 Waiola St., 808/949-2269, www.waiolashaveice.com, 10am-6pm daily). It's tucked away right off Kapahulu Avenue, across from Safeway.

Markets

Tamura's Fine Wines & Liquors (3496 Waialae Ave., 808/735-7100, http://tamurasfinewine.com, 9:30am-9pm Mon.-Sat., 9:30am-8pm Sun.) not only has one of the best selections of beer, wine, and spirits for the best prices in Honolulu, but it also has prepared foods, cheeses, specialty groceries, and is famous for its fresh *poke.*

MO'ILI'ILI
Health Food

Down to Earth (2525 S. King St., 808/947-7678, www.downtoearth.org, 7:30am-10pm daily) is an all-vegetarian, natural, and organic food store with a deli, salad bar, hot foods, and smoothies. Parking is on the roof behind the store. Take the alley right past the entrance and turn up the ramp.

Kokua Market (2643 S. King St., 808/941-1922, www.kokua.coop, 8am-9pm daily) is a natural food store co-op on the other side of University Avenue from Down to Earth. It has bulk foods and natural and organic groceries, but the real draw is the deli, with hot and cold items. The menu includes raw, vegan,

macrobiotic, and natural meats options. There are also freshly baked desserts. Parking is behind the store from Kahuna Lane.

An oasis of charm and natural food on busy and urban King Street, **Peace Café** (2239 S. King St., 808/951-7555, www.peacecafehawaii.com, 11am-9pm Mon.-Sat., 11am-3pm Sun., $9-11) serves vegan home cooking in a comfortable setting. Within its eclectic decorating scheme, Peace Café has sandwiches, salads, stews, and prepared goods like granola for the taking.

Indian

Café Maharani (2509 S. King St., 808/951-7447, http://cafemaharanihawaii.com, 5pm-10pm daily, $14-16) is an award-winning casual restaurant blending natural ingredients and a host of spices to create some of the most sought after Indian food in Honolulu.

Mediterranean

Da Spot (2469 S. King St., 808/941-1313, 11am-9:30pm Mon.-Sat., $6-10) is a roomy Mediterranean café that is completely open to King Street from the front. It offers vegetarian fare, including Thai and Egyptian cuisine and desserts, as well as rustic salads and prepared foods like mango salsa, imported

Leonard's Bakery is the mecca of *malasadas.*

cheeses, olives, and hummus. Take a seat and take advantage of Internet access with your meal.

Steak and Seafood

For modern fine dining on the best in Hawai'i regional cuisine, **Chef Mavro** (1969 S. King St., 808/944-4714, www.chefmavro. com, 6pm-9pm Tues.-Sun., $75-165) offers the quintessential experience. The French-influenced cuisine is award-winning and the ingredients are locally sourced. Seasonal menus are geared toward wine pairings. Children must be 5 years of age or older, and attire is aloha casual.

Renowned chef specializing in Hawai'i regional cuisine Alan Wong pairs fine dining with fresh and local ingredients at his flagship restaurant **Alan Wong's** (1857 S. King St., 808/949-1939, www.alanwongs.com, 5pm-10pm daily, $30-50). Locally raised beef and sustainable seafood combined with O'ahu farm-fresh produce are served up with a completely local flair. In addition to entrées, it offers two set multicourse tasting menus available with wine pairings.

In the same vein of Hawai'i regional cuisine and locally sourced ingredients, **Side Street Inn** (1225 Hopaka St., 808/591-0253, http://sidestreetinn.com, 2pm-10pm Mon.-Thurs., 2pm-11pm Fri., 1pm-11pm Sat., 1pm-10pm Sun., $12-22) has transformed over the years from a little hole-in-the-wall with exceptional food to a big hole-in-the-wall with phenomenal cuisine where local and international chefs go to eat. With the full bar and large portions served pupu style, this is a great place to share the experience of food and drink with family and friends. The bar stays open a couple hours after the kitchen has closed. A second, newer location on Kapahulu Avenue is called Side Street Inn On Da Strip.

IWILEI
Seafood

In the Honolulu Harbor area, seafood is the main attraction. **Nico's at Pier 38** (1129 N. Nimitz Hwy., 808/540-1377, http://nicospier38.com, 6:30am-9pm daily, $13-17) is both a fish market and restaurant. It serves Hawaiian-style seafood with a French twist—gourmet food with plate-lunch delivery. The open-air restaurant also has a full bar. From Nimitz Highway, access Pier 38 from Alakawa Avenue. Open for breakfast, lunch and dinner.

On the way out to Sand Island is one of the few real tiki bars still in operation. **La Mariana** (50 Sand Island Access Rd., 808/848-2800, www.lamarianasailingclub. com, 11am-9pm daily, $14-42) is a steak and seafood restaurant located in the La Mariana Sailing Club. Nestled at the edge of Ke'ehi Lagoon, the restaurant is a veritable museum of Hawaiiana treasures and collectibles, with an unmatched ambience from the warm glow of colorful lights, wood decor, and the grin of tikis all around.

GREATER HONOLULU

Overlooking Pearl Harbor, **Buzz's Pearl City** (98-751 Kuahao Pl., 808/487-6465, 5pm-9pm daily, $17-33) is Buzz's original steak house; the sister location is in Lanikai. Famous for their kiawe broiled steaks, seafood, and no-nonsense cocktails, Buzz's is the perfect finish to a day at Pearl Harbor. Call at 4pm and make reservations.

Local favorite **Taniokas** (94-903 Farrington Hwy., 808/671-3779, www.taniokas.com, 8am-5pm Mon.-Fri., 9am-5pm Sat., 9am-3pm Sun., $5-15) specializes in Hawaiian food, bentos, and *poke*. The extensive menu covers the wide range of flavors found in local food from teriyaki and musubi to stews and kimchi, but seafood, in many preparations, is definitely the cornerstone of the menu.

Information and Services

VISITORS CENTER

The **Hawaii Visitors and Convention Bureau** (2270 Kalakaua Ave., Ste. 801, 808/524-0722 or 800/464-2924, www.gohawaii.com) manages the official visitors center for O'ahu and has all manner of maps, brochures, travel tips and activity ideas.

LIBRARY

Internet access is available at the **Kaimuki Public Library** (1041 Koko Head Ave., 808/733-8422, www.librarieshawaii.org), the **McCully-Moiliili Public Library** (2211 S. King St., 808/973-1099, www.librarieshawaii.org), the **Manoa Public Library** (2716 Woodlawn Dr., 808/988-0459, www.librarieshawaii.org), and the **Hawaii State Library**

(478 S. King St., 808/586-3500, www.librarieshawaii.org). Visitors need a valid HSPLS library card to use an Internet computer. Three-month visitor cards are available for $10. You can reserve Internet computer time online or in person. You can find printed bus schedules, too.

MAIL

Post offices in Honolulu are located in Kaimuki (1130 Koko Head Rd., 808/737-8937), Manoa (2754 Woodlawn Dr., Ste. 7-101, 808/532-5689) in the Manoa Marketplace, Mo'ili'ili (2700 S. King St., 808/275-8777), Ala Moana (1450 Ala Moana Blvd., 808/532-1987) in the Ala Moana Center, and downtown (335 Merchant St., 808/532-1987).

Getting There and Around

GETTING THERE
Air

All commercial flights to O'ahu are routed to the **Honolulu International Airport** (300 Rodgers Blvd., 808/836-6411, http://hawaii.gov/hnl), as are most other flights with neighboring islands as their final destinations. The Honolulu International Airport has three terminals: the Overseas Terminal accommodates international and mainland flights, the Interisland Terminal handles Hawaiian Airlines flights, and the Commuter Terminal handles the small interisland carriers. There is a free intra-airport shuttle service for getting around the airport, and ground transportation is available just outside the baggage claim areas on the lower level, along the center median, where you can get a taxi, catch a shuttle to a rental car agency office, board TheBus, or pick up the other private shuttle buses that ferry visitors to Honolulu, Waikiki,

and beyond. The airport is a mere 10 miles from Waikiki, and 6 miles from downtown Honolulu.

GETTING AROUND
Car

Urban community planning was not top of mind for state officials as Honolulu grew and expanded up and out. Two-way roads suddenly change to one-way only, roads curve and bend with the geography, narrow neighborhood roads have street parking that blocks an entire lane, and it can be extremely frustrating to find a freeway on-ramp. Add to this confusion rush-hour traffic and contra flow, and you're sitting in some of the worst traffic in the United States. Don't be too discouraged, though, because with proper planning and an up-to-date road map, the adventure of getting around Honolulu can be quite exciting.

Making the most of your time in Honolulu

will mean working with the daily tide of traffic. Typical rush hour traffic is 5am-9am, when people flood into downtown from the east and west and the H-1 freeway slows to a crawl. Kapiolani Boulevard and Nimitz Highway are modified with an extra contra flow lane and there are turning restrictions. In the afternoon, rush hour starts up again 3pm-6:30pm, contra flow lanes are added in the opposite direction for traffic to flow out of town, and the H-1 freeway again slows to a crawl. With limited freeway on-ramps, entire side streets will back up for blocks as cars jam onto the H-1. Plan your meals during these periods,or activities where you'll be out of the car and off the road for an extended period of time.

Dealing with parking in Honolulu is another matter in itself. The historic district has metered street parking, which is free on Sundays and holidays, and downtown and Chinatown have ample structure parking. For the best rates, look for the Chinatown municipal parking lots; there are several. You can also park in the high-rises downtown, but the rates are much higher.

Uber and **Lyft** ride-hailing services are available in Honolulu if you prefer not to be the driver. Check out the smartphone apps.

Bus

TheBus (808/848-4500, www.thebus.org) provides islandwide transportation, including transportation from the airport. If you're planning on riding the bus from the airport to your hotel, keep in mind that your bags have to be able to fit under the seat or on your lap without protruding into the aisle. There are several bus stops on the second level of the airport on the center median. Route Nos. 19, 20, and 31 access the airport, and Route No. 19 eastbound will take you to Waikiki. To get to Pearl Harbor, take bus routes 20 or 42 from Kuhio Avenue in Waikiki, or route 20, 42, or 52 from Ala Moana Center or downtown.

There are nine transit centers on O'ahu. The major Honolulu transit centers are the Ala Moana Center Bus Stops, the Alapai Transit Center in downtown, and the Kalihi Transit Center. Fares are $2.50 for adults, $1.25 children ages 6-17, children 5 and under are free if they sit on an adult's lap. The Visitors Pass, a four-consecutive-day pass, is $25 with unlimited use. Call or visit their website for route information, maps, and timetables.

TheBus also has a smartphone app, **DaBus,** which offers real-time information.

Bike

Getting around by bike is not recommended due to the lack of bike lanes, street parking, and bus and traffic congestion. But if you're a diehard and must cruise on two wheels, there is a dedicated, protected, two-way bike lane on King Street that runs from Alapai Street to Isenberg Street for about two miles.

North Shore

J ust 30 miles from Honolulu is the famed North Shore, the big city's polar opposite. Local surfers appropriately make the distinction and have coined the regions "town" and "country."

With an average of 30 inches of rainfall annually, the North Shore is an escape to a verdant, natural haven and a simpler, almost hedonistic lifestyle. It's all about the beaches, diving, fishing, and, of course, surfing.

From the northernmost tip of the island to Ka'ena Point to the west, the North Shore's coastline looks more like a backwards *L*, or even the open jaws of a shark, and captures the powerful open-ocean swells that track across the Pacific during the northern hemisphere's winter. That's the reason for the enormous, powerful surf that pounds the reefs from October through April. Save for the town of Hale'iwa, the gateway to the North Shore, and Turtle Bay Resort, this area has remained commercially undeveloped, a mix between residential and farmland. Locals have taken great pride in their grassroots efforts to establish a marine protected area along Waimea Bay, Three Tables, and Sharks

Cove, to preserve the bluff known as Pupukea-Paumalu that frames the quaint North Shore community and preserve Kawela Bay for perpetuity.

Along the extreme northern stretch of the North Shore, you'll find world-class surf spots like Laniakea, Waimea Bay, the Banzai Pipeline, and Sunset Beach. Because of the quality and sheer number of surf breaks, this part of the North Shore is known as the "Seven Mile Miracle." Hale'iwa, sitting just off the Kamehameha Highway at the bottom of the pineapple fields, is where you'll find shopping, dining, dive and surf rental outfitters, and the famous Matsumoto Shave Ice. Waialua and Mokule'ia comprise the western side of the North Shore and offer quieter, less visited beaches and the rare opportunity to watch polo during the summer months. To those who wish to jump out of a plane and skydive in paradise, head this way.

Previous: Banzai Pipeline; Turtle Bay. **Above:** Waimea Valley botanical garden.

Look for ★ to find recommended sights, activities, dining, and lodging.

Highlights

★ **Waimea Valley:** Part lush tropical botanical garden, part restored ancient cultural site, Waimea Valley is a bastion of beauty and education (page 119).

★ **Waimea Bay Beach Park:** This expansive sandy shore yields to turquoise water that is home to reef fish, spinner dolphins, and green sea turtles. Swim and snorkel the calm waters in summer, or watch surfers ride enormous waves in winter (page 122).

★ **Banzai Pipeline:** Watch expert surfers attempt to ride the barrel at one of the most dangerous breaks in the world (page 126).

★ **Pupukea-Waimea Marine Life Conservation District:** Comprised of Waimea Bay, Three Tables, and Sharks Cove, this mile-long protected shoreline is where marine life abounds. It is the best area for snorkeling and shore diving on the North Shore (page 129).

★ **Skydiving:** Skydiving operators in Mokule'ia offer a once-in-a-lifetime opportunity to tandem skydive, affording you a bird's-eye view of paradise (page 134).

★ **Shopping in Historic Hale'iwa Town:** Quaint Hale'iwa is the official gateway to the North Shore. It's packed with clothing boutiques, surf shops, and art galleries (page 136).

★ **Hawaii Polo:** Enjoy the camaraderie and festive atmosphere of a polo match by the sea. Bring the family, spread out a blanket, open the cooler, and enjoy a perfect summer afternoon (page 137).

North Shore

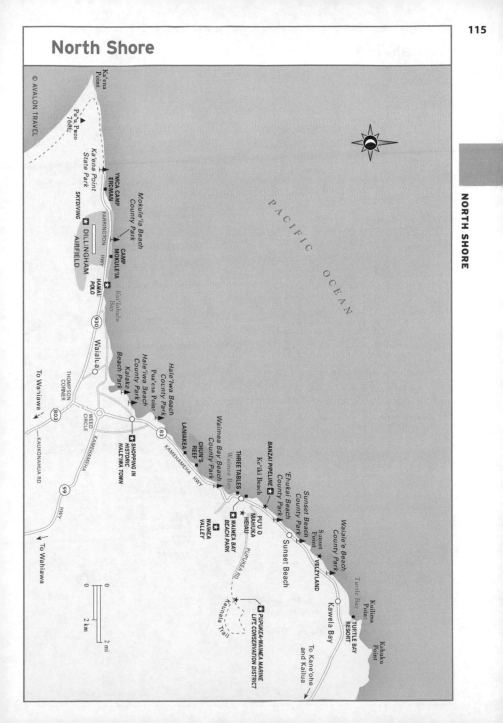

© AVALON TRAVEL

Ka'ena Point

Pu'u Pueo
765ft.

Ka'ena Point
State Park

YMCA CAMP
ERDMAN

SKYDIVING

Mokule'ia
County Park

FARRINGTON

DILLINGHAM
AIRFIELD

CAMP
MOKULE'IA

HAWAI'I
POLO

Kaiʻalohulu
Bay

930

Waialua

THOMPSON
CORNER

803

99
HWY

KAUKONAHUA RD.

To Wahiawa

To Wahiawa

KAMEHAMEHA

WEED
CIRCLE

83

SHOPPING IN
HISTORIC
HALE'IWA TOWN

Kaiaka
Beach Park

Hale'iwa Beach
County Park

Pua'ena Point

Hale'iwa Beach
County Park

LANIAKEA

CHUN'S
REEF

KAMEHAMEHA HWY

Waimea Bay Beach
County Park

THREE TABLES

Waimea Bay

WAIMEA
VALLEY

WAIMEA BAY
BEACH PARK

PU'U O
MAHUKA
HEIAU

PUPUKEA RD.

Kaunala Trail

PUPUKEA-WAIMEA MARINE
LIFE CONSERVATION DISTRICT

BANZAI PIPELINE

Ke'iki Beach

'Ehukai Beach
County Park

Sunset Beach
County Park

Sunset
Point

Sunset Beach

VELZYLAND

Waiale'e Beach
County Park

Kawela Bay

Turtle Bay

Kuilima
Point

TURTLE BAY
RESORT

Kahuku Point

To Kane'ohe
and Kailua

PACIFIC OCEAN

0   2 mi
0   2 km

Hale'iwa

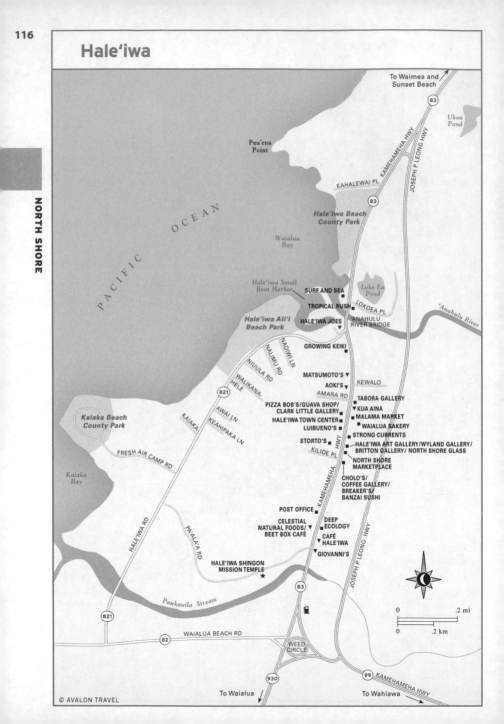

To Waimea and
Sunset Beach

Ukoa
Pond

Pua'ena
Point

KAHALEWAI PL

KAMEHAMEHA HWY

JOSEPH P LEONG HWY

83

Hale'iwa Beach
County Park

Waialua
Bay

PACIFIC OCEAN

Lake Ea
Pond

'Anahulu River

Hale'iwa Small
Boat Harbor

SURF AND SEA

LOKOEA PL

TROPICAL RUSH

Hale'iwa Ali'i
Beach Park

HALE'IWA JOES

'ANAHULU
RIVER BRIDGE

NALIMU LN

NAOIWI LN

GROWING KEIKI

INIULA RD

WALIKANA-
HELE

NIUULA RD

MATSUMOTO'S

AOKI'S

KEWALO

821

AMARA RD

TABORA GALLERY

AWAI LN

KAIAKA

KEAHIPAKA LN

PIZZA BOB'S/GUAVA SHOP/
CLARK LITTLE GALLERY

KUA AINA

MALAMA MARKET

Kaiaka Beach
County Park

HALE'IWA TOWN CENTER

LUIBUENO'S

WAIALUA BAKERY

STRONG CURRENTS

FRESH AIR CAMP RD

STORTO'S

KAMEHAMEHA HWY

HALE'IWA ART GALLERY/WYLAND GALLERY/
BRITTON GALLERY/ NORTH SHORE GLASS

Kaiaka
Bay

KILIOE PL

NORTH SHORE
MARKETPLACE

HALE'IWA RD

PA'ALA'A RD

CHOLO'S/
COFFEE GALLERY/
BREAKER'S/
BANZAI SUSHI

POST OFFICE

CELESTIAL
NATURAL FOODS/
BEET BOX CAFÉ

DEEP
ECOLOGY

CAFÉ
HALE'IWA

JOSEPH P LEONG HWY

GIOVANNI'S

HALE'IWA SHINGON
MISSION TEMPLE

83

Paukauila Stream

0   .2 mi

821

0   .2 km

WAIALUA BEACH RD

82

WEED
CIRCLE

930

99

KAMEHAMEHA HWY

To Waialua

To Wahiawa

© AVALON TRAVEL

PLANNING YOUR TIME

No matter if it's summer or winter, rain or shine, the North Shore shouldn't be missed and can't be rushed. Take advantage of all the natural beauty and ocean activities on offer and plan for a full-day trip to the region. The 33-mile drive from Waikiki to the North Shore, taking the most direct route across the central plateau, will last an hour if all goes well and traffic is light. If your stay on O'ahu is during the summer, drive up in the morning and snorkel in the Pupukea-Waimea Marine Life Conservation District, at Waimea Bay, Three Tables, and Sharks Cove. Park at Three Tables, which is between the other two sites, and utilize the walking trail to visit all three locales without moving the car. Grab a quick lunch at Ted's Bakery at Sunset Beach or at one of the numerous establishments in Hale'iwa, then head out to Mokule'ia for Hawaii Polo, skydiving, or a glider ride. If the mountains are more your style, take a trail ride on the Pupukea bluff or in Kahuku, then head to Turtle Bay for a sunset cocktail at the Hang Ten Bar, right on Kuilima Point.

During the winter the North Shore has a completely different vibe, as powerful waves push across the reefs and surfers flock to the beaches. Snorkeling and diving are out of the picture, as turbulent white water sweeps across the reefs, but watching the surf and the talented surfers taking it on can be mesmerizing. Check out the action at Waimea Bay, Pipeline, and Sunset Beach. Take a break during the day to drive to Kahuku and visit Kahuku Superette for some fresh *poke* and rice, then head back to the beach to eat while wave-watching. Enjoy dinner in Hale'iwa before setting out back to Honolulu.

For a longer, but more scenic trip to the North Shore from Waikiki, follow the Likelike Highway to Kane'ohe and drive up the windward coast in the morning. The roughly 45-mile drive will take about 1.5 hours as the sun rises over the east side. The mellow, gently meandering drive will put you in the right mood for a relaxing day on the North Shore. If you're looking for an O'ahu destination where you can spend a portion or your entire stay surrounded by a rural coastal setting far removed from the city, then a vacation rental along the North Shore Beaches or a room at Turtle Bay Resort are great options. Just be aware that it will take a bit more time and planning for sightseeing and activities in most other island regions.

ORIENTATION

As you descend from the pineapple and coffee fields, the first town you'll come to is Historic Hale'iwa Town, the official gateway to the North Shore. On either side of town, Kamehameha Highway makes a detour through Hale'iwa. If you want to pass around Hale'iwa and continue up the coast, stay on the Joseph P. Leong Highway bypass.

Hale'iwa is full of places to eat, markets, and clothing, souvenir and surf shops, as well as art galleries. Sportfishing, shark tour, and scuba operators are congregated in Hale'iwa Harbor, which has lovely beaches on both sides, though they are better for surfing and stand-up paddling rather than swimming or snorkeling. The **'Anahulu River** empties out by the harbor and beaches, offering potential for stand-up paddling upriver.

Just to the west of Hale'iwa, between the Wai'anae Mountains and the coast as you head toward Ka'ena Point, are **Waialua** and **Mokule'ia.** Both are sleepy, rural agricultural communities. Farrington Highway rejoins the coast through Mokule'ia, where if it's not too windy, the beaches are nice, the water is crystal clear, and solitude surrounds you. Mokule'ia offers polo matches on Sunday afternoons in the summer, skydiving throughout the year, and a seaside hike in a natural reserve at the end of the road to the western tip of the island.

The North Shore Beaches comprise an immaculate stretch of coastline along Kamehameha Highway from **Laniakea**, just past Hale'iwa town, to the legendary **Sunset Beach** to the north. Spinner dolphins frolic in Waimea Bay, sea turtles feed off the shoreline rocks, and reef fish abound along the **Pupukea-Waimea Marine Life**

Your Best Day on the North Shore

Surf, sun, and beaches—the rural North Shore is all about leaving behind the city and tapping into the laid-back atmosphere. Just remember, the North Shore can be very different depending if it's summer or winter.

- Drive up the H-2 freeway, through the central plateau. You'll be able to see the extent of O'ahu's agricultural base—pineapple fields as far as the eye can see. Head directly to the **Pupukea-Waimea Marine Life Conservation District,** the best snorkeling on the North Shore. Whether you post up at Waimea Bay, Three Tables, or Sharks Cove, or visit all three, you'll be amazed at the underwater beauty of the area. Snorkeling is best in the summertime.

- If it's winter during your stay, check out the waves at **Waimea Bay, Pipeline,** or **Sunset Beach.** They attract professional surfers from around the world. The action is spectacular, especially once the waves get really big.

- Stop in at **Ted's Bakery for lunch,** local style, or head out to Kahuku, just a few miles farther north, and visit **Kahuku Superette** for some of the best *poke* on the island.

- Outdoor activities are the hallmark of the North Shore. If you're daring, try **skydiving** in Mokule'ia. If staying on land suits you better, there are two outfitters that offer horseback rides in the fertile mountains above the North Shore beaches.

- During the summer, you can also spend the afternoon stand-up paddling the **'Anahulu River** in Hale'iwa Town or try a shore dive at Sharks Cove or Three Tables.

- For dinner, try **Hale'iwa Joe's** if you're in Hale'iwa town. If you're closer to the northern tip of the island, stop by Turtle Bay Resort and have a great meal at the local favorite, **Lei Lei's.**

Conservation District, which includes **Three Tables** and **Sharks Cove** just north of Waimea Bay, some of the best snorkeling and scuba diving on the island. In the summer, the calm water along this stretch of coast is perfect for swimming and snorkeling, but in the winter, powerful surf draws expert surfers from around the world in search of giant waves at Waimea Bay and Sunset Beach and the awe-inspiring barrels of the Banzai Pipeline. While the most popular beaches might be busy with tourists hopping off buses all year long, a short walk up or down the beach will easily remove you from the melee and most of your cares or worries. For meals you'll mostly find food trucks along the highway, and for accommodations, vacation rentals are the only way to go, save for the only hostel in the region at Three Tables. Sunsets are remarkable from this stretch of coast.

Turtle Bay is the area along Kamehameha Highway from **Kawela Bay** to **Kahuku,** the old sugar town. This region sits at the northern tip of the island and is prone to wind and rain throughout the year. The Turtle Bay Resort on **Kuilima Point** dominates the area, with surf and golf being the main attractions, along with the bars and restaurants that many residents and visitors along the North Shore Beaches make the short drive to indulge in.

Just to the east of Turtle Bay is Kahuku, with a nine-hole golf course of its own. Locals prefer the affordable fees and relaxed atmosphere at the Kahuku course to the resort's professional course. Kahuku is also home to a little market with some of the best *poke* on O'ahu. There is a working ranch here offering horseback trail rides for all levels of riders.

Sights

PU'U O MAHUKA HEIAU

Located on the Pupukea bluff right above Waimea Bay and covering two acres, **Pu'u O Mahuka Heiau** is the largest *heiau* (temple) on O'ahu. Three- to six-foot stacked stone walls are what remain of the original three enclosures thought to have been built in the 17th century. The structure was integral to the social, political, and religious systems for the once-thriving Waimea Valley community. The *heiau* has views of Waimea Valley and the North Shore. There are dirt walking paths around the structure and interpretive signage, but no water or facilities. Follow the trail to the edge of the cliff for a unique view of Waimea Bay. To get there, drive up Pupukea Road and take the first right turn after the switchbacks. The paved road is rough and narrow, so drive slowly and be aware of oncoming vehicles.

the sacred space of Pu'u O Mahuka Heiau

★ WAIMEA VALLEY

Waimea Valley (59-864 Kamehameha Hwy., 808/638-7766, www.waimeavalley.net, 9am-5pm daily) is one of O'ahu's last partially intact *ahupua'a* (a land division stretching from the mountain to the sea), and is part botanical garden and part native Hawaiian cultural site. Once a thriving native Hawaiian community based around the river running down the valley to the sea, it offered sustenance in many forms for native Hawaiians. Today, Waimea Valley is home to many collections of tropical plants, but it is most famous for the hybrid hibiscus collection at the front of the garden and the ginger and heliconia collection at the back of the valley. Peacocks run wild through the gardens, and native birds are common along the stream. There are several native Hawaiian historical living sites along the 0.75-mile paved trail back to the waterfall

Waimea Valley is a botanical garden and cultural heritage site.

and pool. General admission is $16 for adults and $8 for children ages 4-12 and $12 for seniors 60 and over. Golf cart transportation from the ticket booth to the waterfall is available for $4 one way and $6 round-trip.

Guided hikes are led by staff on Thursday and Saturday. Reservations must be made at least three days in advance for these, and additional fees apply. Check the website for the detailed information about the guided hikes.

Beaches

The North Shore beaches are some of the finest on the island. With the natural backdrops of the Pupukea-Paumalu escarpment along the northern portion of the coast and the Wai'anae Range behind Hale'iwa stretching to Ka'ena Point, natural beauty catches your eye in every direction. Ample vegetation separates the sand from the beachfront property, and the coast is broken up by interesting rock and reef formations, sandy bays, and rugged points.

The North Shore also has two distinct personalities: benign and tranquil during the summer, from May until September; and strong and fierce in the winter, from October to April. This duality is caused by powerful storms in the North Pacific that send swell thousands of miles across open ocean, straight to the Hawaiian Islands. The North Shore reefs absorb this energy as giant waves that pound the coast, breaking up to 50 feet from crest to trough. During high surf events in the winter, the water is closed to swimming, and lifeguards monitor the spectators on the beach, as well as the surfers in the water, to make sure everyone is safe. During the biggest swell events, the beaches are closed as well.

On the other hand, summer provides perfect conditions for swimming, snorkeling, and diving. The ocean remains generally calm and flat, and the beaches are at their widest. Sunsets are also better during this time as the sun tracks farther west on the horizon.

HALE'IWA
Ali'i Beach Park
There is a small beach, framed in by rocks, at both sides of **Ali'i Beach Park,** just to the

west of the Hale'iwa Small Boat Harbor, where Hale'iwa town intersects the coast. These are great places for the kids to jump around in the small shore break. Ali'i Beach Park also has a community center, restrooms, and a large, shaded grassy park with palm trees, picnic tables, and shrubs along the vegetation line that offer shade. If there are waves breaking along the outer reef, a strong and dangerous rip current sweeps across the beach. From Kamehameha Highway, turn onto Haleiwa Road, and the beach park is past the entrance to the boat harbor. There is ample parking.

Hale'iwa Beach Park
On the other side of the harbor entrance and the 'Anahulu River, across the famous Rainbow Bridge, is **Hale'iwa Beach Park.** The water is a bit murky and the sand somewhat silty from the river mouth, but the calm waters here are a favorite for kayakers and stand-up paddlers, where you can choose to paddle in the ocean or forge up the 'Anahulu River. There is parking on the side of the road or in the designated parking area. To the north of the parking lot is a big grassy area and restrooms. The beach park is beside Kamehameha Highway. The parking lot and restrooms are closed 10pm-6am daily.

Pua'ena Point Beach Park
You'll have a different experience altogether in **Pua'ena Point Beach Park** to the immediate north of Hale'iwa Beach Park. From Kamehameha Highway, turn onto Kahalewai Place and drive to the parking lot at the end. From there walk through the ironwood trees to the small cove. The beach has lots of shade

and is a great place to explore in and out of the water. Snorkel the inner waters with their mix of sand and reef bottom, or you can walk up the beach to the rocky outcropping of Pua'ena Point.

Mokule'ia Beach Park

Situated on the western flank of the North Shore, **Mokule'ia Beach Park** is a quiet, uncrowded beach across from the Dillingham Airfield. The sand is narrow, but stretches out in both directions, with interesting nooks and crannies along the coast. There are shrubs along the beach and some trees for shade to the east. Mokule'ia Beach Park is great for a long walk on the beach or relaxing in the sun. It's in the path of the trade winds, so it can get blustery. If you plan on swimming or snorkeling, the conditions are best with light winds. There are showers and portable toilets at the beach park along Farrington Highway, close to the end of the road. The parking lot is closed 7pm-7am daily.

NORTH SHORE BEACHES
Laniakea

Famous for the turtles that rest in the sand and feed off of the rocky shelf at the water's edge, **Laniakea** is a beautiful stretch of beach once you get away from the hordes of people that jam onto the small pocket of sand where the majority of the turtles rest. Park in the dirt parking lot on the mountain side of Kamehameha Highway just north of a ranch with horses. Cross the road with extreme caution. Tour buses of all sizes stop here and direct people to the northern corner of the beach. The turtles, however, feed along the rocks that run the length of the beach, so walk to the south to escape the crowds. Where the beachfront properties begin at the southern end of the beach, the sand widens and there are beautiful views of the Wai'anae Mountains and the western side of the North Shore. If you plan on swimming or snorkeling, this is also the best place to enter and exit the water. The farther south you walk along the beach, the better the chance of finding seclusion.

Chun's Reef

A beautiful spot for a beach day, **Chun's Reef** is the next beach north of Laniakea, but without the tour buses and crowds. The wide sandy beach has tidepools in the southern corner up against the rocky point, and the water right off the beach is a bit deeper here and more suitable for swimming and

Hale'iwa Beach Park

snorkeling. The beach gets wider to the north end of Chun's and is lined with tall ironwood trees, providing ample shade. Little waves break over the reef quite a distance offshore almost all year long, so it's a great place for beginners to surf in the summer. It's also a favorite area for stand-up paddle surfers. Park in the dirt on the mountain side of the road across from the beach. There are lifeguards, but no facilities at Chun's.

★ Waimea Bay Beach Park

At the mouth of the Waimea River and Waimea Valley is the scenic **Waimea Bay Beach Park.** The tight bay is lined with beautiful white sand, and the water is crystal clear, perfect for swimming and snorkeling. There are rocky points on both sides of the bay, while the center is all sand, producing light-blue water. Stand-up paddle across the bay, relax on the beach, or jump off the famous Jump Rock, a 20-foot-tall rock spire right off the beach. Spinner dolphins and green sea turtles are frequent visitors. Park in the designated parking area, but if it's full, there is paid parking in Waimea Valley, which is about a 10-minute walk to the beach. Use the white pedestrian bridge to cross the river and access the beach park, which has restrooms, showers, picnic areas, and a grassy park. The beach park is closed 10pm-5am daily.

Three Tables

Once you round Waimea Bay, the first beach you come to heading north is **Three Tables,** named after three flat reef platforms that rise above the ocean surface just off the beach. This is part of the Pupukea-Waimea Marine Life Conservation District, a protected area where fishing is illegal. The resulting copious amounts of reef fish in the water mean the main draw here is snorkeling. Three Tables has a quaint beach, with shallow water stretching between rock outcroppings. Perfect for families, there are shade trees on the beach and picnic tables up by the bike path. There are a few parking spaces in front of the beach on the side of Kamehameha Highway, or you can park in the parking lot just to the north of Three Tables. Turn into the lot at the Pupukea Road traffic signal. There are restrooms here as well, though they are notoriously dingy.

Ke'iki Beach

On the north side of the prominent reef rock point that frames in Sharks Cove, **Ke'iki Beach** is the place to go if you're looking

Waimea Bay Beach Park

Jump In!

In the mid-1900s, sand mining at Waimea Bay unearthed a large rock in the sand. Today that rock is at the water's edge and stands about 20 feet high. People flock to the rock, aptly named **Jump Rock,** to take the plunge into the turquoise water below. The ascent is gradual, starting from the sand to Jump Rock's highest point. Most people jump off the east side. North Shore surfers actually practice a balled-up type of belly flop here to better prepare themselves for any unfortunate wipeouts during the upcoming winter's extra-large surf. If the main jumping point is a bit too high for your liking, the very end of the rock, farthest out into the bay, is only about six feet high.

for solitude. The beach stretches out to the north, and even though the name might change every quarter mile, it's still one beautiful ribbon of sand with aquamarine water pushing up against it. The water gets deep rather quickly here, so it's also great for swimming and snorkeling. From the highway, turn onto Keiki Road and look for parking. There is also intermittent parking along Kamehameha Highway on the ocean side. Follow one of the designated public access paths to the beach. There are no facilities and no shade here.

'Ehukai Beach Park

Across from Sunset Elementary School is a small parking lot for **'Ehukai Beach Park.**

Walk through the small park toward the lifeguard tower and onto the sand. To the immediate left is the world-famous **Banzai Pipeline** surf break. If it's summer, the water is beautiful and clear, but there will be no waves. To the right is 'Ehukai Beach, which stretches north up to Rocky Point. Swimming is great up and down the beach, which is lined with palms and shrubs offering midday shade. During the summer, the snorkeling is better on the Pipeline side of the park, where there is a wide shelf of reef, canyons, and caves to explore. 'Ehukai Beach Park has restrooms and showers, and there are additional public restrooms across the street in front of the school. The beach park is closed 10pm-5am daily.

summertime along 'Ehukai Beach Park

Sunset Beach

To the north of Sunset Elementary School, homes line the ocean side of Kamehameha Highway, and the beach is hidden from view. But once you pass a gas station, **Sunset Beach** is all you see. A wide swath of sand from the highway to the water's edge, Sunset is also famous for its big waves during the winter, but its natural beauty is splendid, waves or not. In the summer, it's perfect for swimming and snorkeling, or you can stand-up paddle up and down the coast from here for a good look at the shore. Take a walk up the point to the north for a great view back toward Hale'iwa. There is parking on the ocean side of the highway, along the bike path. If you luck into one of these spots, it's pleasant enough to relax, have a snack or some coffee, and watch the ocean sparkle. During the winter, it's also a great vantage point for whale-watching. There is another parking lot on the mountain side of the highway where you'll find restrooms and showers.

TURTLE BAY
Kawela Bay

One of the most protected and secluded bays on the North Shore, **Kawela Bay** shelters a small strip of sand and a calm lagoon protected by an outer reef between Sunset Beach and Turtle Bay. It's great for snorkeling, swimming, and getting away from it all. Park on the side of the highway across from the fruit stand and walk through the trees to the beach.

Kuilima Point

Kuilima Point, today known as **Turtle Bay,** is the site of the Turtle Bay Resort, a dramatic coastline, and a sandy beach. To the west of the resort and rugged Kuilima Point is a sand and rock beach that stretches to the eastern point of Kawela Bay. Walk the beach at low tide when there is more sand or snorkel over rock and reef. On the immediate east side of the point and the main resort is a small protected cove great for families and for swimming, but you'll have to share it with the other hotel guests. Farther east of the small bay is a beach seldom visited even though it sits right next to the resort. Walk along the sand or relax under some trees. The reef is shallow right up to the shore, so this is not the best spot for swimming. Visit the beach when the winds are light, as the trade winds blow straight on shore and get quite blustery.

Sunset Beach

Surfing the Seven Mile Miracle

In the surf world, the stretch of coastline from Haleʻiwa to Kuilima Point is known as the **"Seven Mile Miracle."** Unlike anywhere else on planet, the North Shore has just the right combination of geography, geology, wind, weather, and swell to make it one of the most sought-after surfing destinations in the world. The quality, consistency, size, and sheer number of surf breaks along the seven-mile stretch are unmatched. This is truly a surfer's paradise.

Turtle Bay is a great stop if you're looking for a little beach time followed by lunch or dinner.

To get to Kuilima Point from the Kamehameha Highway, turn onto Kuilima Road and follow it to the main resort parking lot. There is beach access on both sides of the main resort tower.

Water Sports

SURFING

Dubbed the "Seven Mile Miracle," this area has more high-quality surf breaks packed into the scenic coastline from Haleʻiwa to Turtle Bay than in any other place in the world. The powerful waves draw surfers from around the world, and for over three decades, professional surfing's elite world tour has wrapped up the title season at the infamous Banzai Pipeline.

The waves on the North Shore are also some of the most dangerous, and deadliest, in the world. With huge breaks, strong currents, and shallow reefs, even top athletes are not immune to severe injury or death. Because of these and other factors, only expert surfers should paddle out. There are lifeguards posted at most North Shore beaches; check with them for ocean conditions and safety. If you're having doubts about the waves and your ability, it's best to have a seat on the beach, enjoy the spectacle, and live to surf another day on a different wave.

Haleʻiwa
HALEʻIWA BREAK

Located in Haleʻiwa town to the west of the harbor, **Haleʻiwa** breaks off Aliʻi Beach. A peak when it's small, the wave becomes exponentially more dangerous the larger it gets,

breaking as a predominant right. The fast waves closeout over a very shallow inside reef ledge known as the Toilet Bowl. A strong rip current is a staple at Haleʻiwa. Paddle out from the west side of the beach, to the left of the Toilet Bowl section.

PUAʻENA POINT

Puaʻena Point is one of the smaller and softer waves on the North Shore, just to the north of the ʻAnahulu River. It has both right- and left-breaking waves and is friendly for longboarders when it's small. The waves can still get big at Puaʻena, but it doesn't happen that often. Paddle straight out from the beach. The parking lot can be a bit suspect, so don't leave any valuables in plain sight.

North Shore Beaches
LANIAKEA

Best on north swells, **Laniakea** is a right pointbreak that breaks over flat reef and sand. Depending on the direction of the swell, the wave is one of the longest on the North Shore. Expert surfers tend to sit up at the point, while novice surfers and longboarders prefer the inside section off the south end of the beach. Paddle out from the south end of the beach. Laniakea is to the immediate north of a ranch, and there is a long dirt parking lot on the mountain side of Kamehameha Highway.

CHUN'S REEF

Just north of Laniakea, the next beach and surf spot you can see from the highway is **Chun's Reef.** Chun's is a soft-breaking right point, but also has a fast-breaking left at the top of the sandy point that most often closes out. Chun's is a favorite wave for beginners, longboarders, and kids. It's one of the most user-friendly waves on the North Shore. Keep in mind that even though the wave itself is good for learning, the shallow bottom is still dangerous, since it's covered by a sharp, flat reef. Chun's is one of the few breaks on the North Shore that also has very small waves in the summer.

LEFTOVERS

A quarter mile north of Chun's Reef, at the next small break in homes along the highway, where you can see the water, and where there is space to park your car, you'll find a wave called **Leftovers.** The wave is a left that breaks into deep water, so there is a defined channel where you can paddle out. A right also breaks off the peak on the very outside. The inside section covers an extremely

shallow and sharp reef. Getting in and out of the water can also be an obstacle, as the beach is covered with rocks and large boulders that stretch out into the water.

WAIMEA BAY

A big wave spot that only starts to break when the waves are 15 to 20 feet on the face, **Waimea Bay** is the only chance for many to see waves of this size, a feat of nature that should not be missed if the bay is breaking. The shore break is also something to see, as huge waves barrel and detonate in spectacular fashion in inches of water. Parking at Waimea fills up quickly when the waves are big. There is limited additional parking along the highway on the west side of the bay heading west, or you can pay to park at Waimea Valley, just past the turnoff to Waimea Bay. You could also park by Three Tables and Sharks Cove and walk back along the highway. Many spectators watch and snap photos from the railing above the rocks on the east side of the bay.

★ BANZAI PIPELINE

The **Banzai Pipeline,** or simply **Pipeline,** is one of the most dangerous waves in the world. Guarded closely by a territorial crew of local surfers, Pipeline is one of those waves where

Waimea Bay doesn't start breaking until the waves reach at least 20 feet.

visiting surfers will find it more to their advantage to sit on the beach and watch its grandeur rather than test their mettle. Breaking just 75 yards off the beach, Pipeline is a spectator's delight. Massive round and hollow lefts explode over a shallow reef, and brave surfers try to place themselves as deep as possible inside the barrel, hoping to emerge out the end on their feet. On the sand, you can feel the waves break on the beach and sense the tension and emotion in the water. Park in the 'Ehukai Beach Park parking lot or along the highway. Pay attention to the sporadic No Parking signs.

'EHUKAI
Also accessible from 'Ehukai Beach Park is the North Shore's only beach break, **'Ehukai.** Depending on the sand and the swells, the waves can break right or left and range from phenomenal shape to junky and lumpy surf.

SUNSET BEACH
Sunset Beach offers one of the most powerful and dangerous waves in the world, breaking from Sunset Point all the way into the bay. Strong currents and closeout sets are the hallmark of Sunset, along with a dredging inside section called **The West Bowl**, which breaks

closest to the beach. A wave for experts only, when the water is gigantic, you'll find surfers attempting to ride the mountainous fluid walls. Bring binoculars to catch all the action way out to sea.

Turtle Bay
KUILIMA POINT
Kuilima Point, known locally as **Turtle Bay,** is a funky, soft wave that breaks along a sharp reef outcropping into deep water. Since the break is just off Kuilima Point, where the Turtle Bay Resort is situated, you can literally watch the surfers from Turtle Bay's pool bar. The inside has soft rolling white water that is perfect for beginners. You can also rent longboards at the resort. The beach and water are open to the public. Paddle out from the rocky shore in front of the bungalows.

Outfitters
Hale'iwa town is full of surf shops that sell apparel, boards, and surf accessories. **Hawaiian Island Creations** (66-224 Kamehameha Hwy., 808/637-0991, www.hicsurf.com, 10am-6pm Mon.-Sat., 9:30am-5pm Sun.) and **Wave Riding Vehicles** (66-451 Kamehameha Hwy., 808/637-2020, www.waveridingvehicles.com, 9am-7pm Mon.-Sat., 10am-6pm

The Banzai Pipeline is one of the most exciting and dangerous waves in the world.

Sun.) are two local surf brands with retail shops, and **Xcel** (66-590 Kamehameha Hwy., 808/637-3248, www.xcelwetsuits.com, 9am-5pm daily) is a local wetsuit company where you can find all manner of wetsuits to stay warm and protect yourself from the sun. **Surf N Sea** (62-595 Kamehameha Hwy., 808/637-9887, http://surfnsea.com, 9am-7pm daily) not only has apparel and new and used boards for sale, but it also rents shortboards and longboards by the hour, day, and week. Shortboards are $5 the first hour, $3.50 each additional hour, $24 daily, and $120 weekly; longboards are $7 the first hour, $6 each additional hour, $30 daily, and $150 weekly. Right across the street is **Tropical Rush** (62-620 Kamehameha Hwy., 808/637-8886, http://tropicalrush.com, 9am-7pm daily), which sells apparel, new surfboards, and gear, and rents boards by the hour, day, and week.

Hawaii Eco Divers (59-059 B Pupukea Rd., 888/349-3864, www.hawaiiecodivers.com, 7:30am-9pm daily) offers surf tours for experienced surfers and lessons for beginners. The surf tours include personalized surf coaching and a video of the session. Tour prices are $150 for a morning session or $250 all day for a group of up to three surfers. Surfboards are not included. Surf lessons run $100 for a three- to four-hour session focusing on catching and riding waves. The lesson rate includes boards and transportation. **Sunset Suratt Surf Academy** (808/783-8657, http://surfnorthshore.com) gives beginner surfing and stand-up paddling lessons. With an arsenal of boards and vans, it drives to where the surf is best suited for learning. Book online. Standard two-hour group lessons start at $80.

Located across from Sharks Cove, **North Shore Surf Shop** (59-053 Kamehameha Hwy., 808/638-0390, 8am-8pm daily) has a huge selection of shortboards, new and used, and carries a lot of the professional surfers' used boards. It rents shortboards for $25 daily, $60 for three days, $125 weekly, and $300 for a month; longboards are $30 daily, $75 for three days, $140 weekly, and $300 for

Summer or winter, Surf N Sea has everything you need for the beach.

a month. It also has a retail location in the town of Hale'iwa.

At Turtle Bay Resort you can rent boards at **Hans Hedemann Surf** (57-091 Kamehameha Hwy., 808/447-6755 or 808/293-7779, www.hhsurf.com, 8am-5pm daily). Shortboards and longboards rent for $15 per hour, $40 for four hours, $50 all day, $60 overnight, $35 each additional day, and $250 per week. Two-hour private lessons go for $150, semiprivate lessons are $125, and group lessons, for up to four surfers, are $95. All equipment is included.

SNORKELING AND DIVING
North Shore Beaches

During the summer, from May to September, when the ocean is flat, the North Shore Beaches are an amazing place to snorkel. With a mix of rocks, reef, sand, calm waters, and favorable winds, just about anywhere you jump in the water will have some interesting underwater topography, coral, and marine life.

★ PUPUKEA-WAIMEA MARINE LIFE CONSERVATION DISTRICT

The most abundant marine life is found at **Three Tables, Sharks Cove,** and **Waimea Bay,** which comprise the **Pupukea-Waimea Marine Life Conservation District.** Established in 1983 to conserve and replenish marine species at Three Tables and Sharks Cove, the reserve was expanded in 2003 to include Waimea Bay, covering 100 acres of coastline about a mile long. Fishing or the taking of any marine species is strictly prohibited in the area. Look for wrasse, surgeonfish, reef squid, puffer fish, the spotted eagle ray, palani, unicorn fish, harlequin shrimp, and frogfish, just some of the creatures that inhabit the area. Waimea Bay is also known for pods of spinner dolphins that frolic in the middle of the bay.

There are boat dives and shore dives available on the North Shore. The shore dives explore Three Tables and Sharks Cove, where there are flourishing reefs teeming with endemic fish and lava tubes, caverns, and walls to explore. The boat dives provide access to the extraordinary underwater topography and pristine offshore reefs of the North Shore Beaches: Atlantis is an area full of trenches, valleys, walls, and lava tubes, and Cathedrals

has rock formations, reefs, and caverns where turtles, eels, and whitetip reef sharks are common; Grand Canyon is a drift dive along the North Shore Beaches where you'll find sponges hanging from the ledges and trevallies and rays in the deep water; two reef sites, Nanny's Reef and Nautilus Reef, are 40 foot dives with a plethora of marine life. Diving the North Shore during the winter is contingent on the size of the surf.

Outfitters

Surf N Sea (62-595 Kamehameha Hwy., 808/637-9887, http://surfnsea.com, 9am-7pm daily) in Hale'iwa is the North Shore's most complete surf and dive shop. It sells new gear, rents beach and ocean-related gear and accessories, and even leads shore and boat dives. It rents dive equipment by the piece at a daily or weekly rate. For snorkel gear, it rents by the piece or in a set, the latter runs $6.50 for four hours, $9.50 daily, and $45 weekly. Its guided dives are operated by **Hawaii Scuba Diving,** which offers shore and boat dives as well as certification courses. The morning dives are for certified divers, while the afternoon charters to shallow reef sites are open to any level diver. One-tank shore dives are $75 for certified divers and $95 for noncertified; two-tank

Sharks Cove is part of a marine protected area.

Snorkel vs. Surf

While Hawai'i's slight seasonal changes in temperature and precipitation might not be apparent to visitors who only stay a week or two at a time, there is one natural phenomenon that differentiates strikingly between summer and winter on the North Shore—waves! During Hawai'i's winter, October-April, and sometimes into spring, storms in the North Pacific create very large, open ocean swells that track toward the equator, passing by the state and expending the wave energy on the reefs and beaches. This is great news for surfers, who follow these swells closely and live to surf the powerful waves, which can break up to 60 feet on the face during the biggest surges on the outermost reefs. For snorkelers and divers, high surf is a worst-case scenario.

Once summer rolls around, the tables turn. From May to September, the North Shore becomes a tranquil swimmer's paradise. The waves usually remain flat the entire period, the sand settles, and the water becomes beautifully clear. Snorkelers and divers revel in the conditions, and the focus on the North Shore shifts from the waves above the surface to the exploration of its underwater world.

shore dives are $100 certified, $125 noncertified; one-tank night dives are $100; two-tank boat dives are $140. Professional Association of Diving Instructors (PADI) diving certification courses are $375 for Open Water Diver, $295 for Advanced Open Water Diver, and $650 for Divemaster.

Banzai Divers Hawaii (808/462-8290, http://banzaidivershawaii.com, 8am-6pm daily) operates diving charters from Hale'iwa Harbor seasonally May through September. Boat dives start at $180 for certified divers.

Hawaii Eco Divers (61-101 Iliohu Pl., 808/499-9177, www.hawaiiecodivers.com, 7:30am-9pm daily), operating from Hale'iwa Harbor, specializes in personalized small-group shore dives. Two-tank shore dives for certified divers, one-tank night dives and one-tank dives for noncertified divers are $109. All gear is included in the rate, along with snacks, refreshments, and photos of the dives. The company will also shoot a video of your dive for $75.

If you get to Sharks Cove and discover you really want to snorkel but don't have any gear, you're in luck: Right across the street is **North Shore Surf Shop** (59-053 Kamehameha Hwy., 808/638-0390, 10am-7:30pm daily). It rents complete snorkel sets for $15 daily and $30 for three days. It also has rash guards for rent for $5, which are great for sun protection while you're snorkeling.

Hawaii Adventure Diving (66-105 Haleiwa Rd., 808/637-3474, http://hawaiiadventurediving.com) has scuba diving and pelagic diving tours and offers a private charter group, two-tank reef dive, maximum six people, for $600. The pelagic snorkel freedive tour takes you to swim and snorkel in deep water with dolphins, whales, sharks and pelagic fish. The two-hour tour has a three-person minimum, six-person maximum and runs $145 per person, $75 ride along.

STAND-UP PADDLING

Hale'iwa is the hub of stand-up paddling and kayaking on the North Shore, largely because of the **'Anahulu River** and the protected and calm waters off **Hale'iwa Beach Park.** You can access the shoreline in the small parking lot next to Surf N Sea or along Hale'iwa Beach Park. From there, you can paddle around the shallow river mouth, north to Pua'ena Point and beyond, or head upriver for a smooth and mellow ride.

On the North Shore, stand-up paddling is popular at **Waimea Bay, Laniakea,** and **Chun's Reef.** The conditions are best in the summer when the ocean surface is flat. Chun's and Laniakea often have very small waves in the summer, so you can even try surfing the stand-up paddleboard.

In Hale'iwa, **Surf N Sea** (62-595 Kamehameha Hwy., 808/637-9887, http://

surfnsea.com, 9am-7pm daily) rents single kayaks for $7 the first hour, $5 for each additional hour, $20 for a half day, and $75 for a full day. The weekly rate is $300. Stand-up paddleboards rent for $10 for the first hour, $8 for each additional hour, and $40 for a full day. The weekly rate is $200. Surf N Sea also rents water bikes and pedal boats and has the distinction of being situated on the bank of the river mouth for easy ocean access.

Hawaii Eco Divers (61-101 Iliohu Pl., 808/499-9177, www.hawaiiecodivers. com, 7:30am-9pm daily) offers a two-hour Hale'iwa Beach and River Tour all year long for $79. In the summer it also has a three-hour Waimea Bay Tour for $109 and a four-mile drift Sunset Beach to Waimea Bay Tour for $125. Snorkeling gear is included for both summer tours.

At the Turtle Bay Resort, **Hans Hedemann Surf** (57-091 Kamehameha Hwy., 808/447-6755 or 808/293-7779, www. hhsurf.com, 8am-5pm daily) rents stand-up paddleboards for $25 per hour, $50 for three hours, $80 all day, $100 overnight, $50 each additional day, and $400 per week. Two-hour private lessons go for $150, semiprivate lessons are $125, and group lessons, up to four surfers, is $75. All equipment is included.

FISHING

During the summer, spearfishing is common along the North Shore, where reef fish and octopus are the desired take. The conditions are prime during this season with the calm, flat ocean surface. Shoreline fishing is also common from Mokule'ia out to Ka'ena Point and along the beach south of Laniakea. Remember that the area from the west side of Waimea Bay to the north side of Sharks Cove is a marine protected area and fishing or taking any marine species is strictly prohibited. Fishing gear is available in Hale'iwa at **Haleiwa Fishing Supply** (66-519 Kamehameha Hwy., 808/637-9876, 10am-8pm daily).

The North Shore is very favorable for sportfishing, with deep water offshore and strong currents from the northwest that continually bring in bait and game fish. Several deep-sea sportfishing operators are located in the Hale'iwa Small Boat Harbor if you're interested in fishing for big game fish like wahoo, mahimahi, tuna, and marlin.

Chupu Charters (66-105 Haleiwa Rd., Slip 312, 808/637-3474, www.chupu.com) operates four boats with amenities like air-conditioning, a custom Pompanette fighting chair, and

Many people stand-up paddle the 'Anahulu River in Hale'iwa.

top-of-the-line rods and reels. Bait, tackle, ice, and fish packaging supplies are provided. Chupu offers full-day exclusive charters starting at $750 for the entire boat, half-day morning private charters starting at $550, and afternoon half-day private charters starting at $550. The charters have a maximum of four to six passengers depending on the boat.

Sport Fishing Hawaii (66-105 Haleiwa Rd., 808/721-8581 or 808/450-7601, www.

sport-fishing-hawaii.com) operates a 47-foot Hatteras and charges $750 for half-day charters and $925 for the full-day, 10-hour charter, with a six-passenger limit.

Kuuloa Kai (66-195 Kaamooloa Rd., 808/637-5783, www.kuuloakai.com) has private charters for up to six anglers and lets you take home enough fish for a couple dinners. It offers full-day charters for $800 and half-day charters for $650.

Hiking, Biking, and Bird-Watching

HIKING

You can hike to **Ka'ena Point,** the western tip of the island, from the North Shore. About five miles round-trip, the route follows an old dirt road to the point. It is a dry, windswept, but extremely beautiful hike, with views of the North Shore the entire way out. Once you reach the nature reserve at the end of the point, cross through the special predator-proof fence to see seabird nesting grounds, monk seals, spinner dolphins, and possibly humpback whales if you're hiking from November to March. Drive to the end of Farrington Highway, past Mokule'ia, park, and proceed on foot. Bring plenty of water. There are no facilities in the area.

At the very end of Pupukea Road is **Kaunala Trail** (a six-mile loop), which runs through the verdant gulches and across the ridges of the Ko'olau foothills above Pupukea. The trail is wide and well graded, with a slight elevation gain. There are great views of the North Shore on the return route. Drive to the end of Pupukea Road and park on the side of the road. Follow the dirt road past the Boy Scout camp and go around the locked gate. The trail is not far ahead to the left of the dirt road. This trail is open on weekends and holidays.

The **Kealia Trail** (seven miles round-trip) is an intermediate hike that climbs the cliff behind Mokule'ia to a summit in the Wai'anae Range. The prize is an overlook of beautiful Makua Valley. After hiking about 4 of the 19 switchbacks you'll find amazing views of the entire North Shore, as well as native trees and shrubs along the trail. To get to the trail, take Farrington Highway through Mokule'ia. As you pass the end of the airport runway, look for an access gate in the fence and turn left. It's open 7am-6pm daily. Go past the runway and park in the lot in front of the control tower. Walk toward the mountain and go through the gate in the fence and immediately turn left.

BIKING

The **North Shore Bike Path** stretches from Waimea Bay to Sunset Beach. Much of the trail is shaded, and there are ocean views along the way. Most of the trail is flat, great for a leisurely cruise or a more relaxing way to beach hop without having to worry about parking.

If you prefer going off-road, mountain bike out to Ka'ena Point on the **Ka'ena Point Trail,** an old railroad bed that is now a dirt road that hugs the coast around the point, a five-mile round-trip. The road is rough and rocky, there is no shade, and the surroundings are arid. Conversely, the scenery of the coastal dunes, the rugged shoreline, and the beautiful water is amazing. In the winter months, huge swells can wrap around the point, creating a cooling sea mist from the white water crashing against the rocks.

In Hale'iwa you can rent bikes at **Surf N Sea** (62-595 Kamehameha Hwy., 808/637-9887, http://surfnsea.com, 9am-7pm daily) for $10 per hour, $20 daily, and $100 weekly.

Across from Sharks Cove, the **North Shore Surf Shop** (59-053 Kamehameha Hwy., 808/638-0390, 10am-7:30pm daily) rents cruisers for $15 per day. **Hele Huli Rental** (57-091 Kamehameha Hwy., 808/293-6024, www.turtlebayresort.com) at Turtle Bay Resort rents bikes for $10 for one hour, $20 for two hours, or $25 per day. **North Shore Bike Rentals** (888/948-5666, www.northshorebikerentals.com) is a bike rental and delivery service. It delivers cruisers to any location from Mokule'ia to Velzyland. It rents cruisers for $19 a day, children's bikes for $10 a day, tandem bikes for $29 a day, pull carriers for $12 a day, and adult cruisers with a pull carrier for $28 a day. For three-day minimum rentals the $10 delivery charge is waived. Free helmets and locks are included with rental.

BIRD-WATCHING

The **James Campbell National Wildlife Refuge** (66-590 Kamehameha Hwy., 808/637-6330, www.fws.gov/jamescampbell) is two separate sections of wetland habitat in between Turtle Bay and Kahuku, 164 acres in total. The wetlands are dedicated to the recovery of Hawai'i's endemic waterfowl, primarily the endangered Hawaiian stilt, Hawaiian moorhen, Hawaiian coot, and the Hawaiian duck. The 126-acre Ki'i Unit is open to the public during the nonbreeding season, October to February. Also utilizing the wetlands is the bristle-thighed curlew. Guided tours are offered twice per week, on Thursday afternoons and Saturday mornings on the first two Saturdays of the month and in the afternoon on the last two Saturdays of the month. Reservations are required.

Adventure Sports

SHARK DIVING

There are two shark diving tour operators out of Hale'iwa Harbor. They travel 3-4 miles offshore and drop a metal shark cage in the water, where guests dive in to see Galapagos, tiger, hammerhead, and other sandbar sharks from a safe underwater vantage point. The tours are weather dependent, and no diving experience is required. If you're lucky, you'll see spinner dolphins, turtles, and even humpback whales during your time at sea. **North Shore Shark Adventures** (808/228-5900, www.hawaiisharkadventures.com) offers two-hour tours throughout the day for $120 adult, $60 children 3-13 years old. If you require transportation from Waikiki, you'll be charged an extra $55. **Hawaii Shark Encounters** (808/351-9373, www.hawaiisharkencounters.com) offers two-hour tours for $115.50 and $82.50 for children under 12 years old.

HORSEBACK RIDING

The North Shore is a rural enclave from Kahuku to Mokule'ia, and farms and ranches are common along the coast. Up on Pupukea, overlooking Waimea Valley and the North Shore is **Happy Trails Hawaii** (59-231 Pupukea Rd., 808/638-7433, www.happytrailshawaii.com). Its trails meander through forest, ranch land, and tropical orchards, offering panoramic mountain and ocean views. Two-hour tours are $99, and one-hour tours are $79. Riders must be at least six years old. **Gunstock Ranch** (56-250 Kamehameha Hwy., 808/293-2026, http://gunstockranch.com), just outside of Kahuku, is a family-owned and -operated working ranch at the base of the Ko'olau Mountains. It has a network of trails and tours for all riding levels, with mountain terrain and beautiful ocean views stretching all the way down the windward coast to Kaneʻohe Bay. Its Scenic Ride is a 90-minute guided ride suitable for all skill levels for $89; the Keiki Experience is a 30-minute horse experience and ride for children ages 2-7 years old for $39; the Advanced Trail Ride is a one-hour ride with trotting and cantering during the ride for $109, and previous riding experience is required. Gunstock also offers a Moonlight Ride, a Picnic Ride, a Sweetheart Ride, a Sunset Ride, and a Dinner Sunset Ride.

★ SKYDIVING

What could be more exhilarating than seeing the entire island of Oʻahu all at once, from 20,000 feet? Jumping out of the plane that took you that high and parachuting back to earth. **Skydive Hawaii** (68-760 Farrington Hwy., 808/637-9700 or 808/945-0222, www.skydivehawaii.com) operates from Dillingham Airfield in Mokuleʻia and specializes in tandem skydiving for first-time jumpers, but its services also extend to experienced skydivers and skydiving students. It makes three jumps a day and offers a free shuttle service from several points in Honolulu. Tandem skydiving from 12,000 feet is $250 with discounted rates for online reservations. Tandem skydive from 20,000 feet is $998. Skydivers must be at least 18 years old. You can also find similar rates and services literally right next door at **Pacific Skydiving Honolulu** (68-760 Farrington Hwy., 808/637-7472, www.pacificskydivinghonolulu.com). It offers online specials for tandem skydiving starting at $139 with free Waikiki pickup.

GLIDER FLIGHTS

For those who would rather stay inside an aircraft yet still partake of those same views of the North Shore and beyond, **Hana Hou Air** (808/222-4235, www.hanahouair.com) at the Dillingham Airfield offers 20-minute scenic glider flights above the Waiʻanae Mountains along the North Shore for $100. Reservations are required. Also accessing the Dillingham Airfield is **Honolulu Soaring** (808/637-0207, www.honolulusoaring.com). It has several planes in its fleet and offers scenic as well as acrobatic glider flights. The average visibility is 30 to 40 miles. One-passenger scenic flights start at $79 for 10 minutes and go to $290 for 60 minutes. Two-passenger scenic flights start at $128 for 10 minutes and go to $390 for 60 minutes. One-passenger acrobatic flights start at $165 for 15 minutes and go to $285 for 60 minutes. Combination scenic and acrobatic flights are also available.

Golf and Tennis

GOLF

Turtle Bay Resort (57-091 Kamehameha Hwy., 808/293-6000 or 800/203-3650, www.turtlebayresort.com/hawaii-golf) is the premier golf destination on the North Shore with two 18-hole championship courses, the **Palmer Course** and the **Fazio Course.** One of the best courses on Oʻahu, the Palmer Course is set across natural wetlands, with its signature 17th hole right on the coast. At 180 acres, there are no interruptions from homes or resort amenities to spoil play. Rates for the Palmer Course are $174 till noon, $140 noon-2pm, $105 2pm-4pm, and $84 after 4pm, which include fees, golf cart, practice balls, and bottled water. The Fazio Course is more forgiving than the Palmer Course and has a walker-friendly layout set among native Hawaiian palms along the coastline. It is designed for short game play. Rates, including fees, golf cart, practice balls, and bottled water, are $115 till noon, $95 noon-2pm, $75 2pm-4pm, and $50 after 4pm. Walking rates are $90 till noon, $70 noon-3pm, and $25 after 3pm. Add $35 to the rate for the course you play in the morning to create a 36-hole package. The resort also has complete practice facilities, including target greens, chipping area, bunkers, and putting greens. You can contact the pro shop to reserve tee times at 808/293-8574.

For a more relaxed and informal round of golf, visit the **Kahuku Golf Course** (56-501 Kamehameha Hwy., 808/293-5842, www1.honolulu.gov/des/golf/kahuku.htm). The nine-hole sporty, seaside course is a walking-only course that can be challenging due to predominantly windy conditions. The greens fee for two nine-hole rounds is $30, twilight or just nine holes is $15. Golf club rental is $12, and handcarts are available for $4.

TENNIS

Public tennis courts can be found on the North Shore at **Sunset Beach Neighborhood Park** (59-360 Kamehameha Hwy., 808/638-7051), which has two courts, and in Waialua at **Waialua District Park** (67-180 Goodale Rd., 808/637-9721), which has four courts. These courts are free to anyone. **Turtle Bay Resort** (57-091 Kamehameha Hwy., 808/293-6000 or 800/203-3650, www.turtlebayresort.com) has a four-court tennis complex. The courts are open 7am-9pm daily. The fee is $25 per hour, and resort guests get one hour per day for free. It also offers clinics and private lessons and rents rackets for $8 and a bag of balls for $4. Call 808/293-6024 to reserve a court.

Yoga and Spas

YOGA

With the focus on healthy living that comes with the ocean-influenced recreational life style of the North Shore, yoga studios abound. In Waialua you'll find **Bikram Yoga North Shore** (67-208 Goodale Ave., 808/637-5700, www.bikramyogahawaii.com), which warms and stretches the muscles. The drop-in rate is $15, one week unlimited is $50, and a 10-class card is $130. The **North Shore Yoga Co-Op** (67-174 Farrington Hwy., 808/561-9639, http://northshoreyoga.org) is a donation-based yoga co-op located at the Weinberg Community Center in Waialua. Students are asked to donate what they feel is appropriate for the instruction and what they can afford. The co-op offers several types of yoga, like vinyasa, yin yoga, yoga for surfers, restorative yoga, and pregnancy yoga. Check the online schedule for class times, complete class list, and descriptions.

Along the North Shore Beaches, **Paumalua Yoga** (59-540 Kamehameha Hwy., 808/221-4258, www.paumaluyoga.com) operates from the Sunset Beach Recreation Center and Waihuena Farm. It leads donation-based hatha, vinyasa, yoga for athletes, and keiki yoga classes. In addition, it offers private and semiprivate yoga instruction at its Pupukea studio, or instructors can come to you. Private rates start at $75 for one 60-90-minute session. Suggested donations are $5-15 per class. The **North Shore Wellness Retreat** (59-142 Kamehameha Hwy., 808/638-8137, http://surfintoyoga.com) offers vinyasa flow, pranayama, yin yoga, and hatha flow classes, as well as Surf into Yoga, its signature class led by professional surfer Rochelle Ballard. The drop-in rate is $10. It also has wellness packages that combine yoga, surfing, spa treatments, and a healthy meal, which start at $130. If you're up at **Turtle Bay Resort** (57-091 Kamehameha Hwy., 808/293-6000 or 800/203-3650, www.turtlebayresort.com), you'll find different types of yoga, Zumba, and other fitness classes for $10 per session. The monthly calendar is online.

SPAS

Spa Luana (57-091 Kamehameha Hwy., 808/447-6868 or 808/293-6000, www.turtlebayresort.com, 8am-8pm daily) is Turtle Bay Resort's luxurious spa. Located in your choice of one of six treatment rooms or an outdoor oceanside cabana, the signature services use local fruit and plant ingredients to complement the spa's relaxing tropical atmosphere. Seaside single massages start at $175 for 60 minutes. There are nine types of massages on the menu, starting at $150 for 60 minutes; six body treatments starting at $160 for 60 minutes; facials and skin care enhancements starting at $150 for 60 minutes;

spa treatment packages and salon services are also available.

At the **North Shore Wellness Retreat** (59-142 Kamehameha Hwy., 808/638-8137, http://surfintoyoga.com), the choice is yours whether to relax inside in the Spa Room or outdoors in the lush tropical garden. It offers three types of massages starting at $135 for 60 minutes. It also offers light body energy work, acupuncture, polarity treatment, body scrubs.

Shopping

HALE'IWA
★ Historic Hale'iwa Town
Historic Hale'iwa Town is packed full of restaurants and shops, most within a comfortable walking distance. Art galleries, surf shops, souvenir shops, and clothing and swimwear boutiques line Kamehameha Highway through this old seaside town established at the turn of the 20th century.

In the **North Shore Marketplace** (66-250 Kamehameha Hwy.), on the south end of town, you'll find **Wyland Galleries** (808/637-8729, www.wyland.com, 10am-8pm Mon.-Thurs., 10am-9pm Fri.-Sat., 10am-7pm Sun.),

featuring a handful of acclaimed artists with works based on ocean and outdoor themes, **Britton Gallery** (808/637-6505, www.brittongallery.com, 10am-6pm daily), with prints, sculpture, jewelry, and Hawaiiana decor from 35 island artists. For women's swimwear check out **Brazilian Showroom** (808/637-1777 or 808/489-9508, http://brazilianshowroomhawaii.com, 9am-5pm Mon.-Fri.).

Directly north of the Marketplace is **Haleiwa Art Gallery** (66-252 Kamehameha Hwy., 808/637-3368, www.haleiwaartgallery.com, 10am-6pm daily), Hale'iwa's oldest gallery. It features the work of 30 island artists

Welcome to Historic Hale'iwa Town.

in media from oil and watercolor to bronze and embroidery.

Haleiwa Store Lots (66-111 Kamehameha Hwy., 808/585-1770, www.haleiwastorelots.com) is a brand-new, plantation-inspired, mixed-use development in Hale'iwa. The open-air mall has plenty of parking in back and features local retailers, dining, general stores, and lots of space to sit, relax, and enjoy the scenery. You'll find **Clark Little Gallery** (Suite #102, 808/626-5319, www.clarklittlephotography.com, 10am-6pm Mon.-Sat., 10am-5pm Sun.), featuring the underwater and wave photography of award-winning local photographer Clark Little. **Greenroom Hawaii** (Suite #201, 808/924-4404, 10am-6pm daily) features famous artists and popular local artist Heather Brown. Check out boutique clothing and beach shop **Guava Shop** (Suite #204, 808/637-9670, http://guavahawaii.com, 10am-6pm daily).

At the north end of town is a popular children's store, the **Growing Keiki** (66-051 Kamehameha Hwy., 808/637-4544, http://thegrowingkeiki.com, 10am-6pm daily), which has unique clothes, locally published children's book, and handmade wooden toys.

Waialua

If you're in Waialua, head to the old Waialua Sugar Mill, where the **North Shore Soap Factory** (67-106 Kealohanui St., 808/637-7627, www.hawaiianbathbody.com, 9am-6pm Mon.-Fri., 8:30am-6pm Sat., 10am-5pm Sun.) specializes in premier Hawaiian bath and body products, the cornerstone being their own handmade and natural soaps.

Entertainment and Events

NIGHTLIFE

Hale'iwa has two popular bars that draw the crowds at night, but also double as restaurants by day. Located in the North Shore Marketplace, **Breakers** (66-250 Kamehameha Hwy., 808/637-9898, www.restauranteur.com/breakers, 8am-2am daily, $11-24) serves breakfast, lunch, and dinner, but the surf-themed restaurant is best known for its full bar and relaxed beach vibe. Packed with surf memorabilia and one of the few places in Hale'iwa that stays open late, it often hosts big parties and has live music.

Many people on the North Shore venture to **Turtle Bay Resort** (57-091 Kamehameha Hwy., 808/293-6000 or 800/203-3650, www.turtlebayresort.com) to visit the only outdoor bar where you can grab a drink and watch the surf, the **Hang Ten Bar & Grill** (808/293-6000, 10am-10pm daily, $8-19), better known as the Pool Bar. Stiff mai tais and other tropical drink concoctions are its specialty. Situated right on the point, this is a great place for a sunset beverage.

Inside the resort there is **Surfer, The Bar** (808/293 6000, 6pm-midnight daily, $12-24), a modern mixed-media bar centered around surfing and its legacy on the North Shore. Along with a light food menu, it offers tropical drinks, wine by the glass, and a bunch of local beers. Check out Talk Story Wednesday, where prominent figures in the surf industry share their stories with the crowd. Video and live music also add to the experience.

FESTIVALS AND EVENTS
★ Hawaii Polo

Experience the fun and sport of seaside polo in beautiful Mokule'ia. Matches at **Hawaii Polo** matches (http://hawaii-polo.org, 2pm Sun. Apr.-Sept., $10 adults, children 12 and under free) are held on Sundays April-September. Game day feels like a giant tailgate party, as people pull their vehicles right up to the field and open blankets under the ironwood trees. Bring a cooler full of food and beverages and enjoy a few chukkers (periods of play). Gates open at noon.

Haleiwa Arts Festival

The **Haleiwa Arts Festival** (62-449 Kamehameha Hwy., www.haleiwaartsfestival.org, July, free) is a weekend-long annual event that takes place at Haleʻiwa Beach Park in the middle of July. The festival features the works of over 100 artists for exhibition and purchase, and has live musical and cultural entertainment, art demonstrations, and children's art activities. Food vendors accompany the open-air festival.

Vans Triple Crown of Surfing

For six weeks every winter, from early November through late December, the **Vans Triple Crown of Surfing** (www.triplecrownofsurfing.com, Nov.-Dec.) takes over the North Shore. This professional surfing event is comprised of three contests, the first at Aliʻi Beach Park in Haleʻiwa, the second at Sunset Beach, and the final one at the Banzai Pipeline. An international field of hundreds of competitors, as well as a cadre of hungry locals, battle it out on the biggest and best days of surf during the holding period for each event. Spectators flock to the beach to watch the action, some of the best surfing in the world. There are food vendors, restrooms,

It doesn't get better than seaside polo on a Sunday afternoon.

drinking water, souvenirs, and giveaways at each event. With limited parking and an influx of people on the North Shore, expect driving delays and plan to either pay for parking or park and walk quite a distance, especially during the Pipeline event.

Food

HALEʻIWA
Coffee

In the North Shore Marketplace, the **Coffee Gallery** (66-250 Kamehameha Hwy., 808/637-5355, www.roastmaster.com, 6:30am-8pm daily) is a popular spot for coffee, both brewed and roasted beans. It has a great selection of bakery goods and sells local coffee by the pound. It also offers free wireless Internet for customers on the rustic covered patio or at outdoor benches.

Quick Bites

Lanikai Juice (66-215 Kamehameha Hwy., 808/637-7774, www.lanikaijuice.com, 8am-7pm daily, $5-10) is great for fresh juices, smoothies and acai bowls.

Storto's (66-215 Kamehameha Hwy., 808/637-6633, 8am-6pm daily, $5-12) is the go-to sandwich deli in Haleʻiwa. The friendly staff makes big sandwiches for big appetites. For a normal serving, order a half sandwich, and don't forget the papaya seed dressing.

The Eddie

Waimea Bay is home to the iconic **Quiksilver in Memory of Eddie Aikau,** an annual one-day event that honors the late North Shore waterman Eddie Aikau and the surfers who dedicate their lives to riding giant waves. Eddie was the first official lifeguard at Waimea Bay and a revered big-wave surfer. In 1978, Eddie was selected to help crew a Polynesian voyaging canoe, a cultural expedition bound for Tahiti. When the canoe encountered treacherous seas outside the Hawaiian Islands and capsized, Eddie struck out fearlessly on a paddleboard back to Hawai'i to save his stranded crew. He was never seen again.

Since 1985, The Eddie is staged every year to test the strongest and best big-wave surfers in the spirit of Eddie's courageous selflessness. The invitational has some impressive criteria: the waves must be at least 20-feet for the entire day of competition. Because of this minimum wave height requirement, The Eddie has only run eight times in 27 years. The waiting period is from December through February and as the saying goes on the North Shore, "The Bay calls the day."

NORTH SHORE FOOD

Café Haleiwa (66-460 Kamehameha Hwy., 808/637-5516, 7am-1:45pm daily, also 6pm-9:30pm Tues.-Sat., $4-10) is a delicious pancakes-and-eggs breakfast restaurant with Mexican specialties and a signature mahimahi plate.

In the mood for shrimp? Visit **Giovanni's** (66-472 Kamehameha Hwy., 808/293-1839, www.giovannisshrimptruck.com, 10:30am-5pm daily, $4-13) shrimp truck. The white truck is an icon on the North Shore, and it has been serving up shrimp plates since 1993. There are three shrimp plates to choose from and hot dogs for the *keiki*. It also has another truck in Kahuku by the old sugar mill that stays open till 6:30pm.

Steak and Seafood

Overlooking the Hale'iwa Harbor, right by the Rainbow Bridge, is **Haleiwa Joe's** (66-011 Kamehameha Hwy., 808/637-8005, http://haleiwajoes.com, 11:30am-9:30pm daily, $19-40). Joe's serves up fresh and delicious seafood with Hawaiian-influenced Pacific Rim preparations. It also has meat selections and great salads. Indoor and patio seating are available or sit in the bar for a more casual experience with the full benefits of the menu. Make reservations to avoid the wait.

Pacific Rim

★ **Rajanee Thai Cuisine** (66-111 Kamehameha Hwy. Suite #1001, 808/

784-0023, 11am-8pm Mon.-Sat., closed Sun., $12-18) has a religious local following. The flavorful Thai cuisine is consistent and delicious. Try a refreshing Thai iced tea with your meal.

Uncle Bo's Pupu Bar & Grill (66-111 Kamehameha Hwy. Suite #101, 808/797-9649, 10am-9pm daily, $12-27) combines American bistro with Pacific Rim cuisine. It has an extensive *pupu* menu, as well as steak, seafood, pasta, and pizza. It is known for large portions meant for sharing.

For sushi, **Banzai Sushi Bar** (66-246 Kamehameha Hwy., 808/637-4404, www.banzaisushibarhawaii.com, noon-9:30pm daily, $6-48) in the North Shore Marketplace is the go-to joint. Sit at a table or try the floor seating for an authentic Japanese experience on a finely decorated outdoor covered lanai. The fish is fresh, the rolls are inventive, and it has a list of premium sake. Vegan options are on the menu, as well as large-party sushi combinations. The tempura avocado is a treat, as is the live music often on hand.

Pizza

A staple in Hale'iwa town for nearly four decades, **Pizza Bob's** (66-145 Kamehameha Hwy., 808/637-5095, http://pizzabobshawaii.com, 7am-9pm Sun.-Thurs., 7am-10pm Fri.-Sat., $11-30) is a casual pizza parlor serving breakfast, lunch, and dinner. It has indoor and patio seating and nightly specials on food and drinks. It also serves burgers and pasta in addition to signature and build-your-own pizzas.

Mexican

★ **Luibueno's** (66-165 Kamehameha Hwy., 808/637-7717, http://luibueno.com, 11am-10:30pm daily, $6-29) serves authentic Mexican and Latin seafood, something that's hard to find on O'ahu. The restaurant decor is modern and colorful, the atmosphere is lively, and the restaurant sources its ingredients locally, including the fish that comes right off the boat at Hale'iwa Harbor.

Cholo's (66-250 Kamehameha Hwy., 808/637-3059, www.cholosmexican.com, 9:30am-9pm Sun.-Thurs., 9:30am-9:30pm Fri.-Sat., $10-15), in the North Shore Marketplace, is a popular eatery, but more for the tequila bar rather than the food, which is the standard taco, burrito, chimichanga affair.

Health Food

Celestial Natural Foods (66-445 Kamehameha Hwy., 808/637-6729, 9am-6pm Mon.-Fri., 10am-6pm Sat.-Sun.) has been the premier health food grocer in Hale'iwa since 1974. It carries organic and natural foods,

organic and local produce, vitamins, cosmetics, and other natural and healthy products.

Next to Celestial Natural Foods, the **Beet Box Café** (66-437 Kamehameha Hwy. Suite #104, 808/637-3000, www.thebeetboxcafe.com, 7am-4pm daily, 6pm-9:30pm Wed.-Sat., $6-11) offers an extensive organic vegetarian menu for breakfast and lunch. Egg dishes served all day, and acai bowls, soup, sandwiches, salads, smoothies, and raw organic vegetable juice are all possibilities.

Sweets and Treats

Established in 1951, **Matsumoto Shave Ice** (66-111 Kamehameha Hwy. Suite #605, 808/637-4827, www.matsumotoshaveice.com, 9am-6pm daily) is an integral part of the history of quaint Hale'iwa town. It has developed a huge following over the years. The result is a long line that snakes around the building just to get a cup of the Hawaiian treat. Be prepared to wait quite a while, especially on the weekends and during the summer. Originally a sundries store, it still sells souvenirs, snacks, and items like sunscreen and sunglasses.

The **Waialua Bakery** (66-200 Kamehameha Hwy., 808/341-2838, 10am-5pm Mon.-Sat.) has much more than just baked goods. The locally owned bakery also

Line up for shave ice.

has juices, a long list of smoothies, and fresh sandwiches. Much of its produce is from the family farm in Mokule'ia.

Markets
Malama Market (66-190 Kamehameha Hwy., 808/637-4520, 7am-8pm Mon., 1pm-8pm Tues., 8am-10pm Wed., 11am-9pm Thurs., 7am-10pm Fri., 10am-9pm Sat.-Sun.) is the big-brand grocery store in the heart of Hale'iwa, with alcohol, produce, dry goods, meats, and groceries.

NORTH SHORE BEACHES AND TURTLE BAY
Quick Bites
Sharks Cove Grill (59-712 Kamehameha Hwy., 808/638-8300, www.sharkscovegrill.com, 8:30am-8:30pm daily) is right across from Sharks Cove and enjoys great ocean views. The food truck serves breakfast, smoothies, and lunch all day and is known for the grilled skewer plates. It has a few covered tables to take in the view while you eat.

Across from Sunset Beach, **Ted's Bakery** (59-024 Kamehameha Hwy., 808/638-5974, www.tedsbakery.com, 7am-8pm daily)

provides homemade bakery goods, pies, salads, burgers, sandwiches, and plate lunches. Expect a wait of 30 minutes during the lunch rush if you order hot food.

Steak and Seafood
When North Shore locals celebrate a big occasion, they go to **Lei Lei's Bar and Grill** (57-049 Kuilima Dr., 808/293-2662, www.turtlebayresort.com, 7am-10pm daily, $22-36). The open-air restaurant and bar has indoor and patio seating, just steps away from the Fazio Golf Course. It serves rich and savory fresh seafood cuisine with Hawaiian favorites like ahi *poke*. The prime rib is also a favorite, as is the escargot appetizer. Lei Lei's is open for breakfast, lunch, and dinner.

Markets
The **Pupukea Foodland** (59-720 Kamehameha Hwy., 808/638-8081, www.foodland.com, 6am-11pm daily) is the only grocery store on the North Shore. Luckily, the big-brand grocery store has everything on premises: produce, meat, groceries, alcohol, and a deli with great made-to-order sandwiches. Expect high prices, even by Hawai'i standards.

Kahuku Superette (56-505

NORTH SHORE FOOD

Hale'iwa Farmers Market is held in Waimea Valley.

Kamehameha Hwy., 808/293-9878, 6am-10pm daily), across from Kahuku High School, is known and treasured for the fresh *poke*, Hawaiian favorites like lomi lomi salmon, and marinated raw meats. It also has alcohol and beverages, beach gear and fishing supplies, and a bare-bones assortment of snacks and groceries.

Farmers Markets

For local farm-fresh produce and prepared foods, **Hale'iwa Farmers Market** (59-864 Kamehameha Hwy., 808/388-9696, http://haleiwafarmersmarket.com, 2pm-6pm Thurs.) is a grassroots community market held at Waimea Valley, rain or shine. It features live music and free arts and crafts for the kids.

Information and Services

VISITOR INFORMATION

The **North Shore Chamber of Commerce** (66-434 Kamehameha Hwy., 808/637-4558, www.gonorthshore.org) is a great place to find detailed visitor information or get a firsthand recommendation. The building is across from the post office on the south end of Hale'iwa town. It hosts a 90-minute walking tour of **Historic Hale'iwa Town** at 3pm Wednesday and 9:30am Saturday for $10 per person. Reservations are required.

LIBRARY

Internet access is available at the **Waialua Public Library** (67-068 Kealohanui St., 808/637-8286, www.librarieshawaii.org) and the **Kahuku Public Library** (56-490 Kamehameha Hwy., 808/293-8935). Visitors need a valid Hawaii State Public Library System (HSPLS) card to use an Internet computer. Three-month visitor cards are available for $10. You can reserve Internet computer time online or in person. You can find printed bus schedules here, too.

MAIL

There are full-service **post offices** in Hale'iwa (66-437 Kamehameha Hwy., 808/637-1711) and in Waialua (67-079 Nauahi St., 808/637-2754).

Getting There and Around

GETTING THERE
Car

To get to the North Shore, you can either take Kamehameha Highway, Route 83 on the windward coast, or travel the H-2 up the middle of the island. At Wahiawa the freeway ends and becomes Wilikina Drive through Schofield Barracks, which turns into Kaukonahua Road and then finally becomes Farrington Highway as you pass Waialua and drive out to Mokule'ia at the end of the road. Or, as the H-2 ends, you can take the Wahiawa off-ramp, exit 8, which puts you on Kamehameha Highway through Wahiawa.

Kamehameha Highway continues through the town of Hale'iwa, across the North Shore, and back down the windward side. You can bypass Hale'iwa on the Joseph P. Leong Highway, Route 83.

Bus

You can get to the North Shore from Honolulu via **TheBus** (808/848-5555, www.thebus.org) on Routes 55 and 88A, the North Shore express, both of which traverse the windward coast. For those looking to leave the car parked for a bit, **TheBus** (808/848-4500, www.thebus.org) offers Route 76, which travels between Waialua and Haleʻiwa. Check out TheBus' app, **DaBus**, for Apple and Android smartphones.

GETTING AROUND

During the Vans Triple Crown of Surfing and periods of high surf on the North Shore, traffic can slow to a crawl from Haleʻiwa to Sunset Beach. There are several notorious choke points along this stretch. Traffic backs up at Laniakea, Chun's Reef, Waimea Bay, and Sunset Beach. Look out for pedestrians crossing the highway. The weekends are notorious for stop-and-go traffic from Haleʻiwa through Chun's Reef.

If the waves are extremely large and Waimea Bay is breaking, traffic gets crazy around the bay as people try to pull off the road to get a view and take photos. Parking on the mountain side of the road is illegal, and there is only limited space on the ocean side shoulder of the highway. It's much safer to park around Sharks Cove and walk back to the bay for photos. Parking laws are strictly enforced in the area.

On the North Shore, parking along the highway is haphazard at best. Be sure not to block residential driveways and be aware of No Parking signs and bus stops. The "No Parking" signs have arrows pointing in the direction of the area where it is illegal to park, and No Parking areas are strictly enforced.

Uber and **Lyft** offer ride-hailing services in the area.

Hanauma Bay and Southeast

The southeast region is like no other on O'ahu.

Ridges lined with mansions and green valleys with quiet communities span from Kahala to Hawai'i Kai, where suburban neighborhoods encircle Koko Marina, which stretches far back to the mountains. Maunalua Bay, a shallow, calm bay with a fringe reef, extends from Black Point in Kahala to the sheer cliffs of Koko Head, an impressive landmark jutting out into the bay. Windswept waves roll across shallow reefs, the turquoise water shimmers in the midday sun and boats cruise from the marina out beyond farthest reaches of the reef.

On the east side of Koko Head is Hanauma Bay State Park, a natural area preserve known for some of the best snorkeling on O'ahu. Past the bay, the scenery changes completely. On the dry, southeastern tip of O'ahu, the area from Koko Head to Makapu'u, also known as the Ka Iwi Coastline, Ka Iwi Sate Scenic Shoreline, and Ka Iwi coast, receives 12-20 inches of rain annually, compared to the 100-inch annual average that Ho'omaluhia Botanical Garden in Kane'ohe receives. There are numerous lookouts to take in the rugged, dry, and wave-pummeled coastline. This stretch is also one of the best locales for whale watching on O'ahu during the humpback whales' annual stay from November to March.

Makapu'u, which means bulging eye in Hawaiian, and Sandy Beach are O'ahu's premier bodysurfing beaches. There is a short hike to the Makapu'u lighthouse, a prime whale-watching vantage point with a great view toward Waimanalo with Manana Island, a seabird sanctuary, in the foreground. For beachcombers, the beaches and tidepools in between Sandy Beach and Makapu'u are full of natural wonders and offer solace from the tour buses that stop at all the major sights in this region.

For botanical enthusiasts, Koko Crater, just inland from Sandy Beach, is home to O'ahu's only dryland botanical garden. A short loop trail circles the inside of the crater with all variety of plants that thrive in the dry conditions. An established plumeria grove, which fragrantly blooms during the summer, graces the entrance of the garden. Hikers can also enjoy a challenge on the Koko Crater stairs, a rigorous climb up an old railway, a remnant from World War II, to the top of the crater for amazing 360-views. On clear days, Moloka'i and Maui can be seen in the distance across the Ka Iwi Channel.

Previous: the rugged Ka Iwi State Scenic Shoreline; Sandy Beach Park. **Above:** Koko Crater Botanical Garden boasts a plumeria grove.

Look for ★ to find recommended
sights, activities, dining, and lodging.

Highlights

© AVALON TRAVEL

★ **Koko Crater Botanical Garden:** With its succulents, cycads, a native Hawaiian *wiliwili* tree stand, and a plumeria grove, you can't miss this garden, especially when the plumeria are in bloom (page 151).

★ **Makapu'u Point State Wayside:** Hike around the point to the lighthouse, whale-watch from November to March, swim and bodysurf at the beach, and explore the black lava tidepools (page 151).

★ **Sandy Beach Park:** The powerful break at Sandy Beach is the place for surfers to test

their mettle—as it detonates right on the sand (page 154).

★ **Hanauma Bay Nature Preserve:** The first marine protected area in the state of Hawai'i, this unique, circular bay lies within an extinct volcanic cone, protected from wind and waves. Live coral reef, 400 species of fish, and endangered sea turtles call it home (page 158).

★ **Hawai'i Kai:** The Hawai'i Kai Marina is the recreation hub of the southeast coast. You'll also find restaurants, shopping, and ample shoreline access along beautiful Maunalua Bay (page 161).

Hanauma Bay and Southeast

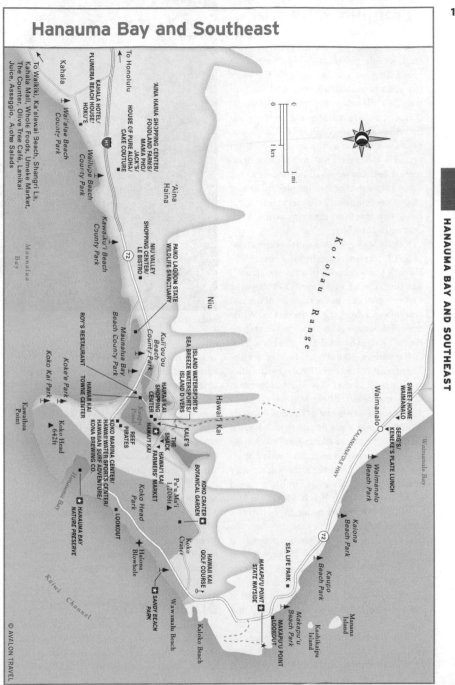

To Honolulu

To Waikiki, Ka'alawai Beach, Shangri La, Kahala Mall, Whole Foods, Umeke Market, The Counter, Olive Tree Cafe, Lanikai Juice, Assaggio, Aloha Salads

Kahala

KAHALA HOTEL/
PLUMERIA BEACH HOUSE/
HOKU'S

Wai'alae Beach
County Park

Wailupe Beach
County Park

'AINA HAINA SHOPPING CENTER/
FOODLAND FARMS/
MAMA PHO/
JACK'S/
HOUSE OF PURE ALOHA/
CAKE COUTURE

Maunalua
Bay

'Aina
Haina

Kawaiku'i Beach
County Park

NIU VALLEY
SHOPPING CENTER/
LE BISTRO

PAIKO LAGOON STATE
WILDLIFE SANCTUARY

Niu

Maunalua Bay
Beach County Park

ROY'S RESTAURANT

Kui'ou'ou
Beach
County Park

ISLAND WATERSPORTS/
SEA BREEZE WATERSPORTS/
ISLAND DIVERS

Hawai'i Kai

Ko'olau Range

Waimanalo

SWEET HOME
WAIMANALO

SERG'S/
KENEKE'S PLATE LUNCH

Waimanalo
Beach Park

KALANIANA'OLE HWY

Waimanalo Bay

Kaiona
Beach Park

Kaupo
Beach Park

Manana
Island

Kaohikaipu
Island

Makapu'u
Beach Park

MAKAPU'U POINT
LOOKOUT

SEA LIFE PARK

MAKAPU'U POINT
STATE WAYSIDE

HAWAI'I KAI
SHOPPING
CENTER

KALE'S

HAWAI'I KAI
FARMERS' MARKET

THE
SHACK

HAWAI'I KAI

REEF
PIRATES

KOKO MARINA CENTER/
HAWAIIAN WATER SPORTS CENTER/
HAWAIIAN SURF ADVENTURE/
KONA BREWING CO.

KOKO CRATER
BOTANICAL GARDEN

Pu'u Ma'i
1,208ft

Koko Head
Park

Koko
Crater

LOOKOUT

Hawai'i Kai

Kamilo
Pond

Koko Kai Park

Koke'e Park

Koko Head
642ft

HAWAI'I KAI
TOWNE CENTER

Kawaihoa
Point

Hanauma Bay

HANAUMA BAY
NATURE PRESERVE

Halona
Blowhole

HAWAI'I KAI
GOLF COURSE

SANDY BEACH
PARK

Wawamalu Beach

Kaloko Beach

Kaiwi Channel

0   6
|———|
0   1 km
|———|
    1 mi

PLANNING YOUR TIME

Southeast Oʻahu is relatively small compared to other Oʻahu regions. It's about 11 miles from Kahala to Makapuʻu. With a 35 mph speed limit on the Kalanianaole Highway, that equates to about a 30-minute drive, sans traffic. While many people take advantage of this scenic-drive corridor as a way to access the windward side—Waimanalo, Kailua, and beyond—from the south shore, the southeast region is a destination all to itself. For sight-seers, a half day would suffice to take in the natural beauty of the area, but for outdoor and recreation enthusiasts, plan on at least a full day to two days to see the many natural wonders without rushing.

Kahala Mall in Kahala and the three shopping centers surrounding the marina in Hawaiʻi Kai—Koko Marina Center, Hawaiʻi Kai Town Center, and Hawaiʻi Kai Shopping Center—are home to the majority of the restaurants and shopping in the region. While the neighborhoods in between Kahala and Hawaiʻi Kai all have hiking trails at the back of the valleys, Hawaiʻi Kai to Makapuʻu is where most of the recreational opportunities are centered. Snorkel, dive, and surf tour outfitters operate out of Koko Marina.

Hanauma Bay is one of the most heavily visited natural areas on the island, known for its spectacular snorkeling, but you'll have to get there early to ensure a parking spot, usually by 8am. Once the lot is full, security guards will turn cars away. The bay is closed every Tuesday. Sandy Beach, Makapuʻu, and Sea Life Park are all major tourist draws with limited parking. They are also the main beaches in the region. There's not much to do to avoid the crowds since the region is so close to Waikiki and the sights are all stops for the tour buses. The stretch of beach from the north end of Sandy Beach to the south end of Makapuʻu headland is your best chance to find a quiet patch of sand.

Since there are no major accommodations in the region, those staying in Waikiki hotels or Kailua vacation rentals will be the closest

Makapuʻu Lighthouse

to the area. While a rental car is always the easiest way to get around, the area is also accessible by taxi, ride-hailing services, and by bus. A taxi ride would run upwards of $50 (one way); ride-hailing services like Uber and Lyft could be pricey, too. The bus, however, is an extremely affordable way to get to specific destinations along the coast without the worry of parking a rental car. The Beach Bus, route 22, runs from Waikiki to Sea Life Park, with stops at Hanauma Bay, Sandy Beach, and Makapuʻu. The bus does not run on Tuesday when Hanauma Bay is closed. Route 57 runs from Kailua to Sea Life Park, where you can transfer to route 22 to access the rest of the Ka Iwi Coastline, Hanauma Bay and on into Waikiki.

ORIENTATION

Stretching from the upscale neighborhood of **Kahala** on the east side of Diamond Head to the easternmost tip of the island at Makapuʻu, the southeast coast has two distinct zones.

Your Best Day in Southeast O'ahu

The Southeast region offers a mix of recreational activities that include mountain, beach, and ocean settings. The region is relatively small, a 30-minute drive from Kahala to Makapu'u, yet the activities are not to be rushed. One could easily spend a few days ticking the boxes of all the things to do along this beautiful stretch of coastline.

- Start the day by snorkeling one of the best reef habitats on O'ahu, **Hanauma Bay Nature Preserve** in Hawai'i Kai. With a beautiful beach set way back in the sheltered bay, spend a couple hours viewing the immense diversity found on a healthy reef ecosystem. Keep in mind that if you arrive after 9:30am, you could be turned away if the parking lot is full. If you'd rather start your morning with a hike, walk the Makapu'u trail to the lighthouse. From November to April, this vantage point is one of the prime locations to view Pacific humpback whales.

- After all that outdoor activity, you'll be in the mood for a delicious meal. Try **Moena Café,** a popular bistro serving breakfast and lunch, or for fresh and delicious poke bowls, check out **Pa'ina Cafe.** They are both located in the Koko Marina Shopping Center in Hawai'i Kai.

- Round out the day at **Sandy Beach.** If you're a strong swimmer and enjoy bodysurfing, you'll be right at home in the barreling shore break. Otherwise, enjoy watching from the sunny beach or take a nature walk along the Ka Iwi Coast, where rocks, tidepools and lava offer a dramatic coastline perfect for exploring on foot. For botanical enthusiasts, stroll through O'ahu's only dryland botanical garden, **Koko Crater Botanical Garden,** and catch the plumeria grove in bloom during the summer.

- For dinner with live music and a relaxing atmosphere overlooking the marina, enjoy pizza, fresh fish, and great local beers on tap at **Kona Brewing Company.** Also located in the Koko Marina Shopping Center in Hawai'i Kai, the bar scene is lively and the food is always fresh and locally sourced.

The first area encompasses the suburban neighborhoods in the valleys and along the ridges from Kahala to **Hawai'i Kai. Aina Haina, Niu Valley,** and **Kuli'ou'ou** are the major valleys along Kalanianaole Highway, the main thoroughfare along this stretch of the island. The Portlock neighborhood lines the western flank of Koko Head and looks west over Maunalua Bay. The other part of the region, known as the Ka Iwi Coast, is dramatically different. As the highway rounds Koko Head, homes disappear and rugged volcanic landscape prevails from Hanauma Bay to Makapu'u. Along this windy and dry stretch of coastline you'll find Koko Crater and Sandy Beach before reaching the Makapu'u headland, the easternmost tip of the island.

Sights

KAHALA
Shangri La

A fitting estate for the upscale neighborhoods of Kahala, **Shangri La** (4055 Papu Cr., 808/734-1941 or 808/532-3853, www.shangrilahawaii.org) was the seasonal home of American heiress and philanthropist Doris Duke. Built in 1937, replete with amazing views from a small cliff above the water's edge, Shangri La was designed to hold Duke's vast collection of Islamic art, and today it serves as a center for Islamic art and culture. Portions of this home that blend Islamic architecture and Hawaiian landscaping are open to the public via guided tours led by the Honolulu Museum of Art. The 12-person group tour begins in the Arts of the Islamic World gallery at the Honolulu Museum of Art, followed by a short video about Duke and her estate, and then a minivan shuttles the group to the estate for a 1.5-hour tour featuring the public rooms of the main house and parts of the grounds. Tours are held 9am, 10:30am, and 1:30pm Wednesday-Saturday. General admission is $25, and reservations are strongly encouraged.

HAWAI'I KAI AND KA'IWI COAST

Maunalua Bay Lookout

There are several lookouts beside Kalanianaole Highway in between Hawai'i Kai and Makapu'u. The coastline is rugged, the road winds precariously close to the edge of the sea cliff, and open ocean swells constantly batter rock outcroppings. The **Maunalua Bay Lookout** is an often forgotten lookout on the mountain side of the highway, just before you arrive at the Hanauma Bay turnoff if you're heading east, with sweeping views of Koko Crater, Hawai'i Kai Marina, and Maunalua Bay, which stretches all the way to Diamond Head.

Hanauma Bay Nature Preserve Park

The first marine protected area in the state of Hawai'i, **Hanauma Bay Nature Preserve Park** (7455 Kalanianaole Hwy., 808/395-2211 or 808/396-4229, 6am-6:20pm Wed.-Mon.) is the most popular snorkeling site on O'ahu. Located just to the east of Koko Head on the southeast shore, the nearly circular bay lies within a volcanic cone, with a semicircular beach and fingers of shallow reef that stretch from the edge of the bay all the way to the beach. If you're driving in, arrive as early as possible, as the parking lot usually fills to capacity by 10am and cars are turned away till others leave, usually around 2pm. There is a $1 parking fee per car and a $7.50 entry fee. Children under 13 are free. You can bring your own snorkel gear or rent snorkel sets for $12 per day. There are also food concessions at the beach. Visitors are required to view a short film and presentation about the preserve and proper etiquette while snorkeling.

Halona Blowhole

Formed by molten lava tubes meeting with the ocean, the **Halona Blowhole** funnels ocean surges through a narrow opening in the rock to create a geyser that can send a plume of

Maunalua Bay and Hawai'i Kai Marina

spray 30 feet into the air. The blowhole isn't always active; it takes a windy day, a high tide, and high surf on the windward side to get the blast really shooting high. However, if you're there on an off day, the view toward Sandy Beach is still worth the stop.

The Halona Blowhole is located along the Kalanianaole Highway, in between Sandy Beach and Makapu'u. There is a good-sized parking lot located on the cliff side of Kalanianaole Highway, and several designated viewing areas along the cliff, right above the blowhole.

★ Koko Crater Botanical Garden

Sited inside arid Koko Crater, **Koko Crater Botanical Garden** (end of Kokonani St., 808/522-7060, www1.honolulu.gov/parks/hbg/kcbg.htm, closed Christmas and New Year's Day) takes advantage of the sheltered spot for plantings of rare and endangered dryland plant species from around the world. Koko Crater is actually two craters in one, an inner and outer crater, of which 60 acres of the basin have been cultivated. A two-mile loop trail takes you from the fragrant and magnificent hybrid plumeria grove in the inner crater, to a stand of native Hawaiian *wiliwili* trees in the back of the outer crater. In between are succulents, cycads, and over 200 species of trees. The plumeria grove is in full bloom April-June. There are no facilities on-site, except for a lone portable toilet, so it's best to use those at nearby Sandy Beach Park.

To get here from Kalanianaole Highway, turn onto Kealahou Street, then turn left onto Kokonani Street. The paved road becomes a dirt road and ends at the garden parking lot. The gardens are open from sunrise to sunset, and there are trail maps at the entrance gate.

MAKAPU'U
★ Makapu'u Point State Wayside

Makapu'u, which translates to "bulging eye" in Hawaiian, marks the rugged and dry eastern tip of O'ahu. The rough black rock is dotted with cacti and small flowering shrubs, like the native Hawaiian *'ilima*, with its cute yellow and orange blossoms. The **Makapu'u Point State Wayside** holds several areas of interest. There are two parking lots at Makapu'u. Coming from Hawai'i Kai on Kalanianaole Highway, the first parking lot offers direct access to the trail that rounds Makapu'u Point and leads to the Makapu'u Point Lighthouse. Roughly a 3-mile round-trip walk, the wide,

SIGHTS

HANAUMA BAY AND SOUTHEAST

Halona Blowhole

paved road gains elevation gradually as it circles the point from the south to face the Pacific Ocean. On a clear day you can see the islands of Moloka'i and Maui in the far distance. The hike has an added bonus of being one of the premier whale-watching venues while the humpback whales breed and rear their young in Hawaiian waters November-March. It is also cooler during this period as well, as the shadeless hike can get rather hot in the midday summer sun. There are informational signs along the trail about humpback whale activity and behavior.

At the end of the hike are a couple lookout platforms and the **Makapu'u Point Lighthouse,** a 46-foot-tall active lighthouse constructed in 1909. The lighthouse itself is off limits to the public, but you can get close enough to take a nice picture with the blue Pacific as the backdrop. Feel free to scamper around the rocks and explore the summit at 647 feet, but be careful as the area is scattered with sharp rocks, boulders, and cacti.

At the second parking lot, just to the north of the first, is a magnificent lookout area with views of the Waimanalo Coast, the rugged southern end of the Ko'olau Range, and two nearby offshore islands, **Manana Island and Kaohikaipu Island State Seabird Sanctuary.** The islands are home to nesting wedge-tailed shearwaters, sooty terns, brown noodies, and several other species. It is illegal to set foot on the islands. Manana Island is commonly referred to as Rabbit Island, because a rancher actually tried to raise rabbits here prior to its designation as a seabird sanctuary.

If you consider yourself an avid hiker, from the lookout you can scramble up the backside of the point to the summit, regain the trail near the lighthouse, and follow the paved path back to the lookout for a nice loop.

Sea Life Park
Sea Life Park (41-202 Kalanianaole Hwy., 808/259-2500, www.sealifeparkhawaii.com, 10:30am-5pm daily) is an aquatic park just north of Makapu'u Point on the *mauka* side of the highway. Focused on education and interaction with exotic sea life and animals, the park is known for its adventure programs that allow guests to literally swim with the dolphins. The Dolphin Royal Swim takes you on a dorsal fin ride with two dolphins and culminates with the foot push, where the dolphins push you around the pool by your feet, $235 and park admission is included. The Dolphin Swim Adventure

Manana Island and Kaohikaipu Island State Seabird Sanctuary

lets you interact with the animals and take a belly ride for $185. The Dolphin Encounter is designed for families with children to interact with dolphins in shallow water for $105. Guests can also swim with sharks, sea lions, or rays. Beyond getting in the water with the sea creatures, the park also offers a Hawaiian shark tank, dolphin shows, sea lion shows, penguins, a kids play area, turtle feeding, and an open-air aquatic theater. Adult general admission is $30, kids age 3-12 $20.

Beaches

Because of the natural geography of Maunalua Bay, there are only a few beaches along this stretch of coast. Houses have been built to the water's edge along the highway and what little beach is accessible at low tide is soon underwater as the tide rises. Fortunately, for those looking to escape the crowds of Honolulu and Waikiki beaches, Kahala beaches offer solace from the congestion.

The beaches along the Ka Iwi Coast, from Hanauma Bay to Makapu'u, are raw, natural, and often windswept, thanks to the pervasive trade winds blowing from northwest to southeast. They are also popular destinations for visitors and locals alike. Sandy Beach and Makapu'u are the main draws with dramatic coastlines, wide beaches, and powerful shore break.

KAHALA
Ka'alawai Beach
Tucked away in the affluent Ka'alawai neighborhood, **Ka'alawai Beach** is a narrow strip of sand that runs from the end of Kulamanu Place to the Diamond Head cliffs. Framed by lavish beachfront properties beyond the vegetation line, the secluded spot draws a younger crowd and is a favorite for topless sunbathers. The shoreline is predominately rock and reef, so getting in the water can involve finding a sandy nook to take a dip. The view to the east of Black Point is picturesque, and the clear water is often choppy from the trade winds.

To access the beach, park on Kulamanu Street and walk down Kulamanu Place to the access point. Follow the sand to the right (west) and find your own spot.

There are also some great tidepools at Ka'alawai. Once through the access point, turn left instead of right and explore. Be aware that the terrain is smooth and slippery in some spots as well as sharp and jagged in others. There are no services in the vicinity.

Waialae Beach Park
From Diamond Head Road, follow Kahala Avenue east toward the Kahala Hotel & Resort. Once you cross the Waialae Stream bridge, turn right into the **Waialae Beach Park** parking lot. Complete with free parking, showers, bathrooms, picnic benches, and a shaded arbor at the beach's edge, Waialae Beach Park is usually uncrowded and a favorite destination for kitesurfers and newlyweds taking wedding pictures. It's a fine place for a barbecue or picnic. The park is actually split in two by the stream, and a beautiful narrow beach unwinds to the west. This quiet stretch of sand, dotted with shells and bits of coral, is fringed by O'ahu's most magnificent homes and mansions. The shallow waters, with a flat sand and rock bottom, are great for snorkeling and perfect for families looking to escape the Waikiki crowds. Unfortunately, the beach is right in the path of the predominant trade winds, so be prepared to tie down umbrellas and keep your light and loose belongings secure. There are several access points along Kahala Avenue from the beach park to Hunakai Street. Park along Kahala Avenue. The beach park is closed 10pm-5am daily.

AINA HAINA
Kawaiku'i Beach Park

In Aina Haina you'll find that **Kawaiku'i Beach Park** is more of a park than a beach. At low tide there is a small strip of coarse sand fronting the park, which has mature shade trees, an expansive lawn, and bathrooms and showers. The inner waters are usually murky and not exactly inviting, but this park is still favored by anglers taking advantage of the shallow bay, and by surfers, windsurfers, kiteboarders, and stand-up paddlers for the surf spots that break along the barrier reef quite a ways out. From Kalanianaole Highway heading east, turn right at Puuikena Drive (there is a traffic signal here) to access the parking lot. Parking is free.

KULI'OU'OU
Kuli'ou'ou Beach Park

Nestled up against the Paiko Lagoon Wildlife Sanctuary in the Kuli'ou'ou neighborhood, **Kuli'ou'ou Beach Park** is one of the few areas along the Maunalua Bay coastline offering a shallow bay beside a well-maintained park. The sandy seafloor of Maunalua Bay is very shallow and dotted with bits of rock, reef, and seaweed. At low tide the water is literally ankle deep, while at high tide, it's waist deep at best. In fact, take a walk all the way out to the barrier reef, roughly 0.25mile out to sea, keeping an eye out for sea cucumbers, crabs, and fish, all within knee-deep water. The park has facilities, picnic benches, and a free parking lot. From Kalanianaole Highway, Bay Street will take you straight there. Kuli'ou'ou Beach Park is closed 10pm-5am daily.

HAWAI'I KAI
★ Sandy Beach Park

A few minutes past the eastern side of Koko Head in Hawai'i Kai, along rugged and dramatic coastline, you'll find the infamous **Sandy Beach Park.** Sandy Beach is notorious for its high-impact shore break and draws bodysurfers, bodyboarders, and surfers to its challenging waves. The beach is rather wide by

the west end of Waialae Beach Park

Hawai'i standards and draws a host of locals and visitors who come to watch the aqua blue waves slam onto the shore. The ocean currents here are dangerous, the sand is studded with rocks, and the surf can get big and extremely powerful, detonating onto dry sand. The shore break has caused injuries and even fatalities, so only expert swimmers should enter the water. However, when the waves are pumping, it is quite a spectacle to watch. Parking in the dirt lot can get somewhat haphazard and choked on the weekends. And while parking is free, theft is common, so take precautions.

Sandy Beach Park is just off Kalanianaole Highway. The turnoff is visible from both directions. At the beach park, a road runs the length of the beach. Wawamalu Beach Park is at the north end. There's no sand here, just jagged lava rock running into the ocean, but it is a great place to stop and stretch or have a bite while watching waves break. There are restrooms and a long park frequented by kite-flying enthusiasts.

Ka Iwi Coast Beaches

About 0.5 mile past Sandy Beach is a traffic signal. Pull off the road to the right just past the signal and park in the hardpack sand to access the beach, which stretches in both directions. The area is great for beachcombers and shell hunters. Walk the coastline, check out the tidepools, post up with an umbrella and enjoy the scenery. The surf tends to be rough, the currents are strong, and the coastline is rocky. Swimming is not recommended.

Makapu'u Beach Park

Makapu'u Point marks the arid southeast tip of O'ahu. Just to the north of the formidable headland, you'll find **Makapu'u Beach Park,** a beautiful crescent of white sand set against the deep-blue ocean and dry, rugged cliffs. The scenery at Makapu'u is breathtaking, complete with Rabbit Island and Black Rock, two seabird sanctuaries, protruding from deep water just offshore. Makapu'u is also known for its pounding shore break, alluring to bodyboarders, bodysurfers, locals and visitors. There are strong currents here, and swimming should be done with caution. Check with the lifeguard for current ocean conditions. On days when the surf is flat and the wind is light, the water becomes very

clear. Snorkeling is best at the south end of the beach, where the rocks and cliff begin. There are restrooms and showers, but parking is limited, so it's best to get there early. There is a small paved parking lot for the beach park, another dirt lot that is severely rutted and only safe for four-wheel-drive vehicles, or you can park up on the highway in the designated lookout area and walk down to the beach.

On the north side of the beach park are the **Makapu'u Tidepools.** The coast is fringed with black lava, creating some wonderful tidepools to explore. Be aware that the surf can wash up onto the tidepools, so it's best to explore the area when the surf is small to flat. To get to the tidepools, you can walk up the coast on dirt paths from Makapu'u Beach Park and meander across the lava as far as you'd like to go, or you can park right at the tidepools. Coming from Koko Head, turn just past Sea Life Park into the oceanside parking area.

Kaupo Beach Park

Just on the other side of the Makapu'u Tidepools you'll come to **Kaupo Beach Park,** a great beach for snorkeling, playing on the sand, fishing or learning to surf, with all the same great views as Makapu'u. Here,

BEACHES

Sandy Beach Park

the lava recedes to offer sandy beaches among the rocks and coastal shrubs. It has character, is safe for kids, and is a favorite for local families on the weekends. It's the perfect spot to take a break from the road and have a dip or bite to eat while enjoying the scenery. As the beach arcs north toward the Makai Research Pier, there are small, gentle waves that break just off the shore. The parking lot for Kaupo Beach Park is at the same turn as the Makapu'u Tidepools, just stay to the left. There is also roadside parking for several vehicles right in front of where the waves break, or you can park down by the research pier. There are restroom and shower facilities in the park's parking lot.

Water Sports

SURFING, BODYSURFING, AND STAND-UP PADDLING

While there are several surf breaks in this region, none of them is both easily accessible and user friendly. Maunalua Bay sees soft and gentle waves most of the year straight out from Hawai'i Kai, but the waves are 0.5 mile out to sea and generally accessed only by boat and surf tour operator. Conversely, the waves along the Ka Iwi Coast at Sandy Beach and Makapu'u are onshore, but extremely dangerous and not for beginners. As a rule of thumb, stand-up paddlers and surfers (longboarders) prefer Maunalua Bay and bodysurfers prefer Sandy Beach and Makapu'u.

The outer reefs of **Maunalua Bay** hold a wealth of surf spots for expert surfers who are comfortable with very long paddles to the breaking waves and surfing over shallow and sharp coral reefs. Because the waves break so far offshore mixed with a lack of shoreline access, it's nearly impossible for the visiting surfer to distinguish between the different breaks and know which break is surfable and which waves are breaking over dry reef.

Luckily, there are a couple surf tour operators who will take visitors out in the bay to one of the gentle, soft waves, perfect for beginner to intermediate surfers. **Hawaiian Surf Adventures** (7192 Kalanianaole Hwy., 808/396-2324, http://hawaiiansurfadventure.

Makapu'u Beach Park

com, 9am-4:30pm Mon.-Sat.) accesses a secluded wave in Maunalua Bay by boat, which is a gentle surf break perfect for beginner surfers. There are no crowds to contend with, just you and the instructor. Group lessons are $89; private lessons are $149. Hawaiian Surf Adventures also offers stand-up paddle lessons and tours of Maunalua Bay starting at $99 as well as outrigger canoe tours. **Island Watersports Hawaii** (377 Keahole St., 808/224-0076, www.islandwatersportshawaii.com, 8am-5pm daily) also taps into the uncrowded waves of Maunalua Bay with two-hour group surf lessons for $99 and 1.5-hour private lessons starting at $125. If you'd rather stand-up paddle the bay, two-hour group lessons are $99 and 1.5-hour private lessons start at $125.

To the east of Koko Head is the infamous **Sandy Beach**. As a favorite of local bodyboarders and bodysurfers, the water's edge fills with heads bobbing up and down, waiting to drop into a heaving barrel, right onto the sand. If this sounds dangerous, that's because it is. Every year people are seriously injured at Sandy Beach, everything from broken limbs to broken necks, even death. The waves can get big, especially in the summer months. If you're not a strong swimmer or comfortable in the surf zone, take solace in the fact that, from the safety of the beach, it's quite amusing to watch surfers getting slammed. Check with lifeguards for current conditions. There are also two surf breaks over a sharp and shallow coral reef, Full Point and Half Point, at the north end of the beach. Local surfers dominate them both.

Much like Sandy Beach, **Makapu'u Beach Park** is known for its powerful shore break, which can get quite big with the right swell conditions. When the surf is smaller, the shore break is a bit more playful and forgiving than Sandy Beach, but you'll still leave the beach with sand in your ears. Surfboards are prohibited in the water, but people will paddle out after the lifeguards have left for the day.

Just north of Makapu'u at **Kaupo Beach Park** there is a gentle little wave called Cockroach that breaks inside the rocky cove, perfect for beginners on big boards. During the winter months, when northeast swells sneak around Rabbit Island, the surf can get big and the currents quite strong.

SNORKELING

Snorkeling in this region is dependent on the weather. The lighter the tradewinds, the better the conditions will be for snorkeling. The

Hanauma Bay is O'ahu's premier snorkeling area.

best bet for seeing an abundance of fish is to snorkel **Hanauma Bay** or go out with a tour operator that can take you to the best place to snorkel for the conditions. If you would like to venture out on your own, try your luck along the Kahala shoreline. You'll need to come prepared with your snorkel set, as there are no outfitters in the vicinity.

★ Hanauma Bay Nature Preserve

Hanauma Bay Nature Preserve (7455 Kalanianaole Hwy., 808/395-2211 or 808/396-4229, www.hanaumabaystatepark.com, 6am-7pm Wed.-Mon., $7.50 admission, $1 parking) is the first Marine Life Conservation District in the state and the most popular snorkeling site on O'ahu. Located just to the east of Koko Head on the southeast shore, the bay lies within a volcanic cone with a semicircular beach and fingers of shallow reef that stretch from the edge of the bay all the way to the beach. After decades of preservation after rampant overuse, Hanauma Bay now boasts about 400 species of fish and an abundance of green sea turtles. Keep in mind that the water close to shore can get quite crowded with snorkelers and you'll have to swim a ways out to find some territory to yourself. If you're

driving in, arrive as early as possible, as the parking lot usually fills to capacity by 10am and cars are turned away till others leave, usually around 2pm. You can bring your own snorkel gear, or snorkel sets are available to rent for $20 per day. There are also food concessions at the beach. Visitors are required to view a short film and presentation about the preserve and proper etiquette while snorkeling. Admission is free for children under 13 and Hawai'i residents. There is also a 3.5-hour tour available on the state sponsored website that includes roundtrip Waikiki transportation, snorkel set and a narrated tour to the bay for $22. There is also a tram from the parking lot to the beach ($1 down, $1.25 up).

DIVING

Island Divers (377 Keahole St., 808/423-8222 or 888/844-3483, www.oahuscubadiving.com, 7am-7pm daily) is a Professional Association of Diving Instructors (PADI) Five Star Dive Center that operates out of the Hawai'i Kai Shopping Center. It caters to all levels of divers and offers PADI certification courses. It has pick-up and drop-off services available from Waikiki hotels, or you can meet at its own private dock. Two-tank boat charter dives with full gear rental start at $119. Island Divers is a

dive tour boats in the Hawai'i Kai marina

Whale-Watching

Humpback whales make an annual migration of 3,500 miles from the Gulf of Alaska to the warm waters of the main Hawaiian Islands every winter. While the greatest pod of whales is found off the windward coast of Maui, humpback whales routinely frequent O'ahu waters during their Hawai'i stay from October to March. Once in the shallow waters, they engage in mating behaviors and give birth to massive calves.

On the windward coast, whales can be seen breaching, tail slapping, and spitting plumes of spray from their blowhole as they cruise along the coast. Fortunately for whale-watchers, humpback whales like to gather in the waters from Makapu'u to Koko Head, and swim very close to shore as they pass by. The lookouts at the Makapu'u Point State Wayside are a great vantage point for watching their exhibitions, as well as the several lookouts along the winding Kalanianaole Highway toward Hanauma Bay.

complete dive center as well, with snorkel and scuba equipment available for rent and sale.

Reef Pirates Diving (7192 Kalanianaole Hwy., 808/348-2700, www.reefpirates.com, 7am-6pm daily) also operates in Hawai'i Kai, but is based in the Koko Marina Shopping Center. It is a complete dive center with sales and rentals and offers PADI certification as well as dive charters. Its two-tank charters start at $125. Ride-along passengers and snorkelers cost $45. Reef Pirates also offers multiple-day dive packages and private charters.

A complete dive shop based in the Koko Marina Center, with scuba and diving sales and rentals, **Hawaii Water Sports Center** (7192 Kalanianaole Hwy. E110, 808/395-3773, http://hawaiiwatersportscenter.com, 8:30am-4pm Mon.-Fri., 9am-4pm Sat.-Sun.) offers 3.5-hour scuba-diving sessions from a dive boat one mile offshore in Maunalua Bay for $69. The boat leaves at 9am every day except Sunday and participants must be at least 10 years old. Call ahead to make reservations.

China Walls

Maunalua Bay, which stretches from Kahala to Koko Head along the southeastern shore, has a wealth of dive sites and several operators that specifically service this region, with charters leaving from the Hawai'i Kai Marina. Special to the area is a dive site known as **China Walls.** This vertical wall dropping off the south side of Koko Head and reaching

down to depths of 75 feet is made up of caves and ledges, and attracts sharks, turtles, jacks, rays, eels, and the endangered Hawaiian monk seal. Whale songs can be heard in the area during the winter months. China Walls is located at the southernmost tip of Koko Head, the headland that frames the eastern side of Maunalua Bay.

Maunalua Bay is home to airplane- and shipwrecks, like the WWII-era Corsair plane, a barge, and a marine landing craft known as an LST. There are also caves, reefs, and overhangs where you'll find turtles, Galapagos sharks, whitetip reef sharks, eels, countless tropical fish, and rare black coral.

Diving in the Maunalua Bay is dependent on ocean and weather conditions, and high winds or high surf can cause diving conditions to deteriorate.

FISHING

The deep waters off the southeast coast are a draw for sport anglers. The dark-blue deep is home to the bigger fish like wahoo, yellowfin tuna, and marlin. **Island Watersports Hawaii** (377 Keahole St., 808/224-0076, www.islandwatersportshawaii.com, 7am-7pm daily) is the only fishing charter operating out of the Hawai'i Kai Marina. Depending on ocean and weather conditions, it trolls for big game fish or fishes the ledges off of Maunalua Bay. The charter is $300 per hour, with a four-hour minimum and a six-passenger maximum. Fishing gear and a captain are included in the price, and you can keep some of your catch, something a lot of charters don't offer. Call the office, located in the Hawai'i Kai Shopping Center, to inquire about discounted rates.

Hiking, Biking, and Bird-Watching

HIKING
Kuli'ou'ou
Even though the southeast corner of O'ahu is one of the drier parts of the island, receiving less than 20 inches of rain annually, once you get off the coast and up into the southern reaches of the Ko'olau Range, the ecosystem changes dramatically. The **Kuli'ou'ou Ridge and Valley Trails** are a great example of this phenomenon. An excellent trek for any level of hiker, the mostly shaded Kuli'ou'ou Ridge trail follows Kuli'ou'ou Stream up Kuli'ou'ou Valley, traverses some switchbacks to the ridgeline, and terminates at a summit of 2,028 feet. With stunning views from Waimanalo and the windward coast all the way to Diamond Head, the five-mile round-trip hike passes through ironwood trees and Cook pines, and native 'ohi'a and lama forests. At about the halfway point there are two covered picnic tables to rest if you've gone far enough. If you prefer, at a signed junction, stay on the Kuli'ou'ou Valley trail, which passes a small pool and waterfall and terminates at a second waterfall, about two miles round-trip.

To get there from Kalanianaole Highway, turn mauka onto Kuli'ou'ou Road and find your way to the very back of the neighborhood, at the back of the valley. There is neighborhood street parking in the cul-de-sac. Take the one-lane paved road down to the stream and the trailhead.

Hawai'i Kai
For a great cardio workout and 360-degree views of the southeast shore, the **Koko Crater Trail** is a daunting 1,048 steps up the south side of Koko Crater. The stairs, actually railroad ties, follow the track of an old World War II military tramway that took supplies to the top of Koko Crater more than 1,000 feet to the summit. At the top you'll find several cement military installations and amazing views all around. From Kalanianaole Highway, turn mauka (to the mountain side) onto Koko Head Park Road and park in the Koko Head District Park parking lot. It's about a 0.25-mile walk to the base of the stairs.

BIRD-WATCHING
Kuli'ou'ou
Just to the west of Kuli'ou'ou Beach Park, the **Paiko Lagoon Wildlife Sanctuary** was established in 1981 to protect native Hawaiian waterbirds, migratory species, and their

Kuli'ou'ou Valley

only 1,048 stairs to the top of Koko Crater

habitat. Hawaiian stilts, plovers, ducks, and other fowl grace the shallow lagoon, which is naturally separated from Maunalua Bay by a small strip of earth complete with plants and trees. It is illegal to remove anything from the area. To get there from Kalanianaole Highway, turn onto Bay Street, which ends at the beach parking lot. The lagoon is directly to the west.

Adventure Sports

★ Hawai'i Kai

Hawai'i Kai Marina and Maunalua Bay are home to all the aquatic thrill rides available in this region for adventure seekers. Wakeboard, water ski, and ride a Bumper Tube and Banana Boat at high speeds in the marina, or Jet Ski, parasail, and drive a sub scooter in the bay. A more recent addition to the lineup is Jetlev flight, using a controlled, water-propelled jet pack that can send you soaring 30 feet into the air.

SeaBreeze Watersports (377 Keahole St., #E-103, 808/396-0100, opens 8:30am daily), based in the Hawai'i Kai Shopping Center, has a wide range of activities. Bumper Tubes and Banana Boat rides are $49 per person, Jet Ski rentals are $49 per person for a two-seater and $69 for a single rider. Jet Ski rates are based on half-hour rides. Parasail flights are $49 per person for a 7-10-minute ride, with two people sailing at a time, and

SeaBreeze is the only outfitter offering the Jetlev flight, starting at $169 for 15 minutes. It also offers snorkeling, scuba, speed sailing, and surfing lessons and has discounts for multiple-activity reservations.

Island Watersports Hawaii (377 Keahole St., 808/224-0076, www.islandwatersportshawaii.com, 7am-7pm daily), also based in the Hawai'i Kai Shopping Center, has the sub scooter, an electric submersible scooter that allows you to explore underwater without diving or scuba gear; $99 for a 20-minute ride. It has two-hour whale-watching cruises November-May for $99 and two-hour turtle-watching and sunset cruises also for $99 per person. In addition, it offers snorkeling, scuba, and fishing adventure packages.

Based in the Koko Marina Shopping Center, behind Kona Brewing Company, **Hawaii Water Sports Center** (7192

Riding the Thermals

The pervasive, fresh trade winds blowing up against the Koʻolau Range, combined with the splendid beauty of clear, tropical waters and verdant cliffs, creates the perfect amphitheater for hang gliding and paragliding. Makapuʻu is the premier ridge-soaring site, with five launch zones and one landing zone on the beach. Pilots also fly in the Kahana area. These are not recreational activities where you can merely rent a hang glider and jump off a cliff, but regulated endeavors for trained pilots, who must register with one of the accredited associations on Oʻahu to fly from specific sites.

Visiting paragliding pilots who have their own gear should contact the **Hawaii Paragliding Association** (53-040 Pokiwai Pl., www.windlines.net). Contact any board member, whose information is listed on the website, to become a member and get in the air. Visiting hang gliding pilots with gear need to contact the **Hawaiian Hang Gliding Association** (45-015 Likeke Pl., http://files.windlines.net/hha/index.htm). Contact information is on the site about becoming a member and flying windward skies.

Kalanianaole Hwy., 808/395-3773, http://hawaiiwatersportscenter.com, 8:30am-4pm daily) is another operator offering a slew of activities. Bumper tube and Banana Boat rides run $35 per person, wakeboarding and waterskiing runs $59 per person, and parasailing is $59 per person and the company flies side-by-side riders. Jet Skis are also available for $52 per person for two riders and $80 for a single-person craft. The center also offers scuba and snorkeling packages and multiple activity discounts.

Golf and Tennis

GOLF
Hawaiʻi Kai

With beautiful views of Koko Crater, the Makapuʻu cliffs, and the Pacific Ocean, which can be seen from every hole, the **Hawaiʻi Kai Golf Course** (8902 Kalanianaole Hwy., 808/395-2358, www.hawaiikaigolf.com/e), with two 18-hole courses, is both enjoyable and challenging. The Championship Course has the largest greens in the state with deep bunkers, and the Executive Course, a much shorter layout with undulating, sloping greens, focuses on putting and chipping for the most advanced golfers. The wind is always a factor here, blowing straight off the ocean and creating another issue to consider on these courses. Greens fees for the Championship Course are $110, $70 twilight (after 1pm), and fees for the Executive Course are $38.50 weekday, $43.50 weekend. The entrance to the golf course is right off Kalanianaole Highway, between Sandy Beach Park and Makapuʻu.

TENNIS

Public tennis courts can be found in Kahala and Hawaiʻi Kai and are located in district parks with restrooms, drinking fountains, and ample parking. District parks close 10pm-6am daily. In Kahala, there are two courts at **Kahala Community Park** (4495 Pahoa Ave., 808/733-7371), but the area around the courts can get extremely crowded on weekdays when the elementary school nearby lets out and the park fills up with kids for baseball and football practice. **Koko Head District Park** (423 Kaumakani St., 808/395-3096) in Hawaiʻi Kai has six similar courts.

Yoga and Spas

YOGA
Kahala
CorePower Yoga (4211 Waialae Ave., 866/441-9642, www.corepoweryoga.com) opened a brand-new studio in 2012 in the Kahala Mall. Located in the lower level directly in front of the Hunakai Street entrance, the climate-controlled venue offers power yoga, hot yoga, power fusion yoga, and yoga sculpt. The studio's complete package includes changing rooms, showers, lockers, and a full apparel boutique. The drop-in rate is $20 per session. Check the website for the schedule. **Power Yoga Hawaii** (4400 Kalanianaole Hwy., www.poweryogahawaii.com) teaches original power yoga and all classes are donation based, meaning there is a suggested cash donation of $15 per class, but you can leave whatever you feel is appropriate. You can use a credit card to rent mats and towels and to purchase water. Check the website for the class schedule. Reservations are not required.

Hawai'i Kai
In Hawai'i Kai, **Yoga Hawaii** (1152 Koko Head Ave., 808/739-9642, www.yoga-hawaii.com) has a real earthy and positive vibe. It offers a wide range of yoga, including beginner yoga, vinyasa, hatha, ashtanga, pregnancy yoga, and yoga for stress. Visit the Om Lounge on-site and pick up yoga apparel and local community-made products. It offers a three-class package for visitors for $45. **Bikram Yoga-Hawai'i Kai** (7192 Kalanianaole Hwy., 808/396-8838, www.bikramyogahawaiikai.com) is in the Koko Marina Shopping Center, on the second floor

across from the movie theater. This small, quiet, and intimate setting is heated by an infrared system. The first class is $15. Check the website for the full schedule.

SPAS
Kahala
Based in the ritzy Kahala Hotel & Resort, **Kahala Spa** (5000 Kahala Ave., 808/739-8938, www.kahalaresort.com/spa, 8am-9pm daily) has 10 lavish, tropically decorated treatment rooms with shower, deep-soak tub, changing area, and wardrobe closet. Known for their award-winning exceptional service, the staff combines the latest trends in spa therapy with organically grown, natural, and locally sourced ingredients from Hawai'i to produce the finest results in healing, relaxing, detoxifying, and rejuvenation. One-hour massages start at $170, with four different styles; 30-minute poolside massages and treatments start at $60; one-hour facials start at $160; and 75-minute signature massages begin at $230. The spa offers teeth whitening, waxing, and nail care services, as well as 90-minute massage and body treatment packages starting at $250.

Hawai'i Kai
Located in the Koko Marina Shopping Center, **J Boutique Salon & Day Spa** (7192 Kalanianaole Hwy., 808/396-1887, www.salonhawaiikai.com, 8:30am-7:30pm Tues.-Fri., 8:30-6 Sat., 8:30-5 Sun.) is a full-service salon with a few spa treatments: 75-minute facials start at $68 and a one-hour massage is $65. It also does makeup, eyelash extensions and tinting, nails, and waxing.

Shopping

KAHALA

Kahala Mall (4211 Waialae Ave., 808/732-7736, www.kahalamallcenter.com, 10am-9pm Mon.-Sat., 10am-5pm Sun.) is the nexus for shopping in Kahala. The small and airy two-story mall is conveniently located right off the H-1 freeway. From Honolulu, take the Waialae Avenue exit and the mall is on your right. You'll find the mall basics like **Macy's** (808/737-5429), **Longs Drugs** (808/732-0784), **Starbucks** (808/737-0283), **Jamba Juice** (808/734-7988), and even **Whole Foods** (808/738-0820). Kahala Mall also has some unique boutique stores that are worth a look, as well as a movie theatre,

Consolidated Theatres Kahala 8 (4211 Waialae Ave., Ste. 3080, 808/733-6243, www.consolidatedtheatres.com/kahala), located on the ground floor.

Milo HNL (808/734-8488) is a local surf shop featuring vintage lines from well-known surf brands. **In My Closet** (808/734-5999) is a small, hip boutique with eclectic and fashionable clothing and accessories. **Island Sole** (808/738-8430) is a one-stop shop for slippers, or what you might call flip-flops or sandals. If you'd like island-themed decorations for your living spaces, check out **SoHa Living** (808/591-9777). The store carries a plethora of shells and beachy knickknacks.

Food

KAHALA

Quick Bites

The Counter (4211 Waialae Ave., E-1, 808/739-5100, www.thecounterburger.com/honolulu, 11am-9pm Sun.-Thurs., 11am-10pm Fri.-Sat., $7-15) is Kahala's premier burger joint. The menu, as well as the interior, is quite modern, and the restaurant's take on the burger is welcoming and refreshing. With signature burgers and a build-your-own menu, there are a wide variety of gourmet and regional toppings and aiolis to choose from, as well as different size burgers, up to one-pound patties. Put all that on a bun or in a bowl, your choice, but either way, it's stacked high. One caution to the brave: because everything is priced individually, your custom burger can cost you a small fortune.

Puka's (4211 Waialae Ave., Ste. 2000, 808/738-0820, www.wholefoodsmarket.com/service/pukas-beerwinepupus, 10am-9pm daily, $8-17), a small pub and restaurant inside Whole Foods Market, offers 20 craft beers on tap, wine, and a small, but delicious selection

of burgers, pizza and other fresh takes on bar food. It offers beer flights, which pair nicely with the IPA-battered fish-and-chips or the fried-green-tomato BLT.

Japanese

★ Located inside Kahala Mall by the movie theater, **Goma Tei** (4211 Waialae Ave., G07, 808/732-9188, www.gomatei.com, 11am-9:30pm Mon.-Thurs., till 10pm Fri.-Sat., till 9pm Sun., $11-15) has some of the best ramen on the island. This busy, popular restaurant offers flavorful broths, fresh vegetables, soft noodles, rich cuts of meat, and crispy gyoza, which are worth any wait.

Steak and Seafood

Plumeria Beach House (5000 Kahala Ave., 808/739-8760, www.kahalaresort.com, 6:30am-10pm daily, $26-45), an open-air seaside restaurant inside the Kahala Hotel & Resort, serves breakfast, lunch, and dinner and has entrée and buffet options. The small menu selection for lunch and dinner means each dish is carefully crafted to capture the best of Hawai'i regional and Pacific Rim cuisine. This comfortable island home setting takes advantage of beautiful ocean views. The Plumeria Beach House is best known for its breakfast buffet, but it also has many other à la carte choices as well.

Also in the Kahala Hotel & Resort is **Hoku's** (5000 Kahala Ave., 808/739-8760, www.kahalaresort.com, 5:30pm-10pm Wed.-Sun., $28-69), an award-winning fine-dining restaurant. The food is a fusion of Hawaiian, Asian, and European cuisine, with steak, duck, lamb, chicken, and fish entrées as well as a sushi menu. An artisan cheese menu makes for a delightful appetizer, and the Sunday brunch, 10am-2pm, features a wide variety of seafood and a prime rib and lamb cutting station.

Italian

Assaggio Bistro (4346 Waialae Ave., 808/732-1011, 11:30am-2:30pm and 5pm-9:30pm Sun.-Thurs., 5pm-10pm Fri. Sat., $16-36) has a huge menu of classic Italian dishes. Its portions come in two sizes, small and large, with the small portion being more than enough for a complete meal. Each main dish has the choice of pasta, potatoes, rice, or vegetables for the side. Reservations are recommended. To get to Assaggio from Hawai'i Kai, take the Waialae Avenue off-ramp and turn right into the parking lot from the ramp. From Waialae Avenue eastbound, turn left onto Kilauea Avenue and then make an immediate right into the parking lot.

Mediterranean

Located on the corner of Kilauea Avenue and Pahoa Avenue is a popular BYOB called the **Olive Tree Café** (4614 Kilauea Ave., Ste. 107, 808/737-0303, 5pm-10pm daily, $11-15). Offering Mediterranean and Greek fare, the menu has plenty of vegetarian as well as meat options. The environment is warm, friendly, and casual, with both indoor and outdoor seating. The café has open seating and there is no wait service. It is a popular joint, so it's best to arrive either early or late to avoid a long wait. Luckily, there is a wine shop just next door.

Health Food

Not only is **Whole Foods** (4211 Waialae Ave., 808/738-0820, www.wholefoodsmarket.com/stores/honolulu, 7am-10pm daily, $3.50 and up) a market where you can pick up organic and locally grown produce and vegetables, but it also makes to order sushi, Chinese food, burgers, Mexican food, sandwiches, pizza, and it has a hot-food bar, salad bar, and dessert and coffee bar. Although known to be high priced, Whole Foods does have $1 street tacos on Tuesday and $2 off per pound from the hot-food bar on Wednesday. It is located in the Kahala Mall, ground level, right off Waialae Avenue.

Lanikai Juice (4346 Waialae Ave., 808/732/7200, www.lanikaijuice.com, 7am-8pm Mon.-Sat., 7am-7pm Sun., $5-8) is a locally owned and operated smoothie shop that uses organic and locally sourced products when available.

Aloha Salads (4211 Waialae Ave., 808/735-8334, www.alohasalads.com, 10am-9pm daily, $6-10) is another locally owned and operated establishment dedicated to using locally sourced products and produce and gourmet meats and cheese. Its menu is simple yet sophisticated, and it has a nice selection of island-inspired soups, sandwiches, and salads. With greens from the North Shore, tomatoes from the windward side, papayas from Moloka'i, and ahi tuna from Hawai'i waters, the food is fresh, delicious, and eco-conscious. The Aloha Passion with grilled steak and the Ono Island Ahi salads are the most popular. Aloha is located inside Kahala Mall on the ground level right next to Whole Foods.

AINA HAINA
Quick Bites

The small community of Aina Haina has a strip mall, the **Aina Haina Shopping Center** (820-850 W. Hind Dr.), along Kalanianaole Highway that has a complete sampling of services and a handful of eateries. **Jack's Restaurant** (808/373-4034, 6:30am-2pm daily, $1-13) serves biscuits and gravy, eggs, omelets, and other seafood breakfast and lunch dishes. Simple and good, the eggs with corned beef hash are a local favorite. You can pick up a big, handmade sandwich at **Foodland Farms** (808/373-2222, 5am-11pm daily), or dig a spoon and chopsticks into some *phô* at **Mama Pho** (808/373-8887, 11am-9pm Sun.-Thurs., 11am-10pm Fri.-Sat., $4-10). Kid's *phô* bowls come with ice cream and a drink.

Sweets and Treats

If you're looking to satisfy your sweet tooth, the Aina Haina Shopping Center has two delicious options. **Cake Couture** (808/373-9750, http://cakecouture.com, 10:30am-6:30pm Mon.-Fri., 10:30am-5:30pm Sat., $3-4) has ridiculously delicious cupcakes in nearly 40 distinctive flavors that rotate throughout the week. Check the website for the flavor schedule.

★ **Uncle Clay's House of Pure Aloha** (808/373-5111, www.houseofpurealoha.com, 11am-6pm Mon.-Thurs., 10:30am-8pm Fri.-Sun., $4-9) indulges in the local favorite, shave ice. Rising above the competition with handmade syrups actually produced from locally sourced ingredients and friendly, family-style service, Uncle Clay's takes shave ice to a new culinary level. The small shop also has healthy grab-bag snacks for sale.

NIU VALLEY
Steak and Seafood

The Niu Valley Shopping Center in Niu Valley has one noteworthy tenant on the food front, **Le Bistro** (5730 Kalanianaole Hwy., 808/373-7990, 5:30pm-9pm Wed.-Mon., $25-40). This contemporary French restaurant, casual yet elegant, is a fixture in the Honolulu dining scene. The chef recommends his legendary short ribs, a staple on the menu since the restaurant opened over a decade ago, and the beef quartet, a sampler entrée chosen by the

chef himself. Robust soups, stews, and salads round out the menu.

HAWAI'I KAI
Quick Bites

The Shack (377 Keahole St., 808/396-1919, 11am-2am daily, $7-24) is the quintessential pub and sports bar in the Hawai'i Kai area. Being dark, a bit musty, having dark wood furniture, darts, billiards, TVs all around, classic bar food, including ribs, and interesting, even curious, decorations makes this bar come alive. Not to mention, it's located right on the water in the Hawai'i Kai Shopping Center, with outside seating as well. And the *pau hana* (happy hour) and daily specials will make you extra happy.

Steak and Seafood

At the water's edge in the Koko Marina Center in Hawai'i Kai is the ★ **Kona Brewing Co.** (7192 Kalanianaole Hwy., 808/396-5662, http://konabrewingco.com, 11am-10pm daily, $12-28), a local brewpub serving fresh steak and seafood, all with a twist—its signature brew is incorporated in some way into most of the recipes. It has a huge pizza menu, specialty beers on tap you can't find in the stores, and brews to go. Kona also has a great weekday happy hour 3pm-6pm: half off draft beers and select appetizer specials.

For fine dining in Hawai'i Kai, ★ **Roy's** (6600 Kalanianaole Hwy., 808/396-7697, 5:30pm-9pm Mon.-Thurs., 5:30pm-9:30pm Fri., 5pm-9:30pm Sat., 5pm-9pm Sun., $15-45) is a must. It serves signature Hawaiian fusion cuisine with exemplary service and attention to detail, and its sushi creations pair wonderfully with the entrées. It also has indoor and lanai bar seating that is first-come, first-served, accompanied by soft, live music, a much more casual option than the main, second floor dining room with beautiful views of Maunalua Bay.

Health Food and Cafés

In the Hawai'i Kai Shopping Center is **Kale's**

Natural Foods (377 Keahole St., 808/396-6993, www.kalesnaturalfoods.com, 8am-8pm Mon.-Fri., 8am-5pm Fri.-Sat., $6-10), a market and deli serving natural products and organic produce. The small kitchen specializes in vegetarian, vegan, macrobiotic foods, and free-range meat options. The food is fresh, homemade, and surprisingly creative.

Moena Café (7192 Kalanianaole Hwy., #D-101, 808/888-7716, www.moenacafe.com, 6:30am-3pm daily, $9-18) is a local favorite, serving breakfast and lunch. Located in the Koko Marina Center across from the theater, the small dining room is clean and bright. It offers delicious fruit bowls, Panini sandwiches, salads, pancakes, eggs Benedict and a mean short rib loco moco. There are only a handful of tables and its very popular, so be prepared for a wait. It also uses local ingredients throughout the menu.

Pa'ina Café (7192 Kalanianaole Hwy., #E-123A, 808/356-2829, www.painacafe. com, 11am-7:30pm Sun.-Thurs., 11am-8pm Fri.-Sat., $7-12) is a small, take-out café in the Koko Marina Center. It offers a variety of fresh and delicious poke bowls, salads, and a few tasty sandwiches. If you're in the mood for poke, this is the place in Hawai'i Kai. There is plenty of outdoor seating around the marina to enjoy your meal.

Sweets and Treats

After lunch or dinner, **Bubbies** (7192 Kalanianaole Hwy., #D-103 808/396-8722, http://bubbiesicecream.com, 10am-11pm Sun.-Thurs., 10am-midnight Fri.-Sat., $3-8) is a must. The shop is reminiscent of an old-school ice-cream parlor and has been making ice cream and desserts in Hawai'i for over 30 years. It specializes in traditional, creamy ice cream, sorbet, and mochi ice cream. If you're visiting for an event, it's a great place to pick up a homemade ice-cream cake.

MAKAPU'U
Quick Bites

Inside Sea Life Park you'll find **Pink's Hot Dogs** (41-202 Kalanianaole Hwy., 808/259-7933, 10am-3:30pm daily, $4-9). Yes, it's true. The Hollywood legend has opened a signature location on O'ahu. You'll find the same burgers and hot dogs piled high with all manner of toppings. A quirky location, you have to pay the parking attendant a small fee to park for one hour and then you'll be reimbursed when you leave with proof of receipt from Pink's.

Information and Services

LIBRARY

Internet access is available at the **Aina Haina Public Library** (5246 Kalanianaole Hwy., 808/377-2456, http://ainahainalibrary. org, 1pm-8pm Tues., 10am-5pm Wed.-Sat.), and the **Hawai'i Kai Public Library** (249 Lunalilo Home Rd., 808/397-5833). Visitors need a valid Hawaii Public Library System (HSPLS) card to use an Internet computer. Three-month visitor cards are available for $10. You can reserve Internet computer time online or in person. You can also find printed bus schedules, too.

MAIL

Post offices on the southeast shore are located in Kahala (4354 Pahoa Ave., 808/737-8937) on the ocean side of Kahala Mall, in the Aina Haina Shopping Center (820 W. Hind Dr.), and in Hawai'i Kai (7040 Hawai'i Kai Dr., 808/396-6431).

Getting There and Around

CAR

Getting around the southeast coast is very simple, because, for the most part, the highway is hemmed in by the Pacific Ocean on one side and the Ko'olau Mountains on the other. On the southeast shore, the H-1 becomes Kalanianaole Highway (Highway 72) as it merges with Waialae Avenue. Kalanianaole Highway circles the southeastern tip of O'ahu and runs through Waimanalo before pulling away from the coast and intersecting the Pali Highway (Highway 61) at the Kamehameha Highway (Highway 83) junction in the Maunawili area. Kamehameha Highway runs north/south through the town of Kane'ohe, regaining the coast for the rest of the way to the North Shore.

To get there from Waikiki, you can take the scenic drive around Diamond Head and through Kahala on Kahala Avenue. Take Kealaolu Avenue to get back to the H-1. From there heading east, the freeway immediately turns into Kalanianaole Highway. The highway is the only main thoroughfare around this side of the island.

BUS

TheBus (808/848-5555, www.thebus.org) has several routes accessing southeast locales. If you're traveling from Waikiki, get to Kahala, Hanauma Bay, Sandy Beach and Sea Life Park by using Routes 22 or 23. From Honolulu, get to Hawai'i Kai via Routes 80, 80A, or 82. From Kailua, Routes 56, 57, and 57A go to Sea Life Park, where you'll need to jump on the 22 to get from there to Kahala. TheBus' app, **DaBus,** is available for Apple and Android smartphone users.

RIDE-HAILING

Uber and **Lyft** are available in the area.

Kailua and Windward

Look for ★ to find recommended sights, activities, dining, and lodging.

Highlights

★ **Ho'omaluhia Botanical Garden:** Backed right up to the Ko'olau Mountains, this botanical garden is known for its lake, canopy trees, and myriad species of palms from around the world. The bird-watching is phenomenal (page 175).

★ **La'ie Point State Wayside:** A dramatic offshore, wave-battered sea arch sits just off a rugged point jutting sharply out into the Pacific. It's a great place to pull up and enjoy a quiet lunch or fish from the rocks. There's a cliff-jumping spot on the south side—if you dare (page 177).

★ **Waimanalo Beach Park:** Empty white-sand beach, ironwood trees, and calm water: Waimanalo has everything you need (page 179).

★ **Kailua Beach Park:** Kailua Beach Park is the destination for ocean activities like swimming, stand-up paddling, kayaking, fishing, kiteboarding, and sailboarding (page 179).

★ **Kahana Bay Beach Park:** Where the valley opens to the ocean, you'll find this perfectly moon-shaped beach of fine, soft sand. The water is shallow and calm, and towering trees shade the deep-set bay. Remnants of an ancient Hawaiian fishpond still stand on the south side of the bay (page 183).

© AVALON TRAVEL

★ **Mokulua Islands:** Don't miss paddling out to the Mokulua Islands. When you reach an islet, turn around and looking back to the mainland, for an amazing view with the Ko'olaus rising up behind the beach (page 187).

Known for its ample rainfall, the lush and dramatic corduroy cliffs, the windward side of O'ahu, the eastern shore of the island, spans the entire length of the Ko'olau Mountain Range.

Kamehameha Highway, which winds along the shoreline, provides excellent opportunities to pull off the highway and find a nook of beach to enjoy. Windward towns, save for Kailua and Kane'ohe, are primarily residential and historically rooted in agriculture and aquaculture: *kalo lo'i* (taro), banana plantations, papaya, and fishponds. A drive up the windward coast is a trip back in time, with weathered wooden fruit stands offering family farm goods. It's a leisurely drive that should be enjoyed at every turn in the road.

The vegetation on the windward side of O'ahu is owed, in large part, to the wet weather. The predominant trade winds blow out of the northeast and push air heavy with moisture up against the Ko'olau Range. As the warm, humid air rises, it cools, condenses, and forms clouds, which become saturated and dump their payload, freshwater raindrops, down on the coast and the mountains.

In addition to the stunning landscape,

Kailua and Kane'ohe have developed into major population centers and desirable destinations, each with its own draw. Kailua is full of hip shops, restaurants, and some of the best fine-white-sand beaches on O'ahu. It's also known for kitesurfing and kayaking, with several islets just offshore (two of which are only accessible via kayak). Kane'ohe town definitely caters to locals with its dining options and shopping services, but there are more than enough reasons for a visit to the Ho'omaluhia Botanical Garden and the famous Kane'ohe Bay Sandbar, perfect for a half-day kayaking adventure.

Here, on the windward side, other than the ranch tours at Kualoa Ranch and the Polynesian Cultural Center, everything is centered around the ocean. Whether you're snorkeling, fishing, stand-up paddling, or walking along a deserted stretch of sand, the beaches and the scenery are the main attractions. If you see a nice spot along your drive and feel

Previous: Kailua Beach Park; Kane'ohe Bay. **Above:** bird-watching on the edge of the Kawainui Marsh.

Kailua and Windward

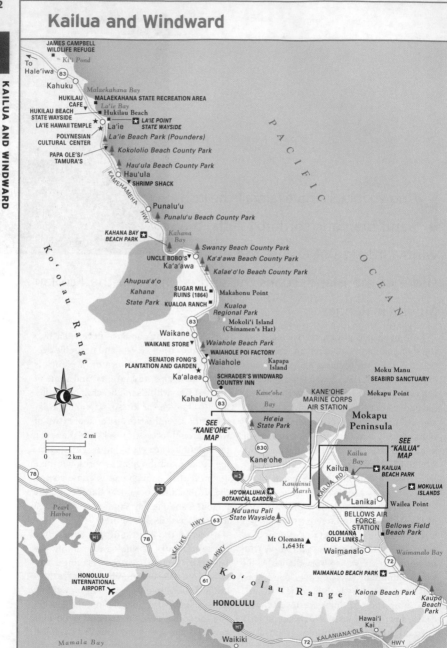

To Hale'iwa

JAMES CAMPBELL WILDLIFE REFUGE
Ki'i Pond
83
Kahuku
Malaekahana Bay
HUKILAU CAFE
MALAEKAHANA STATE RECREATION AREA
La'ie Bay
HUKILAU BEACH STATE WAYSIDE
Hukilau Beach
LA'IE HAWAII TEMPLE
La'ie
LA'IE POINT STATE WAYSIDE
POLYNESIAN CULTURAL CENTER
La'ie Beach Park (Pounders)
PAPA OLE'S/ TAMURA'S
Kokololio Beach County Park
Hau'ula Beach County Park
Hau'ula
KAMEHAMEHA HWY
SHRIMP SHACK

Punalu'u
Punalu'u Beach County Park

Kahana Bay
KAHANA BAY BEACH PARK
Swanzy Beach County Park
UNCLE BOBO'S
Ka'a'awa Beach County Park
Ka'a'awa
Kalae'o'io Beach County Park

Ahupua'a o Kahana State Park

Ko'olau Range

SUGAR MILL RUINS (1864)
Makahonu Point
KUALOA RANCH
Kualoa Regional Park
83
Mokoli'i Island (Chinamen's Hat)
Waikane
WAIKANE STORE
Waiahole Beach Park
WAIAHOLE POI FACTORY
SENATOR FONG'S PLANTATION AND GARDEN
Waiahole
Kapapa Island
Ka'alaea
SCHRADER'S WINDWARD COUNTRY INN
Kahalu'u
83
Kane'ohe Bay

Moku Manu SEABIRD SANCTUARY
Mokapu Point

KANE'OHE MARINE CORPS AIR STATION

Mokapu Peninsula

SEE "KANE'OHE" MAP
He'eia State Park
830
Kane'ohe
H3
HO'OMALUHIA BOTANICAL GARDEN

SEE "KAILUA" MAP
Kailua Bay
Kailua
KAILUA RD
KAILUA BEACH PARK
Kawainui Marsh
Lanikai
MOKULUA ISLANDS
Wailea Point

PACIFIC OCEAN

78
H3
Pearl Harbor
H1
78
LIKELIKE HWY
63
Nu'uanu Pali State Wayside
PALI HWY
61
HONOLULU INTERNATIONAL AIRPORT
Mt Olomana 1,643ft
Ko'olau Range
BELLOWS AIR FORCE STATION
Bellows Field Beach Park
OLOMANA GOLF LINKS
Waimanalo
72
Waimanalo Bay
WAIMANALO BEACH PARK
Kaiona Beach Park
Kaupo Beach Park

HONOLULU
H1
Waikiki
72
KALANIANA'OLE HWY
Hawai'i Kai
HWY

Mamala Bay
Diamond Head
Maunalua Bay

0   2 mi
0   2 km

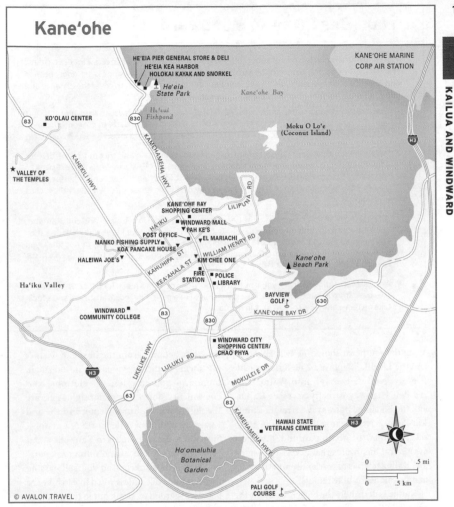

Kane'ohe

the need to pull over and swim, do it! The closer you look, the more you'll find the hidden gems. Don't forget, there are a few good hikes, if you don't mind mud and mosquitoes.

PLANNING YOUR TIME

The windward side of O'ahu, from Waimanalo in the south to La'ie up north, spans about 35 miles. With a 35 mph speed limit on both the Kalanianaole Highway and Kamehameha Highway, it's not a drive you want to rush (or can rush, for that matter). You'll want to

earmark at least half a day to take the scenic drive up to La'ie town from Waimanalo. If you're interested in sights and beach activities in addition to the drive, you'll likely want two days to really explore this region.

With its beautiful scenery and ample recreational activities, the windward side draws many people. There are no hotels; however, you'll find plenty of vacation rentals and B&Bs in Kailua and Lanikai. For those driving in from Waikiki, there are three options to access the windward side: the Kalanianaole Highway

Your Best Day in Windward

The windward region is a mix of suburban and rural communities and covers a lot of coastline. Framed by the Pacific Ocean and the Koʻolau mountain range, the coastline is strikingly diverse and beautiful. To experience the area to its fullest, a rental car is a must to cover the distance and have the flexibility for a change of plans if the weather dictates.

- Grab breakfast and a coffee, then from Waikiki take the Likelike Highway to Kaneʻohe and start your morning with a walk through **Hoʻomaluhia Botanical Garden.** Or, continue on to **Kualoa Ranch** and take a tour of the ranch and the surrounding area.

- Head back south toward Kailua. For lunch, head into Waimanalo and try out **I Love ʻIA,** for a healthy lunch, or make your way into Kailua Town and pick up a sandwich at **Kalapawai Market.** Head to **Kailua Beach Park** or **Lanikai** for a beach day. Lanikai has beautiful views of the Mokulua Islands; Kailua Beach is one of the most beautiful white-sand beaches on Oʻahu.

- After taking in all that beauty from the beach, you'll want to get in the water and cruise around. The best way to do that is to rent a kayak. Kailua town is the hub for kayak rentals. Either stick around in Kailua and paddle to **Flat Island** and the **Mokulua Islands,** or put the kayak on the roof and go exploring. Other great areas for kayaking are **Kaneʻohe Bay, Kualoa Beach Park,** and **Kahana Bay.**

- After all that outdoor activity, you'll be in the mood for a delicious meal. Try **Buzz's,** just across the street from Kailua Beach Park, for a great steak. For a more relaxed atmosphere and a local take on Pan-Latin fare, try **Cactus** in Kailua.

along the southeast shore, the Pali Highway, and the Likelike Highway. The Kalanianaole Highway will deliver you into Waimanalo, the Pali Highway directly accesses Kailua, and the Likelike Highway is a straight shot to Kaneʻohe. A rental car will provide the greatest flexibility for getting around, but there are several bus routes that access the region too. Kailua town is bike friendly and there are many options for bike rentals.

Kailua is definitely the biggest draw for the area. The town offers upscale shopping and dining and the beaches are amazing: calm, clean water, white sand, and beautiful scenery. Kailua could be a day trip in itself, but plan for at least half a day here if you're driving in. It's a great locale for a nice dinner at the end of a busy day. Kailua is densely populated and gets a large amount of daily visitor traffic, so the town frequently sees heavy traffic and the main beach parks get very crowded on the weekends and beautiful, sunny days.

Waimanalo is a great stop for a beach day and lunch, and the beaches north of Kaneʻohe

Bay are a getaway from the bustle of Oʻahu's big towns. In these regions you'll find small, mom-and-pop eateries, gas stations, and convenience stores. The major sights here are the Polynesian Cultural Center in Laʻie and Kualoa Ranch, a few miles north of Kaneʻohe. Since there are no beaches in Kaneʻohe and it generally serves a local and military population, you'll most likely find yourself passing through Kaneʻohe unless you'd like to hike the botanical garden or kayak out to the sandbars in the bay.

The weather changes fast on the windward side. A typical day might start out with sun in the morning, then clouds by midday, and finally heavy showers by the afternoon. Still, typical rain showers are often fleeting localized events. Just because a shower is passing by doesn't mean you need to pack up the beach gear for the day. The best thing to do if you're planning a beach day on the windward side is to hope for the best and prepare for the worst. At least it's still warm when it rains.

ORIENTATION

The Makapu'u headland is the easternmost tip of the island. To the immediate north is Waimanalo, an agricultural town with a few food trucks, plate-lunch eateries, and white-sand beaches lined by tall wispy ironwood trees. Waimanalo is known for its local farms, ranches, and beach camping. The Kalanianaole Highway runs through Waimanalo to Kailua, where it intersects the Pali Highway.

To the north of Waimanalo is Kailua. Kailua offers boutique shopping and upscale restaurants, while the beaches are some of the prettiest on the island—fine white sand stretching for miles along the coast. The beaches are generally windy and known for kitesurfing and windsurfing. To the immediate south of Kailua is the quaint Lanikai neighborhood, where the Mokulua Islands sit right offshore.

Complete with a mall and ample fast food, Kane'ohe is one of the larger and more congested towns on the windward coast. It's to the north of Kailua. Because of the bay there are no beaches, but the sheltered waters offer great potential for kayaking in the bay and out to the Kane'ohe Bay Sandbar. Fishing is also the draw here.

Once you travel past the northern neighborhoods of Kane'ohe, Kamehameha Highway hugs the coast from one beach town to the next. Most are quite small—maybe a food truck and convenience store—and others are strictly residential. But they all have beautiful beaches in common. Kualoa Regional Park and Kualoa Ranch are points of interest in the Kualoa area. Ka'a'awa leads to Kahana Bay, with the remnants of an ancient Hawaiian fishpond and hiking in the valley. Farther north is Punalu'u, then Hau'ula, and finally La'ie, a town defined by its connection to the Church of Jesus Christ of Latter-day Saints and the home of the Polynesian Cultural Center, which is under the church's wing.

Sights

KAILUA
Ulupo Heiau State Historic Site

The massive stone platform of the **Ulupo Heiau State Historic Site** was supposedly built by the legendary *menehune* and shows remarkable skill with stone, measuring 140 feet wide by 180 feet long by 30 feet high at its tallest edge, although the stepped front wall has partially collapsed under a rockfall. The *heiau* overlooks Kawainui Marsh, and below the *heiau*, you can see traditional *kalo lo'i*, taro growing in small ponds. Ulupo Heiau was one of three *heiau* that once overlooked the former fishpond. The other two, located on the west side of the marsh, are Pahukini and Holomakani Heiau. Some restoration has been done to Pahukini Heiau, but both remain largely untouched and inaccessible.

To get to Ulupo Heiau as you approach Kailua on the Pali Highway, turn left at the Castle Medical Center onto Uluoa Street, following it one block to Manu Aloha Street, where you turn right. Turn right again onto Manu O'o and park in the Windward YMCA parking lot. The *heiau* is directly behind the YMCA building.

KANE'OHE
★ Ho'omaluhia Botanical Garden

Ho'omaluhia Botanical Garden (45-680 Luluku Rd., 808/233-7323, www1.honolulu.gov/parks/hbg/hmbg.htm, 9am-4pm daily, closed Christmas and New Year's Day) is a botanical gem nestled at the base of the Ko'olau Range. With 400 acres of geographically organized gardens—covering the Philippines, Hawai'i, Africa, Sri Lanka, India, Polynesia, Melanesia, Malaysia, and

Tropical America—and a network of trails interconnecting the plantings, one could spend an entire day in the garden. The visitors center is staffed with extremely knowledgeable docents who can help identify birds and interesting plants in flower during your visit. You can also grab a trail map there. A paved road links all the plantings and there are separate parking lots for each, so you can pick and choose where you'd like to spend your time. Drive slowly on the road, as the path is a lovely, popular walk for residents and garden guests. Ho'omaluhia also boasts its own lake, Lake Waimaluhia. Catch-and-release fishing is permitted on the weekends 10am-2pm. The garden is serene, quiet, lush, and often wet, so be prepared for the passing shower, mud, and mosquitoes. Rustic camping is also permitted from Friday afternoon till Monday morning. Check in at the visitors center for a pass. The garden is located in a residential area on Luluku Road, which you can access from both Kamehameha Highway and the Likelike Highway.

Ho'omaluhia Botanical Garden

Coconut Island

Coconut Island (808/235-9302, http://coconutislandnews.blogspot.com), tucked away deep in Kane'ohe Bay, literally had its 15 seconds of fame as part of the opening reel of scenic shots for the 1960s TV sitcom hit *Gilligan's Island*. But the island has a much more eclectic and interesting history than just appearing on television. Once fertile fishing grounds belonging to Kamehameha I and Bernice Pauahi Bishop, the island was purchased in the 1930s and expanded by a young heir to the Fleischmann's Yeast company. He transformed it into a zoo and aquarium, as well as a tuna-fish packing plant, the remnants of which are still visible on the island. The island changed hands several more times over the decades and today is the Hawai'i Institute of Marine Biology and one of the seminal locations for marine research on O'ahu. The education outreach arm of the institute offers tours once or twice a month, depending on docent availability, for a nominal fee based on the number of people in your party. Call for a reservation or visit the blog for more information.

If you wish to simply view the island from shore, you can get a great view of the island from the elevated vantage of Lilipuna Road as it hugs the coastline. There is no public parking on Lilipuna for the institute, but you can find street parking a little way south of the dock and walk back to the point to snap some pictures. Be careful walking along the road, as there is no shoulder or designated pedestrian area. Turn onto Lilipuna Road from Kamehameha Highway at the north end of Kane'ohe town, by the Windward Mall.

Valley of the Temples

Located along the Kahekili Highway just north of Kane'ohe town, **Valley of the Temples** (47-200 Kahekili Hwy., 808/239-8811, www.valley-of-the-temples.com) is a memorial park with lush landscaping and a wealth of gardens and temples to honor many faiths. The memorial park is open to the public, and the peaceful and serene setting is only amplified by the natural amphitheater of cliffs of the Koʻolaus.

KUALOA TO LAʻIE

Chinaman's Hat

Just offshore from **Kualoa Regional Beach Park** (49-479 Kamehameha Hwy.) is the curious islet known as **Chinaman's Hat**. Mokoliʻi Island is its Hawaiian name. The island is a quick kayak trip from the beach and has a tiny private alcove of sand on the back side. You can hike, or rather scramble, up to its 213-foot summit.

Kualoa Ranch

Kualoa Ranch (49-560 Kamehameha Hwy., 808/237-7321, www.kualoa.com) is both a 4,000-acre working cattle ranch, activity, and cultural center and the site for many of the Hollywood blockbuster movies filmed in Hawaiʻi (*Jurassic Park*, *Godzilla*, and *50 First Dates*, to name a few). It offers historical and cultural tours like its Movie Sites and Ranch Tour, Jungle Expeditions Tour, Ancient Fishing Grounds, and Tropical Garden Tour, or Kahiko Hula Lessons starting at $24 adult, $15 children. For adventure tours, it provides one- and two-hour ATV or horseback

packages, starting at $69. It also has venues for weddings and corporate events and even has tours that include lunch or dinner. Cultural/historic tour package tours start at $59, adventure tour packages start at $99.

★ Laʻie Point State Wayside

The **Laʻie Point State Wayside** is a hidden marvel, the perfect place to pull up to the edge of the rugged point, relax, have a snack, and watch waves crash against a small seabird sanctuary just offshore, a little island noteworthy for its sea arch. There are trashcans, but no services in the area. It is also a popular spot for cliff jumping. On the south face of the cliff is a small area where jumpers plunge roughly 30 feet to the warm water below. There is a nook in the cliff to climb out of the water and up an extremely sharp and rocky gorge to the top of the cliff. It's best to watch a few others jump and get back up before you try. There are no lifeguards, so you're on your own, quite far from a sandy beach.

Tucked away at the back of a neighborhood and out of view from the highway, turn off of Kamehameha Highway onto Anemoku Street, then hang a right onto Naupaka Street and follow it to the end of the point. Anemoku Street

Coconut Island

is across the highway from the Laʻie Village Center.

Laʻie Hawaii Temple

Built in 1919, the **Laʻie Hawaii Temple** (55-600 Naniloa Loop, 808/293-2427, www.ldschurchtemples.com/laie, 9am-8pm daily) was the first temple erected by the Church of Jesus Christ of Latter-day Saints outside the state of Utah, and also the first in Polynesia. You can tour the grounds and gardens of this stark-white, grand edifice, and there's an accompanying visitors center free to the public.

Beaches

The **beaches** along Oʻahu's windward coast, from Waimanalo to Laʻie, are raw, natural, and often windswept, thanks to the pervasive trade winds blowing from northwest to southeast. The different ribbons of sand tend to be bastions of solitude, where you can pull off the highway and find a quiet nook under *naupaka* and palm trees. A barrier reef stretching the length of the windward coast keeps waves at most beaches to a minimum. You'll find driftwood, rocks, fine white sand, shells, and spectacular views of the lush Koʻolau Mountains from the water's edge. Beachgoers should be prepared for passing showers, as the trade winds also bring rain. Kailua beaches, especially at the two main beach parks, are usually the most crowded in the area.

WAIMANALO
Kaiona Beach Park

About a mile north of the research pier on Kalanianaole Highway in Waimanalo is a small grassy park with restrooms and showers and a narrow but beautiful beach. **Kaiona Beach Park** is a favorite area for local families, with shallow, clean, and clear water great for swimming and snorkeling. The ocean floor, a combination of white sand and reef, gives the water a magnificent azure color. Just to the south of the beach access is Pahonu Pond, an ancient Hawaiian turtle pond. Today, it's perfect for the youngest of kids to get comfortable in the water in a calm and sheltered setting. The locals also call the beach Shriners after the Shriners Beach Club at the

Laʻie Point State Wayside

Disappearing Sands

It's no secret: O'ahu's beaches are its top attractions and best commodities, for recreational, social, and cultural reasons. But in some locales where urban development has marched right up to the high tide mark, the beaches are in serious danger of disappearing, if they're not gone already. There are natural processes in Hawai'i, like large swell events, seasonal currents, and storms with heavy rainfall, that move sand up and down the beach, offshore, and then back again. This natural and transient process is called coastal erosion and has been going on for centuries and will continue to shape the beaches until the island erodes back into the Pacific altogether.

In the meantime, recent human alteration of the shoreline has played a detrimental leading role in the disappearance of sand and entire beaches altogether. On O'ahu, when the ocean shoreline encroaches within 20 feet of a structure, property owners can be granted a variance that allows them to build a seawall to protect the property. Once the natural beach dune system is stripped away and replaced with a seawall, the beach has no way to store or replenish sand for periods of natural coastal erosion, leading to a permanent state of beach erosion. You'll find this phenomenon in Kahala, Lanikai, and on other stretches of beach along the windward coast where dwellings have been built right up to sand. Where the shoreline is armored, the beaches have washed away.

---

water's edge. The free parking lot is small and fills up quickly. Use caution if you park along the road. The restroom at the beach park closes 7pm-7am daily.

★ Waimanalo Beach Park

Right in the heart of Waimanalo town, **Waimanalo Beach Park** offers the same fine white sand, great snorkeling, swimming, and azure water as all along the Waimanalo coast. The beach park has free parking, showers, restrooms, and a grassy camping area, which is predominantly used by the homeless. While lean-tos and laundry lines don't sound like paradise, the camping area is just a small portion of the three-mile beach, one of the longest on O'ahu. The beach is also lined with ironwood trees, so it's easy to duck into the shade if the sun becomes too intense. Mostly uncrowded during the week, the beach shows a different face during the weekends as families post up, fish, relax, and have a good time. It can get pretty rowdy, though. The beach park is closed 9:30pm-7am daily.

Bellows Beach Park

At the north end of Waimanalo town, Bellow Air Force Station harbors **Bellows Beach Park.** It's open to the public every

Friday-Sunday. Here you'll find more of Waimanalo's signature white sand, ironwood-lined beaches. Camping complete with facilities is also available at Bellows by permit. Take the well-marked Bellows AFB turnoff from Kalanianaole Highway and follow the road to the beach, where parking is free.

KAILUA
★ Kailua Beach Park

This ocean activity hub of the windward coast offers everything—swimming, bodyboarding, kitesurfing, sailboarding, stand-up paddling, and kayaking. **Kailua Beach Park,** at the south end of Kailua, marks the start of the world-famous Kailua Beach, composed of fine grains of white sand and stretching 2.5 miles up the coast in a gentle arc. The water is shallow and often calm, perfect for families and swimming, but there can be small shore-breaking waves along parts of the beach.

Because the ocean floor is sand, ditch the snorkel mask and fins and get on top a kayak. There are outfitters within walking distance to the beach and along Ka'elepulu Stream. Popoi'a Island, better known as Flat Island, is a quick paddle offshore. There is also a boat ramp where residents launch their watercraft. Locals tend to gravitate to the small beach on the south side of the boat ramp, where they can park their trucks and anchor just off the beach.

Kailua Beach Park has restrooms, showers, and three free parking lots that fill to maximum capacity nearly every day. The park is clean, with manicured landscaping, a walking path, and beautiful canopy trees. There is also a restaurant and market right across the street. Weekends are always more crowded than weekdays, but summer weekends see the crowds swell in both the park and along the beach. Police adamantly ticket illegally parked vehicles.

To get to Kailua Beach Park from Honolulu, the Pali Highway turns into Kalanianaole Highway, which becomes Kailua Road. From Waimanalo, turn right onto Kailua Road from Kalanianaole Highway. Continue straight on Kuulei Road as Kailua Road veers right and into Kailua's shopping district. Follow Kuulei Road until it dead-ends at South Kalaheo Avenue. Turn right, then make a left at Kailua Road to access the first parking lot, or continue on Kalaheo Avenue and over the bridge as the road turns into Kawailoa Road. The next parking lot is on the left, just on the south side of the stream. At the stop sign, take a left onto Alala Road and the third parking lot is on the left side of the boat ramp. All three

lots border Kailua Beach Park and are closed 10pm-5am daily. The restrooms are locked until 6am.

Lanikai Beach

Lanikai Beach fronts the affluent and quaint Lanikai neighborhood. The aesthetics of Lanikai Beach are the same as Kailua, except Lanikai Beach gets narrower as you head south, until it disappears altogether and a seawall and multimillion-dollar homes take its place. The draw at Lanikai Beach, apart from the great swimming and calm, turquoise water, is the Mokulua Islets. A trip to "The Moks," as they are locally referred to, is the quintessential kayak destination on O'ahu. You can take a tour or paddle the 0.75 mile solo to the islands. Most people land on Moku Nui, the larger and more northerly of the two islets. It has a small beach that offers a postcard-perfect view of the mainland and the Ko'olau Mountains, a perspective most visitors will never attain. There is also a trail to the back of the island. It is against the law to deviate from the trail, as the island is also home to nesting seabirds. Parking for Lanikai Beach is on the street through the neighborhood. There are no sidewalks, so be mindful of

Kailua Beach Park is famous for its fine white sand.

Kailua

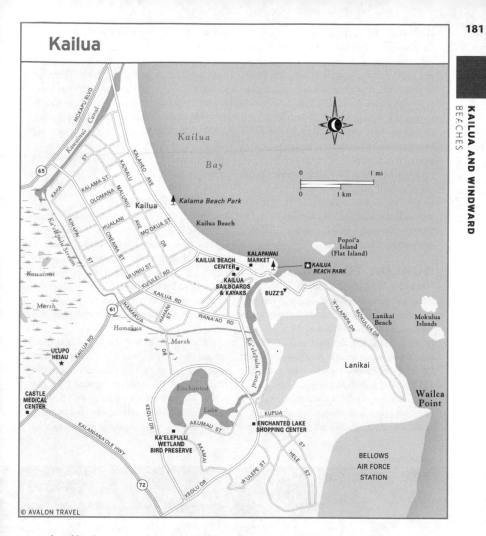

residents' landscaping and driveways. There are several public beach access walkways in between the homes, which are obvious and well signed.

Mokulua Islands

On the western shore of **Moku Nui,** the larger and more northern of the **Mokulua Islands,** is a small beach, the perfect respite after making the kayak crossing from Kailua or Lanikai. Once here, you'll find an amazing view of the leeward coast from a unique vantage point. The water is clear and blue, and the vibe on the beach is often festive. You can spot the burrows of the island's nesting seabirds from the white-sand beach. Moku Nui is a bird sanctuary, so public access is limited to the beach and a narrow footpath that circles the island. Paddling across via kayak, stand-up paddleboard, or other watercraft is the only way to access the beach. There are no facilities here.

Kalama Beach Park

At the north end of Kailua Beach is a wooded park that has a soft, manicured lawn, showers, and restrooms: **Kalama Beach Park.** The beach here is slightly less crowded than at Kailua Beach Park, and at Kalama Beach Park you'll avoid many of the kitesurfers and kayakers. Walk either way up or down the beach from the beach park to nab your own swath of sand and surf. From Kuulei Road, turn left onto North Kalaheo Avenue. You'll see the small parking lot for the beach park on the right where parking is free. The gate gets locked 6pm-7am daily. If the lot is full or if you're planning on staying after hours, park on neighborhood streets.

KUALOA TO LA'IE
Kualoa Regional Park

After you pass through Kahalu'u, Waikane, and Waiahole on Kamehameha Highway, all set in Kane'ohe Bay, with nearshore mudflats instead of beaches, the next beautiful sandy beach you come to is at **Kualoa Regional Park** (49-479 Kamehameha Hwy., 808/237-8525, www1.honolulu.gov/parks/programs/beach/kualoa.htm). The water is clear and calm, and the ocean bottom is a mix of sand, rock, and reef, a good place to swim and snorkel. Kualoa Regional Park is also a kayaker's destination because of the Mokoli'i Islet just offshore. Chinaman's Hat, as it's known, has a small beach on the north side. There are showers and restrooms, but no outfitters here, so you'll need to rent a kayak either in Kailua or in Honolulu. There is camping by permit in the park. The parking lot is free, and the entrance to the park is signed and visible from the highway. The park is closed and gated 8pm-7am daily.

Ka'a'awa Beaches

Just north of Kualoa you'll pass through Ka'a'awa. The Pacific Ocean pushes right up to Kamehameha Highway along much of Ka'a'awa, but there are a couple sandy nooks worth a stop. The first beach you'll come to is **Kalae'o'io Beach Park.** Simply pull off the highway under the trees. There's a grassy area, picnic tables, and a clean beach with light-blue water. The beach is usually empty.

Ka'a'awa Beach Park is just a skip to the north up the highway. You'll see the restrooms and showers from the road, and notice there are only three parking spaces. If they're taken, just pull off the highway and park on the shoulder. This narrow beach is a local favorite for fishing and camping and can be

Lanikai Beach

packed on the weekends. The restrooms are closed 9pm-6:30am daily.

Beyond the beach park, across from the U.S. Post Office and gas station is **Swanzy Beach Park,** where camping is allowed with a permit. The beach is small and a mix of sand and rock, but it's a great zone for snorkeling when the winds are calm. The beach park has restrooms, showers, and an expansive grassy area with no shade. The views of the Ko'olaus from Swanzy are quite extraordinary. The parking lot is closed 10pm-6am daily.

★ Kahana Bay Beach Park

Kahana Bay Beach Park (52-222 Kamehameha Hwy., 808/237-7767, www.hawaiistateparks.org), found in dramatic Kahana Bay, offers camping by permit, a great area for a picnic, and calm, sheltered water for stand-up paddling. At the base of the bay, the Kahana Valley meets the sea and Kahana Stream spills into the Pacific, depositing fine silty sand along the beach and out into the bay. The water is often murky and a bit chilly, but remains shallow quite a ways out. The area is perfect for families with kids. Parking is right off Kamehameha Highway on the ocean side, and there are restrooms and showers. The remnants of the ancient Huilua fishpond are

on the south side of the bay. The beach park and facilities are open during daylight hours.

Kokololio Beach Park

Kokololio Beach Park, at the north end of Hau'ula, offers a wide beach by Hawai'i standards, with a shoreline fringed with tropical almond canopy trees and *naupaka*. The ocean floor is sandy and the water is clear when the winds are light. During the winter months, when the surf is up, the shore break can get quite powerful, and a surf break appears on the outer reef. Swimming becomes dangerous during periods of high surf due to strong currents. There are restrooms and showers in the park, as well as a generous grassy area with a large parking lot. Camping is allowed with a permit, and on the weekends, especially during the summer, the park is filled with local residents and families. The beach is also a favorite for fishing. The gated parking lot is locked 8pm-6:45am daily.

La'ie Beach Park

Just to the north, on the other side of an outcropping of limestone cliffs that marks the end of Kokololio Beach Park, is **La'ie Beach Park.** The beach park is also known as Pounders, named after the bodysurfing area near the cliffs, where the shore break can get

Ka'a'awa has a few narrow but beautiful beaches.

big and powerful during the winter months. The beach is relatively small and often lined with organic debris, but the park is beautiful and dotted with picnic benches. Swimming here is better in the summer months. Stroll to the north to find another small beach on the other side of the point. There are no facilities at this beach park, but a paved parking lot is right off the highway.

Hukilau Beach

On the north end of La'ie town sits the lovely **Hukilau Beach,** a long, crescent-shaped sandy beach with dunes covered in *naupaka*. During the summer months the water is great for swimming, but the surf and currents make for poor conditions during the winter months. Throughout the year, this area has the propensity for strong trade winds, which can also create unfavorable beach and swimming conditions. The park itself is beautiful, with shade from ironwood trees, grass, and picnic benches—beachgoers are always welcome. There are showers, but no restrooms, and a dirt parking lot off Kamehameha Highway, which is closed on Sunday.

Malaekahana State Recreation Area

Continuing up the same crescent of sand from Hukilau Beach, you'll come to the **Malaekahana State Recreation Area** (808/537-0800, www.hawaiistateparks.org), framed in by Kalanai Point and Goat Island to the north. When the wind is not whipping onshore from the northwest and the surf is flat, the sandy bottom makes for great swimming and crystal clear water. There is more rock and reef to the north end of the beach, which is better for snorkeling if all the other weather conditions are favorable. The beach is also a favorite for fishing. Malaekahana State Recreation Area has showers, restrooms, and picnic tables, and camping is allowed with a permit on the south side of Kalanai Point. On the north side, or Kahuku side of Kalanai Point is Malaekahana Park-Kahuku section, a private 37-acre camping area. The entrance to Malaekahana State Recreation Area is off Kamehameha Highway and is well marked; the beach is not visible from the highway. Follow the road back to the parking lot, which is known as a high theft area. The entrance to the Malaekahana Park-Kahuku section is just north of the state recreation area. Look for a small faded blue sign on the side of the road. From Labor Day to March 31 the recreation area is open 7am-6:45pm daily. From April 1 to Labor Day it remains open till 7:45pm daily.

Water Sports

SURFING, STAND-UP PADDLING, AND KITESURFING

The windward side is typically just that, windy, a weather condition that can adversely affect surfing conditions unless the winds are blowing offshore. Unfortunately, the windward side usually sees onshore winds, leaving little in the way of consistent, good-quality waves for surfing. On the other hand, sports like sailboarding and kitesurfing that flourish in the windy conditions are popular in this region, centered around Kailua, where most of the outfitters are located.

Waimanalo

Just north of Makapu'u at **Kaupo Beach Park** there is a gentle little wave called Cockroach that breaks inside the rocky cove, perfect for beginners on big boards. During the winter months, when northeast swells sneak around Rabbit Island, the surf can get big and the currents quite strong.

Kailua

All along Kailua beaches, from Lanikai to Kalama Beach Park, the ocean conditions are usually just right for stand-up paddling. With a soft, sandy bottom, little to no shore break, and generally calm water, the area around **Kalama Beach Park** is perfect for distance paddling up and down the coast. If you paddle out from **Kailua Beach,** there is **Flat Island** to explore. And if you're paddling from **Lanikai Beach,** there is a bit more rock and reef off the beach, so you can explore the nearshore waters or paddle out to the **Mokulua Islands.** During the winter months, there are two surf breaks that reveal themselves on either side of Moku Nui, the larger of the two islands. Keep in mind that if the surf is big enough for waves to be breaking on the outer reefs, the ocean currents will be much stronger. Stand-up paddle surfing should only be attempted by expert stand-up paddlers.

Stand-up paddling can become more of a chore than a pleasurable experience in extremely windy conditions. When the wind does pick up and the ocean surface becomes choppy and bumpy, sailboarders and kitesurfers take to the water in Kailua instead.

You can rent stand-up paddleboards at **Kailua Beach Adventures** (130 Kailua Rd., Ste. 101B, 808/262-2555 or 888/457-5737, www.kailuasailboards.com, 8am-5pm daily) for $59 half day and $69 full day, with multiday prices and free carts to walk the board to the beach. It also offers two-hour group lessons for $129, including hotel pickup and one-hour private lessons for $174, two-hours for $229, three-hours for $289. The retail outlet is within walking distance of Kailua Beach Park. **Windward Watersports** (33 Hoolai St., 808/261-7873, www.windwardwatersports.com, 9am-5pm daily) is a complete water-sports shop selling new and used boards and gear for many activities. It rents stand-up paddleboards starting at $49 half day and $59 full day, with two-hour lessons for $125. Kiteboard rentals start at $30 for one day. Actual rental of the kite is contingent upon your skill level, or beginners can take a one-hour course with a certified instructor. Located in Kailua town, the shop will help you put racks and watercraft on your vehicle for the short drive to the beach. **Hawaiian WaterSports** (167 Hamakua Dr., 808/262-5483, www.hawaiianwatersports.com, 9am-5pm daily), also located in Kailua, rents stand-up paddleboards starting at $59 for a full day with multiday rentals. It has a wide range of boards 7-14 feet and boards for all

Kailua Beach Park

skill levels, and you can exchange your board at any time during your rental period. Group lessons start at $104 for 1.5 hours. Sailboard rentals with beginner gear starts at $79 full day, $99 full day for advanced gear, and the shop also offers 1.5-hour lessons—groups of two start at $140, private are $199. Kiteboards are also available for rent starting at $29 per day. Different lessons are offered depending on your skill level. Private lessons start at $199 for 1.5 hours of instruction. Book online for discounted rates.

Kualoa to La'ie

Just after you pass the row of oceanfront homes across from Kualoa Ranch, the road bends and Kualoa Valley opens up to your left and the beach comes into view on your right. There's immediate roadside parking for a washy surf spot called **Rainbows.** Shallow patches of flat reef amid a sandy bottom create a few different zones where mushy waves break haphazardly. Usually windblown and choppy, this break is favored by beginner surfers and longboarders. The closest outfitters for gear rentals are in Kailua.

Kahana Bay is a great spot to stand-up paddle. The bay is somewhat protected from the pervasive trade winds, and the water is usually calm and flat, with only tiny waves lapping up onshore. The sandy bottom stays shallow all around the bay, and you can paddle up to the fishponds on its southern edge or explore around the point to the north.

On the southern edge of La'ie town, pull off Kamehameha Highway into the La'ie Beach Park parking lot and walk just to the south toward the jagged limestone cliff jutting out into the ocean. The shorebreak next to the cliff is known as **Pounders.** It gets big and powerful during the winter months when swells out of the north arrive on O'ahu shorelines. During the summer, it's usually flat and a great place to swim.

SNORKELING

This region has some great snorkeling locales, but it's up to you find the best spots during your stay. Because of the dips and bends in the coastline, ocean conditions can vary greatly from beach to beach, so it can be as much of an adventure to find the perfect spot to snorkel as it is to explore the water.

The windward side is heavily affected by the trade winds, which create chop on the ocean surface and wind waves can stir up sediment in the water—the stronger the trades, the choppier the ocean. Beaches with an outer reef that block the surf and shallow, protected inner waters with a mix of rock, reef, and sand are best. And unless you're heading to Kailua, where the snorkeling is subpar, you'll need to have your own gear ready at hand because there are no shops to rent equipment along the windward coast.

Beyond Makapu'u Point, most of the windward coast is fringed by an outer reef, which creates calm and shallow nearshore waters. Add an ocean floor mostly covered in rock and reef to that equation and you have the perfect conditions for snorkeling. **Waimanalo** is much like Kailua Beach with a sandy bottom. You won't see any reef fish, but you might glance a sea turtle. **Kualoa** has more potential for spotting reef fish with its reef and rock bottom. Snorkel in the area right off the beach and out toward Chinaman's Hat. **Ka'a'awa** also has some great snorkeling potential if the winds are light. Get in the water near the beach park or along the straight stretch of coast just to the south of Kahana Bay. **Hau'ula** and **La'ie** also have great beaches to explore in mask and fins, as long as weather conditions are also cooperating. You'll find a similar reef and rock bottom no matter where you jump in the water in these two towns. Just steer clear of any river mouths. Hau'ula and La'ie are also prone to high surf in the winter months, which creates dangerous ocean currents and can stir up the usually crystal clear water.

Most windward towns are small residential communities without snorkeling or diving outfitters renting or selling gear, with the exception of a few options in Kailua. **Kailua Beach Adventures** (130 Kailua Rd., Ste.

101B, 808/262-2555 or 888/457-5737, www. kailuasailboards.com, 8am-5pm daily) rents mask, snorkel, and fins for $12 half day, $16 full day, and $48 per week. **Twogood Kayaks** (134B Hamakua Dr., 808/262-5656, www.two-goodkayaks.com, 9am-6pm Mon.-Fri., 8am-6pm Sat.-Sun.) has snorkel sets for $12 day, for weekly rentals pay for three days and get the next two for free. **Aaron's Dive Shop** (307 Hahani St., 808/262-2333 or 888/847-2822, www.hawaii-scuba.com, 7am-7pm Mon.-Fri., 7am-6pm Sat., 7am-5pm Sun.) also rents and sells snorkel gear.

KAYAKING
Kailua
KAILUA BEACH PARK

For all the same reasons that make **Kailua Beach Park** an attractive destination for swimming, stand-up paddling, and relaxing on the beach—white-sand beaches, shallow and calm water, and beautiful views all around—it is also the hub for kayaking on O'ahu. You can launch from Kailua Beach Park and paddle out to Flat Island, or paddle up and down the coast. Another popular place to launch from is Lanikai.

Those not comfortable with a little swell or chop on the ocean surface can also kayak in Ka'elepulu Stream, which spills into the ocean at Kailua Beach Park. The stream opens up into Ka'elepulu Pond, a wetland area that was flooded to create the Enchanted Lake neighborhood. The water in the stream will contain urban runoff, and if the mouth of the stream has not opened in some time, it can be a bit stinky. On the other side of the coin, the water will be smooth, calm, and more protected from the wind. Just try not to get wet. For first-time kayakers, a group tour is a great way to get acquainted with the kayak and the water.

★ MOKULUA ISLANDS

The **Mokulua Islands,** less than a mile offshore from Kailua Beach, are a popular draw. You can actually land on **Moku Nui,** the larger, more northern island. There's an inviting beach on the leeward side, just make sure to pull your kayak all the way up to the rocks to allow other people to land. Pack a lunch and put your camera in a dry sack because the view of mainland O'ahu from the island is breathtaking. There is a trail that circles the island. Remain on the trail because the island is a seabird nesting sanctuary.

kayaking to Moku Nui, the largest of the Mokulua Islands

OUTFITTERS

In Kailua, you can rent kayaks at **Hawaiian WaterSports** (167 Hamakua Dr., 808/262-5483, www.hawaiianwatersports.com, 9am-5pm daily). Single kayaks start at $59 full day, and double kayaks start at $59 half day and $69 full day. All rentals include life vests, paddles, seats, backrests, and dry bags. Add a snorkel set to a kayak rental for an extra $15. The shop also offers 1.5- and three-hour group and private excursion to Flat Island, Lanikai Beach, and the Mokulua Islands. 1.5-hour group and private kayak adventures start at $104 and three-hour group and private excursions start at $168. Inquire about excursions to Kaneʻohe Bay and the sandbars.

Windward Watersports (33 Hoolai St., 808/261-7873, www.windwardwatersports.com, 9am-5pm daily) rents single kayaks starting at $49 half day, $59 full day, and double kayaks for $55 half day and $65 full day. Triple kayaks are $79 half day and $89 full day. Kayaks can be picked up at the retail store or dropped off and ready for you at the beach. Windward offers a four-hour, self-guided tour for $49 and a four-hour, guided tour for $159 going to Flat Island, Lanikai Beach, and the Mokulua Islands.

Twogood Kayaks (134B Hamakua Dr., 808/262-5656, www.twogoodkayaks.com, 9am-6pm Mon.-Fri., 8am-6pm Sat.-Sun.) rents single kayaks for $45 half day, $55 full day and tandem kayaks for $55 half day, $65 full day. Rentals come with a paddle, but there is an additional charge for a dry bag and backrest. Twogood offers free delivery of kayaks to Kaʻelepulu Stream at Kailua Beach Park and basic instruction. It will deliver kayaks to other Kailua areas for $15. Twogood Kayaks has two packages that run 9am-3pm: an Adventure Package for $75 per person with kayak rental, life jacket, paddle, lunch, and round-trip transportation from Waikiki and a Guided Tour for $125 per person with extras like a guide, snorkel gear, dry bag, and backrest.

Just across the street from Kailua Beach Park you'll find **Kailua Beach Adventures** (130 Kailua Rd., Ste. 101B, 808/262-2555 or 888/457-5737, www.kailuasailboards.com, 8am-5pm daily). It rents single kayaks for $59 half day, and high-performance single kayaks and double kayaks for $69 half day. Dry bag, cooler, and backrest are an additional fee. Tour options are: a four-hour guided tour for beginners that includes snorkeling, transportation from your hotel, and lunch for $129 adults and $114 children 8-12; a two-hour guided kayak tour with a one-hour massage after your paddle for $229; a four-hour guided adventure of Kailua Bay, Flat Island, and the Mokulua Islands with snorkeling, lunch, and hotel transportation for $179; and a six-hour exploration tour for experienced kayakers with snorkeling, lunch, and hotel pickup for $249.

Kaneʻohe
KANEʻOHE BAY

Kaneʻohe Bay is a unique natural treasure in Hawaiʻi, the largest sheltered body of water in the islands, and has several worthwhile sights that make kayaking in the bay quite an extraordinary experience. Devoid of beautiful sandy beaches, the draw in Kaneʻohe Bay is what's in the bay. Coconut Island is just a stone's throw from the Kaneʻohe coast, but a world all its own. The entire island is a marine research facility, so the public cannot go onshore, but the reefs surrounding the island are protected and pristine, home to species of coral found only in Kaneʻohe Bay. The water is crystal clear, and the reefs teem with fish. Farther to the north is the Kaneʻohe Bay Sandbar, also known as Sunken Island. At low tide, the expansive sandbar, the size of a football field, is a favorite destination for locals and visitors. Sailboats pull right up on the sand, kayakers stop for rest, and people set up beach chairs in the sand and just relax. On the northern fringes of the bay, you'll also find the remains of several ancient fishponds.

OUTFITTERS

In Kaneʻohe, **Holokai Kayak and Snorkel Adventures** (46-465 Kamehameha Hwy., 808/781-4773, www.holokaiadventures.com, 8:30am-2pm Mon.-Sat.) rents tandem kayaks and offers a three-hour guided tour of the bay for $120 per adult, $100 per child (4-12) kayaking from Coconut Island to the Heʻeia fishpond. It offers a free shuttle service to and from Waikiki and a 15 percent discount for booking online. Otherwise, you'll need to have your kayak already in tow. Many of the outfitters in Kailua or Honolulu offer free racks for your vehicle.

Kualoa to Laʻie
KUALOA REGIONAL PARK

You can put your kayak in the water and paddle out to Chinaman's Hat, a small island with a distinctive profile just off the shore, from **Kualoa Regional Park.** The ocean floor off the beach is a mix of sand, reef, and rock, so there is much to see in the water. It's also very shallow, which keeps the surface rather calm. There are no outfitters in the area, so you'll need to have your kayak already on top of the car. Aside from a nice kayak adventure, the park makes a comfortable setting for a picnic lunch.

FISHING

Shoreline fishing and spearfishing are popular activities on the windward coast, whether for hobby, sport, or sustenance. Between Waimanalo and Laʻie, there are miles of accessible coastline where you can pull out the rod and reel, or hold your breath, and fish.

You can shoreline fish from the beaches of **Waimanalo, Kailua, Kaʻaʻawa, Kahana, Punaluʻu, Hauʻula, Laʻie Point State Wayside,** and **Malaekahana State Recreation Area.** In Kaneʻohe Bay, people often fish from **Heʻeia Pier.** In some areas, especially from Kualoa to Kahana, where the ocean pushes right up again the highway, you can find a place to pull off on the shoulder, pop up a tent, and cast a line. Spearfishing is also popular along the shallow nearshore waters where rock and reef make up the ocean bottom. Waimanalo, Kualoa, Kaʻaʻawa, and Malaekahana State Recreation Area are all good spots to spearfish, and octopus, locally known as tako, is abundant in these areas—if you can find them.

If you're inclined to get out on the open water to fish, kayak fishing is the easiest way to go. Waimanalo, Kailua, and Kaneʻohe Bay are more protected from the wind and better for fishing from a kayak. Kaʻaʻawa also has nice long stretches of nearshore water to troll as well, but is more prone to the trade winds.

If you're coming from Honolulu and forget your fishing gear, you'll need to stop at **Nanko Fishing Supply** (46-003 Alaloa St., 808/247-0938, www.facebook.com/ NankoFishingSupply, 8am-6pm Mon., 8am-7pm Tues.-Sat., 9am-2pm Sun.), the hub of fishing gear for the windward side. Also, **Longs** (46-047 Kamehameha Hwy., 808/235-4511, 7am-midnight daily) in the Kaneohe Bay Shopping Center sells basic fishing supplies and three-prong spears.

Hiking, Biking, and Bird-Watching

HIKING
Kailua

There is a popular walking trail along **Kawainui Marsh,** one of the few wetland ecosystems on Oʻahu and home to several species of native waterbirds like the Hawaiian coot, Hawaiian moorhen, and the Hawaiian stilt along with a host of other feathered inhabitants. The mile-long path is a raised, paved trail that crosses the marsh from Kailua Road to Kaha Street, off Oneawa Street on the north end of the Kailua neighborhood known as Coconut Grove.

Maunawili Falls is a short hike in the shadow of Olomana that follows Maunawili Stream and terminates at the falls. From

Fishponds

an ancient Hawaiian fishpond at Kahama Bay

Ancient Hawaiian communities were organized by *ahupuaʻa,* land divisions that stretched in giant swaths from the mountains all the way into the sea. Fishing was just as important as farming, and precontact Hawaiians were experts at both. Fishponds were constructed in shallow, nearshore waters by the people of the *ahupuaʻa* to store fish for food, because high surf and adverse ocean conditions often kept them onshore. Fishponds guaranteed a catch. Even more important, the fishponds were constructed as spawning grounds to ensure sustainability of certain species. In fact, Hawaiian fishponds were the first marine protected areas in Hawaiʻi, and the people were not allowed to catch the fish that were spawning and considered *kapu,* off limits.

The fishponds were made by building a wall of stone on the reef that would enclose a body of water. The remnants of these fishponds are visible up and down the windward coast, and some are being restored and put into practice. There is the Moliʻi fishpond at Kualoa Ranch, the Huilua fishpond in Kahana Bay, the Kahaluʻu fishpond, the Pahonu Pond at Kaiona Beach Park in Waimanalo, which was also used to keep turtles, and the Heʻeia fishpond on the north end of Kaneʻohe Bay. Friends of Heʻeia Fishpond is a nonprofit organization dedicated to maintaining the working fishpond for the community.

The Ko'olau Range

The drastic, verdant, and corduroy cliffs of Ko'olau Range are not actually mountains in the traditional sense, but the remnants of the western half of the **Ko'olau Volcano**, which erupted nearly two million years ago. The caldera and eastern portion are thought to have slid cataclysmically into the ocean in prehistoric times. As erosion has chipped away at the peaks over hundreds of thousands of years, the tallest peak, **Pu'u Konahuanui,** now measures only 3,100 feet, but was once thought to be about three times that height. Spanning the entire windward coast, the smaller and more recent volcanoes we refer to today as Diamond Head, Punchbowl Crater, Hanauma Bay, Koko Crater, Koko Head, and Tantalus were all created by eruptions from the Ko'olau Volcano.

Kalanianaole Highway, turn into A'uola Road in the Maunawili neighborhood. Immediately fork left onto Maunawili Road and follow it through the subdivision and a forested area to the end at Kelewina Street. Park near the intersection and continue on foot on the one-lane private road. A sign indicates the way to the falls, which in part is on private land, so stay on the trail. Along the stream look for *'ape*, a plant with huge, elephant-ear-shaped leaves. A ridgeline section offers views of Ko'olau Range, Olomana and Kane'ohe Bay. Regain the stream and follow it to a large, deep pool and Maunawili Falls. On the hike you'll cross the stream several times and the trail can be quite muddy. It is also very popular and heavily used on the weekends. There is a second smaller pool at the top of the falls and the trail continues back from there if you wish to continue exploring the forest.

Kualoa to La'ie

Just north of Ka'a'awa is the lush Kahana Valley, a state park designed to foster native Hawaiian culture. There are two trails that intermingle, loop, and wind through the valley, the **Kapa'ele'ele Trail** and the **Nakoa Trail.** The Kapa'ele'ele Trail is a one-mile loop passing cultural sites with views of Kahana Bay. And the Nakoa Trail is a 2.5-mile with *koa* and *hau* tree forests, pools along the stream, and a mountain apple grove. From Kamehameha Highway, turn *mauka* into the Ahupua'a O Kahana State Park. There is an Orientation Center, where you can find trail maps and other information, as well as restrooms. Be prepared for mud and mosquitoes on the hike.

BIKING
Kailua

Kailua is the most bike-friendly town on O'ahu. The beaches and neighborhoods are in relatively close proximity to the town center, where all the dining, shopping, and services are located. The town is flat, the weather is exceptional, and the traffic is usually so congested that it's faster to get around on two wheels. In addition to riding around town, bikes are allowed on the trail that crosses the Kawainui Marsh.

The Bike Shop (270 Kuulei Rd., 808/261-1553, www.bikeshophawaii.com, 9am-8pm Mon.-Fri., 9am-5pm Sat., 10am-5pm Sun.) is a full-service bicycle shop. It rents 21-speed cruisers for $20 per day, road bikes for $40 per day, and performance mountain bikes for $85 per day. **Kailua Beach Adventures** (130 Kailua Rd., Ste. 101B, 808/262-2555 or 888/457-5737, www.kailuasailboards.com, 8am-5pm daily) rents bikes for $20 half day, $25 full day, and $85 for seven days. **Rusty Chain Cyclery** (28 Oneawa St., 808/263-7878, www.rustychaincyclery.com, 10am-6pm Mon., Tues., Thurs., Fri., 10am-3:30pm Wed. and Sat.) rents and sells bikes. Beach cruisers and multi-speed city bikes rent for $13 and up for two hours, mountain bikes rent for $45 and up per day, and road bikes start at $35 per day. Kid trailers start at $10 for two hours.

BIRD-WATCHING
Kailua

There are several areas perfect for bird-watching in Kailua. The 800-acre **Kawainui Marsh** is the largest wetland area in the state. A paved trail traverses it from Kailua Road to Kaha Street, about a mile long. Look for native Hawaiian waterbirds, migrant waterfowl, and other curious residents, like the black-crowned night heron with its large black beak and piercing red eyes. Binoculars are a must for this area.

If you don't have binoculars and want to get an up-close look at a Hawaiian moorhen or a Hawaiian stilt, check out the **Hamakua Marsh,** which parallels Hamakua Drive. In the parking lot behind Down to Earth market is a viewing area with informative signs about the residents of the marsh. Though the parking lot leaves much to be desired for a natural setting for bird-watching, many of the native Hawaiian waterbirds congregate here in large numbers.

Another area close by to view waterbirds is in the Enchanted Lake neighborhood. The **Ka'elepulu Wetland Bird Preserve** is a small wetland area bordered by homes, and this little nook is a favorite for waterbirds. In addition to the Hawaiian duck, stilt, moorhen, and coot, look for red-footed boobies and great frigatebirds. From Keolu Drive, turn into Kiukee Place, a short dead-end road. Park and watch the birds from the sidewalk.

Kane'ohe

Ho'omaluhia Botanical Garden, nestled up against the base of the Ko'olau Mountains

Hawaiian coot

in Kane'ohe, is frequented by a wide range of urban and forest birds. Within several different areas corresponding to regional plantings, there are myriad trails and tropical foliage where you can search for birds. Bring binoculars as the gardens have canopy trees as well as interesting flowering plants and palm. Stop by the visitors center to speak with a docent about the birds that are around the garden during your stay and the best areas for sightings. You can get to the gardens, in a residential area on Luluku Road, from both Kamehameha Highway and the Likelike Highway.

Golf and Tennis

GOLF
Waimanalo

Just outside of Waimanalo town, on the Kailua side, is **Olomana Golf Club** (41-1801 Kalanianaole Hwy., 808/259-7926, www.pacificlinks.com/olomana), an 18-hole, par-72 course. The front nine has level fairways and water hazards at every hole, while the back nine features rolling hills and sand bunkers. The course also has stunning views of the Ko'olau Mountains. Play 18 holes with a cart for $100. Twilight greens fees are $85 after 2:15pm.

Kane'ohe

Bay View Golf Park (45-285 Kaneohe Bay Dr., 808/247-0451, www.bayviewgolfcourse.us) is an affordable 18-hole course in Kane'ohe that has a double-decker range facility and is open for night play during the week. Visitor rates are $21 weekday, $29 weekend, $15 cart fee for 9 holes, and $29 weekday, $37 weekend, $19 cart fee for 18 holes. Club rentals are $25 and pull cart is $3.

For a more scenic and lush experience, visit the 18-hole **Pali Golf Course** (45-050 Kamehameha Hwy., 808/266-7612, www.honolulu.gov/des/golf/pali.html). This challenging, hillside course has three sets of tees for different skill levels. Greens fees are $55 daily. Twilight fees are $27.50 and cart rental for 18 holes is $20.

TENNIS

Public tennis courts can be found from Waimanalo to Kane'ohe and are generally located in district parks with restrooms, drinking fountains, and ample parking. District parks close 10pm-6am daily. **Waimanalo District Park** (41-415 Hihimanu St.) has four courts, **Kailua District Park** (21 S. Kainalu Dr.) has eight public courts, and **Kane'ohe District Park** (45-660 Keaahala Rd.) has six courts.

Kane'ohe

Yoga and Spas

YOGA
Kailua

The **Yoga School of Kailua** (326 Lala Pl., 808/292-9642, www.yogakailua.com) is a satellite school of the International Yoga College, a trauma healing center, and a teacher-training facility. The nonprofit organization offers public group classes in asana/prananyama yoga four days a week, one class per day. Donations are requested. Check the website for classes and times.

Mindful Matters (407 Uluniu St., #412, 808/230-2476, www.mindfulmatterskailua.com) is right in the heart of Kailua town in the Kailua Medical Arts Building. This complete wellness center offers tai chi/qigong, massage, naturopathy, acupuncture, Pilates, and a host of different forms of yoga to suit every function or need. Ashtanga, core stability, hatha, power flow, restorative, vinyasa, and yoga for pregnancy are some of the disciplines they cover. The first-time drop-in rate is $10 followed by $15 each additional drop-in session.

Hot Yoga By The Sea (320 Uluniu St., Ste. 6, 808/469-1541, www.hotyogabythesea.com) is tucked away by the Kailua Wellness Center, in suite 6, down the alleyway. Look for a Buddha statue outside the door. It practices hot ashtanga, power, vinyasa, and yoga basics. Drop-ins are welcome on a first-come, first-served basis, and the rates start at $18, with 3-, 5-, 10-, and 20-class packages.

Aloha Yoga Kula (38 Kaneohe Bay Dr. or 1300 Kailua Rd., 808/772-3520, www.alohayogakula.com) has two studios in Kailua and offers nine forms of yoga to suit your needs, from kids/family yoga to vinyasa and ashtanga. There is no registration necessary, and mats and props are available in the studios. The drop-in rate is $10 per class. The Pali Studio, off Kailua Road near Castle Medical Center, has free parking at the Christ Church Uniting Disciples and Presbyterians, and the Aikahi Studio, across from the Aikahi Shopping Center, has parking at the Windward United Church of Christ.

SPAS
Kailua

Honu You Hawaiian Spa (122 Oneawa St., 808/261-1268, www.honuyou.com) focuses on balance and simplicity. It has treatments on par with the major hotel spas and, in addition, employ an educated staff focused on providing the individual with designer treatments. Facials start at $116 and a 50-minute organic facial therapy is $95. Fifty-minute massages start at $80 for lomilomi, deep tissue, or Swedish. Honu You provides waxing and nail care services as well. There is also a location next to the Kailua Wellness Center on the other side of the Kailua town center (320 Ulumiu St., 808/261-5200, 9am-5pm Tues.-Sat.).

Located on the second floor of Kailua Square, **Lomilomi Hana Lima Healing Center and Spa** (315 Uluniu St., 808/263-0303, http://lomilomihanalima.com, 9am-5pm Mon.-Sat.) is a healing center specializing in lomilomi, aromatherapy, organic facials, microdermabrasion and body scrubs. Sixty-minute massages start at $90, 90-minute body treatments start at $130, and the spa offers many packages and add-on services like steam bath, foot bath, facials, and aromatherapy.

Shopping

KAILUA

In downtown Kailua, park the car, get outside, and walk around the busy town center, where most of Kailua businesses are located. There are definitely some great finds in Kailua town.

Get your fill of reading material at **BookEnds** (600 Kailua Rd., 808/261-1996, 9am-8pm Mon.-Sat., 9am-11pm Sun.), a great independent bookstore (one of the few left) with volumes stacked ceiling to floor. The knowledgeable staff can get you into the perfect book for your stay. For records, CDs, and other music paraphernalia, check out **Hungry Ear Records** (418 Kuulei Rd., 808/262-2175, http://hungryear.com, 10:30am-6pm Mon.-Sat.), a classic independent record store with a great selection of new and used music. Hungry Ear is a must for record collectors. If you'd rather play than listen to music, **Coconut Grove Music** (167 Hamakua Dr., #200, 808/262-9977, www.coconutgrovemusic.com, 10am-6pm Mon.-Sat., 11am-4pm Sun.), a complete music store selling new, used, and vintage instruments. **Oliver Men's Shop** (49 Kihapai St., 808/261-6587, www.oliverhawaii.com, 10am-6pm Mon.-Fri., 10am-5pm Sat.-Sun.) is a hip boutique for men—think groovy T-shirts, printed walking shorts, vintage surf brands and other trinkets and goods that harken back to a more nostalgic era in the islands. Two doors down is **Olive Boutique** (43 Kihapai St., 808/263-9919, www.iheartolive.com, 10am-6pm Mon.-Fri., 10am-5pm Sat.-Sun.) for the ladies. It features beachy clothing and unique gifts, eclectic knickknacks and decorations.

For local farm-fresh produce and prepared foods, hit up the **Kailua at Night** farmers market (609 Kailua Rd., 5pm-7:30pm Thurs.). The market sets up in the covered parking lot by Longs.

There is also a Sunday market featuring all local farmers and vendors: **Kailua Town Farmers' Market** (315 Kuulei Rd., 808/388-9696, http://haleiwafarmersmarket.com, 9am-1pm Sun.) sets up in the Kailua Elementary School parking lot. Just look for the rows of white tents.

KANE'OHE

On the corner of Kamehameha Highway and Haiku Road in Kane'ohe, the **Windward Mall** (46-056 Kamehameha Hwy., 808/235-1143, www.windwardmall.com, 10am-9pm Mon.-Sat., 10am-5pm Sun.) serves the windward side of the island with national brands and a few local retailers. **Macy's** and **Sears** are the big department stores and there is the **Regal Cinemas 10,** but the mall is more a hangout where local families congregate and grab a bite to eat, and not necessarily geared toward the visitor.

Entertainment and Events

NIGHTLIFE
Kailua

Located at the intersection of Hamakua Drive and Hahani Street, **Boardriders Bar & Grill** (201 Hamakua Dr., 808/261-4600, noon-2am daily, $9-15) is better known as a bar than a grill, but it does serve pizza, salad, steak, stir-fry, and classic bar munchies. Boardriders has a couple pool tables and is the best venue for catching live music on the windward side. The bar sees local, national, and international artists and favors reggae and jawaiian (Hawaiian reggae) music. *Pau hana* is 4pm-6pm daily.

Nestled next to the Hamakua Marsh is a small but friendly blue-collar bar called the **Creekside Lounge** (153 Hamakua

Dr., 808/262-6466, http://creeksidelounge.com, 8am-2am daily). Established in 1982, the Creekside is a biker bar with a cadre of friendly female bartenders. The bar shows live sporting events and is no frills, but it has a huge local following. Smoking is allowed on the patio overlooking the marsh, where most patrons regularly spill out to.

CULTURAL TOURS AND LU'AU

The windward side has two venues for cultural tours and lu'au. **Kualoa Ranch** (49-560 Kamehameha Hwy., 808/237-7321, www.kualoa.com) offers historical and cultural tours of the working ranch, "bordering" valleys, and coastline. Established in 1850 the ranch is steeped in tradition and has a unique perspective and story to tell about the area. There is an Ancient Fishing Grounds and Tropical Gardens Tour, Ocean Voyage Tour, Secret Island Beach Tour, and Jungle Expedition Tour. The tours are $35 adult and $25 child. On the northern end of the windward side, in La'ie, the **Polynesian Cultural Center** (55-370 Kamehameha Hwy., www.polynesianculturalcenter.com, 800/367-7060, noon-9pm Mon.-Sat.) introduces visitors to the people and cultures of Hawai'i, Samoa, Maori New Zealand, Fiji, Tahiti, Marquesas, and Tonga as you walk through and visit the different villages and interact with the people demonstrating their specific arts and crafts. There is also a canoe ride that explores the villages as well. Dining is paramount to the experience, and you can choose between the Island Buffet with a mix of local Hawaiian fare, Prime Dining with prime rib, crab legs, and sushi in a secluded setting, or the famous Ali'i Luau, with authentic Hawaiian food, including traditional *imu* pork, a large pig cooked in an earthen oven. An evening show called "Ha: Breath of Life" is a culmination of story, dance, Polynesian music, and fire. General admission, which is for the day experience only,

is $59.95 adult, $47.96 child (5-11). Admission, buffet, and evening show will run $79.95 adult, $63.96 child, and packages for admission, the lu'au, and show start at $99.95 adult, $79.99 child.

CINEMA

If you're keen to grab a movie and popcorn on the windward side, there are two theaters. **Regal Cinemas 10** (46-056 Kamehameha Hwy., 808/234-4006) is on the south side of the Windward Mall and shows major motion pictures, art films, digital presentations, and 3-D, RPX, and IMAX movies. General admission is $11, matinee (before 6pm) is $8. In La'ie you'll find **Laie Palms Cinemas** (55-510 Kamehameha Hwy., 808/232-0006, www.laiepalmscinemas.com) in the Laie Shopping Center strip mall. General admission is $10, matinee (before 5pm) is $7, children (3-11) are $7. The theater does not show R-rated films and is closed on Sunday.

FESTIVALS AND EVENTS
Kailua

The **"I Love Kailua" Town Party** (last Sunday of April) is a daytime festival in the heart of downtown Kailua. Kailua Road is closed to vehicular traffic, and people from all over the island come out to eat, shop, and celebrate Kailua. There are activities for the kids and local restaurants and retail outlets line the street with tents full of merchandise and delicious fare.

Kane'ohe

Orchids are a big deal in Hawai'i and the **Windward Orchid Society** holds an annual spring show and plant sale in the King Intermediate School gym (46-155 Kamehameha Hwy., www.windwardorchidsociety.org). The two-day event showcases the best in orchid cultivars as well as other unusual plants.

Food

WAIMANALO

Quick Bites

Waimanalo has a few places to stop and grab a quick bite as you make your way along the Kalanianaole Highway. **Keneke's Plate Lunch & BBQ** (41-857 Kalanianaole Hwy., 808/259-9811, 9:30am-5:30pm daily, $2-7) serves up the typical Hawaiian plate lunch and is very popular. **Serg's** (41-865 Kalanianaole Hwy., 808/259-7374, 11am-8pm Mon.-Sat., opens at 8am Sun., $3-12) brings Mexican food to Waimanalo with carnitas, carne asada, carne al pastor, and its famous flauta. **'Ai Love Nalo** (41-1025 Kalanianaole Hwy., 808/259-5737, 9am-5pm daily, $5-10) mixes Hawaiian-style cooking with the principles of sustainability, sourcing its ingredients locally and using organic when possible. The menu is strictly fish and vegetarian and the restaurant works closely with a Waimanalo farm for all aspects of its operation. It also serves smoothies and breakfast bowls.

KAILUA

Steak and Seafood

★ **Buzz's Lanikai** (413 Kawailoa Rd., 808/261-4661, http://buzzssteakhouse.com/lanikai.htm, 11am-9:30pm daily, $19-44) is famous for its kiawe charcoal-broiled burgers and steaks as well as its salads. The small, popular restaurant is quirky and fun, complete with a tree right in the middle of the lanai seating. It's right across from Kailua Beach Park, so it's usually packed, with a wait. Buzz's is also known for its signature mai tai, a mix of rum with a cherry on top. If you'd like a juice mixer with it, order the B.F.R.D. Don't forget to ask what that stands for. No tank tops after 4:30pm.

Formaggio Grill (305 Hahani St., 808/263-2633, www.formaggio808.com, 11:30am-11pm Mon.-Thurs., 11:30am-1am Fri.-Sat., 11am-11pm Sun., $12-69) blends Italian dishes with favorites from the grill like prime rib, lamb chops, barbecued ribs, and filet mignon. Thin-crust pizzas and rich lobster bisque complement the dishes, as does the wine-by-the-glass selection, over 50 bottles. Parking is extremely limited in front of the restaurant. Try the lot across the street by Macy's.

Quick Bites

Kalapawai Market (306 S. Kalaheo Ave., 808/262-4359, www.kalapawaimarket.com, 7am-9pm daily, $4-24) is right at Kailua Beach Park, with another location in downtown Kailua (750 Kailua Rd., 808/262-3354, 6am-9pm Mon.-Thurs., 6am-9:30pm Fri., 7am-9:30pm Sat., 7am-9pm Sun., $8-24). The beach park location has a small sandwich deli and a limited grocery store that also sells beer and wine. The downtown location is strictly a café and deli with a coffee and wine bar and bakery. Open for breakfast, lunch, and dinner, with indoor and outdoor seating, Kalapawai Market has made-to-order sandwiches and a selection of prepared gourmet foods.

Boots & Kimo's Homestyle Kitchen (151 Hekili St., 808/263-7929, 7:30am-2pm Mon.-Fri., 7am-2:30pm Sat.-Sun., $4-14) is all about pancakes, and people line up for them—macadamia nut pancakes to be exact. It also serves other traditional breakfast items and Hawaiian-style favorites all day long, with a few lunch items as well. The restaurant is awash in sports memorabilia.

★ **Morning Brew** (600 Kailua Rd., 808/262-7770, http://morningbrewhawaii.com, 6am-6pm daily, $1-9) is the go-to coffeehouse and bistro in Kailua. With good coffee, a great assortment of bakery goods, sandwiches, snacks, free Internet, and two stories of seating, plus outdoor seating, it's an easy all-day hangout if you have some work to do.

La'ie Town

If you drive through La'ie town on a Sunday, it might take a few minutes to notice that there's something different here that you won't find anywhere else on O'ahu—or in Hawai'i, for that matter. Everything is closed. Everything, that is, except for the places of worship of the Church of Jesus Christ of Latter-day Saints. Mormons first came to La'ie in the mid-1800s and purchased a 6,000-acre parcel in 1865. By 1919, the first Mormon temple outside of Utah had been built, the Hawaii Temple.

The town of La'ie, O'ahu's only "dry" town, has developed in concert with the growth of the church in Hawai'i and reflects the values of the religious institution. The Latter-day Saints erected their signature, private Brigham Young University next door, and built the Polynesian Cultural Center, providing jobs for the students and capitalizing on tourism to spread their message to the masses.

Mexican

Cactus (767 Kailua Rd., 808/261-1000, http://cactusbistro.com, 11am-10pm daily, $6-24) offers a blend of locally sourced ingredients and Central and South American cuisine, including influences from Cuba, Puerto Rico, and Mexico. The restaurant has a modern style, complete with regional wines and premium rums, tequilas, and liquors. It serves lunch and dinner and opens at 10am for breakfast on Saturday and Sunday.

In the Kailua Shopping Center, **Mexico Lindo** (600 Kailua Rd., 808/263-0055, www.mexicolindohawaii.com, 10am-9pm Sun.-Thurs., 10am-10pm Fri.-Sat., $7-20) has the standard beans and rice, tacos and tostadas, Corona and tequila menu. Large portions and the yellow, white, and red decor make the stop worthwhile.

Japanese

Noboru (201 Hamakua Dr., A-102, 808/261-3033, http://noborukailua.com, 5pm-9pm Mon.-Thurs., 5pm-9:30pm Fri., 4:30pm-9:30pm Sat., 4:30pm-9pm Sun. $4-29) is the premier sushi restaurant in Kailua. It also serves teishoku, shabu-shabu, chanko nabe, and has a modern sake bar with over 25 different kinds of sake.

Thai

Check out **Saeng's Thai Cuisine** (306 Kuulei Rd., 808/263-9727, www.restauranteur.com/saengs, 11am-9:30pm daily, $7-11). It offers a wide range of vegetarian options alongside soups, salads, curries, seafood, meat, and noodle dishes. It is closed from 2pm-5pm to change from lunch to dinner service.

Health Food

Down to Earth (201 Hamakua Dr., 808/262-3838, www.downtoearth.org, 7:30am-10pm daily) is an all-vegetarian organic and natural food store. In addition to groceries, vitamins, cosmetics, bulk items, and produce, it has a hot-food bar and bakery. There are a few tables in front of the store where you can enjoy your meal. Hamakua Marsh is just across the parking lot.

Whole Foods (629 Kailua Rd., #100, 808/263-6800, www.wholefoodsmarket.com/stores/kailua, 7am-10pm daily) has a hot-food bar, sandwiches, cold prepared foods, fresh pizza, Chinese food, burgers, burritos, even a few beers on tap, and a comfortable outdoor lanai for sitting down and enjoying your grub.

KANE'OHE

Kane'ohe is a town that has not been largely altered by tourism, the proof being that you won't find any fine-dining restaurants or chic clothing boutiques. Instead, Kane'ohe is littered with local and national fast-food chains and small and simple ethnic eateries.

Quick Bites

Once you pass through Kane'ohe, it's all about mom-and-pop places where you can grab a quick bite. And at the top of the list is the **Waiahole Poi Factory** (49-140 Kamehameha Hwy., 808/239-2222, http://waiaholepoifactory.com, 11am-5pm daily, $5-11). Serving up real Hawaiian food like squid and beef lu'au, kalua pig, lomi salmon, lau lau, and chicken long rice, it has mini plates that come with rice and lomi salmon and combo plates for a larger appetite. It also sells hand-pounded poi, which has a firmer texture and lighter flavor than milled poi.

Just past the Poi Factory, the **Waikane Store** (48-377 Kamehameha Hwy., 808/239-8522, 8:30am-5pm daily) is a historical landmark on the Hawai'i Register of Historic Places. Established in 1898, it's still serving up many of the snacks and treats it's been selling for decades: boiled peanuts, fresh cooked chicken, local fruits, and homemade peanut butter cookies.

Breakfast

For a local-style diner breakfast, stop by **Koa Pancake House** (46-126 Kahuhipa St., 808/235-5772, 6:30am-2pm daily, $2-8). It's a popular breakfast spot on the weekends and is usually packed all morning, so expect a wait. The parking lot is very small, and if it's full, park on Kawa Street.

Korean

Kim Chee Restaurant (46-010 Kamehameha Hwy., 808/235-5560, 9am-9pm Mon.-Sat., 7am-9pm Sun., $8-27) is revered as the best local-style Korean food eatery on the windward side. The big portions come with different styles of kimchi. The menu is full of choices, but the kalbi is a must. One downside, there are only a couple parking spots in front of the restaurant.

Chinese

Pah Ke's (46-018 Kamehameha Hwy., 808/235-4505, http://pahke.com, 10:30am-9pm daily, $6-24) Chinese restaurant is just down the street from Kim Chee Restaurant and equally as popular. It's a big venue that can accommodate large parties quite easily, although it does fill up for dinner. The dishes tend to be simple combinations of a protein, vegetable, and sauce.

Thai

If you're in the mood for Thai, try **Chao Phya** (45-480 Kaneohe Bay Dr., 808/235-3555, 11am-9pm Mon.-Sat., opens at 5pm Sun., $8-10) in the Windward City Shopping Center next to Starbucks. It's a good option for take-out as well.

Mexican

There is a very small Mexican restaurant in Kane'ohe called **El Mariachi** (45-1151 #B Kamehameha Hwy., 808/234-5893, 11am-9pm daily, $10-27) right behind the Aloha gas station on the *makai* side of Kamehameha Highway. With just a few tables available, it serves traditional Mexican food like burritos, enchiladas, and chile rellenos. It also has seafood selections.

Delis

★ **He'eia Pier General Store & Deli** (46-499 Kamehameha Hwy., 808/235-2192, www.heeiapier.com, 7:30am-4pm Tues.-Sun., $9-13) is a breath of fresh air in terms of high-quality, fresh local food. Whether you order guava chicken, fresh fish, or burgers and fries, the deli is known for sourcing organic and local produce and meats. It also has a few old-time dishes on offer.

Steak and Seafood

For a sit-down, true steak and seafood dining experience, ★ **Haleiwa Joe's** (46-336 Haiku Rd., 808/247-6671, http://haleiwajoes.com, 5pm-9pm Mon.-Thurs., 4:30pm-10pm Fri.-Sat., 9:30am-10pm Sun., $24-35) is Kane'ohe's answer. Nestled in a lush garden setting, Joe's serves up prime rib, fresh fish, and a handful of local favorites like poke, sashimi, sizzling mushrooms, and sticky ribs. It also has a Sunday brunch.

KA'A'AWA TO LA'IE
Quick Bites

Next to the post office in Ka'a'awa is a great mom-and-pop barbeque joint called **Uncle Bobo's** (51-480 Kamehameha Hwy., 808/237-1000, www.unclebobos.com, 11am-5pm Tues.-Fri., 11am-6pm Sat.-Sun., $5-16). It offers beef and pork barbecue plates, burgers, hot dogs, chili, and daily specials like a BLT. It even has fruit smoothies for good measure.

In Hau'ula you'll find the **Shrimp Shack** (58-360 Kamehameha Hwy., 808/256-5589 http://shrimpshackoahu.com, 10am-5pm daily, $10-24), a big yellow food truck serving up garlic and coconut shrimp, mahi, crab, mussels, calamari, and even steak.

Papa Ole's Kitchen (54-316 Kamehameha Hwy., 808/293-2292, www.papaoles.com, 7am-9pm Thurs.-Mon., 7am-3pm Tues., $3-12) is a Hawaiian food family restaurant open for breakfast, lunch, and dinner with loco moco, plate lunches, and fresh baked desserts.

In La'ie, stop by **Hukilau Cafe** (55-662 Wahinepee St., 808/293-8616, 6:30am-2pm Tues.-Fri., 7am-11:30am Sat., $5-13) for Hawaiian breakfast and lunch plates. Think burgers with egg and kalua pork with two scoops of white rice. The food is delicious, and the portions are ample. Cash only.

Markets

Tamura's (54-316 Kamehameha Hwy., 808/232-2332, 8am-9pm daily) is a small, but fully stocked grocery store and the last place you'll be able to buy alcoholic beverages until you get to the North Shore.

You can also pick up groceries in La'ie at **Foodland** (55-510 Kamehameha Hwy., 808/293-4443, 5am-midnight Mon.-Sat.). This location does not sell alcohol and is closed on Sundays.

Information and Services

LIBRARY

Internet access is available at the **Kailua Public Library** (239 Kuulei Rd., 808/266-9911), and the **Kane'ohe Public Library** (45-829 Kamehameha Hwy., 808/233-5676). Visitors need a valid Hawaii State Public Library System (HSPLS) card to use an Internet computer. Three-month visitor cards are available for $10. You can reserve Internet computer time online or in person. You can find printed bus schedules, too.

MAIL

Post offices on the windward side can be found in Kailua (335 Hahani St., 808/266-3996), Kane'ohe (46-036 Kamehameha Hwy., 808/235-1055), Ka'a'awa (51-480 Kamehameha Hwy., 808/237-8372), and Hau'ula (54-316 Kamehameha Hwy., 808/293-5057).

Getting There and Around

CAR

Getting around the windward coast is fairly simple, because for the most part, the highway is hemmed in by the Pacific Ocean on one side and the Ko'olau Mountains on the other. Kalanianaole Highway circles the southeastern tip of O'ahu and runs through Waimanalo before pulling away from the coast and intersecting the Pali Highway (Highway 61) at the Kamehameha Highway (Highway 83) junction in the Maunawili area. Kamehameha Highway runs north/south through the town of Kane'ohe, regaining the coast for the rest of the way to the North Shore. There is a parallel highway in Kane'ohe, the Kahekili Highway (Highway 83), which mirrors Kamehameha Highway, but bypasses the town closer to the mountains with fewer traffic signals.

There are three ways to go to get to the windward side from Honolulu or Waikiki: the Kalanianaole Highway takes you along the southeast shore, from Kahala to Kailua; the Pali Highway puts you directly into Kailua; and the Likelike Highway puts you directly into Kane'ohe. From Kane'ohe to the North Shore, the Kamehameha Highway unfolds with the Pacific Ocean on one side and the dramatic Ko'olau Mountains on the other.

To get to Kailua directly from Honolulu without going around the southeastern tip of O'ahu, simply take the H-1 to the Pali Highway. Once you are descending the Pali on the windward side, the Pali Highway becomes Kalanianaole Highway for a short way until you reach Castle Medical Center, where Kalanianaole Highway takes a right turn toward Waimanalo. Kailua-bound traffic continues straight ahead on Kailua Road and straight into Kailua town.

To get to Kane'ohe directly from Honolulu, take the H-1 to Likelike Highway (Highway 63). Once you are descending on the Likelike, you can either take the Kahekili Highway turn off and continue heading north toward the North Shore, bypassing Kane'ohe town, or continue to the Kamehameha Highway intersection. Turning left, or north, takes you toward the North Shore. Turning right, south, takes you to the Pali Highway and Kalanianaole Highway junction.

BUS

TheBus (808/848-5555, www.thebus.org) has several routes accessing windward locales. Bus 55 goes from Ala Moana Center, over the Pali Highway, and through Kane'ohe all the way up the windward coast to Hale'iwa on the North Shore. Bus 56 travels from Ala Moana Center, over the Pali Highway, dips into Kailua Town, and then heads over to Kaneohe. Bus 77 goes in between Waimanalo and Kane'ohe, but will skip Kailua. Bus 57 goes from Ala Moana Center, over Pali Highway into Kailua, then through Waimanalo and to Sea Life Park. Bus 57A follows a similar route, but circles Kailua and heads back to Honolulu. Check out TheBus' smartphone app, **DaBus,** for real-time information.

Ko Olina and Leeward

The leeward coast, also known as the Wai'anae Coast, is arid and rugged, with ridgelines that extend to the coast, where reef, rocks, and cliffs often take the place of sandy beaches.

Still, there is much to recommend here. The leeward coast has an unobstructed view for every day's precious sunset, where green flashes occur on a regular basis. The deep waters off the coast are prime grounds for sportfishing and a few surf spots break year-round, the most famed being Makaha, home to the first world championship professional surfing event. Spinner dolphins, humpback whales, and sea turtles frequent the waters, and the conditions are usually perfect for diving. Don't forget to look inland, where the verdant valleys of the Wai'anae Range lie in stark contrast to the parched land along the coast.

If luxury, pampering, golf, and fine dining better suit your taste, then Ko Olina, at the southwestern tip of the island, is a prime destination. A sprawling community of condos, timeshares, hotels, dining, golf, and four artificial lagoons on private land, Ko Olina is an oasis in the desert. Geared to be the next Waikiki, the area offers full-service amenities, but the price is definitely on the high side.

PLANNING YOUR TIME

If you're planning on any activity in the Ka'ena Point State Park, whether it be hiking to the natural reserve at the tip of the point, or mountain biking the dirt road to the point, or kayaking in Yokohama Bay, then head there first, as early as possible, to beat the heat of the midday sun. If you have booked a fishing or diving charter departing from the Wai'anae Small Boat Harbor, then you'll need to leave Honolulu very early to account for morning traffic. After a half day in the state park, head back south and take in the sights and snap some pictures along the way. The beaches and valleys will be perfectly lit by the afternoon sun. Finish up with dinner in Ko Olina at one of its premier restaurants.

For a west side beach day it is absolutely essential to bring an umbrella, plenty of water,

---

Previous: the arid and rugged leeward coast; Ko Olina lounging. **Above:** Ka'ena Point.

Highlights

★ **Kane'aki Heiau:** This restored stone structure is a historic and spiritual window into Hawaiian culture and perseverance (page 206).

★ **Ka'ena Point State Park:** Stretching from breathtaking Yokohama Bay to the western tip of the island, Ka'ena Point State Park includes verdant valleys, a secluded beach, and a dramatic volcanic coast (page 207).

★ **Ko Olina Lagoons:** Four ocean-fed lagoons offer a safe and beautiful environment for a family day at the beach (page 208).

★ **Makaha Beach Park:** Steeped in surfing history, this dramatic point offers one of the best waves on O'ahu, which breaks nearly year-round. The wide, sandy beach forms a small bay where trees provide shade for picnicking and surf-gazing (page 210).

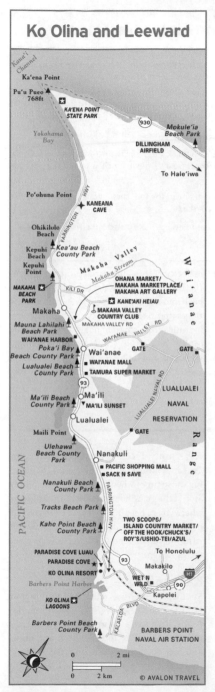

Ko Olina and Leeward

Kaua'i Channel

Ka'ena Point

Pu'u Pueo 768ft

KA'ENA POINT STATE PARK

930

Mokule'ia Beach Park

DILLINGHAM AIRFIELD

Yokohama Bay

To Hale'iwa

Po'ohuna Point

KANEANA CAVE

Ohikilolo Beach

Kepuhi Beach

Kepuhi Point

Kea'au Beach County Park

Makaha Valley

Makaha Stream

OHANA MARKET/ MAKAHA MARKETPLACE/ MAKAHA ART GALLERY

MAKAHA BEACH PARK

KILI DR

KANE'AKI HEIAU

Makaha

MAKAHA VALLEY COUNTRY CLUB

MAKAHA VALLEY RD

Wai'anae

Mauna Lahilahi Beach Park

WAI'ANAE HARBOR

Poka'i Bay Beach County Park

Lualualei Beach County Park

Wai'anae

WAI'ANAE VALLEY RD

GATE

GATE

WAI'ANAE MALL

TAMURA SUPER MARKET

93

Ma'ili Beach County Park

Ma'ili

MA'ILI SUNSET

LUALUALEI

LUALUALEI NAVAL RD

NAVAL RESERVATION

Lualualei

Maili Point

GATE

Wai'anae Range

Ulehawa Beach County Park

Nanakuli

PACIFIC SHOPPING MALL

SACK N SAVE

Nanakuli Beach County Park

PACIFIC OCEAN

Tracks Beach Park

Kaho Point Beach County Park

TWO SCOOPS/ ISLAND COUNTRY MARKET/ OFF THE HOOK/CHUCK'S/ ROY'S/USHIO-TEI/AZUL

FARRINGTON HWY

To Honolulu

PARADISE COVE LUAU

PARADISE COVE

KO OLINA RESORT

93

Makakilo

WET N WILD

H1

Barbers Point Harbor

90

Kapolei

KO OLINA LAGOONS

KALAELOA BLVD

Barbers Point Beach County Park

BARBERS POINT NAVAL AIR STATION

0   2 mi

0   2 km

© AVALON TRAVEL

and sunscreen. Shade is sparse in the region. If you're heading west just for the sunset, don't wait too late in the afternoon, as rush-hour traffic heading west could spoil your sunset plans. Lounge in one of the Ko Olina Lagoons all afternoon or post up at one of the leeward beaches, where you'll be in a prime sunset-viewing location. Keep in mind that Ko Olina is a busy resort, so there will be many people with the same sunset ideas. You'll need to keep heading west if you're in the market for your own piece of private beach real estate to watch the sun go down on another day.

If golfing is your main reason for heading to the leeward side, you can choose from two courses. The course in Wai'anae Valley is very affordable while the Ko Olina resort community offers a world-class golf experience and a shorter drive. For those staying in Ko Olina, you'll have to contend with morning rush-hour traffic heading into Honolulu as you strike out to other island locales.

ORIENTATION

Ko Olina and the windward coast are about 25 miles from downtown Honolulu. As you travel west on the H-1 to reach the locale, you'll pass Pearl Harbor and O'ahu's arid southwestern plain, home to several growing residential communities. 'Ewa—miles and miles of apartment complexes, condominiums, and homes—is to the west of Pearl Harbor. 'Ewa Beach stretches out west to Kalaeloa and the Kalaeloa Airport, an old military operation now used for light, local air traffic. To the west of 'Ewa on the 'Ewa Plain is Kapolei, a brand-new planned community on the south side of the H-1 freeway. You'll also pass by Pearl City, Waipio, Waipahu, and Makakilo, all to the north of the H-1.

Ko Olina is a private resort and lifestyle community located on the coast between Barbers Point and Nanakuli, right where the highway meets the coast after crossing the 'Ewa Plain. Ko Olina has its own exit off Farrington Highway and a gated entrance manned by resort staff. This high-end community is home to three major resort hotels

Your Best Day on the Leeward Coast

The Leeward Coast is rough, rugged, and beautiful in its own right. This side of O'ahu tends to be hot and dry, so be prepared with sunscreen, hats, and plenty of water.

- If you're interested in nature, plan on hiking to **Ka'ena Point.** Mitigate the heat by arriving as early as possible, preferably as the sun is coming up. Explore the **Ka'ena Point Natural Area Reserve.** You'll most likely see Hawaiian monk seals and nesting seabirds.

- On your return to your vehicle, take a refreshing dip in the ocean at **Yokohama Bay.**

- Head south down the Leeward Coast. Grab a quick snack at **Ohana Market** in Makaha. Continue south until you get to **Ko Olina.** Have a sit-down lunch at one of the poolside restaurants at the three resort properties.

- Families should spend a playful afternoon in one of the four sheltered lagoons in Ko Olina. Couples can schedule a treatment at **Laniwai Spa.**

- For dinner, try **Roy's** for Hawaiian fusion cuisine, or **Monkeypod Kitchen** for the best in locally sourced fare.

and four artificial lagoons for both resort guests and the public. It is also the main locale for accommodations and services in the region.

The leeward coast stretches about 20 miles from Barbers Point to Yokohama Bay in Ka'ena Point State Park, and is connected by one thoroughfare, Farrington Highway. The majority of the commercial property is along the highway, as the neighborhoods snake back into the dry valleys between the massive ridges that extend to the coast. The main communities from south to north are **Nanakuli, Ma'ili, Wai'anae,** and **Makaha.** The highway dead-ends at Ka'ena Point State Park, the westernmost tip of the island.

Sights

MAKAHA
★ Kane'aki Heiau

Located deep in Makaha Valley is one of the best-preserved *heiau* on O'ahu, the **Kane'aki Heiau.** Begun in 1545, the final structure was only completed by 1812, during the reign of King Kamehameha. Two restoration phases of construction occurred to preserve the physical, spiritual, and historic aspects of the *heiau.* Originally dedicated to Lono, the Hawaiian god of harvest and fertility, it was later converted to a *luakini heiau* for human sacrifice. The thatched huts used as prayer and meditation chambers, along with a spirit tower and carved images, have all been replicated. Because the *heiau* is within a private gated community, access is limited to 10am-2pm Tuesday-Sunday. It may be closed even during those times when it's too rainy or muddy. Stop at the guardhouse and let the guard know where you're heading, at which time you will need to show your identification and car registration or car rental agreement before you are signed in.

Kaneana Cave

Spelunkers rejoice, just off Farrington Highway on the edge of Makua Valley is the **Kaneana Cave,** a sacred ancient Hawaiian site. At 100 feet high and about 450 feet deep, this cave, *ana,* is spoken of in Hawaiian legend as the womb of the

Hawaiian monk seal

★ Ka'ena Point State Park

Ka'ena Point State Park (www.hawaiistate-parks.org/parks/oahu) is the most scenic, raw, and naturally breathtaking area on the leeward side. It is also an embodiment of all things found on the leeward coast. Located at the end of Farrington Highway and stretching all the way out to the western tip of O'ahu, Ka'ena Point State Park provides outdoor and ocean recreational activities, wildlife viewing, native plant life, green valleys, a secluded white-sand beach with turquoise water, and a dramatic volcanic coast all under the hot west-side sun. It is truly about as far removed from Honolulu and Waikiki as you can get on O'ahu.

As you round the last bend in the road with a slight elevation, the gentle arcing white sand of Yokohama Bay, also known as Keawa'ula Bay, stretches out in front of you to the west. Pristine and uncrowded, it begs for you to pull the car over and take in the serenity. Look back into the valley to catch a glimpse of the unspoiled, verdant mountains of the Wai'anae Range. As you come to the end of the paved road, a rutted, rocky dirt track completes the way to Ka'ena Point. You can walk or mountain bike out to the western tip of the island, where you'll find the **Ka'ena Point Natural Area Reserve.** This is prime territory for wildlife viewing. Look for spinner dolphins and green sea turtles in the water; on the beach you'll probably see Hawaiian monk seals basking in the sun; and the sand dunes are a protected site for nesting seabirds.

earth, where mankind emerged and spread throughout the Wai'anae coast. It is named after Kane, the god of creation. In Hawaiian lore it is also thought to be the home of Nanaue, the shark man. The cave is dark and often slippery, so bring a flashlight. It is also unmaintained, and there are several side tunnels off the main cavern that should be avoided for your own safety. Look for the painted cement road barrier that marks the entrance.

Soul's Leap

Ka'ena Point is a sacred place, and not just for its natural beauty. Ancient Hawaiians thought Ka'ena Point to be a jumping-off point for the spirits of the dead to enter the afterlife. Legend has it that humankind emerged from the depths of **Kaneana Cave,** the womb of the earth goddess, and spread across the Wai'anae coast. The souls of the deceased would find their way to Ka'ena Point by following the sun past the sunset, to the eternal night. Their leap would take them to Po, the realm of ancestral spirits, a spiritual place akin to heaven and described as being a sea of eternity. Once in Po, the soul is thought to have completed the cycle of life.

Beaches

If you're feeling adventurous and don't mind an hour's drive across the island, the beaches of leeward O'ahu offer wide swaths of white sand under clear, sunny skies. As the trade winds blow across the island from east to west, the leeward coast's waters remain calm and protected, offering beautiful conditions for swimming, surfing, fishing, snorkeling, diving, or just soaking up the sun. Waves are common along leeward beaches all year long, but generally get the biggest in the winter, from October to March. Make sure to exercise caution and assess the ocean conditions before entering the water. Check with a lifeguard for the safest place to swim.

KO OLINA
Paradise Cove

Just past the entrance gate to Ko Olina and next to Paradise Cove Luau is a small, yet beautiful sandy cove and lagoon called **Paradise Cove.** In the past it has been called Lanikauka'a and then Lanikuhonua Beach. Paradise Cove is one of three sacred lagoons in the immediate area where Queen Ka'ahumanu was said to have bathed and performed religious ceremonies. The shallow lagoon is protected from ocean swells by a raised reef rock shelf on its ocean side. There are trees on the beach for shade and tidepools. All in all, it's a great out-of-the-way nook to take the kids and explore. Parking is a little tricky, though. Take a right into the third driveway past the entrance gate. On the right is a small, free public parking area for about 10 cars. The sidewalk leads to a sandy pathway between two tall fences down to the beach.

★ Ko Olina Lagoons

Ko Olina has four lagoons open to the public from sunrise to sunset. The **Ko Olina Lagoons** are numbered 1-4, heading from west to east, and also have the Hawaiian names Kohola, Honu, Napa, and Ulua, respectively. They are more widely known and referred to by their number. The lagoons are artificially constructed semicircles cut from the sharp and rugged reef rock shelf that creates the shoreline. Channels were cut into the shelf to allow ocean water to flow in and out

Paradise Cove in Ko Olina

Ko Olina has four manmade lagoons.

leeward beaches. Each lagoon has its own access road from Aliinui Drive, the main road through Ko Olina. Turn right on Kamoana Place to reach Lagoon 1. The next three consecutive streets will lead to a lagoon and its parking area. There are no lifeguards on duty, but there is plenty of security, known as the Aloha Patrol, monitoring the lagoons from golf carts. Ever vigilant, they will be sure to let you know if you're breaking any rules from the long list of prohibited actions and items. Parking is free but very limited at each lagoon, with Lagoon 4 having the most available spots.

MA'ILI
Ma'ili Beach Park
Marking the beginning of Ma'ili town and its long stretch of beach, **Ma'ili Point** is one of the more dynamic and picturesque settings along the leeward coast. There is a small park with picnic tables and grass on the southern side of the point. The shoreline rocks extend out into the water and meet up with the shallow reef here, creating a lot of whitewater and surf action to watch while relaxing or having a snack. On the north side of the point, **Ma'ili Beach Park** runs the length of Ma'ili town. Situated between two streams that run down from the mountains, the sandy beach is widest during the

of the lagoons while blocking any surf from entering. With sandy beaches, grassy parks, a fair bit of shade from palms and trees, and a meandering pathway connecting all four lagoons, this oasis provides a sheltered, manufactured, resort-style beach experience, completely opposite to the rest of the

Master-Planned Paradise

If you notice that there's something too good to be true about Ko Olina's four clamshell-shaped lagoons, that's because the coastline has been severely altered to create Lagoons 1-4, part of the master-planned resort and lifestyle community. Before Ko Olina and the lagoons were developed, the rugged shoreline was quite inhospitable. Four- to six-foot cliffs of extremely sharp fossil reef rock protruded from the land into the sea, dropping straight into the surging waves. The area was devoid of sandy beaches. To create safe and desirable shoreline access for resort guests, channels were cut into the reef rock shelf to allow the flow of natural ocean water into half-moon lagoons, while keeping the surf and ocean currents at bay. Add sand, grass, and a few tall palm trees, and you have an artificial tropical paradise in a safe and controlled setting. It's not for everyone, but some consider it the ideal vacation.

summer when the waves are smaller, and the gently arcing beach is great for swimming and snorkeling. During the winter, however, the sand tends to migrate elsewhere with the more frequent high surf, revealing a rock shelf along the shore. There are restrooms, picnic areas, and camping on the weekends by permit only. Ma'ili Beach Park is closed 10pm-5am daily.

WAI'ANAE
Poka'i Bay Beach Park

Between the small boat harbor and Kane'ilio Point sits a beautiful sheltered bay and wide sandy beach called **Poka'i Bay Beach Park.** There is a breakwater offshore and a reef in the middle of the bay that keep the water calm along the shoreline year-round, making this a perfect spot for swimming and families. Small waves break over the reef during the winter, which attracts novice surfers. In addition to the beautiful beach, the **Ku'ilioloa Heiau** is also out on the point and has three terraced platforms. The *heiau* is thought to have been a place for learning the arts of fishing, navigation, and ocean-related skills. The beach park is closed 10pm-5am daily.

MAKAHA
★ Makaha Beach Park

A world-class surf break with a recent history entwined with the birth of international professional surfing, **Makaha Beach Park** is the hub of surfing on the leeward coast. The beautiful beach is framed at both ends by rocky headlands, the north end being the site of the surf break and the sharp reef that absorbs the ocean's energy. The surf here breaks all year but is biggest in the winter months, when waves can reach 40-50 feet high on the face during the biggest swell episodes. In the summer, swimming is best in the middle of the beach, or if the waves are completely flat, you can snorkel over the reef shelf. There are restrooms, showers, and a few shade trees and hau bushes along the road where everyone parks. If there is surf during your stop at Makaha, check with the lifeguards for the best place to enjoy the water.

Makua Beach

At the north end of Makua Valley, the only valley in the area fenced off and privately held by the U.S. Army, is a small parking area on the ocean side of the road under some trees with access to **Makua Beach.** This

Ma'ili Beach Park

undeveloped, secluded white-sand beach is a great place to find solitude. When the waves are flat, it's also fine for swimming and snorkeling, but during high surf the ocean is dangerous at Makua Beach.

Yokohama Bay

Referred to on maps and by many as **Yokohama Bay,** Keawaʻula Bay offers by far the most picturesque beach on the leeward coast. Part of **Kaʻena Point State Park,** the white sand beach curves to the northwest and points the way toward the western tip of the island, Kaʻena Point. The turquoise water sees waves throughout the year and is extremely dangerous for swimming during times of high surf. The surf breaks in the area are for expert surfers only. When the water is calm, the ocean is ideal for swimming. There is no shade on the beach, so be prepared with an umbrella or tent to mitigate the piercing sun. To complete the stunning views, behind the bay are several valleys that change from a dry, reddish hue to verdant green the farther back your eye takes you. There are public restrooms and lifeguards on duty.

Surfing

Much of the surf on the leeward side breaks over sharp and shallow reef, making it best suited for expert surfers. Scaling rocks and reef to enter and exit the water can be a challenge for newcomers, and the locals are quite territorial when it comes to their surf breaks. Still, with the right attitude, there's definitely a wave to be had on the leeward coast.

The leeward coast basically faces west, so it is prone to waves all year long. Southerly summer swells and the northwesterly winter swells both offer opportunities for quality surf. Winter swells can get quite big—scary big actually. When a high surf advisory is called for the coast and waves are above the 20-foot mark, it's best to leave the surfboard at home and watch the locals who are familiar with the challenging breaks.

Yokohama Bay

MA'ILI
Ma'ili Point

Ma'ili Point is one of the best waves on this stretch of coastline. A predominantly left-breaking point break, the wave breaks over a shallow coral shelf, which can be a nearly dry reef at low tide. On south swells, the wave is a bit slopey and sometimes rights will break off the main peak. On northwesterly swells, Ma'ili Point is a freight-train wave, with fast breaking and barreling lefts suited for experts only. Park in the parking lot on the north side of the point. Getting in and out of the water can be tricky because of the rocky shelf along the beach, so watch or ask one of the local surfers the best way to get in without getting hurt.

WAI'ANAE
Poka'i Bay

Inside the breakwater in Poka'i Bay in Wai'anae is a rolling wave perfect for beginners. Longboarders, stand-up paddlers, and first-time surfers can get the feel of a board under their feet at this soft break. The wave breaks over a wide reef and is small and calm, even when the surf is larger elsewhere.

MAKAHA
Makaha Beach Park

Makaha is a right-hand point break steeped in surf history. The site of the Makaha International Surfing Championships 1954-1971, the waves at Makaha can range from fun and playful to massive and life threatening. Makaha breaks in summer and winter, with the largest waves occurring during the wintertime high surf advisories. The wave breaks over shallow reef at the top of the point and runs into deeper water with a sandy bottom near the beach, famous for its backwash. Makaha gets crowded and has a well-established pack of locals of all ages. If you paddle out at Makaha, smile, say hello, and don't hassle anyone for a wave, or you'll be on the beach before you know it. At Makaha, you'll find people pursuing ocean sports of all kinds: surfing, bodyboarding, stand-up paddling, and bodysurfing. Parking along the road is the safest so you can keep an eye on your car.

Yokohama Bay

About eight miles past Makaha, in the Ka'ena Point State Park at the end of the road, are several challenging, barreling surf breaks. Nestled in the beautiful and secluded Keawa'ula Bay, better known as **Yokohama**

Makaha Beach Park

Bay, swells approach out of deep water from the north and the south and detonate along the bay's shallow reefs. The waves are very dangerous as they break on extremely shallow reef shelves close to shore. This is a favorite spot for expert surfers and bodyboarders.

Outfitters

Hale Nalu (85-876 Farrington Hwy., #A2, 808/696-5897, http://halenalu.com, 10am-5pm daily) has new and used boards and rents bodyboards starting at $14 per day, shortboards starting at $20 per day, longboards starting at $30 per day, and stand-up paddleboards starting at $50 per day. It also has discounts for three-day and week rentals.

West Oahu SUP (84-1170 Farrington Hwy., 808/729-2229, http://westoahusup.com, 9am-5pm daily) rents bodyboards for $30 per day, $65 per five-day week; shortboards $30 per day, $100 per week; longboards $7.50 hourly, $30 full day, and $100 per week; and stand-up paddleboards with paddle for $15 hourly, $55 full day, and $165 per week.

Water Sports

SNORKELING

When the surf is flat and the ocean is calm, generally during the summer, the leeward coast is a snorkeler's dream come true. Crystal clear turquoise water, ample rock outcroppings and patches of reef beside white sandy beaches, and calm nearshore waters protected from the trade winds make for excellent snorkeling all along the coast. Look for areas where a sandy beach connects to rock and reef for the best opportunities to see marine life with safe and easy passage in and out of the water. While there are many places to just pull off the road and jump in the water, it's always safer to swim or snorkel by lifeguards and first check with them about the current ocean conditions. And remember that strong currents accompany high surf, even if there are no waves breaking in your immediate locale. Green sea turtles and spinner dolphins are common sights on the leeward side.

A popular dive and snorkel spot is Kahe Point Beach Park. Getting in and out of the water can be tricky as small waves break on the beach, but the water becomes calm almost immediately past the shorebreak. With plenty of reef on the ocean floor, you'll see fish and turtles and plenty of corals. The visibility improves as you swim away from the beach.

Makaha also offers great snorkeling when the waves are flat. Enter the water from the beach and snorkel up the point or down the beach to the south to see live corals, fish and turtles. If there are surfers in the water, do not attempt to snorkel where the waves are breaking. If there are small waves along the point, try the south end of the beach.

Outfitters

The best bet is to bring your snorkel gear with you from your point of origin, because if you find yourself on the west side in need of snorkel gear, you'll have to drive to Wai'anae or Makaha to rent or purchase equipment. Hale Nalu (85-876 Farrington Hwy., #A2, 808/696-5897, http://halenalu.com, 10am-5pm daily) is a sporting goods store located in Wai'anae across from Poka'i Bay renting snorkel gear for $10 per day, $20 for three days, and $35 per week. In Makaha, West Oahu SUP (84-1170 Farrington Hwy., 808/729-2229, http://westoahusup.com, 9pm-5am daily) rents snorkel sets for $15 full day and $50 five days. Inside the same retail space you'll also find Paradise Isle (87-2070 Farrington Hwy., #B-2, 808/695-8866), a fish and dive shop where you can purchase new gear.

DIVING

Nestled in the lee of the trade winds, the west side has some of the best conditions for diving on a consistent basis. The underwater world has shallow reef diving with lava tubes and arches, the Makaha caverns and rock formations—a favorite for turtles and monk seals—and several wrecks, including a plane fuselage, a landing craft unit, an airplane, and a minesweeping vessel. Look for octopus, whitemouth morays, porcupine puffer fish, whitetip reef sharks, Hawaiian stingrays, and spinner dolphins.

Outfitters

Patrick's Diving Adventures (725 Auahi St., 808/589-2177, http://pearlharbordivers. com), is based in Honolulu, but dives the west side in addition to the south and southern coasts. Its two-tank boat dives from the Wai'anae Small Boat Harbor are $99 per person. It also offers a special three-tank Ka'ena Point drift dive once or twice a month for $109. It has scuba courses in Honolulu, offering NAUI certification starting at $379 group and $449 private.

KAYAKING

From the water, the leeward coast is nothing less than spectacularly beautiful. Its rugged coastline, a combination of white-sand beaches, rock and reef outcroppings, and jagged cliffs, is only complemented by the deep valleys lying in succession all the way up the coast. Sea kayaking affords a perspective unmatched and unobtainable by land, far from the spiderweb of power lines over the neighborhoods and the bustle of Farrington Highway. In addition, the crystal clear water runs from turquoise to deep blue, and humpback whale-watching is at its best on this side of the island during their annual stay from November to March.

As the trade winds rise over the Wai'anae Range, they create pristine conditions for ocean activities. Calm nearshore waters afford easy paddling and abundant ocean life. You can enter the water from Tracks, at the south end of the leeward coast, but be prepared to deal with small waves along the shore. From here, you can explore the jagged cliffs and find small pockets of sand only accessible from the water. Sheltered Poka'i Bay in Wai'anae is perfect for launching the kayaks. For the best views of the valleys, put in at Makaha, Makua Beach, or Yokohama Bay, but only if the surf is flat, which is more likely to occur in summer.

West Oahu SUP (84-1170 Farrington Hwy., 808/729-2229, http://westoahusup.com, 9am-5pm daily) rents single-rider kayaks for $25 hourly, $50 full day, and $175 per five-day week. Two-person kayaks rent for $25 hourly,

the rugged leeward coast

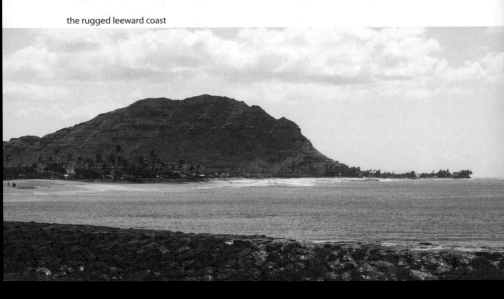

$60 full day, and $215 per week. The shop also rents roof racks and tie-downs for $10.

SAILING

If you prefer to charter a catamaran and let someone else do the navigating for you so you can focus on taking in the sights, **Wild Side Hawaii** (87-1286 Farrington Hwy., 808/306-7273, http://sailhawaii.com) has three tours that leave from Wai'anae Small Boat Harbor: Morning Wildlife Cruise is a three-hour nearshore cruise with snorkeling, spinner dolphin swims, and seasonal whale-watching for $115; Best of the West is a 3.5-hour tour with dolphin swims, whale-watching, and tropical reef snorkeling, with a maximum of six guests for $195 per person; the Deluxe Family Charter is a mid-morning three-hour cruise focusing on hands-on learning about Hawaii's marine creatures with dolphin swims, snorkeling instruction, and whale-watching for $175 adult, $145 child. It also has a full-day cruise departing from Honolulu to the leeward coast for $335.

E O Waianae Tours (2101 Nuuanu Ave., 808/538-9091, www.eowaianaetours.com) has morning and afternoon west-side catamaran tours with snorkeling and kayaking. Adults $120, children ages 5-12 $100, children ages 4 or younger $45. It also offers transportation from Waikiki.

FISHING

While shoreline fishing is common from the cliffs and beaches in the region—papio, kumu, and moana being the sought-after take—fishing charters also run out of the area and take advantage of the frequently calm ocean conditions and the steep ledges offshore attracting pelagic fish. There is a 3,000-foot ledge just three miles from Wai'anae Harbor and another 6,000-foot ledge just seven miles out. It's also not uncommon to see people fishing from kayaks just offshore along the coast.

In the Ko Olina Marina there are several fishing charter operators. **Hawaii Charter Boat** (808/372-3868, http://hawaiicharterboat.com) offers deep-sea excursion off Ko Olina and the west coast on their luxury 43-foot fishing yacht. Their private charters are for a maximum of six passengers: the four-hour charter is $700, six hours go for $850, and eight hours will run you $950. **Holopono Sportfishing Charters** (808/330-9890, www.holoponosportfishing.com) trolls for big game fish. Its four-hour charter is $700, six hours is $900, and eight hours will run you $1,100. It also offers private whale-watching tours and sunset cruises.

In the Wai'anae Small Boat Harbor you'll find **Boom Boom Sportfishing** (85-371 Farrington Hwy., Pier A, 808/306-4162, www.boomboomsportfishing.com), which offers private and shared charters for a maximum of six passengers, with two departure times daily. Four-hour private charters are $625, six hours $725, 8-10 hours $900, and 12 hours $1,300. Shared charters start at $160 for four hours and free round-trip transportation or a 10 percent discount for Ko Olina Resort guests.

Live Bait Sportfishing (808/696-1604, www.live-bait.com) also operates out of the Wai'anae Harbor, from slip B-2, and provides all equipment and tackle. You are responsible for bringing food and drinks. The company primarily fishes for marlin, wahoo, tuna, and mahimahi, and give a meal-sized portion of the catch to passengers. Half-day trips are $550 and full-day trips are $750, with a four-passenger maximum.

For fishing gear and tackle retailers, check out **Westside Tackle and Sports Shop** (87-701 Manuaihue St., 808/696-7229) in Wai'anae or **Paradise Isle** (87-2070 Farrington Hwy., #B-2, 808/695-8866) in Makaha.

Hiking, Biking, and Bird-Watching

HIKING
Leeward

The leeward side is notoriously dry, sunny, and hot, so hiking is best done early in the morning or late in the day. No matter when you go, bring plenty of water, a hat, and sunscreen.

In **Ka'ena Point State Park** (www.hawaiistateparks.org), hiking out to **Ka'ena Point** is a special experience. The rough and rocky trail, a little over five miles round-trip, follows a well-worn dirt road along the cliff out to the point. The volcanic coast is breathtaking, with tidepools, natural stone arches, and surf surging onto rock outcroppings. The road has washed away not far from the point, so follow the narrow side trail around the cliff. You'll reach a formidable fence designed to keep out invasive species; enter through the double doors. Once you are inside the **Ka'ena Point Natural Area Reserve** (www.state.hi.us/dlnr/dofaw/kaena/index.htm), an ecosystem restoration project, it is of the utmost importance to stay on the marked trails so as not to disturb the seabird nesting grounds. The dunes are covered with native Hawaiian plants and home a handful of Hawaiian and migratory seabirds. Continue down to the shoreline past some old cement installments and look for Hawaiian monk seals basking in the sun. There are no facilities along the hike and no water, so bring plenty of fluids. To get to the trail, follow Farrington Highway to Yokohama Bay. Drive along the beach till the paved road ends. Park in the dirt parking area and proceed down the dirt road on foot. The state park is open from sunup to sundown.

Explore the deep valley behind Wai'anae, in the shadow of O'ahu's tallest peak, Mount Ka'ala. The six-mile **Wai'anae Kai** loop trail is full of ups and downs, with a final climb to an overlook. It then follows an ancient Hawaiian trail back to the main route. You'll find native Hawaiian trees, shrubs, and herbs along the hike and the likes of the Japanese bush warbler. There are views of Wai'anae, Lualualei, and Makaha Valleys. The trail is unimproved and rough, so proper footwear is essential. To get there, follow Waianae Valley Road to the back of the valley. Continue on it after it turns into a one-lane dirt road. Park in the dirt lot across from the last house at the locked gate. Continue past the locked gate and follow the dirt road on foot.

BIKING

The leeward coast does have a gem of a mountain biking trail, the road to **Ka'ena Point.** Part of **Ka'ena Point State Park** (www.hawaiistateparks.org), the trail is flat, so there's no climbing or downhill involved, but the rocky, rutted, and curving cliffside dirt road is a challenging ride nonetheless. At 2.7 miles

the dusty and rocky road to Ka'ena Point

Predator-Proof Fence

Ka'ena Point is a 59-acre Natural Area Reserve.

Ka'ena Point has long been home to a variety of Hawaii's wildlife, a chorus of flora and fauna on land and in the sea. In years past, human impact took a devastating toll on the fragile ecosystem: off-road vehicles tore up the dunes, destroying native vegetation and disturbing seabird nesting sites, and feral cats, dogs, rats, and mongooses decimated seabird populations, namely the wedge-tailed shearwater and Laysan albatross that nest in the dunes, by eating eggs and killing juvenile birds.

Today, because of the **Ka'ena Point Natural Area Reserve Ecosystem Restoration Project,** Ka'ena Point is a natural restoration success story. Integral to the return of native plant species, native insects, and nesting seabirds is the predator-proof fence. Completed in 2011, the 6.5-foot-high fence uses a fine mesh technology to protect the 59-acre reserve from predation by invasive species. Spanning 700 yards and following an old railroad track roadbed around the point, the fence is also buried underground, with the ability to keep two-day-old mice from entering. A double-gated entry system ensures unwanted pests cannot sneak in, as only one door can open at a time. The fence is unobtrusive and colored to blend in with the natural vegetation and geography. Since its completion, native vegetation has returned and nesting seabird populations are steadily increasing.

one way from the parking area to the point, the ride is extremely scenic, passing rocky coves, sea arches, and crashing waves. Once at the fence, to keep out invasive species from the natural reserve portion of the park, you can bike around the point, along the perimeter of the fence, to the Mokule'ia side and continue up the North Shore, or you can walk your bike through the double doors in the fence. However, the trails inside the reserve are narrow and sandy. The sun is intense, and there is

no shade in the area, so bring plenty of water and wear sunscreen.

To get to the trail, follow Farrington Highway to Yokohama Bay. Drive along the beach until the paved road ends. Park in the dirt parking area and proceed down the dirt road on foot. The state park is open from sunup to sundown.

Hale Nalu (85-876 Farrington Hwy., #A2, 808/696-5897, http://halenalu.com, 10am-6pm Mon.-Fri., 10am-5pm Sat.-Sun.), in

Wai'anae, rents mountain bikes for $30 per day, $60 for three days, or $90 for one week.

BIRD-WATCHING

The **Pearl Harbor National Wildlife Refuge** (808/637-6330, www.fws.gov/pearl-harbor) is a sanctuary for native Hawaiian waterbirds and migratory waterfowl. There are two small conservation areas, which are not open to the public, but you can view the refuge from the Pearl Harbor Bike Path as it rounds Middle Loch. Since you can't physically enter the refuge, bring binoculars.

The **Ka'ena Point Natural Area Reserve** (www.state.hi.us/dlnr/dofaw/kaena/index.htm) inside the Ka'ena Point State Park is the premier bird-watching area on the leeward coast. The 59-acre reserve is an active ecosystem restoration project designed to restore the native ecosystem on the point and bolster the number of endangered species, both flora and fauna, that call the area home. Look for Laysan albatross, wedge-tailed shearwater, and white-tailed tropicbird that nest in dunes. Nesting begins in November, with the adults departing in late spring and juveniles leaving the nests by late June. The area is also home to several species of native Hawaiian birds, including the great frigatebird, red-footed,

the sand dunes at Ka'ena Point Natural Area Reserve

brown, and masked boobies, sooty and white terns, and the Hawaiian short-eared owl. Other migratory birds, like the wandering tattler and the Pacific golden plover, also frequent the area.

Golf

KO OLINA

The manicured **Ko Olina Golf Club** (92-1220 Aliinui Dr., 808/676-5300, http://www.koolinagolf.com) is the region's premier golf destination. The beautiful Ted Robinson layout features views of the Wai'anae Mountains and the Pacific Ocean. The 18-hole course has expansive landing areas and multitiered greens for golfers of all skill levels. It also has an internationally recognized golf shop and offers private, group, and corporate classes at the Ko Olina Golf Academy, with a Professional Golfers Association (PGA) teaching staff.

Greens fees start at $189, with discounted rates for Ko Olina Resort guests.

MAKAHA

In Makaha you'll find the **Makaha Valley Country Club** (84-627 Makaha Valley Rd., 808/695-7111, www.pacificlinks.com/makahaeast) surrounded by the ridges of the Wai'anae Mountains in the expansive Makaha Valley. Opening out to the Pacific Ocean, the 18-hole, par-71 course has a rolling topography known for its challenging par-3 holes. Greens fees start at $90.

Spas

KO OLINA

Inside the **Aulani, A Disney Resort and Spa** (92-1185 Ali'inui Dr.) In Ko Olina you'll find the **Laniwai** (808/674-6300, https://resorts.disney.go.com/aulani-hawaii-resort/spa-fitness). In addition to standard spa services like massage, facials, and body treatments, it offers full salon and nail services, as well as spa fitness, even spa treatments for teens and kids. Fifty-minute massages start at $155, 50-minute facials start at $155, and 50-minute body treatments start at $155. For men, the spa offers facials and back rejuvenation starting at $155. Couples can get side-by-side massages by choosing from any of the services offered. Prices are per person. Laniwai also has several complimentary fitness group classes like a guided lagoon walk, aqua Job, beach workout, and Zumba. 60-minute yoga sessions are $15. Contact the spa for the current schedule of classes.

Inside the **Marriott's Ko Olina Beach Club** (92-161 Waipahe Pl.) you'll find the **Spa by the Sea** (808/382-5798, www.marriott.com/hotels/hotel-information/fitness-spa-services/hnlko-marriotts-ko-olina-beach-club/). It features three cabanas and reasonably priced spa treatments, like women's and men's facials, body treatments, wraps, and scrubs. Massages start at $60.

Entertainment

KO OLINA

Paradise Cove Luau (92-1089 Aliinui Dr., 808/842-5911 or 800/775-2683, www.paradisecovehawaii.com) is located just inside the Ko Olina main entry gate. Set on 12 oceanfront acres, the luau probably has one of the best sunset views on O'ahu. An evening at Paradise Cove actually begins before sunset. For about two hours, guests can explore the beautiful property, trying traditional arts and crafts, playing traditional Hawaiian games, shopping, or sipping mai tais. Guests can even partake in a *hukilau*, pulling fishing nets up onto the shore. After a sunset ceremony, the feast starts with traditional luau favorites, then begins the Paradise Cove Hawaiian Revue. Packages start at $80 adult, $70 youth, and $60 children. Two packages with higher rates offer better seats. Reservations are available online.

Expressly Pineapple

Dole Plantation

Ananas comosus of the family Bromeliaceae is a tropical fruit that originated in southern South America. During the 1500s and 1600s, voyaging ships' captains took this unusual and intriguingly sweet fruit around the world on their journeys. **Pineapples** seem to have been brought to Hawaii from somewhere in the Caribbean in the early 1800s, but it wasn't until the mid-1880s that any agricultural experimentation was done with them. James Dole planted the first commercial pineapple plots for production on the Leilehua Plateau at Wahiawa just after the turn of the 20th century. To preserve the fruit, he built an on-site cannery in 1903 and later a second in Iwilei in Honolulu. Expanding his operation, Dole bought the island of Lana'i in 1922 and proceeded to turn the Palawai Basin into one huge pineapple plantation—some 18,000 acres at its greatest extent. The Lana'i plantation produced a million pineapples a day during peak harvest. Relying heavily on canning, Dole made the "king of fruits" a well-known and ordinary food to the American public.

Pineapple production is a lengthy process. First the ground must be tilled and harrowed to ready the soil for planting. The crowns of the pineapple fruit (which themselves look like miniature pineapple plants) or slips from the stem are planted by hand into long rows—some 30,000 plants per acre. A drip-irrigation system is then installed and the soil covered with ground cloth to help control pests and weeds. Fertilizers and pesticides are sprayed as needed, and the plants grow in the warm tropical sun. After 11-13 months these plants fruit. Generally each plant yields one fruit, which grows on a center stalk surrounded by sharp and spiky curved leaves. The plant sprouts again and, about 13 months later, a second crop is taken. Sometimes a third crop is also harvested from these same plants, before the remainders are tilled into the soil and the process begins again. Pineapples are picked by hand—a hot, dusty, and prickly job—and then placed on a boom conveyor that dumps them into trucks for transportation to the cannery. There, all are pressure-washed and sorted by size and quality before being canned or fresh-packed into boxes and shipped to market. Generally about two-thirds are sold as fresh fruit; the remainder is canned. All aspects of production are rotated to keep pineapples available for market throughout the year. There are no longer any pineapple canneries on O'ahu.

Food

MA'ILI
Steak and Seafood

For a sit-down meal overlooking the ocean, check out **Maili Sunset Bar & Grill** (87-064 Farrington Hwy., 808/679-9080, 4pm-2am daily, $8-24). Open for dinner and late-night shenanigans, it's just about the only restaurant on the west side with a great location, modern décor, full bar, and a sit-down menu. The cuisine is a combination of steak, seafood, and bar food prepared local style. It also has live music and entertainment on occasion.

MAKAHA
Markets

In the Makaha Marketplace, on the corner of Farrington Highway and Makaha Valley Road, you'll come to **Ohana Market** (84-1170 Farrington Hwy.), your last chance for snacks, local sundries, and beverages if you're headed to Ka'ena Point.

KO OLINA

If you're looking for a traditional sit-down, white-tablecloth meal on the west side, then drop into Ko Olina, where top chefs have set up shop to cater to the resort guests.

Quick Bites

Off the Hook (92-1185 Aliinui Dr., 808/674-6200, http://resorts.disney.go.com/aulani-hawaii-resort, 9am-11pm daily, $9-15) is an open-air, beachside lounge in the Aulani Resort, resembling a seaside fishing shack with Hawaiiana-inspired décor. The appetizer menu features Asian-influenced fare with the option to build your own seafood platter priced per piece. The full bar specializes in tropical cocktails.

Island Country Markets (92-1048 Olani St., 808/671-2231, 6:30am-11pm daily) and **Two Scoops Ice Cream** (92-1048 Olani St., 808/680-9888, www.twoscoopsicp.com, 11am-9pm daily, $3-9) are both located in the

Ko Olina Center & Station, near the Ko Olina entrance on the mountain side of the golf course and train tracks. The market has a full deli with hot and cold prepared foods, groceries, produce, raw foods, and alcohol. It also has tourist garb like towels, shirts, and souvenirs. Two Scoops is a locally owned ice-cream parlor with sundaes, frozen drinks, smoothies, and coffee drinks. In addition to supreme ice cream, a jumbo hot dog and Philly cheesesteak are also on the menu.

Steak and Seafood

Monkeypod Kitchen (92-1048 Olani St. Ste. 4-107, 808/380-4086, www.monkeypodkitchen.com/ko-olina/, 11am-11pm Mon.-Fri., 9am-11pm Sat.-Sun., $14-38) is leading the charge for handcrafted and sustainable cuisine. It uses only socially conscious ingredients, like range-free Maui beef and sustainably caught fish. It serves hand-tossed, wood-fired pizza, burgers, fish, steaks, and noodle dishes like saimin, and boasts an extensive beer and wine list. Monkeypod Kitchen is can't-miss dining.

Inside the Marriott Beach Club, **Chuck's Steak & Seafood** (92-161 Waipahe Pl., 808/678-8822, www.chuckshawaii.com/steakseafood.html, 4:45pm-9:30pm Mon.-Thurs., 4:45pm-10pm Fri.-Sun., $20-45) serves classic, no frills steak and seafood dishes. Enjoy indoor or outdoor seating and a full bar with two nightly happy hours.

A Hawaii staple, **Roy's** (92-1220 Aliinui Dr., 808/676-7697, www.roysrestaurant.com, 11am-2pm and 5:30pm-9:30pm Mon.-Fri., 11am-2pm and 5pm-9pm Sat.-Sun., $15-45) offers lunch and dinner in the Ko Olina Golf Club. Known for its signature Hawaiian fusion cuisine, Roy's blends fresh ingredients with European sauces and Asian spices. A prix fixe menu includes wine pairings and the exceptional desserts are made fresh to order. Indoor and outdoor seating overlooks the golf course.

Getting There and Around

CAR

To get to the leeward coast from Waikiki or Honolulu, take the H-1 freeway west. Right before Ko Olina the H-1 turns into Farrington Highway, Route 93. Farrington Highway runs the entire length of the leeward coast. The drive from Honolulu to Ko Olina takes about 45 minutes if traffic is flowing. If Ko Olina is your destination, take the Ko Olina exit, which puts you right onto Aliinui Drive, Ko Olina's main road. If you have questions about where to go once inside the community, ask the attendant at the gate as you enter Ko Olina.

Getting around the leeward side is simple; there is only one major road running north and south along the coast—Farrington Highway. Farrington Highway loops past Ko Olina and shoots up the west side, parallel to the coast, all the way to the Ka'ena Point State Park, where it ends. Farrington Highway has two lanes in each direction. From Nanakuli to Makaha, there are a lot of traffic signals, so the short-distance drive can take upwards of 45 minutes. Road construction, which is quite common, will bring the highway down to one lane in each direction and cause immediate traffic delays. Even though the west side is still rugged and underdeveloped compared to most other communities on O'ahu, there are still frequent gas stations, several grocery stores, and places to stop and eat if you don't mind fast food.

BUS

TheBus (808/848-4500, www.thebus.org) routes C, 40, 401, 402, and 403 service the leeward side, and there is a transfer station in Wai'anae. Route C is an express route from Ala Moana Center in Honolulu to Makaha. Route 40 runs from Ala Moana Center to Makua, while routes 401, 402, and 403 service the leeward valleys and neighborhoods. **DaBus,** TheBus' smartphone app, is a useful tool, which provides real-time information.

Where to Stay on Oʻahu

Waikiki

With over 60 hotels and resorts packed in between the Ala Wai Canal and the Pacific Ocean, Waikiki's options for accommodations to suit your needs, and your budget, can seem daunting. Selecting a hotel here is all about setting your priorities during your stay. Are you after a beachfront hotel with sand and ocean activities just steps from your room, or is location not a factor because you plan on spending little time in Waikiki? Are you on a romantic getaway where ocean views are a must, or are you traveling with the family and looking for an affordable two-bedroom suite? For business or leisure, Waikiki has it all, including the beautiful beaches, weather, and water it's famous for.

UNDER $100

Pacific Ohana Hostel (2552 Lemon Rd., 808/921-8111, www.hawaiihostelwaikiki.com, $34-95) has female dorms, coed dorms, semi-private single and double rooms, and private rooms. Its private rooms with air-conditioning are an additional $10 per night. All rooms have private bathrooms and some units have full kitchens. There is a community kitchen open 8am-8pm. There is a small charge for linens and towels, and there's coin-operated laundry on-site.

Also on Lemon Road on the east end of Waikiki, **Waikiki Beachside Hostel** (2556 Lemon Rd., 808/923-9566, www.waikiki-beachsidehostel.com, $34-273) is the largest hostel on O'ahu. It offers small and large coed and female dorms. The semiprivate rooms have two beds, air-conditioning, lockers, private lanai, and a shared kitchen, while the small and large private suites sleep 2-4 and include full kitchen, bathroom, lockers, closet, and electronic door locks. The facility has free wireless Internet access, coffee and toast in the morning, and free local calls from every room. The hostel also has a storage room for $5 per day if you need to leave personal items for an extended period of time.

The **Waikiki Sand Villa** (2375 Ala Wai Blvd., 808/922-4744, www.sandvillahotel.com, $105-175) is a traditional high-rise hotel for budget travelers. Located on Ala Wai Boulevard, the tower has city views and premium rooms have golf course views for a slightly higher rate. The suites have kitchenettes.

On the beautiful stretch of coast closer to Diamond Head and away from the bustle of Waikiki, **Diamond Head Beach Hotel** (2947 Kalakaua Ave., 808/922-1928, www.obrhi.com/hawaii/diamond-head-beach-hotel, $95-175) offers discount vacation rentals in a 15-floor pyramid-shaped tower. The studio, one- and two-bedroom condos are fully furnished, with the best views toward the top of the building. There is also a private oceanfront lounge and private beach access from the property.

$100-250

For families or large parties looking for multiple-room accommodations, the **Aston at the Waikiki Banyan** (201 Ohua Ave., 808/922-0555, www.astonwaikikibanyan.com, $175-269) is a condo resort where every suite has separate bedrooms, full kitchens, private lanai, and free wireless Internet. There is a focus on recreation, with a swimming pool, jet spas, sauna, tennis, basketball court, putting green, and playground.

The **Waikiki Gateway Hotel** (2070 Kalakaua Ave., 808/942-6006, www.waikiki-gateway.com, $129-209), located in Gateway

---

Park, has stylish and modern standard rooms, while premium rooms have a private lanai. Most of the rooms in the tower offer unobstructed views of the ocean, city, and Fort DeRussy Beach Park. The hotel also has larger rooms with kitchenettes designed for extended stays.

The Equus (1696 Ala Moana Blvd., 808/949-0061, www.equushotel.com, $129-169) is on the western outskirts of Waikiki, near the Ala Wai Harbor and Ala Moana Center. The contemporary, equestrian-themed decor is a departure from most hotel island-style furnishings. All 67 rooms have a midsize refrigerator and wireless Internet access. There is a small plunge pool as well.

Boasting beautiful views of Fort DeRussy Beach Park, **Luana Waikiki Hotel & Suites** (2045 Kalakaua Ave., 808/955-6000, www.aquaresorts.com/hotels/luana-waikiki, $145-500) is decorated in contemporary island style, with standard rooms, studios with kitchenettes, and suites with full kitchens starting at $230. There is a swimming pool, sundeck, and fitness center at the hotel.

For accommodations closer to Diamond Head and outside the pulse of Waikiki in this price range, check out the **New Otani Kaimana Beach Hotel** (2863 Kalakaua Ave., 808/923-1555, www.kaimana.com, $187-400). With beachfront at Kaimana Beach and right across from Kapi'olani Park, the well-appointed modern rooms have ocean or park views, free Internet, private lanai, and refrigerators. Rooms in the Diamond Head Wing also have a microwave and kitchen sink. With Kaimana Beach right out front and the zoo nearby, it's the perfect family location.

Known for award-winning service, the **Aqua Waikiki Pearl** (415 Nahua St., 866/970-4162, www.aquawaikikipearl.com, $110-425) is a good choice for families looking for affordable multi-bedroom accommodations. The one-, two-, and three-bedroom suites are simply decorated with an island

theme and have full kitchens complete with dinnerware and cookware and a private lanai with city views. Two-bedroom suites with 986 square feet are $325 a night, and three-bedroom suites with 1,157 square feet are $425 a night.

Located on one of the busiest corners in Waikiki, the **Sheraton Princess Kaiulani** (120 Kaiulani Ave., 808/922-5811, www.princess-kaiulani.com, $175-257) has three distinct buildings that comprise the hotel. All rooms in the Kaiulani Wing and Ainahau Tower have a private lanai. There is a pool in the center courtyard, and the hotel has suites and family rooms. The rooms have a simple and clean feel, with light colors and wood furnishings.

The **Aqua Pacific Monarch Hotel** (2427 Kuhio Ave., 808/923-9805, www.aquapacific-monarch.com, $169-229) is a small condominium resort just a couple blocks from famous Kuhio Beach Park. It has studios with kitchenettes and one-bedroom suites with full kitchens. One-bedroom suites start at $252 with partial ocean views. The suites have floor-to-ceiling glass doors that open up to the trade winds. There is also a rooftop pool.

Queen Kapiolani Hotel (150 Kapahulu Ave., 808/954-7418, www.queenkapiolani.com, $218) is all about location. With great views of Kapi'olani Park and the ocean looking toward Diamond Head, the beach is right across the street, as are the park and the Honolulu Zoo.

Across from Kuhio Beach is the **Pacific Beach Hotel** (2490 Kalakaua Ave., 808/922-1233, www.pacificbeachhotel.com, $165-235). With 839 rooms in two towers, the hotel is able to offer very reasonable rates for ocean-view rooms, starting at $180.

The **Holiday Inn Waikiki Beachcomber** (2300 Kalakaua Ave., 808/922-4646, www.waikikibeachcomberresort.com, $199-299) has a central location, and the rooms are bright, with light tropical accents. There is a swimming pool on the sundeck and a large

Where to Stay in Waikiki

Name	Type	Price	Features	Why Stay Here?	Best Fit For
Aqua Bamboo	boutique hotel	$139-199	studios and suites with kitchens	luxury suites with outdoor lanai	couples, honeymooners
Aqua Waikiki Pearl	condo hotel	$110-425	full kitchens, private lanai	affordable suites	families
Aston at the Waikiki Banyan	condo resort	$175-269	free Wi-Fi, full kitchen, private lanai, pool, jet spa	family focus	families, large groups
Aqua Pacific Monarch	condo resort	$169-229	studios and suites with kitchens, rooftop pool	location, affordable	families, couples
Aston Waikiki Beach Tower	hotel	$465-710	all suites, gourmet kitchens	location, spacious suites	families, groups
Courtyard by Marriott	hotel	$229-382	high-speed Internet, business center	open spaces for business	business travelers
Diamond Head Beach Hotel	vacation rental	$95-175	studio and multi-room condos, private beach	oceanfront, near Diamond Head	couples, budget travelers
DoubleTree Alana	hotel	$249-385	pool, 24-hour fitness center	modern rooms, high-tech	business travelers, couples
Embassy Suites	hotel	$309-409	all suites, mini-kitchens, fitness center	condo experience in Waikiki	couples, families
The Equus	hotel	$129-169	in-room Wi-Fi	location	business travelers, budget travelers
★ Halekulani	historic hotel	$530	deep soak tubs, spa, fine dining	elegant, oceanfront	couples, honeymooners
Hawaii Prince Hotel Waikiki	hotel	$269-369	oceanfront, day spa, fitness center	luxury oceanfront resort	golfers, luxury lovers

Name	Type	Price	Features	Why Stay Here?	Best Fit For
Hilton Hawaiian Village	resort	$209-409	oceanfront, pools, saltwater lagoon	self-contained resort	couples, families, honeymooners
Holiday Inn Waikiki Beachcomber	hotel	$199-299	sundeck, swimming pool	location	families, couples
Hotel Renew	boutique hotel	$189-291	Wi-Fi	emphasis on nature	couples
Hyatt Regency Waikiki Beach	hotel	$309-379	spa, mall	location	beach lovers, couples, families
Ilikai	hotel	$249-289	full kitchens	affordable ocean views	couples, families
★ Moana Surfrider	historic hotel	$278-432	oceanfront pool, spa, dining	historic hotel, great location	couples, honeymooners
★ The Modern Honolulu	boutique hotel	$319-479	pool, sundeck, plush furnishings	luxury experience	couples, honeymooners
New Otani Kaimana Beach Hotel	hotel	$187-400	ocean and park views, free Wi-Fi, private lanai	oceanfront, near Diamond Head	families, couples
Luana Waikiki Hotel & Suites	hotel	$145-500	pool, sundeck, fitness center, full kitchens	affordable suites	families, budget travelers
Outrigger Reef on the Beach	hotel	$209-309	free high-speed Internet, restaurants, shops, pool	beachfront location	groups, families, couples
★ Outrigger Waikiki on the Beach	hotel	$199-409	pool, oceanfront location	beachfront location	beach lovers, couples, families
Pacific Beach Hotel	hotel	$165-235	almost 1,000 rooms in two towers	affordable, ocean views	families, couples
Pacific Ohana Hostel	hostel	$34-95	private bathrooms, full kitchens	affordable	budget travelers, backpackers

Where to Stay in Waikiki (continued)

Name	Type	Price	Features	Why Stay Here?	Best Fit For
Queen Kapiolani Hotel	hotel	$218	ocean and park views	location	families, couples
★ Royal Hawaiian	historic hotel	$380-625	authentic decor, tropical gardens, spa, fine dining	historic, beachfront location	couples, honeymooners
Sheraton Princess Kaiulani	hotel	$175-257	private lanai, pool	location	families, couples
★ Sheraton Waikiki	hotel	$252-449	infinity pool, bars, restaurants	oceanfront location	couples, families, honeymooners
Waikiki Beach Marriott	hotel	$219-299	pool, spa, private lanai	location	couples, families
Waikiki Beachside Hostel	hostel	$34-273	lockers, free Wi-Fi	affordable, location	budget travelers, backpackers
Waikiki Gateway Hotel	hotel	$129-209	ocean, city, and park views; studios	affordable, extended stay	business travelers, budget travelers
Waikiki Parc	hotel	$215-440	contemporary, urban luxury	luxury and services	couples, honeymooners
Waikiki Sand Villa	hotel	$105-175	suites, kitchenettes	affordable, private	budget travelers

workout center. Oceanview one-bedroom suites start around $700.

Decked out in cool, tropical, and Asian-influenced decor from the pool and lobby to the guest rooms, **Aqua Bamboo** (2425 Kuhio Ave., 808/922-7777, www.aquabamboo.com, $139-199) has standard rooms, studio kitchenettes, and one- and two-bedroom suites. The boutique hotel's sky-high luxury bedroom has an outdoor lanai with a gas grill and patio furniture.

Hotel Renew (129 Paoakalani Ave., 808/687-7700, www.hotelrenew.com, $189-291) is a small, modern boutique hotel with a sophisticated interior focused on balance and harmony. Wireless Internet, use of beach gear, and morning coffee or tea are complimentary in all 72 rooms, themed to echo the natural environment. The oceanview rooms start at $291 a night.

The **Waikiki Parc** (2233 Helumoa Rd., 808/921-7272, www.waikikiparc.com, $215-440) offers contemporary urban style and luxury. It's modern, the guest rooms are plush, and it's billed as the chicest boutique hotel in Waikiki. Guests also have access to services at its sister hotel, Halekulani, across the street.

$250-400

On the west end of Waikiki with mountain, ocean, and park views is the contemporary **DoubleTree Alana** (1956 Ala Moana Blvd., 808/941-7275, http://doubletree3.hilton.com, $249-385). The smart design with Hawaiian accents complements the chic and modern rooms with the latest in technology and amenities. There is a small heated outdoor pool and 24-hour fitness center. The DoubleTree offers smoking and nonsmoking rooms, and the high-end suites have private outdoor decks.

A beachfront hotel on the western end of Waikiki, the **Outrigger Reef on the Beach** (2169 Kalia Rd., 808/923-3111, www.outriggerreef-onthebeach.com, $209-309) offers restaurants, shops, and renewed accommodations in an elegant modern style. The moderate-rate rooms have no view, but there is free high-speed Internet access throughout the hotel. For families and large groups, the hotel also has one-bedroom ocean and city-view suites, and two-, three-, and four-bedroom oceanview suites.

The **Hawaii Prince Hotel Waikiki** (100 Holomoana St., 888/977-4623, www.princeresortshawaii.com/hawaii-prince-hotel-waikiki, $269-369) is an all-oceanfront accommodation, meaning that its design affords every room a floor-to-ceiling ocean view overlooking Ala Moana Harbor and Ala Moana Beach and Park. Located on the western edge of Waikiki near Ala Moana Center, the sophisticated hotel has 57 luxury suites, restaurants, a day spa, and a fitness center, and caters to golfers, with packages for play at the Hawaii Prince Golf Club in 'Ewa. One-bedroom suites start at $439, and two-bedroom suites start around $599.

The **Courtyard by Marriott** (400 Royal Hawaiian Ave., 808/954-4000, www.marriott.com/hotels/travel/hnlow-courtyard-waikiki-beach, $229-382), just behind the Duty Free Shopping Galleria on Kuhio Avenue, has comfortable rooms with soft colors and wood decor. With high-speed Internet throughout the hotel, a business center, and flexible open spaces in the lobby, the hotel is geared toward business travel.

The **Waikiki Beach Marriott** (2552 Kalakaua Ave., 808/922-6611, www.marriott.com/hotels/travel/hnlmc-waikiki-beach-marriott-resort-and-spa, $219-299) is a resort right across the street from Kuhio Beach Park. There are shops and restaurants on the 5.2-acre property, plus a swimming pool and spa, and the rooms are stylish, with wood accents and private lanai.

Located on the west side of the Hilton Hawaiian Village, fronting the Ala Wai Boat Harbor, the **Ilikai** (1777 Ala Moana Blvd., 808/949-0892, www.ilikaihotel.com, $249-289) has 30 stories of ocean views. It also has mountain-view and oceanview full kitchen rooms starting at $339, as well as mountain- and oceanview two-bedroom suites starting at $399.

For accommodations right in the heart of Waikiki on Waikiki Beach, check out the ★ **Outrigger Waikiki on the Beach** (2335 Kalakaua Ave., 808/923-0711, www.outrigger.com/hotels-resorts/hawaiian-islands, $199-409). Perfect for visitors interested in taking advantage of all of Waikiki's ocean activities, the hotel also has one of the best, and most famous, restaurants in Waikiki, Duke's Waikiki. The guest rooms are Hawaiian themed, with dark wood furnishings.

Overlooking the Ala Moana Small Boat Harbor, ★ **The Modern Honolulu** (1775 Ala Moana Blvd., 808/954-7427, www.themodernhonolulu.com, $319-479) mixes sophistication and smart modern design with a laid-back surf culture vibe. The Sunrise Pool has a warm, wood deck with potted shade trees, and the Sunset Pool, an adults-only blue-tiled pool, is surrounded by sand imported from neighboring islands. The luxurious rooms have innovative design features and plush furnishings. One-bedroom suites are available.

The **Hilton Hawaiian Village** (2005 Kalia

Rd., 808/949-4321, www.hiltonhawaiianvillage.com, $209-409), a 22-acre oceanfront mega-resort on the west end of Waikiki, is practically its own town. Nestled right up to the sand on Duke Kahanamoku Beach, the widest beach in Waikiki, with calm water perfect for the family, the resort has swimming pools, waterslides, and waterfalls, a saltwater lagoon, its own luau, 18 restaurants, retail shops, and a Friday night fireworks show. For accommodations, there are five towers: the Rainbow Tower is right on the beach with amazing views; the Aliʻi Tower focuses on luxury, with separate check-in, a private pool, whirlpool, and fitness center; and three Village Towers offer lower-rate rooms.

The **Hyatt Regency Waikiki Beach** (2424 Kalakaua Ave., 808/923-1234, http://waikiki.hyatt.com, $309-379) holds prime real estate across from Waikiki Beach and is the perfect hub for travelers looking to take advantage of all the beach activities Waikiki has to offer. Within its central location, is a spa, a mall on ground level, and several well-known restaurants. The rooms are simple but classy with a light tropical feel. The suites are modern and sophisticated.

Another beachfront resort that towers over the Pacific, the ★ **Sheraton Waikiki** (2255 Kalakaua Ave., 808/922-4422, www.sheraton-waikiki.com, $252-449) has stylish and comfortable accommodations, two pools, and on-site dining and shopping. The infinity edge pool is a treat for guests 16 and older. There is no beach in front of the hotel, but there is a pathway that runs along the edge of the water and offers beach access in both directions.

Situated in the Waikiki Beach Walk outdoor mall, a hub for Waikiki shopping and dining, **Embassy Suites** (201 Beach Walk St., 808/921-2345, http://embassysuiteswaikiki.com, $309-409) is an all-suite hotel that offers a condo-like experience. One- and two-bedroom suites have complimentary high-speed Internet, made-to-order breakfasts, and mini kitchens. There is also a fitness center.

The first hotel in Waikiki, opened in 1901, the ★ **Moana Surfrider** (2365 Kalakaua Ave., 808/922-3111, www.moana-surfrider.com, $278-432) is a historic icon along the Waikiki shoreline. Situated in the heart of Waikiki on Waikiki Beach, the original, stately building remains, with additional wings and towers to offer over 800 rooms. The hotel offers an oceanfront spa, a pool,

Waikiki's first hotel, the Moana Surfrider

The Royal Hawaiian is also known as the Pink Palace of the Pacific.

and dining on the veranda under the historic banyan tree. The room decor is modern, yet captures the legacy of the hotel.

$400-650

The ★ Halekulani (2199 Kalia Rd., 808/923-2311, www.halekulani.com, $530) has a long history of hospitality in Waikiki going back nearly 100 years. Today, the Halekulani is a mark of elegance and sophistication. The rooms and suites are light and bright, with marble vanities, deep soaking tubs, and glassed-in showers. The oceanfront hotel has a full service spa and several fine dining restaurants.

Just steps from Kuhio Beach, the **Aston Waikiki Beach Tower** (2470 Kalakaua Ave., 808/926-6400, www.astonwaikikibeachtower.com, $465-710) is an all-suites hotel specializing in spacious two-bedroom suites with fully equipped gourmet kitchens and in-room washer and dryer. Perfect for families that want to be close to the beach.

Opening in 1927, the ★ **Royal Hawaiian** (2259 Kalakaua Ave., 808/923-7311, www.royal-hawaiian.com, $380-625) is a landmark hotel also known as "The Pink Palace of the Pacific." The classic elegance of the guest rooms has been preserved, down to the hand-carved wooden doors in the main building. There is also a tower in addition to the historic original hotel. There are garden-view rooms of the tropical gardens and coconut grove, and a range of oceanview rooms and suites on the beachfront on hopping Waikiki Beach. Spa, fine dining, shopping, and a pool and hot tub round out the services.

Honolulu

Even though it is the biggest metropolis in the middle of the Pacific, there aren't many places to stay in Honolulu, most likely because Waikiki is practically next door. There are a few hotels near the airport for those who have an overnight layover and don't wish to take a taxi into Waikiki, one hotel downtown serving a strictly business clientele, and a two more hotels near Ala Moana Center.

ALA MOANA
Under $100

The **YMCA Central Branch** (401 Atkinson Dr., 808/941-3344, www.ymcahonolulu.org, $45-75), next to the Hawai'i Convention Center and across from Ala Moana Center, is the largest YMCA facility on O'ahu. It has partially furnished single and double rooms for men, women, and couples and offers rooms with a private shower and bathroom for an additional $10 a day. The double rooms with private baths have a mini fridge and microwave, and all guests can use the laundry and fitness facilities. There is no smoking or alcohol permitted on the premises. Weekly and monthly rates are available.

The **YMCA Nu'uanu Branch** (1441 Pali Hwy., 808/536-3556, www.ymcahonolulu. org, $42) is a male-only facility just north of downtown and Chinatown and has 70 single rooms for $42 per night. For women, the **YWCA Fernhurst** (1566 Wilder Ave., 808/941-2231, www.ywca.org, $45) offers a secure residence with 24-hour electronic access located in the downtown historic district. Double-occupancy rooms are $45 per night and singles are $65 per night. The rooms are equipped with telephones and free Internet access. It also has a free computer lab.

$100-250

The **Pagoda Hotel** (1525 Rycroft St., 808/948-8356, www.pagodahotel.com, $119-149), near the Ala Moana Center, is a great option for travelers on a budget who won't be spending a lot of time at their hotel and don't feel the necessity to stay in Waikiki. The Asian-influenced design and décor is complete with Japanese gardens, koi ponds, and waterfalls. The 359-room hotel has standard guest rooms in the main tower and studios, one-, and two-bedroom units with kitchenettes in the five-story terrace wing.

Just on the outskirts of Waikiki and situated between the Ala Moana Center and the Hawai'i Convention Center is the **Ala Moana Hotel** (410 Atkinson Dr., 808/955-4811, www.alamoanahotelhonolulu.com, $189-269). A bargain compared to some of the beachfront hotels in Waikiki, the location lends itself to those attending a convention or visitors wanting the flexibility of getting out the door and on the road without worrying about the congestion of Waikiki. The two towers offer ocean and city skyline views, and the rooms have free Internet access. The hotel also has one-bedroom suites. And with Ala Moana Center next door, there are plenty of dining options a quick walk from the hotel.

GREATER HONOLULU
$100-250

Built in 1912 in lush Manoa Valley and listed in the National Register of Historic Places, the **Manoa Valley Inn** (2001 Vancouver Dr., 808/947-6019, www.manoavalleyinn. com, $155-195) is a bed-and-breakfast set in a luxurious Victorian inn filled with European antiques. Nestled in verdant Manoa Valley, the intimate retreat is peaceful and unique, with six rooms and a country cottage available. The residence is surrounded by a tropical garden and has a heated saltwater swimming pool with a meandering waterfall. There are four friendly dogs and a cat on the premises.

Where to Stay in Honolulu

Name	Type	Price	Features	Why Stay Here?	Best Fit For
Airport Honolulu Hotel	budget hotel	$169	Wi-Fi, microwave, 24-hour airport shuttle	close to airport	business and budget travelers
Ala Moana Hotel	hotel	$189-269	Internet access	location for business	business and budget travelers
Best Western the Plaza Hotel	budget hotel	$179-189	Wi-Fi, microwave, 24-hour airport shuttle, pool	close to airport	business and budget travelers
Manoa Valley Inn	bed and breakfast	$155-195	saltwater pool	peaceful garden setting	couples, honeymooners
Pagoda Hotel	hotel	$119-149	Japanese gardens, multi-room suites	location	families, budget travelers
Sand Island State Recreation Area	camping	$18	basic facilities	only camping in Honolulu	budget travelers, backpackers
YMCA Central Branch	hostel	$45-75	rooms for men, women, and couples; monthly rates	affordable for extended stay	budget travelers, backpackers
YMCA Nu'uanu Branch	hostel	$42	men only	Chinatown location	budget travelers, backpackers
YWCA Fernhurst	hostel	$45	women only, free Internet, computer lab	downtown location	budget travelers, backpackers

The **Airport Honolulu Hotel** (3401 N. Nimitz Hwy., 808/836-0661, www.outrigger.com/hotels-resorts/hawaiian-islands/oahu-waikiki/airport-honolulu-hotel, $169) has basic 300-square-foot rooms with free wireless high-speed Internet, microwave, refrigerator, and free 24-hour airport shuttle service to the hotel.

Clean and scenic for a hotel near the airport, the **Best Western the Plaza Hotel** (3253 N. Nimitz Hwy., 808/836-3636, http://bestwesternhawaii.com/hotels/best-western-the-plaza-hotel, $179-189) offers 274 rooms with microwaves, refrigerator, and free high-speed Internet. It also has free airport shuttle service. There's even a pool if you need to take a quick dip and can't make it to the beach.

PEARL HARBOR
$100-250

The **Harbor Shores** (98-145 Lipoa Pl., 808/227-8796, www.harborshoreshi.com, $120) is an apartment hotel located on the shore of Pearl Harbor. It has basic, no frills two-bedroom units with full-size kitchens, private lanai, microwave, refrigerator, toaster oven, wireless Internet access, and a swimming pool. It caters to military families and budget and business travelers. Rates depend on the number of guests per room, and it offers weekly rates as well.

In similar fashion, the **Harbor Arms** (98-130 Lipoa Pl., 808/488-5556, www.harborarms.com, $113-125) apartment hotel has one- and two-bedroom suites with partial or full kitchens, private lanai, and free cable TV and wireless Internet. It also has a swimming pool and offers weekly rates.

North Shore

Keeping true to the North Shore's rural and relaxed atmosphere, the high-rise hotels that identify Waikiki won't be found here, though many visitors would love to spend their entire vacation in this beautiful region. Turtle Bay Resort has the distinction of being the only high-occupancy accommodation on the North Shore, a designation reflected in its room rates. Luckily for travelers enamored by the North Shore, the community is full of vacation rentals. The North Shore is more family friendly in the summer, when the surf is flat and the conditions for swimming and snorkeling are perfect.

NORTH SHORE BEACHES
Under $100

Hawaii Backpackers (59-788 Kamehameha Hwy., 808/638-7838, http://backpackers-hawaii.com, $30-150) is the North Shore's only hostel and is a collection of several properties around the Three Tables area. It has three location choices for hostel beds and four locations for private rooms and studios. Hostel beds start at $30 per night; private rooms with shared kitchen and bath start at $70 per night; private studio apartments with a beachfront patio and a full bath start at $130 per night; and private cabins sleeping 4-8 with full kitchens start at $150 per night. A 10 percent discount is offered on weekly rates.

$100-250

★ **Ke Iki Beach Bungalows** (59-579 Ke Iki Rd., 808/638-8829, http://keikibeach.com, $160-230) is located on Ke Iki Beach, just to the north of Sharks Cove and not far from Pipeline. The studio, one-, and two-bedroom bungalows are clean, stylishly appointed in tropical décor, and could not be in a more beautiful location, fronted by the Pacific Ocean and surrounded by tropical foliage. The five beachfront bungalows sleep 3-5 people and start at $195 per night. Six garden-view bungalows sleep 2-8 and start at $160 per night. Extra cleaning fees apply.

TURTLE BAY
$250-400

★ **Turtle Bay Resort** (57-091 Kamehameha Hwy., 808/293-6000, www.turtlebayresort.com, $320-430) is the North Shore's premier hotel and resort. The property is spread across almost five miles of beachfront and the family-friendly, surfer-friendly, and golfer-friendly resort has a wide range of accommodations, including 375 guest rooms and 25 suites ($330-660) in its six-story main hotel, 42 beach cottages ($500), and luxury ocean villas with beachfront locations along Kuilima Cove. The pool and waterslide will keep the kids busy all day. There is a surf break right off Kuilima Point, where the hotel sits, and the resort is home to two championship golf courses. Package rates for golf and accommodations are also available.

Where to Stay on the North Shore

Name	Type	Price	Features	Why Stay Here?	Best Fit For
Hawaii Backpackers	hostel	$30-150	private rooms, ocean views	accommodates large groups	backpackers, budget travelers
Kaiaka Bay Beach Park	camping	$50	beach camping	natural setting	nature lovers, budget travelers
★ Ke Iki Beach Bungalows	cottages	$160-230	bungalows, five beachfront	affordable, natural setting	nature lovers, couples, honeymooners
★ Turtle Bay Resort	resort	$320-430	suites, beach cottages, villas	only resort on the North Shore	nature lovers, couples, honeymooners, families

Southeast and Windward

On the southeast shore you'll find the only resort in this region, the high-class Kahala Hotel & Resort, and vacation rentals in Hawai'i Kai. On the windward coast, camping is prevalent in the beach parks, just be prepared for rain and wind, common weather conditions on this side of the island. Kailua boasts an array of bed-and-breakfast accommodations and vacation rentals to service the seaside hamlet, a great option for escaping from the Waikiki scene to one of the prettiest white-sand beaches on the island.

SOUTHEAST O'AHU
$400-650

At the end of Kahala Avenue, in the affluent Kahala neighborhood, is the luxurious **Kahala Hotel & Resort** (5000 Kahala Ave., 808/739-8888, www.kahalaresort. com, $316-796). The rooms and suites are decorated in a light tropical palette with island accents, and guests can enjoy the secluded white-sand beach just steps away. The hotel has its own private lagoon where guests can interact with dolphins and other sea creatures. A swimming pool, high-end

spa with 10 private treatment suites, and a beachfront fitness center are a few of the amenities.

KAILUA
$100-250

Just a few blocks away from Kailua Beach, **Pillows in Paradise** (336 Awakea Rd., 808/262-8540, www.pillowsinparadise.com, $110-130) offers two units: a private one-bedroom unit and a spacious studio suite with king- and queen-size beds, perfect for families. Both units have private bathrooms and entrances, coffeemaker, refrigerator, microwave, and other kitchen items. A swimming pool graces the tropical garden. There is a $50 cleaning fee.

Set on the Ka'elepulu Stream, four blocks from Kailua Beach, **Sharon's Kailua Serenity Bed & Breakfast** (127 Kakahiaka St., 808/262-5621, www.sharonsserenity.com, $105-160) has two rooms and one suite available and serves a continental breakfast. Casual and homey, the Blue Room has one queen-size bed, and the Poolside Room has a king and a twin bed. The suite is designed for a family of

Where to Stay on the Southeast and Windward Coast

Name	Type	Price	Features	Why Stay Here?	Best Fit For
Ahupua'a O Kahana	camping	$18	beachfront camping	close to valley hiking	couples, nature lovers, budget travelers
Bellow Field Beach Park	camping	$30	lifeguards, gated campground	campsite on active military base	families, budget travelers, couples
Hau'ula Beach Park	camping	$50	pavilion, convenient store	location	budget travelers
Hawaii's Hidden Hideaway Bed and Breakfast	B&B	$175-250	private bathrooms, kitchenettes, laundry	location	couples, honeymooners
Ho'omaluhia Botanical Garden	camping	$30	basic facilities	fishing, bird-watching	groups, families, nature lovers
★ Kahala Hotel and Resort	resort	$316-796	beachfront, private lagoon, spa	luxury, beach location	luxury lovers, couples, honeymooners
Kokololio Beach Park	camping	$50	beachfront	fishing	budget travelers

3-4. There are no cleaning fees. There is also a dog on the premises.

The **Sheffield House Bed & Breakfast** (131 Kuulei Rd., 808/262-0721, www.hawaiisheffieldhouse.com, $139-194) is just steps away from Kailua Beach and has two suites with private entrances, Mexican-tile floors, wireless Internet, kitchenettes, and off-street parking. The Ginger Studio with Secret Garden sleeps 2-3 and has a tropical garden and fountain outside the entrance. The Garden Suite sleeps 2-4 and can be combined with the Ginger Studio to form a two-bedroom, two-bath rental. There are cleaning fees in addition to the rate and a complimentary breakfast on the first morning of the stay.

Located 0.5 mile from the beach, **Papaya Paradise** (395 Auwinala Rd., 808/261-0316, http://windward-oahu.com/papaya/papaya.htm, $100) has a large swimming pool, great views of the Ko'olau Mountains, and a covered lanai for relaxing, reading, and enjoying the daily complimentary continental breakfast on. The rooms have wireless Internet, private entrances, private baths, two beds, and tropical furnishings. It also has beach accessories on hand to borrow.

Name	Type	Price	Features	Why Stay Here?	Best Fit For
Kualoa Regional Park	camping	$30-50	basic facilities	fishing and recreation	couples, families, nature lovers
★ Lanikai Bed and Breakfast	B&B	$175-250	suites, king-size bed, kitchenettes	beautiful setting	couples, honeymooners
Papaya Paradise	bed and breakfast	$100	pool, Wi-Fi, mountain views	family oriented	couples, families
Pillows in Paradise	bed and breakfast	$110-130	private bathrooms, pool, kitchen	location, privacy	couples, families
Sharon's Kailua Serenity Bed & Breakfast	bed-and-breakfast	$105-160	pool, Wi-Fi	family oriented	families
Sheffield House Bed & Breakfast	bed and breakfast	$139-194	private entrance, Wi-Fi, kitchenettes	beach location, privacy	couples, families
Waimanalo Bay Beach Park	camping	$50	shaded beach, basic facilities	beautiful beach	budget travelers, nature lovers, couples

Just south of Kailua in the Lanikai enclave, **Hawaii's Hidden Hideaway Bed and Breakfast** (1369 Mokolea Dr., 808/262-6560, www.ahawaiibnb.com, $175-250) has several suites surrounded by tropical foliage with private entrances, private bathrooms, kitchenettes, dining areas, lanai, wireless Internet, and laundry facilities. The Deluxe Studios each sleeps two and offers a choice of king, queen, or twin beds. The Peacock Suite sleeps 2-3 and has a large lanai with an outdoor spa.

The units can be connected, and there are additional cleaning fees of $55 per unit.

★ **Lanikai Bed and Breakfast** (1277 Mokulua Dr., 808/261-7895, http://lanikaibedandbreakfast.com, $175-250) is 100 yards from Lanikai Beach. The Garden Studio has teak and bamboo furnishings, an outdoor dining area, and a king-size bed. The Tree House is a spacious upstairs two-bedroom suite surrounded by mature trees. Both units have high-speed Internet and kitchenettes.

Ko Olina and the Leeward Coast

Ko Olina is a great family destination for those seeking a controlled and manicured resort atmosphere without the crowds and nightlife of Waikiki. Inside Ko Olina you'll find the amenities of luxury resorts, hotels, and vacation rentals, but you'll also sacrifice Waikiki's selection of restaurants, ocean activities, and nearby sights, as Ko Olina is very isolated on the southwestern tip of the island. Makaha has vacation rentals in condominium towers right on the beach. There is also camping at westside beach parks.

LEEWARD COAST
$100-250

You'll find visitor accommodations only at Makaha. The **Hawaiian Princess** (84-1021 Lahilahi St., 800/776-2541, www.hawaiian-princessmakaha.com, $149-209) is one of the more stylish and well-maintained condominium buildings along Makaha Beach. Its one- and two-bedroom units have 180-degree views of the Pacific, full kitchens, washer/dryer, and private lanai. There is also a pool, hot tub, barbecue area, tennis court, and recreation room. One-bedroom units start at $149, and two-bedrooms rent for $209.

Makaha Shores (84-265 Farrington Hwy., 808/696-4186, www.makahashores.com, $219) rents simple studio apartments with full-size kitchens and private lanai. There is a barbecue area by the swimming pool, and beautiful Makaha Beach is steps away. Other than ocean activities, there's not much to do in the area, or places to eat out, so guests should be comfortable with being self-sufficient on this quiet nook of coastline. Discounts are offered for longer stays.

KO OLINA
$400-650

Three swimming pools, seven whirlpool spas, and a beautiful seaside lagoon make the **Marriott's Ko Olina Beach Club** (92-161 Waipahe Pl., 808/679-4700, www.marriott.com/hotels/travel/hnlko-marriotts-ko-olina-beach-club, $414-839) the ultimate kid-friendly resort. Its one-, two-, and three-bedroom villas with fully equipped kitchens and tableware provide for a family

Disney's Aulani

Where to Stay on the Leeward Coast

Name	Type	Price	Features	Why Stay Here?	Best Fit For
★ Aulani	resort	$494-699	aquatic park, spa, fine dining, suites	family-oriented Disney resort	families
Harbor Arms	apartment hotel	$113-125	suites, pool, Wi-Fi, cable	long-term stay	military families, business travelers
Harbor Shores	apartment hotel	$120	two-bedroom units, full kitchen, private lanai	long-term stay	military families, business travelers
Hawaiian Princess	condominium	$149-209	full kitchens, laundry, private lanai, ocean views	slow pace	couples, families
Kea'au Beach Park	camping	$50	grassy campsites	affordable	budget travelers
Ko Olina Beach Villa Resort	luxury villas	$405	two- and three-bedroom villas, ocean views	private, long-term stay	luxury-loving families, couples, honeymooners
Ma'Ili Beach Park	camping	$30	basic facilities	fishing	budget travelers
Makaha Shores	apartments	$219	studios with full kitchens, pool	slow pace	couples, families
Marriott's Ko Olina Beach Club	villas and suites	$414-839	full kitchens, lanai, washer/dryer	family oriented	couples, families
Nanakuli Beach Park	camping	$50	shaded campsites	fishing	budget travelers

vacation that is much more comfortable, and the master suites with oversize soaking tubs and king-size beds are the ultimate in relaxation for couples. The villas also have private lanai, washer/dryer, and wireless high-speed Internet.

★ **Aulani** (92-1185 Aliinui Dr., 808/674-6200 or 714/520-7001, http://resorts.disney.go.com/aulani-hawaii-resort, $494-699), A Disney Resort & Spa, is set on one of the trademark Ko Olina lagoons, and its Hawaiian theme is everything you'd expect from Disney. At the center of this family-oriented resort is Waikolohe Valley. The aquatic adventure park has a winding river with two tubing adventures, including one with rapids and caverns; an enormous swimming pool with waterslides; a private snorkeling lagoon with tropical fish; and an interactive play area for the littlest ones. There are also hot tubs and a separate pool away from the main pool for parents wanting to enjoy some peace and quiet. During the day, Disney characters make appearances, and after the sun goes down there are age-specific theme parties for the kids. The rooms are modern and luxurious, and there are several types of views that dictate the room rate. The suites are designed for large families. A spa and fine- and casual-dining restaurants are also at the resort.

For families or couples after a romantic getaway, the **Ko Olina Beach Villa Resort** (92-106 Waialii Pl., 808/679-4088 or 877/333-3808, www.beachvillaresort.com) features private villa suites, each with a unique floor plan and an elegant and sophisticated interior design. The two- and three-bedroom villas have separate living and dining areas, private lanai, and partial to full ocean views. One-bedroom villas are only available during the low season for $405 per night. All rooms have a seven-night minimum stay.

Background

The Landscape

When Papa, the Hawaiian earth mother, returned from vacationing in Tahiti, she was less than pleased on learning through a gossiping messenger that her husband, Wakea, had been playing around. Besides simple philandering, he'd been foolish enough to impregnate Hina, a lovely young goddess who bore him island children. Papa, scorned and furious, showed Wakea that two could play the same game by taking a handsome young lover, Lua. Their brief interlude yielded the man-child O'ahu, sixth of the great island children.

Geologically, O'ahu is the second oldest main island after Kaua'i. It emerged from beneath the waves as hissing lava a few million years after Kaua'i and cooled to form Hawai'i's third-largest island. With four distinct shores—north, south, windward, and leeward—O'ahu is 44 miles long and 30 miles wide. There are 227 miles of shoreline, a mix of sandy beaches, armored shoreline, harbors, a major port, rocks, and cliffs. O'ahu is 72 miles southeast of Kaua'i across the Kaua'i Channel, and only 26 miles west of Moloka'i, separated by the treacherous Ka'iwi Channel.

GEOGRAPHY

Ancient Hawaiians worshipped Madame Pele, the fire goddess, whose name translates equally well as Volcano, Fire Pit, or Eruption of Lava. When she was angry, she complained by spitting fire, basaltic lava actually, which cooled and formed land. Two separate and extremely large shield volcanoes were behind the development of O'ahu. The Wai'anae Volcano is about 2.2 million-3.8 million years old, and the Ko'olau Volcano is roughly 1.8 million-2.6 million years old. The Wai'anae and Ko'olau Mountain Ranges are the constantly eroding remnants of the two extinct volcanoes. Over the centuries, wind and rain have sculpted the dramatic *pali*, or cliffs, on the windward side, while streams cut the deep valleys along the leeward coast.

The island is also dotted by smaller tuff cone volcanoes—Diamond Head, Punchbowl, Koko Crater, Koko Head, and Hanauma Bay—which are believed to have erupted from 500,000 to just 20,000 years ago.

There are two distinct types of lava on O'ahu for which the Hawaiian names have become universal geological terms: 'a'a and pahoehoe. They're easily distinguished by appearance, but chemically they're the same. 'A'a is extremely sharp, rough, and spiny. Conversely, pahoehoe, is billowy, ropelike lava that can mold into fantastic shapes. While O'ahu has had no recent lava flows, examples of both are still visible across the island.

O'ahu has no navigable rivers, but there are hundreds of streams. O'ahu has the state's longest stream, **Kaukonahua,** which begins atop Pu'u Ka'aumakua at 2,681 feet in the central Ko'olau Range and runs westward 33 miles through the Leilehua Plateau, emptying at the North Shore. En route, it runs through the Wahiawa Reservoir, which, at 302 acres, forms the second-largest body of freshwater in Hawai'i. Two of O'ahu's taller, accessible waterfalls are Manoa Falls, at the back of Manoa Valley, and **Waihe'e Falls** in Waimea Valley on the North Shore, which has a drop of more than 40 feet. The only sizable and natural freshwater bodies of water on O'ahu, both altered by man, are Salt Lake in Honolulu and Enchanted Lake in Kailua.

CLIMATE
Temperature
O'ahu has comfortable weather year-round.

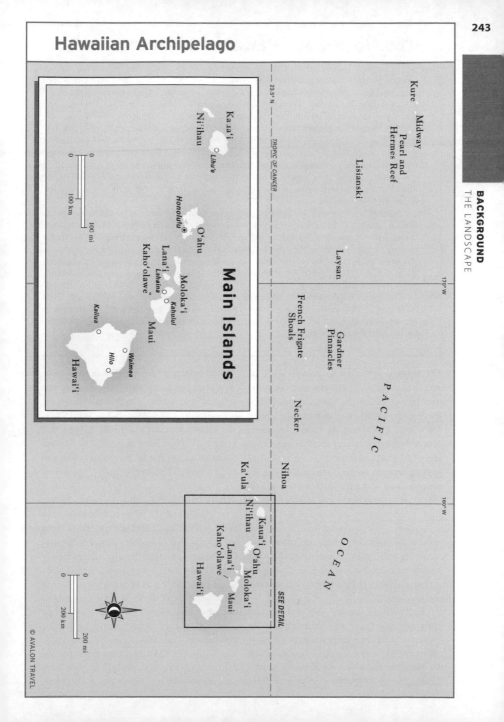

Hawaiian Archipelago

Kure
Midway
Pearl and
Hermes Reef

Lisianski

Laysan

French Frigate
Shoals

Gardner
Pinnacles

Necker

Nihoa

Ka'ula

P A C I F I C

O C E A N

23.5° N
TROPIC OF CANCER

170° W

160° W

Main Islands

Kaua'i
Ni'ihau
Lihu'e

O'ahu
Honolulu

Moloka'i
Lana'i
Lahaina
Kaho'olawe

Kahului
Maui

Kailua
Waimea
Hilo
Hawai'i

0   100 km
0   100 mi

SEE DETAIL

Kaua'i
Ni'ihau
O'ahu
Moloka'i
Lana'i
Kaho'olawe
Maui
Hawai'i

0   200 km
0   200 mi

© AVALON TRAVEL

The Northwest Hawaiian Islands

Like tiny gems of a necklace, the Northwest Hawaiian Islands stretch across the vast Pacific. Popularly called the Leewards, most were discovered in the 19th century. The Leewards are the oldest islands of the Hawaiian chain, believed to have emerged from the sea 25 million-30 million years ago. Slowly they floated west-northwest past the suboceanic hot spot as the other islands were built. Measured from **Nihoa Island,** about 100 miles off the northwestern tip of Kaua'i, they span just under 1,100 miles to **Kure Atoll.** There are islets, shoals, and half-submerged reefs in this chain: Kure, Midway, Pearl, and Hermes Atolls and Lisianski, Maro Reef, Gardner Pinnacles, French Frigate Shoals, Necker, and Nihoa. Most have been eroded flat by the sea and wind, but a few tough volcanic cores endure. Together they make up a landmass of approximately 3,500 acres, the largest being the three Midway islands, taken together at 1,580 acres, and the smallest is **Gardner Pinnacles** at 6 acres.

Politically, the Leewards are administered by the City and County of Honolulu, except for Midway, which is under federal jurisdiction. None, except Midway, is permanently inhabited, but there are some lonely wildlife field stations on Kure and the French Frigate Shoals. All, except for Midway Atoll, are part of the **Hawaiian Islands National Wildlife Refuge,** established at the turn of the 20th century by President Theodore Roosevelt. In 1996, following the closure of the Naval Air Base on Midway Island, Midway Atoll was turned over to the Department of the Interior and is now administered as the **Midway Atoll National Wildlife Refuge.** In June 2006, this 140,000-square-mile string of 10 islands and atolls and their surrounding waters, roughly 1,400 miles long and 100 mile wide, were officially designated a **Marine National Monument** (www.hawaiireef.noaa.gov), effectively creating the nation's largest wilderness preserve and the world's largest marine preserve.

The average daytime high temperature in winter is about 82°F, and the average summer day high raises the thermometer only a few degrees to 87.5°F. Nighttime temperatures drop about 10 degrees. Elevation, however, does reduce temperatures about 3 degrees for every 1,000 feet you climb.

Temperatures are both constant and moderate because of the trade winds, prevailing northeast breezes that blow at about 10-20 miles per hour. You can count on the trades to be blowing on an average of 300 days per year, hardly missing a day during summer and occurring half the time in winter. Although usually calm in the morning, they pick up during the heat of the afternoon, then weaken at night.

The Tropic of Cancer runs through the center of Hawai'i, yet the latitude's usually oppressively hot and muggy weather is most often absent in the islands. Honolulu, on the same latitude as sweaty Hong Kong and Havana, has an acceptable 60-75 percent daily humidity factor.

Winds blowing from the south and southwest are known as kona winds. *Kona* means leeward in Hawaiian. Kona winds bring hot, humid air and unstable weather. If they persist for more than a couple days, they also bring vog, a thick haze caused by the Kilauea Volcano on the Big Island. Kona winds are most common October to April.

Rainfall

Precipitation is the biggest differentiating factor in O'ahu's climate. Rainfall is most often localized and comes in waves of passing showers. Precipitation also occurs mostly at and below the 3,000-foot level, with O'ahu's mountains acting as rain magnets. As the trade winds push warm, moist air up against the mountains, the air rises, cools, and drops a payload of rain to the ground. Generally, the heaviest rainfall occurs on the windward side of O'ahu and over both mountain ranges, and dry conditions prevail on the leeward side and south shore. Wai'anae, Honolulu International Airport, and Waikiki

Polynesian Triangle

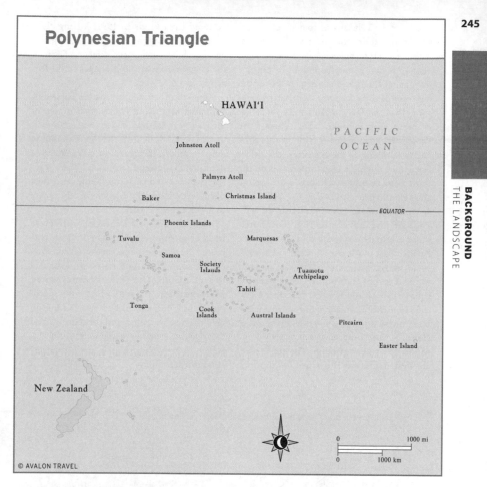

HAWAI'I

PACIFIC
OCEAN

Johnston Atoll

Palmyra Atoll

Baker   Christmas Island

EQUATOR

Phoenix Islands

Tuvalu   Marquesas

Samoa
        Society
        Islands   Tuamotu
                                   Archipelago
                Tahiti

Tonga   Cook
             Islands   Austral Islands

                                        Pitcairn

                                        Easter Island

New Zealand

0   1000 mi

0   1000 km

© AVALON TRAVEL

average only 20-25 inches of rain per year. The Leilehua Plateau in the center of the island averages 40 inches per year. Rain falls much more frequently and heavily in the Koʻolau Mountains and along the windward coast. The bay town of Kaneʻohe sees 75-90 inches per year, while the Nuʻuanu Reservoir in the mountains above Honolulu gets a whopping 120-130 inches yearly.

Localized weather means that weather patterns are very specific. If it's raining where you are, simply relocate to another part of the island or just wait a few minutes for the precipitation to pass. You can usually depend on the beaches of Waikiki and the leeward side to be sunny and bright. Ocean temperatures run 75-80°F year-round.

Severe Weather

Tsunami is the Japanese word for tidal wave. Oʻahu's location in the middle of the Pacific Ocean puts it in the path of tsunamis as they travel from their point of origin and spread across the Pacific. A Hawaiian tsunami is actually a seismic sea wave that has been generated by an earthquake or landslide that could easily have originated thousands of miles away in Japan, South America, or Alaska. Not actual waves that break like the ones seen along Oʻahu's reefs, tsunamis show up as a series of 3-5 tidal surges that affect coastal waters and shorelines over several hours, with about 30 minutes between each surge. Tsunamis can range from simply a larger than usual fluctuation in sea level over the duration of the event to a devastating tidal surge that can floor and damage shoreline property, especially the harbors, and cause loss of life. For visitors staying in shoreline hotels with six or more stories, the safest place to be during a tsunami event is on the third floor or higher. Otherwise, shoreline areas should be evacuated.

Hurricanes are also a threat in Hawai'i. They are rare, but destructive. Most hurricanes originate far to the southeast, off the Pacific coast of Mexico and Latin America; some, particularly later in the season, start in the midst of the Pacific Ocean near the equator, south of Hawai'i. Hurricane season is generally considered June-November. Most hurricanes pass harmlessly south of Hawai'i, but some, swept along by kona winds, do strike the islands. The most recent and destructive was Hurricane 'Iniki, which battered the islands in 1992, killing eight people and causing an estimated $2 billion in damage. It had its greatest effect on Ni'ihau, the Po'ipu Beach area of Kaua'i, and the leeward coast of O'ahu.

Kona storms are another matter. These subtropical low-pressure storms develop west of the Hawaiian Islands, and as they move east, they draw winds up from the south. Common only in winter, they can cause considerable damage to crops and real estate. There is no real pattern to kona storms. Some years they come every few weeks, whereas in other years they don't appear at all.

O'ahu is equipped islandwide with severe weather warning sirens, which indicate tsunamis, hurricanes, and earthquakes. They are tested at 11am on the first working day of each month. **The Hawai'I Emergency Management Agency** (http://www.scd.hawaii.gov/index.htm) has information on civil defense warnings and procedures. You can also find tsunami preparedness information at http://www.prh.noaa.gov/hnl/pages/tsunami_safety.php.

During tsunami events, boats leave the harbor for safer waters offshore.

Hurricanes in Hawai'i

A **tropical depression** is a low-pressure system, or cyclone, with winds below 39 mph. A **tropical storm** is a cyclone with winds 39-73 mph. A **hurricane** is a cyclone with winds over 74 mph. These winds are often accompanied by torrential rains, destructive waves, high water, and storm surges.

The National Weather Service issues a **Hurricane Watch** if hurricane conditions are expected in the area within 36 hours. A **Hurricane Warning** is issued when a hurricane is expected to strike within 24 hours. The state of Hawai'i has an elaborate warning system against natural disasters using sirens high atop poles along many beaches and coastal areas to alert the public of potential or imminent natural disasters, like tsunamis and hurricanes. Over the decades, hurricanes have caused a great deal of property damage, but, thankfully, the loss of life has been minimal.

MAJOR HURRICANES SINCE 1950

- Hurricane Hiki: Occurred in August 1950, on Kaua'i. Resulted in one death.

- Hurricane NIna: Occurred in December 1957, on Kaua'i. No reported damages.

- Hurricane Dot: Occurred in August 1959, on Kaua'i. Resulted in damages of $5.5 million.

- Hurricane Fico: Occurred in July 1978, on the Big Island. No direct damage, since it didn't make landfall.

- Hurricane Iwa: Occurred in November 1982, on Kaua'i and O'ahu. Resulted in one death and $234 million of damage.

- Hurricane Estelle: Occurred in July 1986, on Maui and the Big Island. Resulted in $2 million of damage.

- Hurricane 'Iniki: Occurred in September 1992, on Kaua'i and O'ahu. Resulted in eight deaths and caused $2 billion of damage.

Plants and Animals

The Hawaiian Islands, about 2,500 miles from any continental landfall, are the most isolated landmass on the planet. Spawned from volcanic activity in the middle of the Pacific, the islands were originally devoid of plant or animal life. Over time, as plants, animals, and insects found their way to the islands, they slowly evolved into highly specialized organisms occupying the gamut of each island's microclimates. In Hawai'i, it is not uncommon for a particular plant species only to be found in a single valley across the entire island chain.

The unique plants and animals found only in Hawai'i are known as endemic, those species naturally occurring in Hawai'i but found elsewhere in the world are known as native, and those brought to the islands by people are called introduced species. Introduced species that are fast growing, rapidly increase in number, and easily spread over a region are referred to as invasive species. Invasive species and loss of habitat have been detrimental to the survival of Hawai'i's highly specialized native and endemic flora and fauna. Hawai'i is also known as the endangered species capital of the world, with most of its endemic plants and animals listed as rare and endangered, with many species having already gone extinct. The majority of the remaining pockets of native Hawaiian flora on O'ahu have been relegated to inaccessible valleys and steep mountain cliffs.

INTRODUCED PLANTS

Before settlement, Hawai'i had no fruits, vegetables, coconut palms, edible land animals, conifers, mangroves, or banyans. The early Polynesians brought in 27 varieties of plants that they needed for food and other purposes, like banana, sweet potato, breadfruit, sugarcane, and taro. They also carried along gourds to use as containers, *'awa* to make a basic intoxicant, and the *ti* plant to use for offerings or to string into hula skirts. About 90 percent of plants on the Hawaiian Islands today were introduced after Captain James Cook first set foot here. Non-Hawaiian settlers over the years have brought mangoes, papayas, passion fruit, pineapples, and the other tropical fruits and vegetables associated with the islands. Also, most of the flowers, including protea, plumeria, anthuriums, orchids, heliconia, ginger, and most hibiscus, have come from every continent on earth. Tropical America, Asia, Java, India, and China have contributed their most beautiful and delicate blooms.

Ti was one of the 28 plants Polynesian settlers brought to Hawai'i in their canoes.

TREES

Koa and *'ohi'a* are two endemic Hawaiian trees still seen on O'ahu. Both have been greatly reduced by the foraging of introduced cattle and goats, and through logging and forest fires. The *koa* (*Acacia koa*) is Hawai'i's finest native tree. It can grow to more than 70 feet high and has a strong, straight trunk, which can measure more than 10 feet in circumference. The Hawaiians used *koa* as the main log for their dugout canoes, and elaborate ceremonies were performed when a log was cut and dragged to a canoe shed. *Koa* wood was also preferred for paddles, spears, and even surfboards. Today it is still considered an excellent furniture wood. To protect fine specimens found in reserves, *koa* is now being grown on plantations for future harvesting for commercial purposes.

The *'ohi'a* (*Metrosideros polymorpha*) is a survivor and a pioneer plant, one of the first types of plants to colonize lava flows. It is the most abundant of all the native Hawaiian trees. Coming in a variety of shapes and sizes, it grows as miniature trees in wet bogs or as 100-foot giants on cool slopes at higher elevations. The *'ohi'a* produces a tuft-like flower—usually red, but occasionally orange, yellow, or white, the latter being very rare and elusive—that resembles a bottlebrush. The flower was considered sacred to Pele; it was said that she would cause a rainstorm if *'ohi'a* blossoms were picked without the proper prayers. The flowers were fashioned into lei that resembled feather boas. The strong, hard wood was used to make canoes, poi bowls, and especially for temple images. *'Ohi'a* logs were also used as railroad ties and shipped to the mainland from the Big Island. It's believed that the "golden spike" linking rail lines between the U.S. East and West Coasts was driven into an *'ohi'a* log from the Big Island when the two railroads came together in Ogden, Utah.

The All-Purpose Kukui Tree

Reaching heights of 80 feet, the *kukui* (candlenut) tree was a veritable department store to the Hawaiians, who made use of almost every part of this utilitarian giant. Its nuts, bark, and flowers were ground into potions and salves to be taken as a general tonic, applied to ulcers and cuts as an effective antibiotic, or administered internally as a cure for constipation or asthma attacks. The bark was mixed with water, and the resulting juice was used as a dye in tattooing, tapa-cloth making, and canoe painting, and as a preservative for fishnets. The oily nuts were burned in stone holders as a light source, and they were ground and eaten as a condiment called 'inamona. Polished nuts took on a beautiful sheen and were strung as lei. Finally, the wood was hollowed into canoes and used as fishnet floats.

MARINE LIFE

Although decades of overfishing have taken their toll on the marine life along O'ahu's reefs, entire populations of reef dwellers are bouncing back in specific locations thanks to managed Marine Protected Areas. **Hanauma Bay**, the **Waikiki Marine Life Conservation District**, and the **Pupukea-Waimea Marine Life Conservation District** are protected and managed no-take zones designed to give all types of marine species an environment and promote reef health and bolster populations of reef-dwelling species. In turn, these healthy areas allow populations of fish to grow rapidly and reproduce in exponentially larger numbers, spilling over into unprotected waters and benefiting species higher up the food chain. Hawai'i has over 200 species of native fish.

Whales and dolphins are also common in Hawaiian waters. The most famous whale, and commonly seen, is the North Pacific humpback, but others include the sperm, killer, false killer, pilot, Cuvier's, Blainsville, and pygmy killer. There are technically no porpoises, but dolphins include the common, bottlenose, white-sided, broad- and slender-beaked, and rough-toothed. Small and sleek spinner dolphins are the ones you'll often see near the shore. The mahimahi, a favorite food fish found on many menus, is commonly

the curly leaves of *koa*

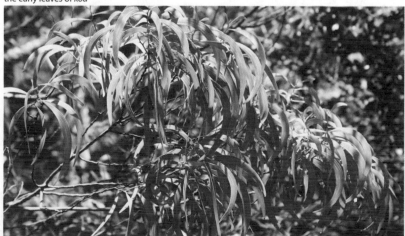

referred to as dolphin fish but is unrelated and is a true fish, not a cetacean.

The **Hawaiian monk seal** is one of only two mammals native to Hawai'i (the Hawaiian hoary bat is the other). These curious seals are critically endangered and protected by law. Monk seals frequently relax on the beach and have a nap in the sun. If you see a monk seal, give it ample space and do not disturb or touch the seal in any way. Green sea turtles are also common along O'ahu's shorelines and share the endangered designation. Also protected, they should be given the same respect as the seals.

BIRDS

Due to the lack of native mammals and reptiles in precontact Hawai'i, native birds flourished, becoming widespread and highly specialized. Not to mention, they were able to feast on over 10,000 species of native insects. However, one of the great tragedies of natural history is the continuing demise of Hawaiian birdlife. Perhaps only 15 original species of birds remain of the more than 70 native families that thrived before the coming of humans. Since the arrival of Captain Cook in 1778, 23 species have become extinct, with 31 more in danger. And what's not known is how many species were wiped out before white explorers arrived. Experts believe that the Hawaiians annihilated about 40 species, including seven species of geese, a rare one-legged owl, ibis, lovebirds, sea eagles, and honeycreepers—all gone before Captain Cook showed up. Hawai'i's endangered birds account for 40 percent of the birds officially listed as endangered or threatened by the U.S. Fish and Wildlife Service. Almost all of O'ahu's native birds are gone, and few indigenous Hawaiian birds can be found on any island below the 3,000-foot level.

The shores around O'ahu, especially those off Koko Head, Ka'ena Point, and on the tiny islets of Moku Manu, Manana, and others on the windward side are home to thriving colonies of marine birds. On these diminutive islands it's quite easy to spot several birds from the tern family, including the white, gray, and sooty tern. Along with the terns are shearwaters and enormous Laysan albatross with its seven-foot wingspan. Tropicbirds, with their lovely streamer-like tails, are often seen along the windward coast.

If you're lucky, you can also catch a glimpse of the *pueo* (Hawaiian owl) in the mountainous areas of Wai'anae and the Ko'olau Range. Also, along trails and deep in the forest from

Hawaiian monk seal

Tantalus to the Wai'anae Range you can sometimes see elusive birds like the *'elepaio, 'amakihi,* and the fiery red *'i'iwi.* The *'amakihi* and *'i'iwi* are endemic birds not endangered at the moment. The *'amakihi* is one of the most common native birds; yellowish-green, it frequents the high branches of the *'ohi'a, koa,* and sandalwood trees looking for insects, nectar, or fruit. It is less specialized than most other Hawaiian birds, the main reason for its continued existence. The *'i'iwi,* a bright red bird with a salmon-colored, hooked bill, is found in the forests above 2,000 feet. *'apapane* is abundant in Hawai'i, and being the most common native bird, is the easiest to see. It's a chubby, red-bodied bird about five inches long with a black bill, legs, wingtips, and tail feathers.

O'ahu's exotic birds are the most common in the beach parks and in urban areas: black myna birds with their sassy yellow eyes are common mimics around town; sparrows, introduced to Hawai'i through O'ahu in the 1870s, are everywhere; and munia, first introduced as caged birds from Southeast Asia,

have escaped and can be found almost anywhere around the island.

O'ahu is also home to several game birds found mostly in the dry upland forests. These include three varieties of dove, the Japanese quail, both the green and ring-necked pheasant, and Erckel's francolin.

INTRODUCED ANIMALS

Almost all of the mammals on O'ahu are introduced, and many have had severe and detrimental consequences for Hawai'i's natural environment and native species. Rats, mice, and mongooses thrive on O'ahu and are responsible for disease and the decline of ground-nesting bird populations. Feral ungulates like pigs and goats destroy native forests as they root up and eat vegetation, creating fetid pools of water where mosquitoes thrive, contributing to the decline of forest bird populations through disease. In years past, grazing cattle was responsible for the deforestation of watersheds that led to landslides. Geckos, anoles, and chameleons are a few of the introduced reptiles that are common on O'ahu.

History

HAWAI'I'S SETTLERS

The great "deliberate migrations" from the southern Pacific islands seem to have taken place AD 500-800, though the exact date is highly contested by experts. It's generally agreed that the first planned migrations were from the violent cannibalistic islands called the Marquesas, 11 islands in extreme eastern Polynesia. The islands themselves are harsh and inhospitable, breeding toughness into the people that enabled them to withstand the hardships of long, unsure ocean voyages and years of resettlement. They were masters at building great double-hulled canoes with the two hulls fastened together to form a catamaran, and a hut in the center provided shelter in bad weather. The average voyaging canoe was 60-80 feet long and could comfortably hold

an extended family of about 30 people. These small family bands carried all the staples they would need in the new lands.

For five centuries the Marquesans settled here and lived peacefully on the new land. The tribes coexisted in relative harmony, especially because there was no competition for land. Cannibalism died out. There was much coming and going between Hawai'i and Polynesia as new people came to the settlement over the course of hundreds of years. Then, it appears that in the 12th century a deliberate exodus of warlike Tahitians arrived and subjugated the islanders. This incursion had a terrific significance on the Hawaiian religious and social system. The warlike god Ku and the rigid *kapu* system were introduced, through which the new rulers became dominant. Voyages between Tahiti and Hawai'i continued for about 100 years, and Tahitian customs, legends, and language became the Hawaiian way of life. Then suddenly, for no recorded or apparent reason, the voyages discontinued and Hawai'i returned to total isolation.

CAPTAIN COOK

The islands remained forgotten for almost 500 years until the indomitable English seafarer, Captain James Cook, sighted O'ahu on January 18, 1778, and stepped ashore at Waimea on Kaua'i two days later. At that time Hawai'i's isolation was so complete that even the Polynesians had forgotten about it. The Englishmen had arrived aboard the 100-foot flagship HMS *Resolution* and its 90-foot companion HMS *Discovery*. The first trade was some brass medals for a mackerel. Cook provisioned his ships by exchanging chisels for hogs, while common sailors gleefully traded nails for sex. Landing parties were sent inland to fill casks with freshwater. After a brief stop on Ni'ihau, the ships sailed away, but both groups were indelibly impressed with the memory of each other.

Almost a year later, when winter weather forced Cook to return from the coast of Alaska, the *Discovery* and *Resolution* found safe anchorage at Kealakekua Bay on the kona coast of the Big Island on January 16, 1779. By the coincidence of his second arrival with religious festivities, the Hawaiians mistook Cook to be the return of the god Lono. After an uproarious welcome and generous hospitality for over a month, it became obvious that the newcomers were beginning to overstay their welcome. During the interim a sailor named William Watman died, convincing the Hawaiians that the *haole* were indeed mortals, not gods. Inadvertently, many *kapu* were broken by the English, and once-friendly relations became strained. Finally, the ships sailed away on February 4, 1779.

After plying terrible seas for only a week, *Resolution*'s foremast was badly damaged. Cook sailed back into Kealakekua Bay, dragging the mast ashore on February 13. The natives, now totally hostile, hurled rocks at the sailors. Confrontations increased when some Hawaiians stole a small boat and Cook's men set after them, capturing the fleeing canoe, which held an *ali'i* named Palea. The Englishmen treated him roughly, so the Hawaiians furiously attacked the mariners, who abandoned the small boat.

Next, the Hawaiians stole a small cutter from the *Discovery* that had been moored to a buoy and partially sunk to protect it from the sun. For the first time, Captain Cook became furious. He ordered Captain Clerk of the *Discovery* to sail to the southeast end of the bay and stop any canoe trying to leave Kealakekua. Cook then made a fatal error in judgment. He decided to take nine armed mariners ashore in an attempt to convince the venerable King Kalani'opu'u to accompany him back aboard ship, where he would hold him for ransom in exchange for the cutter. The old king agreed, but his wife prevailed upon him not to trust the *haole*. Kalani'opu'u sat down on the beach to think while the tension steadily grew.

Meanwhile, a group of mariners fired on a canoe trying to leave the bay, and a lesser chief, No'okemai, was killed. The crowd around Cook and his men reached an estimated 20,000, and warriors outraged by the killing of the chief armed themselves with clubs and protective straw-mat armor. One bold warrior advanced on Cook and struck him with his *pahoa* (dagger). In retaliation Cook drew a tiny pistol lightly loaded with shot and fired at the warrior. His bullets spent themselves on the straw armor and fell harmlessly to the ground. The Hawaiians went wild. Lieutenant Molesworth Phillips, in charge of the nine mariners, began a withering fire; Cook killed two natives.

Overpowered by sheer numbers, the sailors headed for boats standing offshore, while Lieutenant Phillips lay wounded. It is believed that Captain Cook stood helplessly in knee-deep water instead of making for the boats because he could not swim. Hopelessly surrounded, he was knocked on the head, then countless warriors passed a knife around and hacked and mutilated his lifeless body. A sad Lieutenant King lamented in his diary, "Thus fell our great and excellent commander."

UNIFICATION OF THE HAWAIIAN ISLANDS

In the 1780s, the islands were roughly divided into three kingdoms: Kalaniʻopuʻu ruled Hawaiʻi and the Hana district of Maui; wily and ruthless warrior-king Kahekili ruled Maui, Kahoʻolawe, Lanaʻi, and later Oʻahu; and Kaeo, Kahekili's brother, ruled Kauaʻi. War ravaged the land until a remarkable chief, Kamehameha, rose and subjugated all the islands under one rule. Kamehameha initiated a dynasty that would last for about 100 years, until the independent monarchy of Hawaiʻi forever ceased to be.

Hawaiʻi under Kamehameha was ready to enter its "golden age." The social order was medieval, with the *aliʻi* as knights, owing their military allegiance to the king, and the serf-like *makaʻainana* paying tribute and working the lands. The priesthood of *kahuna* filled the posts of advisers, sorcerers, navigators, doctors, and historians. This was Polynesian Hawaiʻi at its apex. But like the uniquely Hawaiian silversword plant, the old culture blossomed, and as soon as it did, it began to wither. Ever since, all that was purely Hawaiian has been supplanted by the relentless foreign influences that began bearing down upon it.

MISSIONARIES AND WHALERS

Kamehameha was as gentle in victory as he was ferocious in battle. Under his rule, which lasted until his death on May 8, 1819, Hawaiʻi enjoyed a peace unlike any the warring islands had ever known. However, the year 1819 was of the utmost significance in Hawaiian history. With the death of Kamehameha came the overthrow of the ancient *kapu* system, the arrival of the first whalers in Lahaina, and the departure of Calvinist missionaries from New England determined to convert the heathen

islanders. Great changes began to rattle the old order to its foundations. With the *kapu* system and all of the ancient gods abandoned (except for the fire goddess Pele of Kilauea), a great void opened the souls of the Hawaiians. In the coming decades Hawaiʻi, also coveted by Russia, France, and England, was finally consumed by America. The islands had the first American school, printing press, and newspaper west of the Mississippi. Lahaina, in its heyday, became the world's greatest whaling port, accommodating more than 500 ships of all types during its peak years.

In 1823, the first mission was established in Lahaina, Maui, under the pastorate of the Reverend William Richards and his wife. Within a few years, many of the notable *aliʻi* had been, at least in appearance, converted to Christianity. By 1828 the cornerstones for Waineʻe Church, the first stone church on the island, were laid just behind the palace of Kamehameha III.

THE GREAT MAHELE

In 1840, after moving the royal court to Honolulu, the new center of commerce in the islands, Kamehameha III ended his autocratic rule and instituted a constitutional monarchy. This brought about the Hawaiian Bill of Rights, but the most far-reaching change was the transition to private ownership of land, known as The Great Mahele. Formerly, all land belonged to the ruling chief, who gave wedge-shaped parcels called *ahupuaʻa* to lesser chiefs to be worked for him. The commoners did all the real labor, their produce heavily taxed by the *aliʻi*. The fortunes of war, the death of a chief, or the mere whim of a superior could force a commoner off the land.

The Hawaiians, however, could not think in terms of owning land. No one could *possess* land, one could only *use* land, and its ownership was a foreign concept. As a result, naive Hawaiians gave up their lands for a song to unscrupulous traders, and land ownership issues remain a basic and unrectified problem to this day. In 1847 Kamehameha III and his advisers separated the lands of Hawaiʻi into three groupings: crown land (belonging to the king), government land (belonging to the chiefs), and the people's land (the largest parcels). In 1848, 245 *ali'i* entered their land claims in the *Mahele Book,* assuring them ownership. In 1850, the commoners were given title in fee simple to the lands they cultivated and lived on as tenants, not including house lots in towns. Commoners without land could buy small *kuleana* (farms) from the government at $0.50 per acre. In 1850, foreigners were also allowed to purchase land in fee simple, and the ownership of Hawai'i from that day forward slipped steadily from the hands of its indigenous people.

THE END OF A KINGDOM

Like the Hawaiian people themselves, the Kamehameha dynasty in the mid-1800s was dying from within. King Kamehameha IV (Alexander Liholiho) ruled 1854-1863; his only child died in 1862. He was succeeded by his older brother Kamehameha V (Lot Kamehameha), who ruled until 1872. With his passing the Kamehameha line ended. William Lunalilo, elected king in 1873 by popular vote, was of royal lineage, but not of the Kamehameha bloodline. He died after only a year in office, and being a bachelor, he left no heirs. He was succeeded by David Kalakaua, known far and wide as the "Merrie Monarch," who made a world tour and was well received wherever he went. He built 'Iolani Palace in Honolulu and was personally in favor of closer ties with the United States, helping to push through the Reciprocity Act. Kalakaua died in 1891 and was replaced by his sister, Lydia Lili'uokalani, last of the Hawaiian monarchs.

REVOLUTION AND ANNEXATION

When Lili'uokalani took office in 1891, the native population was at a low of 40,000, and she felt that the United States had too much influence over her homeland. She was known to personally favor the English over the Americans. She attempted to replace the liberal constitution of 1887 (adopted by her pro-American brother) with an autocratic mandate in which she would have had much more political and economic control of the islands.

When the McKinley Tariff of 1890 brought a decline in sugar profits, she made no attempt to improve the situation. Thus, the planters saw her as a political obstacle to their economic growth; most of Hawai'i's American planters and merchants were in favor of a rebellion. A central spokesperson and firebrand was Lorrin Thurston, a Honolulu publisher who, with a core of about 30 men, challenged the Hawaiian monarchy. Although Lili'uokalani rallied some support and had a small military potential in her personal guard, the coup was relatively bloodless—it took only one casualty. Naturally, the conspirators could not have succeeded without some solid assurances from a secret contingent in the U.S. Congress as well as outgoing President Benjamin Harrison, who favored Hawai'i's annexation. Marines from the USS *Boston* went ashore to "protect American lives," and on January 17, 1893, the Hawaiian monarchy came to an end.

Sanford B. Dole, who became president of the Hawaiian Republic, headed the provisional government. Lili'uokalani surrendered not to the conspirators, but to U.S. Ambassador John Stevens. She believed that the U.S. government, which had assured her of Hawaiian independence, would be outraged by the overthrow and would come to her aid. Incoming President Grover Cleveland *was* outraged, and Hawai'i wasn't immediately annexed as expected.

In January 1895, a small, ill-fated counterrevolution headed by Lili'uokalani failed, and she was placed under house arrest in 'Iolani Palace. Officials of the Republic insisted that she use her married name (Mrs. John Dominis) to sign the documents, forcing her to abdicate her throne. She was also forced to swear allegiance to the new Republic. Lili'uokalani went on to write *Hawaii's Story* and the lyric ballad "Aloha O'e." She never forgave the conspirators and remained queen

Land Ownership

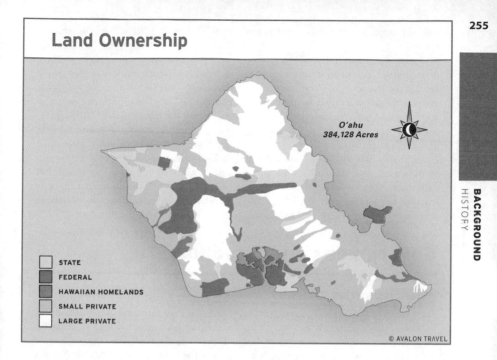

O'ahu
384,128 Acres

STATE
FEDERAL
HAWAIIAN HOMELANDS
SMALL PRIVATE
LARGE PRIVATE

© AVALON TRAVEL

BACKGROUND
HISTORY

in the minds of Hawaiians until her death in 1917.

On July 7, 1898, President McKinley signed the annexation agreement, arguing that the U.S. military must have Hawai'i in order to be a viable force in the Pacific.

PEARL HARBOR ATTACK

On the morning of December 7, 1941, the Japanese carrier *Akagi,* flying the battle flag of Admiral Togo of Russo-Japanese War fame, received and broadcast over its public address system island music from Honolulu station KGMB. Deep in the bowels of the ship a radio operator listened for a much different message, coming thousands of miles from the Japanese mainland. When the ironically poetic message "east wind rain" was received, the attack was launched. At the end of the day, 2,325 U.S. soldiers and 57 civilians were dead; 188 planes were destroyed; 18 major warships were sunk or heavily damaged; and the United States was engaged in World War II. Japanese casualties were ludicrously light. The ignited

conflict would rage for four years until Japan, through the atomic bombing of Nagasaki and Hiroshima, was brought into total submission. By the end of hostilities, Hawai'i would never again be considered separate from America.

Statehood

Several economic and political motivations explain why the ruling elite of Hawai'i desired statehood, but put simply, the vast majority of people who lived there, especially after World War II, considered themselves Americans. The first serious mention of making the Hawaiian Islands a state was in the 1850s under President Franklin Pierce, but the idea wasn't taken seriously until the monarchy was overthrown in the 1890s. For the next 50 years statehood proposals were made repeatedly to Congress, but there was stiff opposition, especially from the southern states. With Hawai'i a territory, an import quota system beneficial to mainland producers could be enacted on produce, especially sugar. Also, there was prejudice against creating a state in a place where the majority of the populace was not white.

During World War II, Hawai'i was placed under martial law, but no serious attempt to confine the Japanese population was made, as it was in California. There were simply too many Japanese, and many went on to gain the respect of the American people through their outstanding fighting record during the war. Hawai'i's own 100th Battalion became the famous 442nd Regimental Combat Team, which gained notoriety by saving the Lost Texas Battalion during the Battle of the Bulge and went on to be *the* most decorated battalion in all of World War II. When these GIs returned home, *no one* was going to tell them that they were not loyal Americans. Many of these Americans of Japanese Ancestry (AJAs) took advantage of the GI Bill and received higher education. They were from the common people, not the elite, and they rallied grassroots support for statehood. When the vote finally occurred, approximately 132,900 voted in favor of statehood, with only 7,800 votes against. Congress passed the Hawaii State Bill on March 12, 1959, and on August 21, 1959, President Dwight Eisenhower announced that Hawai'i was officially the 50th state.

Government and Economy

GOVERNMENT

There are only two levels of government in the state of Hawai'i: the state and the county. With no town or city governments to deal with, considerable bureaucracy is eliminated. Hawai'i, in anticipation of becoming a state, drafted a constitution in 1950 and was ready to go when statehood came. Politics and government are taken seriously in the Aloha State, which at one time consistently turned in the best national voting record per capita. These days, residents give greater importance to and show greater turnout for state elections. In the election to ratify statehood, hardly a ballot went uncast, with 95 percent of the voters opting for statehood. The bill carried every island of Hawai'i except Ni'ihau, where most of the people (total population 250 or so) are of relatively pure Hawaiian blood.

When Hawai'i became a state, Honolulu became its capital. Since statehood, the Democratic Party has dominated the legislative and executive branches of state government. Breaking a 40-year Democratic hold on power in the state and becoming the first woman to hold the position, former Maui mayor and Republican Linda Lingle was elected as governor in 2002 and reelected in 2006.

City and County of Honolulu

O'ahu has been the center of government for about 160 years, since King Kamehameha III permanently established the royal court here in the 1840s. In 1879-1882, King David Kalakaua built 'Iolani Palace as the central showpiece of the island kingdom. Lili'uokalani, the last Hawaiian monarch, lived in the nearby residence, Washington Place, after her dethronement. While Hawai'i was a territory, and for a few years after it became a state, the palace was used as the capitol building, with the governor residing in Washington Place. Modern O'ahu, besides being the center of state government, governs itself as the City and County of Honolulu. The county covers not only the entire island of O'ahu, but also all the far-flung Northwestern Islands except for Midway, which is under federal jurisdiction.

The island of O'ahu houses three times as many people as the other islands combined. Nowhere is this more evident than in the representation of O'ahu in the bicameral state legislature. O'ahu claims 18 of the 25 state senators and 35 of the 51 state representatives. These lopsided figures make it obvious that O'ahu has plenty of clout, especially the Honolulu urban districts, which elect more than 50 percent of Oʻahu's representatives. Frequent political battles ensue because what's good for the City and County of Honolulu isn't always good for the rest of the state. More often than not, the political moguls of Oʻahu, backed by huge business interests, prevail.

Like the rest of the state, the voters on the island of Oʻahu are principally Democratic in orientation, but not in as great a percentage as on the other islands. The mayor in 2016 is Kirk Caldwell (D). An elected county council consisting of nine members, one from each council district around the island, assists him. The Oʻahu state senators are overwhelmingly Democrats. Democratic state representatives also outnumber Republicans, but not by quite as huge a margin. For more information about the City and County of Honolulu, visit www.honolulu.gov.

ECONOMY

Hawaiʻi's mid-Pacific location makes it perfect for two primary sources of income: tourism and the military. Tourists come in anticipation of endless golden days on soothing beaches, while the military is provided with a strategic global position. Each economic sector nets Hawaiʻi billions annually. Also contributing to the state revenue are manufacturing, construction, and agriculture.

Economically, Oʻahu dwarfs the rest of the islands combined. A huge military presence, an international airport that receives the lion's share of visitors, and, unbelievably, half of the state's best arable land keep Oʻahu the leader in revenue. The famous "Big Five" and other major businesses all maintain their corporate offices in downtown Honolulu, from which they oversee vast holdings throughout Hawaiʻi and the mainland. The Big Five—C. Brewer and Co., Theo. H. Davies & Co., Amfac Inc., Castle and Cooke Inc. (Dole), and Alexander and Baldwin Inc., historically Hawaiʻi's major economic powerhouses—controlled the economic lifeblood of the islands through their web of subsidiary corporations and holding companies and for all practical purposes controlled politics on the islands through their

influence in government until World War II. Based in about the same spots as when their founders helped overthrow the monarchy, they're still going strong, whereas the old royalty of Hawaiʻi has vanished.

Tourism

The flow of visitors to Oʻahu has gone on unabated ever since tourism outstripped sugar and pineapples in the early 1960s as Hawaiʻi's top moneymaker. Visitor expenditures bring in over 11 billion a year, and this is only the amount that can be directly related to the hotel and restaurant trades. Of the more than seven million people who visit the state yearly, more than half stay on Oʻahu. On any given day, Oʻahu plays host to about 90,000 visitors. And nearly all of the state's visitors at least pass through Oʻahu. While many travel to Hawaiʻi with a group or on a package tour, independent travelers make up the majority of the state's visitors. Hotels directly employ more than 16,000 workers, nearly half the state's total, not including all the shop assistants, food servers, taxi drivers, and everyone else needed to ensure a carefree vacation. Of the state's 77,000 accommodation units, Oʻahu claims 35,000; of those, about 29,000 are in Waikiki. The Oʻahu hotels consistently have some of the highest occupancy rates in the state, hovering around 81 percent. In contrast, the average daily room rate is the lowest in the state, making accommodations on Oʻahu slightly more of a bargain than on the other islands. The visitor industry generates more than $11 billion in annual revenue.

The Military

Hawaiʻi is the most militarized state in the United States, and all five branches of service are represented on Oʻahu. Based in Honolulu, USPACOM (U.S. Pacific Command) is one of six U.S. Unified Combat Commands of the armed forces, which is responsible for more than 50 percent of the earth's surface, from California to the east coast of Africa and to both poles. The U.S. military presence dates back to 1887, when Pearl Harbor was given to the navy as part of the Sugar Reciprocity Treaty.

About 325,000 military and civilian personnel are assigned to USPACOM. The U.S. Marine Corps has about 85,000 personnel, the U.S. Air Force has roughly 40,000, the U.S. Army has 60,000, and the U.S. Coast Guard has 27,000. The combined services are one of the largest landholders, with more than 238,000 acres, accounting for 6 percent of Hawaiian land. The two major holdings are the 100,000-acre Pohakuloa Training Area on Hawai'i and 81,000 acres on O'ahu, which is a full 21 percent of the island. The Army controls 63 percent of the military lands, followed by the Navy at 22 percent, the Marines with 11 percent, and the remainder goes to the Air Force and a few small installations to the Coast Guard.

Agriculture

You'd think that with all the people living on O'ahu, coupled with the constant land development, there'd hardly be any room left for things to grow, but that's not the case. The land is productive, although definitely stressed.

Although O'ahu has the smallest average size of farms in the state, it still manages to produce a considerable amount of pineapples and the many products of diversified agriculture and floriculture. Pineapples cover 9,100 acres, with the biggest holdings in the Leilehua Plateau belonging to Dole. As a result of demand and diversification, O'ahu now also raises a variety of organic greens, freshwater shrimp, coffee, and flowers. Only about 100 acres have been put into coffee, the smallest acreage of any of the islands—on land between Wahiawa and Hale'iwa—but this land produces a respectable 50,000 pounds per year. In the hills, entrepreneurs raise *pakalolo*, or marijuana, which has become one of the state's most productive cash crops. O'ahu is also a huge agricultural consumer, demanding more than four times more vegetables, fruits, meats, and poultry to feed its citizens and visitors than the remainder of the state combined.

People and Culture

POPULATION

Of the nearly 1.4 million people that reside in Hawai'i, 963,607 live on O'ahu, with slightly less than half of these living in the Honolulu metropolitan area. Statewide, city dwellers outnumber those living in the country by nine to one. For the island of O'ahu, 96 percent of the population is urban, whereas only 4 percent live rurally. O'ahu's population accounts for 70 percent of the state's population, yet the island comprises only 9 percent of the state's land total. Sections of Waikiki can have a combined population of permanent residents and visitors as high as 90,000 per square mile, making cities like Tokyo, Hong Kong, and New York seem roomy by comparison. The good news is that O'ahu *expects* all these people and knows how to accommodate them comfortably.

About 400,000 people live in greater Honolulu, the built-up area from 'Aiea to Koko Head. The next most populous urban centers after Honolulu are the Kailua/Kane'ohe area on the windward side with about 100,000 residents, Mililani and Wahiawa on the Leilehua Plateau with about the same number, followed by Pearl City and Waipahu with a combined total of about 70,000 or so. The strip of towns on the leeward coast, including Wai'anae, totals about 40,000 inhabitants. Since 2000, Mililani and 'Ewa have had the greatest increase in population.

PEOPLE

Nowhere else on earth can you find such a kaleidoscopic mixture of people as in Hawai'i. Every major race is accounted for, and more than 50 ethnic groups are represented throughout the islands, making Hawai'i the most racially integrated state in the country. Ethnic breakdowns for the state include 25.3 percent Hawaiian/part Hawaiian, 20.5 percent Caucasian, 18.4 percent Japanese, 10 percent Filipino, 8.9 percent Hispanic/Latino, and 4.2 percent Chinese. These statistics mirror the population demographics on O'ahu very closely.

Of the major ethnic groups, you'll find the Hawaiians clustered around Wai'anae and on the windward coast in Waimanalo and near Waiahole; Caucasians tend to be in Wahiawa, the North Shore, around Koko Head, in Waikiki, and in Kailua/Kane'ohe; those of Japanese ancestry prefer the valleys heading toward the *pali*, including Kalihi, Nu'uanu, and Tantalus; Filipinos live just east of the airport, in downtown Honolulu, and in Wahiawa; the Chinese are in Chinatown and around the Diamond Head area. Of the minor ethnic groups, the highest concentration of African Americans is around Schofield Barracks; Samoans live with the Hawaiians in Wai'anae and the windward coastal towns, although they are most concentrated in downtown Honolulu; Koreans and Vietnamese are scattered here and there, but mostly in Honolulu.

Ni'ihau, a privately owned island, is home to about 160 pure-blooded Hawaiians, representing the largest concentration of Hawaiians, per capita, in the islands. The Robinson family, which owns the island, restricts visitors to invited guests only. The second largest concentration is on Moloka'i, where 2,700 Hawaiians, living mostly on a 40-acre *kuleana* of Hawaiian Home Lands, make up 40 percent of that island's population. The majority of mixed-blood Hawaiians, 240,000 or so, live on O'ahu, where they are particularly strong in the hotel and entertainment fields.

Native Hawaiians

When Captain Cook first sighted Hawai'i in 1778, there were an estimated 300,000 natives living in relative harmony with their ecological surroundings; within 100 years a scant 50,000 Hawaiians remained. Today, although more than 240,000 people claim varying degrees of Hawaiian blood, experts say that fewer than 1,000 are pure Hawaiian.

Ancient Hawaiian society was divided into rankings by a strict caste system determined by birth, and from which there was no chance of escaping. The highest rank was the *ali'i*, the chiefs and royalty. The impeccable genealogies of the *ali'i* were traced back to the gods themselves, and the chants (*mo'o ali'i*) were memorized and sung by a rank of a *ali'i* called *ku'auhau*. Ranking passed from both father and mother, and custom dictated that the first mating of an *ali'i* be with a person of equal status.

A *kahuna* was a highly skilled person whose advice was sought before any major project was undertaken, such as building a house, hollowing a canoe log, or even offering a prayer. The *mo'o kahuna* were the priests of Ku and Lono, and they were in charge of praying and following rituals. They were very powerful *ali'i* and kept strict secrets and laws concerning their various functions.

Besides this priesthood of *kahuna,* there were other *kahuna* who were not *ali'i*, but commoners. The two most important were the healers (*kahuna lapa'au*) and the sorcerers (*kahuna 'ana'ana*), who could pray a person to death. The *kahuna lapa'au* had a marvelous pharmacopoeia of herbs and spices that could cure over 250 diseases common to the Hawaiians.

The common people were called the *maka'ainana*, "the people of land"—the farmers, craftspeople, and fishers. The land they lived on was controlled by the *ali'i*, but they were not bound to it. If the local *ali'i* was cruel or unfair, the *maka'ainana* had the right to leave and reside on another's lands. The *maka'ainana* mostly loved their local *ali'i*, much like a child loves a parent, and the feeling was reciprocated. *Maka'ainana* who lived close to the *ali'i* and could be counted on as warriors in times of trouble were called *kanaka no lua kaua* (a man for the heat of battle). They were treated with greater favor than those who lived in the backcountry, *kanaka no hi'i kua,* whose lesser standing opened them up to discrimination and cruelty. All *maka'ainana* formed extended families called *'ohana* who usually lived on the same section of land, called *ahupua'a.* Those farmers who lived inland would barter their produce with the fishers who lived on the shore, and thus all shared equally in the bounty of land and sea.

A special group called *kauwa* was an untouchable caste confined to living on reservations. Their origins were obviously Polynesian, but they appeared to be descendants of castaways who had survived and became perhaps the aboriginals of Hawai'i before the main migrations. It was *kapu* for anyone to go onto *kauwa* lands; doing so meant instant death. If a human sacrifice was needed, the *kahuna* would simply summon a *kauwa,* who had no recourse but to mutely comply. To this day, to call someone *kauwa,* which now supposedly only means servant, is still considered a fight-provoking insult.

Occasionally there were horrible wars, but mostly the people lived quiet and ordered lives based on the strict caste society and the *kapu* system of rigidly observed cultural taboos and laws. Famine was known, but only on a regional level, and the population was kept in check by birth control, crude abortions, and the distasteful practice of infanticide, especially of baby girls. The Hawaiians were absolutely loving and nurturing parents under most circumstances and would even take in *hanai* (an adopted child or oldster), a lovely practice that lingers to this day.

A strict division of labor existed among men and women. Men were the only ones permitted to have anything to do with taro. This crop was so sacred that there were a greater number of *kapu* concerning taro than concerning a man himself. Men pounded poi and served it to the women. Men were also the fishers and the builders of houses, canoes, irrigation ditches, and walls. Women tended to other gardens and shoreline fishing and were responsible for making tapa cloth. The entire family lived in the common house called the *hale noa.*

Certain things were *kapu* between the sexes. Primarily, women could not enter the *mua* (men's eating house), nor could they eat with men. Certain foods, such as pork, coconut, red fish, and bananas were forbidden to women, and it was *kapu* for a man to have intercourse before going fishing, engaging in battle, or attending a religious ceremony. Young boys lived with the women until they underwent a circumcision rite called *pule ipu.* After this was performed, they were required to keep the *kapu* of men. A true Hawaiian settlement required a minimum of five huts: the men's eating hut, women's menstruation hut, women's eating hut, communal sleeping hut, and prayer hut. Without these five separate structures, Hawaiian society could not happen because the *i'a kapu* (forbidden eating between men and women) rules could not be observed.

Ali'i could also declare a *kapu* and often did so. Certain lands or fishing areas were temporarily made *kapu* so that they could be revitalized. Even today, it is *kapu* for anyone to remove all the *'opihi* (a type of limpet) from a rock. The greatest *kapu, kapu moe,* was afforded to the highest-ranking *ali'i:* anyone coming into their presence had to prostrate themselves. Lesser-ranking *ali'i* were afforded the *kapu noho:* lessers had to sit or kneel in their presence. Commoners could not let their shadows fall on an *ali'i,* nor enter the house of an *ali'i* except through a special door. Breaking a *kapu* meant immediate death.

RELIGION

The Polynesian Hawaiians worshipped nature. They saw its forces manifested in a multiplicity of forms to which they ascribed godlike powers, and they based daily life on this animistic philosophy. Handpicked and specially trained storytellers chanted the exploits of the gods. These ancient tales, kept alive in a special oral tradition called *mo'olelo,* were recited only by day. Entranced listeners encircled the chanter; in respect for the gods and in fear of their wrath, they were forbidden to move once the tale was begun.

Any object, animate or inanimate, could be a god. All could be infused with *mana*, especially a dead body or a respected ancestor. *'Ohana* had personal family gods called *'aumakua* on whom they called in times of danger or strife. There were children of gods called *kupua* who were thought to live among humans and were distinguished either for their beauty and strength or for their ugliness and terror. It was told that processions of dead *ali'i*, called "Marchers of the Night," wandered through the land of the living, and unless you were properly protected, it could mean death if they looked upon you. There were simple ghosts known as *akua lapu* who merely frightened people. Forests, waterfalls, trees, springs, and a thousand forms of nature were the manifestations of *akua li'i*, "little spirits" who could be invoked at any time for help or protection. It made no difference who or what you were in old Hawai'i; the gods were ever present, and they took a direct and active role in your life.

Behind all of these beliefs was an innate sense of natural balance and order. It could be interpreted as positive-negative, yin-yang, life-death, or light-dark, the main idea being that everything had its opposite. The time of darkness when only the gods lived was *po*. When the great gods descended to the earth and created light, this was *ao*, and humanity was born. All of these *mo'olelo* are part of *The Kumulipo*, the great chant that records the Hawaiian version of creation. From the time the gods descended and touched the earth at Ku Moku on Lana'i, the genealogies were kept. Unlike in the Bible, these included the noble families of female as well as male *ali'i*.

Ancient Hawaiians performed religious ceremonies at *heiau*, temples. The basic *heiau* was a masterfully built and fitted rectangular stone wall that varied in size from about as big as a basketball court to as big as a football field. Once the restraining outer walls were built, the interior was backfilled with smaller stones, and the top dressing was expertly laid and then rolled, perhaps with a log, to form a pavement-like surface. All that remains of Hawai'i's many *heiau* are the stone platforms or walls. The buildings on them, constructed in perishable wood, leaves, and grass, have long since disappeared.

The Hawaiian people worshipped gods who took the form of idols fashioned from wood, feathers, or stone. The eyes were made from shells, and until these were inlaid, the idol was dormant. The hair used was often human hair, and the arms and legs were usually flexed. The mouth was either gaping or formed a wide figure-eight lying on its side, and more likely than not was lined with glistening dog teeth. Small figures made of woven basketry were expertly covered with feathers. Red and yellow feathers were favorites, taken from specific birds by men whose only work was to roam the forests in search of them.

In the 1820s, missionaries brought Congregational Christianity and the "true path" to heaven to Hawai'i, setting out to convert the pagan Hawaiians and "civilize" them. Catholics, Mormons, Adventists, Episcopalians, Unitarians, Christian Scientists, Lutherans, Baptists, Jehovah's Witnesses, the Salvation Army, and every other major and minor denomination of Christianity that followed in their wake brought their own brand of enlightenment. Chinese and Japanese immigrants established major sects of Buddhism, Confucianism, Taoism, and Shintoism. Today, Allah is praised, the Torah is chanted in Jewish synagogues, and nirvana is available at a variety of Hindu temples, even the Church of Scientology is selling books and salvation.

LANGUAGE

In Hawai'i, English is the primary language spoken, yet the beat and melody of the local dialect is noticeably different. Hawai'i has its own unmistakable linguistic regionalism. The many ethnic people who make up Hawai'i have enriched the English spoken with words, expressions, and subtle shades of meaning that are commonly used and understood throughout the islands. The greatest influence on the English spoken here comes from the Hawaiian language, and words such as *aloha, hula, lu'au,* and *lei* are familiarly used and understood by all.

Pidgin

Other migrant peoples, especially the Chinese, Japanese, and Portuguese, influenced the local dialect to such an extent that the simplified plantation lingo they spoke has become known as "pidgin." English is the official language of the state, business, and education, but pidgin is the language of the people. Hawaiian words make up most of pidgin's non-English vocabulary, but it includes a good smattering of Chinese, Japanese, and Samoan as well. The distinctive rising inflection is provided by the melodious Mediterranean lilt of the Portuguese. Pidgin is not a stagnant language. It's kept alive by new slang words introduced by younger generations of speakers. *Maka'ainana* of all socioethnic backgrounds can at least understand pidgin. Most islanders are proud of it, but some consider it a low-class jargon.

Hawaiian

The Hawaiian language sways like a palm tree in a gentle wind. Its words are as melodious as a love song. With its many Polynesian root words easily traced to Indonesian and Malay, Hawaiian is obviously from this same stock. The Hawaiian spoken today is very different from old Hawaiian. Its greatest metamorphosis occurred when the missionaries began to write it down in the 1820s. Still, it nearly vanished. There has been a movement to reestablish the Hawaiian language over the last couple of decades. Not only are courses offered at the University of Hawai'i, but there is also a successful elementary school immersion program in the state, some books are being printed in it, and more and more musicians are performing in Hawaiian.

Hawaiian is, by and large, no longer spoken as a language except on Ni'ihau and in Hawaiian-language immersion classes and family settings; the closest tourists will come to it is in place names, street names, and words that have become part of common usage, such as *aloha* and *mahalo.* There are sermons in Hawaiian at some local churches. Kawaiaha'o Church in downtown Honolulu is the most famous of these, but each island has its own.

Thanks to the missionaries, the Hawaiian language is rendered phonetically using only 12 letters. They are the five vowels, a-e-i-o-u, sounded as they are in Spanish, and seven consonants, h-k-l-m-n-p-w, sounded exactly as they are in English. Sometimes "w" is pronounced as "v," but this only occurs in the middle of a word and always follows a vowel. A consonant is always followed by a vowel, forming two-letter syllables, but vowels are often found in pairs or even triplets. A slight oddity about Hawaiian is the glottal stop called *'okina.* This is an abrupt break in sound in the middle of a word, such as "oh-oh" in English, and is denoted with a reverse apostrophe ('). A good example is the one in *ali'i* or, even better, the O'ahu town of Ha'iku, which actually means Abrupt Break.

Pronunciation Key

For those unfamiliar with the sounds of Spanish or other Romance languages, the vowels are sounded as follows:
A—pronounced as in "ah" (that feels good!). For example, *tapa* is "tah-pah."
E—short "e" is "eh," as in "pen" or "dent" (thus *hale* is "hah-leh"). Long "e" sounds like "ay" as in "sway" or "day." For example, the Hawaiian goose (*nene*) is a "nay-nay," not a "nee-nee."
I—pronounced "ee" as in "see" or "we" (thus *pali* is pronounced "pah-lee").
O—pronounced as in "no" or "oh," such as "oh-noh" (*ono*).
U—pronounced "oo" as in "do" or "stew." For example, "kah-poo" (*kapu*).

Diphthongs and Stresses

Eight vowel pairs are known as "diphthongs" (ae-ai-ao-au-ei-eu-oi-ou). These are the sounds made by gliding from one vowel to another within a syllable. The stress is placed on the first vowel. In English, examples would be **soil** and **bail**. Common examples in Hawaiian are *lei* and *heiau*.

The best way to learn which syllables are stressed in Hawaiian is by listening closely. It becomes obvious after a while. There are also some vowel sounds that are held longer than others; these can occur at the beginning of a word, such as the first "a" in "'aina," or in the middle of a word, like the first "a" in *lanai*. Again, it's a matter of tuning your ear and paying attention. When written, these stressed vowels, called *kahako*, are noted with a macron, or short line, over them. Such stressed vowels are not indicated in this book.

Many Hawaiian words are commonly used in English, appear in English dictionaries, and therefore would ordinarily be subject to the rules of English grammar. The Hawaiian language, however, does not pluralize nouns by adding an "s"; the singular and plural are differentiated in context. For purposes of this book, and to highlight the Hawaiian culture, the Hawaiian style of pluralization will be followed for common Hawaiian words. The following are some examples of plural Hawaiian nouns treated this way in this book: *haole* (not *haoles*), *kahuna*, lei, and lu'au.

No one is going to give you a hard time if you mispronounce a word. It's good, however, to pay close attention to the pronunciation of street and place names because many Hawaiian words sound alike; a misplaced vowel here or there could be the difference between getting where you want to go and getting lost.

FOOD

Thanks to Hawai'i's plantation past, immigrants from around the world also brought their cuisine to the islands, and many of the dishes remain local favorites to this day. You'll find Chinese dim sum and bao, char siu stuffed steamed buns called manapua, Korean kimchi, Vietnamese *phô*, Puerto Rican pasteles, Portuguese malasadas, tonkatsu from Japan, and SPAM, biscuits, and gravy from World War II Americans in ethnic eateries and on menus across O'ahu.

While local Hawaiian food is rooted in Polynesian techniques and flavors, it is also an amalgam of the cuisine from the immigrants who became an integral part of Hawaiian culture. Plate lunches, found mainly at O'ahu's drive-in restaurants (island-style fast food), are served with two scoops of rice, macaroni salad, and a protein, including chicken katsu, kalbi, or kalua pork. This affordable and filling meal incorporates Japanese, Korean, American, and Hawaiian cooking. Loco moco is another favorite plate for lunch as well as breakfast: two fried eggs and a hamburger patty over rice smothered in gravy—talk about East meets West.

The food served at lu'au is very similar to what you'll find at a Hawaiian food restaurant, and there are several staple dishes no matter where you go. Kalua pig is a favorite, a smoky-flavored pulled pork tossed with cabbage. Traditionally, it is cooked in an *imu*, an underground earthen oven. Chicken long rice has bits of thigh meat cooked with ginger, green onions, and long rice noodles in a chicken broth. Lau lau is fish, pork, or chicken wrapped in taro leaves and steamed in *ti* leaves, lomi salmon is raw cubed salmon tossed with tomatoes, onion, and chile peppers, and squid luau is young taro leaves and squid cooked in coconut milk, the end product a tasty dish resembling creamed spinach. *Poke* (pronounced like okay with a p), is a raw fish salad made with ahi tuna, soy sauce (called shoyu in Hawai'i), and sesame oil. There are all different kinds of *poke*, some have onions and seaweed, some are spicy, some are mayonnaise based, and sometimes the fish is replaced with *tako* (octopus). No Hawaiian lu'au is complete without poi, a staple starch made from pounded taro root, and haupia, a coconut milk-based dessert usually served as a congealed pudding.

THE ARTS
Music

Ancient Hawaiians passed along stories

The Lu'au Tradition

The lu'au is an island institution. Local families have big lu'au for a baby's first birthday, anniversaries, graduations, and family reunions. Commercial operators have packaged the lu'au as nightly dinner and entertainment so visitors can get a glimpse of the tradition and traditional Hawaiian fare—kalua pig, lau lau, chicken long rice, lomi salmon, white rice, and poi. For a fixed price, you can gorge yourself on a tremendous variety of island foods, sample a few island drinks, and have an evening of entertainment as well. Generally, lu'au run 5pm-8:30pm. On your lu'au day, eat a light breakfast and skip lunch.

All commercial lu'au have pretty much the same format, though the types of food and entertainment differ somewhat. The tourist variety of lu'au is a lot of food, a lot of fun, but definitely a show. To have fun at a lu'au you have to get into the swing of things, like the Polynesian Revue. Local performers dance and lead the tourist hula—the fast version with swaying hips and dramatic lighting—a few wandering troubadours sing Hawaiian standards, and a muscular, sweaty man will swing flaming torches. Some offer an *imu* ceremony, where the pig is taken from the covered oven, as well as traditional games, arts, and crafts. Food is usually served buffet style, although a few do it family style. Most tourist lu'au have American and Asian dishes for those less adventurous souls.

To cook the pig, the lu'au master starts the *imu* on the morning of the gathering. He lays the hot stones and banana stalks to create an underground oven, which must maintain a perfect 400°F. In one glance, the lu'au master can gauge the weight and fat content of a succulent porker and decide just how long it should be cooked. The water in the leaves covering the pig steams and roasts the meat so that it falls off the bone. Local wisdom has it that "All you can't eat in the *imu* are the hot stones."

through chants, in which the emphasis was placed on historical accuracy, not melody. The missionaries were the first to introduce the Hawaiians to melody through Christian hymns, and soon singing became both an individual and group pastime. Early in the 1800s, Spanish vaqueros from California were imported to teach the Hawaiians how to be cowboys. With them came guitars and moody ballads. Immigrants who came along a little later in the 19th century, especially from Portugal, helped create Hawaiian-style music. Their biggest influence was a small, four-stringed instrument called a *braga* or *cavaquinho,* the prototype of the homegrown Hawaiian instrument that became known as the ukulele. Jumping flea, the translation of ukulele, is an appropriate name devised by the Hawaiians when they saw how nimble the fingers were as they jumped over the strings. Over many decades, Hawaiian music has evolved through techniques like slack key tuning, the twang and easy slide of the steel guitar, and the smooth falsetto singing that

accompanies the relaxed melodies. Today, popular Hawaiian music has fused with the beat of reggae, creating a style of music locally known as jawaiian.

Hula

The hula is more than an ethnic dance; it is the soul of Hawai'i expressed in motion. It began as a form of worship during religious ceremonies and was danced only by highly trained men. It gradually evolved into a form of entertainment, but in no regard was it sexual. It was history portrayed in the performing arts. In the beginning an androgynous deity named Laka descended to earth and taught men how to dance the hula. In time the male aspect of Laka departed for the heavens, but the female aspect remained. The female Laka set up her own special hula *heiau* at Ha'ena on the Na Pali coast of Kaua'i, where it still exists. As time went on women were allowed to learn the hula. Scholars surmise that men became too busy wresting a living from the land to maintain the art form.

Men did retain one type of hula for themselves called *lua*. This was a form of martial art employed in hand-to-hand combat that evolved into a ritualized warfare dance called *hula ku'i*. During the 19th century, the hula almost vanished because the missionaries considered it vile and heathen. King Kalakaua is generally regarded as having saved it during the late 1800s, when he formed his own troupe and encouraged the dancers to learn the old hula. Many of the original dances had been forgotten, but some were retained and are performed to this day.

Today, hula *halau* (schools) are active on every island, teaching hula and keeping the old ways and culture alive. Hula combines the chanting of the *mele* (story) and is accompanied by traditional instruments like the *ipu* (gourd). Performers spend years perfecting their techniques telling stories through dance. They show off their accomplishments during the fierce competition of the Merrie Monarch Festival in Hilo every April. The winning *halau* is praised and recognized throughout the islands.

Weaving and Carving

Hawaiians became the best basket makers and mat weavers in all of Polynesia. *Ulana* (woven mats) were made from *lau hala* (pandanus) leaves. Once split, the spine was removed and the leaves stored in large rolls. When needed they were soaked, pounded, and then fashioned into various floor coverings and sleeping mats. Intricate geometric patterns were woven in, and the edges were rolled and well fashioned. A wide variety of basketry was made from the aerial root *'ie'ie*, and the shapes varied according to use. Some baskets were tall and narrow, some were cones, others were flat like trays, and many were woven around gourds and calabashes.

Wood was a primary material used by Hawaiian artisans. They almost exclusively used *koa* because of its density, strength, and natural luster. It was turned into canoes, woodware, calabashes, and furniture for the *ali'i*. Temple idols were another major product

of woodcarving. A variety of stone artifacts were also turned out, including poi pounders, fish sinkers, and small idols.

The most respected artisans in old Hawai'i were the canoe makers. With little more than a stone adze and a pump drill, they built canoes that could carry 200 people and last for generations—sleek, well-proportioned, and infinitely seaworthy. The main hull was usually a gigantic *koa* log, and the gunwale planks were minutely drilled and sewn to the sides with sennit rope. Apprenticeships lasted for years, and a young man knew that he had graduated when one day he was nonchalantly asked to sit down and eat with the master builders. Small family-sized canoes with outriggers were used for fishing and perhaps carried a spear rack; large oceangoing double-hulled canoes were used for migration and warfare. On these, the giant logs had been adzed to about two inches thick. A mainsail woven from pandanus was mounted on a central platform, and the boat was steered by two long paddles. The hull was dyed with plant juices and charcoal, and the entire village helped launch the canoe in a ceremony called "drinking the sea."

Lei Making and Featherwork

Any flower or blossom can be strung into lei, but the most common are orchids or the lovely smelling plumeria. Lei are all beautiful, but special lei are highly prized by those who know what to look for. Of the different stringing styles, the most common is *kui*—stringing the flower through the middle or side. Most "airport-quality" lei are of this type. The *humuhumu* style, reserved for making flat lei, is made by sewing flowers and ferns to a *ti*, banana, or sometimes *hala* leaf. A *humuhumu* lei makes an excellent hatband. *Wili* is the winding together of greenery, ferns, and flowers into short, bouquet-type lengths. The most traditional form is *hili*, which requires no stringing at all but involves braiding fragrant ferns and leaves such as *maile*. If flowers are interwoven, the *hili* becomes the *haku* style, the most difficult and most beautiful type of lei.

Every major island is symbolized by its own lei made from a distinctive flower, shell, or fern. Each island has its own official color as well, although it doesn't necessarily correspond to the color of the island's lei. O'ahu, "The Gathering Place," is symbolized by yellow, the color of the tropical sun. Its flower is the delicate *'ilima,* which ranges in color from pastel yellow to a burnt orange. The blooms are about as large as a silver dollar, and lei made from *'ilima* were at one time reserved only for the *ali'i,* designating them as a royal flower.

The highly refined art of featherwork was practiced only on the islands of Tahiti, New Zealand, and Hawai'i, but the fashioning of feather helmets and idols was unique to Hawai'i. Favorite colors were red and yellow, which came only in a very limited supply from a small number of birds such as the *'o'o, 'i'iwi, mamo,* and *'apapane.* Professional bird hunters in old Hawai'i paid their taxes to *ali'i* in prized feathers. The feathers were fastened to a woven net of *olona* cord and made into helmets, idols, and beautiful flowing capes and cloaks. These resplendent garments were made and worn only by men, especially during battle, when a fine cloak became a great trophy of war. Featherwork was also employed in the making of *kahili* and lei, which were highly prized by the noble *ali'i* women.

Tapa Cloth

Tapa, cloth made from tree bark, was common throughout Polynesia and was a woman's art. A few trees such as the *wauke* and *mamaki* produced the best cloth, but a variety of other types of bark could be utilized. First the raw bark was pounded into a felt-like pulp

The delicate yellow *'ilima* blossom is a cultural symbol for O'ahu.

and beaten together to form strips (the beaters had distinctive patterns that helped make the cloth supple). The cloth was then decorated by stamping (a form of block printing) and dyed with natural colors from plants and sea animals in shades of gray, purple, pink, and red. They were even painted with natural brushes made from pandanus fruit, with an overall gray color made from charcoal. The tapa cloth was sewn together to make bed coverings, and fragrant flowers and herbs were either sewn or pounded in to produce a permanent fragrance. Tapa cloth is still available today, but the Hawaiian methods have been lost, and most tapa comes from other areas of Polynesia.

Essentials

Transportation

GETTING THERE
Air
All commercial flights to Oʻahu are routed to the **Honolulu International Airport** (300 Rodgers Blvd., 808/836-6411, http://hawaii.gov/hnl), as are most other flights with neighbor islands as final destinations. The Honolulu International Airport has three terminals: the Overseas Terminal accommodates international and mainland flights, the Interisland Terminal handles Hawaiian Airlines flights, and the Commuter Terminal handles the small interisland carriers. There is a free intra-airport shuttle service for getting around the airport and ground transportation is available just outside the baggage claim areas on the lower level, along the center median. The airport is a mere 10 miles from Waikiki, and 6 miles from downtown Honolulu.

Everyone visiting Hawaiʻi must fill out a *Plants and Animals Declaration Form* and present it to an airline flight attendant or the appropriate official upon arrival in the state. Anyone carrying any of the listed items must have those items inspected by an agricultural inspection agent at the airport. These items include but are not limited to fruits, vegetables, plants, seeds, and soil, as well as live insects, seafood, snakes, and amphibians. For additional information on just what is prohibited, contact any U.S. Customs Office or check with an embassy or consulate in foreign countries.

Also remember that before you leave Hawaiʻi for the mainland, all of your bags are subject to an agricultural inspection before you enter the ticketing line to check luggage and get your boarding pass. There are no restrictions on beach sand from below the high-water line, coconuts, cooked foods, dried flower arrangements, fresh flower lei, pineapples, certified pest-free plants and cuttings, and seashells. However, papaya must be treated before departure. Some other restricted items are berries, fresh gardenias, jade vines, live insects and snails, cotton, plants in soil, soil itself, and sugarcane. Raw sugarcane is acceptable, however, if it is cut between the nodes, has the outer covering peeled off, is split into fourths, and is commercially prepackaged. For any questions pertaining to plants that you want to take to the mainland, call the Agricultural Quarantine Inspection office (808/861-8490) in Honolulu.

GETTING AROUND
Car
The easiest way for independent travelers to get around Oʻahu is by car, and there are plenty of rental car companies. There are six on-airport car rental agencies and several off-airport companies. If you haven't booked a rental car online prior to your arrival, the registration counters are located in the baggage claim area. All car rental shuttles stop in the designated area along the center median on the ground level of the airport, just outside the baggage claim areas. Offices for the on-airport companies are located on the ground level opposite Baggage Claim G. Keep in mind that if you're staying at a hotel in Waikiki, there will most likely be an additional daily parking fee for your rental car.

Once you've acquired your ride, there is an H-1 freeway on-ramp at the east end of the airport. From the freeway you can head east to Honolulu and Waikiki or west to the windward side via the H-3, the North Shore via the H-2, or out to the leeward side of the island. If

---

Pacific Crossroads

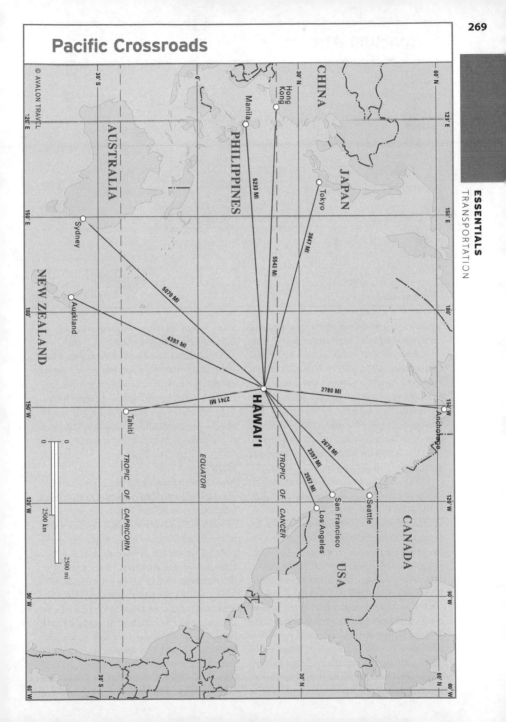

© AVALON TRAVEL

CHINA

Hong Kong
Manila

PHILIPPINES

AUSTRALIA

Sydney

NEW ZEALAND

Auckland

JAPAN

Tokyo

5233 MI

5545 MI

3847 MI

5070 MI

4393 MI

2741 MI

Tahiti

HAWAI'I

2780 MI

2678 MI

2397 MI

2557 MI

Anchorage

Seattle

San Francisco

Los Angeles

CANADA

USA

EQUATOR

TROPIC OF CAPRICORN

TROPIC OF CANCER

0   2500 km

0   2500 mi

Honolulu Airport

To Pearl Harbor ← H1
NIMITZ HWY
COMMUTER TERMINAL
POST OFFICE
HONOLULU AIRPORT HOTEL
ROGERS BLVD
THE PLAZA HOTEL
KOAPAKA ST
PAEA ST
To Honolulu and Waikiki
H1 →
UALENA ST
AOLELE ST
ARRIVALS GROUND LEVEL
LEI
IN →
OUT ↑ IN ↓
INTERISLAND TERMINAL
GATES
DEPARTURES TOP LEVEL
BANK
PARKING
CAR RENTALS
GATES
MAINLAND AND INTERNATIONAL TERMINAL
GATES
GATES
GATES

© AVALON TRAVEL
SCALE NOT AVAILABLE

you're leaving from a car rental agency located on Nimitz Highway, head east under the freeway until you come to a junction where you can continue to Waikiki via Nimitz Highway, enter the H-1 freeway east to Honolulu or Waikiki, or access Dillingham Boulevard for Honolulu. Driving west on Nimitz will take you to an on-ramp for the H-1 freeway. From there you can access the H-3 to the windward side, the H-2 to the North Shore, or continue on the H-1 to the leeward side.

On O'ahu, there are several local courtesies to follow on the road. Drivers don't generally honk their horns except to say hello or in an emergency. It's considered rude to honk to hurry someone along. Hawaiian drivers reflect the climate: They're relaxed and polite. Often on small roads, they'll brake to let you turn left when they're coming at you. They may assume you'll do the same, so be ready, after a perfunctory turn signal from another driver, for him or her to turn across your lane. The more rural the area, the more apt this is to happen. On all roadways, it is customary to let a signaling motorist change lanes in front of you, and if you need to change lanes and someone lets you in, always give a thank-you wave. When merging, people generally allow every other car into the lane.

O'ahu has a seat belt law as well as a ban on cell phones while driving. Speed limits change periodically along the highways, particularly when they pass through small towns. Police routinely check the speed of traffic with radar equipment, often hiding in a blind spot to radar and ticket speeding motorists.

Bus

From the airport, there are several shuttle services to hotels and resorts in the Waikiki area and beyond. Pick up shuttles along the center median on the ground level in front of the baggage claim areas. There is a complete list of shuttle service providers at the Honolulu International Airport website. **Roberts Hawaii** (808/539-9400 or 800/831-5541, www.robertshawaii.com) Express Shuttle has round-trip service from the airport to Waikiki hotels. **SpeediShuttle** (877/242-5777, www.speedishuttle.com) provides on-demand door-to-door service from the airport to Waikiki hotels, Kahala Resort, Ko Olina, Turtle Bay Resort on the North Shore, and residences around the

Interisland Air Routes

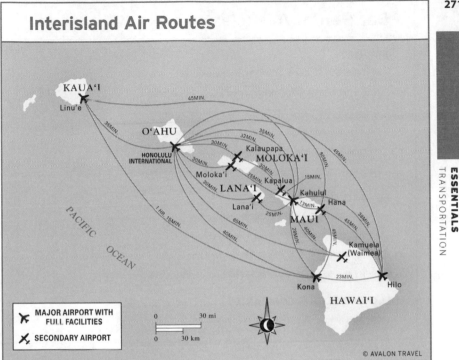

KAUA'I
Linu'e
45MIN.
35MIN.
O'AHU
HONOLULU INTERNATIONAL
35MIN.
32MIN.
30MIN.
Kalaupapa
MOLOKA'I
30MIN.
30MIN.
30MIN.
60MIN.
45MIN.
Moloka'i
28MIN.
Kapalua
15MIN.
LANA'I
30MIN.
Kahului
1 HR. 15MIN.
Lana'i
13MIN.
Hana
65MIN.
25MIN.
MAUI
38MIN.
45MIN.
40MIN.
28MIN.
40MIN.
45MIN.
Kamuela
(Waimea)
23MIN.
Kona
Hilo
HAWAI'I

PACIFIC OCEAN

✈ MAJOR AIRPORT WITH FULL FACILITIES
✈ SECONDARY AIRPORT

0   30 mi
0   30 km

© AVALON TRAVEL

ESSENTIALS
TRANSPORTATION

island. Passengers are allowed two bags and a carry-on for free. Rates are based on the destination, and there are additional fees for bicycles, surfboards, golf bags, and extra baggage.

TheBus (808/848-4500, www.thebus. org) provides islandwide transportation, including from the airport. If you're planning on riding the bus from the airport to your hotel, keep in mind that your bags have to be able to fit under the seat or on your lap without protruding into the aisle. There are several bus stops on the second level of the airport on the center median. Route Nos. 19, 20, and 31 access the airport, and Route No. 19 eastbound will take you to Waikiki. Fares are $2.50 for adults, $1.25 children ages 6-17, children 5 and under are free if they sit on an adult's lap. The Visitors Pass, a four-consecutive-day pass, is $25 with unlimited use. Call 808/848-5555 for route information or download TheBus' smartphone app **DaBus** (www.

honolulu.gov/mobile/dabus.html), which provides real-time information.

Taxi

Taxi service is available at the Honolulu International Airport from the center median fronting the baggage claim areas. Look for attendants in green shirts that say "Taxi Dispatch." From the terminal to Waikiki costs about $35-40 during non-rush hour periods, with a maximum of four passengers. The fare is by meter only, and there is a charge of $0.35 per bag.

To get around by taxi, it's best to call and make arrangements directly from a company or driver, rather than trying to hail one from the curb, as it is technically illegal for taxi drivers to cruise around looking for a fare. For taxi service call **Charley's Taxi** (808/233-3333 or 877/531-1333, http://charleystaxi.com), **City Taxi** (808/524-2121, www.citytaxihonolulu.com), and **TheCAB** (808/422-2222, www.

Car Rental Agencies

AIRPORT

- Avis (808/834-5536 or 800/321-3712, www.avis.com)
- Budget (808/836-1700 or 800/527-0700, www.budget.com)
- Dollar (808/944-1544 or 800/800-4000, www.dollar.com)
- Enterprise (808/836-2213 or 800/736-8222, www.enterprise.com)
- Hertz (808/831-3500 or 800/654-3011, www.hertz.com)
- National (808/834-6350 or 800/227-7368, www.nationalcar.com)

BEYOND THE AIRPORT

- A-1 (808/833-7575, http://a1rentacarhawaii.com)
- Advantage (808/834-0461, www.advantage.com)
- Alamo (808/833-4585 or 800/327-9633, www.alamo.com)
- Thrifty (808/952-4238 or 800/367-5238, www.thrifty.com)

ECO-CONSCIOUS COMPANIES

- Eco Cab (808/979-1010, www.ecocabhawaii.com)

thecabhawaii.com). For earth-conscious travelers, try **Eco Cab** (808/979-1010, www.ecocabhawaii.com). If you need some special attention like a limousine service, try **Cloud 9 Limousines** (808/524-7999, www.cloudninelimos.com). It is one of about 50 limo services on the island.

Uber (www.uber.com/cities) and **Lyft** (www.lyft.com/cities) riding-hailing companies are also available. Download the smartphone apps or visit their websites.

Recreation

Outdoor activities are at the heart of the Hawai'i lifestyle, and a major draw to most visitors in the islands. With comfortable weather year round, warm ocean water and ample nature from mountain to sea, O'ahu holds the opportunity for outdoor enthusiasts to pursue their activity of choice in a beautiful, tropical setting.

SURFING

The art of riding waves for pleasure and athletic challenge was born in Hawai'i and legendary beachboy, waterman, and Olympic gold-medal swimmer Duke Kahanamoku shared it with the world in the early 20th century, putting on expos in California and Australia. Today, surfing is enjoyed by people around the globe. Whether you're an expert surfer, a weekend warrior, or a beginner, O'ahu has surf breaks suited for surfers of all experience levels around the island.

For beginners and novice surfers, Waikiki is the perfect place to learn how to get on your feet or catch a few fun waves. While summer sees the most consistent surf, there's usually something rolling into Canoes that you can paddle into. Beginners usually stick to Canoes, the gentle surf break directly in front of the Moana Surfrider hotel. Talk to the beachboys who work at the beach services stands along Waikiki for lessons and rentals. Longboards are generally the surfboard of choice in Waikiki. Seasoned surfers who are looking for quality waves should paddle out to Publics, the break to the west of Canoes, or Queen's, which is the peak right in front of Kuhio Beach Park.

In the winter months, the North Shore sees nearly continual wave action, with powerful breakers reaching up to 50 feet at top surf breaks like Waimea Bay. North Shore surf breaks are for experts only, and draw surfers from around the world riding all types of boards. There are several surfboard rental outfitters in Hale'iwa town and at Shark's Cove, but if you're experienced enough to surf the big waves on the North Shore, you'll most likely have your own equipment in tow.

STAND-UP PADDLING

Stand-up paddling was invented by the Waikiki beachboys, who would paddle around the Waikiki lineups using canoe paddles on top of their longboards. Stand-up paddling is very similar today, with the paddles being more refined, lighter, and easier to use. The boards are long, thick, and wide, making them very stable on top of the ocean surface. Stand-up paddling is done with the feet parallel, like skiing, whereas surfers stand one foot in front of the other. Stand-up paddle surfing is when paddlers use specifically designed stand-up paddleboards to surf waves, as opposed to just paddling around the ocean, going from one place to another.

Stand-up paddling is most enjoyable in favorable ocean conditions: light winds, smooth ocean surface, and little to no surf. The sport is very popular in Waikiki year-round and on the North Shore during the summer months, when the surf is flat. You can also paddle up the 'Anahulu River in Hale'iwa town. Stand-up paddling is also popular in Kailua, but the predominant trade winds make choppy wave conditions a common occurrence.

All the beach services in Waikiki rent stand up paddleboards and paddles, as well as give lessons. You can find the same rental and lesson services in Kailua and Hale'iwa as well, but you won't find boards to rent along the North Shore beaches. You'll need to rent a board and some racks in Hale'iwa town and keep driving north to the beach of your choice.

KAYAKING

Kayaking is a great activity to get out in the water, exercise, and cover some distance over the reefs. The majority of recreational kayaking on O'ahu is done on the North Shore in the summer, and on the windward coast, where you'll find several islets to explore that offer a remarkable retreat and perspective of O'ahu.

Kailua Beach Park and Lanikai are the most popular destinations for kayaking. There are outfitters right by the beach park that offer single and double kayaks for rent, as well as tour packages. If you're comfortable in the ocean and with your physical abilities, rent a kayak and trek out on your own. Explore the Mokulua Islands, Flat Island, or drive to Kane'ohe Bay and paddle out to the sandbar, a unique natural phenomenon in the middle of the bay. Drive north even farther on the windward side to Kualoa Ranch and paddle around Chinaman's Hat, a small islet just offshore. Kahana Bay, just north of Kualoa, also has great kayaking potential in the deep sheltered bay. If you like the idea and safety of kayaking with a guide, or are new to the sport altogether, take a tour and enjoy the added information about the area that you won't get on a solo adventure. (Not to mention, most tours offer lunch.)

On the North Shore, kayaking is a summer activity. Hale'iwa town has outfitters that rent kayaks right on the beach at Hale'iwa Beach Park, a great place to kayak. You can also paddle up the 'Anahulu River. If you're feeling

Snorkeling

© AVALON TRAVEL

adventurous, rent some racks, put the kayak on top the car and drive north to the North Shore beaches and explore the coast.

SNORKELING

While you can snorkel just about anywhere around O'ahu, the best opportunity to see lots of marine life like fish and coral is over the island's healthiest reefs. You'll find these reefs in marine protected areas, where fishing is illegal. Like all ocean activities, the most pleasurable snorkeling experience requires certain conditions, namely light winds, calm seas, and a smooth ocean surface. Sunny days help bring out the colors in the reef and the fish.

At the South Shore, you'll find a small marine protected area in Waikiki, along Queen's Surf Beach, and the ever-popular Hanauma

Bay in Hawai'i Kai. Hanauma Bay boasts hundreds of species of fish in the waters and, apart from the crowds in the water and on the beach, you won't be disappointed by the bounty of life in the ocean. You can rent snorkel gear in Waikiki or at Hanauma Bay.

On the North Shore, Waimea Bay, Three Tables, and Sharks Cove make up the Pupukea-Waimea Marine Life Conservation District. A less-structured experience than Hanauma Bay, the three consecutive beaches along the coast offer unique underwater topography and viewing possibilities. You'll find the best conditions to snorkel these areas in the summer. If you plan on snorkeling here, it's best to have your snorkel gear with you. There are outfitters in Hale'iwa and one outfitter at Sharks Cove.

DIVING

O'ahu is a great place to scuba dive. There are a host of reefs, interesting underwater geography, and wrecks to dive. There are boat dives, drift dives, shore dives, and night dives. Dive charters operate primarily out of Kewalo Basin in Honolulu, the Hawai'i Kai Marina in Hawai'i Kai, Hale'iwa Harbor in Hale'iwa on the North Shore, and on the Leeward side out of Wai'anae Harbor in Wai'anae.

The wreck dives are on the South and West Shores, and shore dives at Sharks Cove, in addition to boat dives, are common on the North Shore. The North Shore is known for its lava tubes, caves, and other interesting underwater geography. Hawai'i Kai is famous for the vertical walls off Koko Head crater that fall 70 feet into the blue Pacific. The South Shore has plane- and shipwrecks, and the windward side has the opportunity for a drift dive from Ka'ena Point down the coast.

Dive operators offer experiences for all levels of divers and instruction for many different types of certification. Many also offer transportation from and to Waikiki hotels. All dive operators will offer packaged rates including gear rental and some have retail outlets if you have your own gear.

HIKING

For all the ocean lovers that flock to O'ahu, there are equal opportunities for hikers to explore O'ahu's mountains, valleys, forests, and waterfalls. There are two main mountain ranges on O'ahu. The Ko'olau Mountains run the length of the windward coast, with valleys and rises spread along the South Shore and inland urban Honolulu neighborhoods. The mountains are verdant, with many native Hawaiian species of shrubs, ferns, and trees in the upper elevation reaches of the range. The Ko'olaus are best known for the dramatic cliffs stretching from Waimanalo to Kualoa. The Wai'anae Range spans the leeward coast and is home to the highest peak on the island. The mountains are also green and lush in the upper portions, with many native Hawaiian

species as well, but dry out significantly as the ridges push into the hot and dry leeward coast.

If you plan on doing some serious hiking, it's best to stop by a bookstore and pick up one of the several hiking trail guides for O'ahu. There are also many resources online that provide specific route descriptions and topographical maps.

Many of the shorter, more accessible hikes are located in the valleys above Honolulu. They are easy to get to and offer great opportunities ranging from a short walk in the wilderness to an all-out day hike with water falls and summits. Hiking in the Ko'olaus on the windward side is more apt to be a muddy, slippery experience with mosquitoes and possible showers at any time, especially the higher up you venture. Hiking in the Wai'anae Mountains is a rockier, drier experience. Hikers should set out early to beat the midday sun and heat. The North Shore also has a few trails on the Pupukea bluff and on the north-facing side of the Wai'anae Range, which receives more rainfall than the leeward side of the mountains.

Not many trails are managed, so it's best to hike with others for safety. Be prepared for rain and wind, and let someone else know where you set out to hike before you begin. Bring ample water and sunscreen, and stay on marked trails. Don't leave valuables in your car when parking at trailheads.

GOLF

With 38 (and counting) public, private, municipal, and military golf courses scattered around such a relatively small island, golf is a main draw for residents and visitors alike. The courses range from modest nine-holers to world-class courses whose tournaments attract the biggest names in golf today. Prices range from $10 per round up to $175. An added attraction of playing O'ahu's courses is that you get to walk around on some of the most spectacular and manicured pieces of real estate on the island. Some afford sweeping

Campgrounds

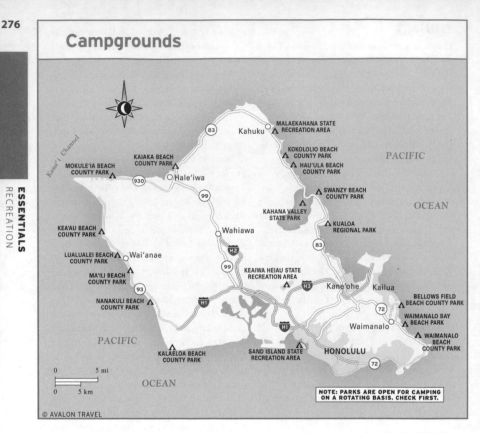

NOTE: PARKS ARE OPEN FOR CAMPING ON A ROTATING BASIS. CHECK FIRST.

© AVALON TRAVEL

views of the coast, whereas others have a lovely mountain backdrop. Tough or easy, flat or full of definition, O'ahu's courses provide ample opportunity and variety for any golfer.

Municipal and public courses are open to everyone. Resort courses cater to the public as well as to resort guests. Semiprivate courses set aside most of their time for members but do have specified days and times when they are open to the public. Private courses are strictly for members only and their guests. Military personnel and dependents, Department of Defense personnel, and those who have access to military bases are welcome to golf at the military courses. Some are also open to the public. If you wish to golf at courses other than municipal or public courses, be sure to call ahead to verify accessibility.

Most golf courses offer lessons. Many have driving ranges, some lighted. Virtually all have pro shops and clubhouses with restaurants and lounges or snack shops. Many courses offer reduced special time rates, twilight hour rates, and summer specials. Be sure to ask about these rates because they often afford substantial savings. On the other hand, some courses charge higher fees for non-U.S. residents. Military courses charge different greens fees for civilians than for military personnel, and the military fees might differ depending on rank.

For ease of use of municipal golf courses, the City and County of Honolulu has an automated tee time reservation and information system (808/296-2000) to make or check your reservation or to have your inquiry answered.

Golf Courses

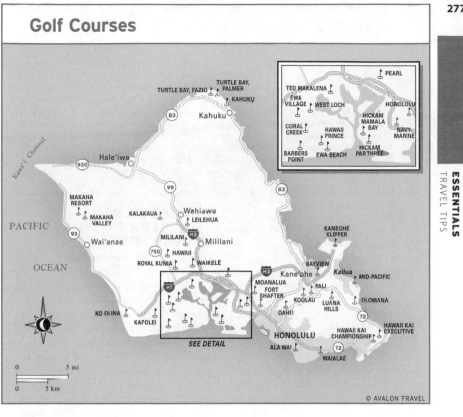

Travel Tips

WHAT TO PACK

While Oʻahu might be isolated in the middle of the Pacific Ocean, it still has all the products, services, and conveniences of a big city. When filling your suitcase, pack light: lightweight clothing and footwear. Leave the jeans at home and choose comfortable, casual wear. Even if you're planning on a fancy night out or two, guys can get away with an aloha shirt and slacks, while the ladies can wear a nice sundress. If you don't have any flip-flops, you can always pick them up when you arrive, as well as anything else you might find yourself in need of, like that colorful aloha shirt. Just

make sure at the top of your clothing list is board shorts or a bikini.

For sports enthusiasts, bringing the necessary equipment is usually a matter of preference. Expert and professional surfers bring their own boards to the islands, but most visitors just rent boards. The airlines charge high fees for checking in surfboards. If you golf and don't want to lug your clubs around the airport, all the courses rent clubs. Hikers should bring their own boots, which will most likely get muddy. For convenience, tennis players should bring their own rackets.

Traveling With Pets

Hawai'i has a very rigid pet quarantine policy designed to keep rabies and other mainland diseases from reaching the state. All domestic pets are subject to a **120-day quarantine** (a 30-day quarantine and 5-day-or-less quarantine are allowed by meeting certain pre-arrival and post-arrival requirements; service animals with proper documentation may qualify for same day release.). The process is expensive and time-consuming, and there are additional airline fees as well. Unless you are contemplating a move to Hawai'i, it is not feasible to bring pets. Exceptions to the quarantine are made for animals originating in other rabies-free locales like Guam, Australia, New Zealand, and the British Isles. For complete information, contact the **Department of Agriculture, Animal Quarantine Division** (99-951 Halawa Valley St., 'Aiea, HI 96701, 808/483-7151, http://hawaii.gov/hdoa/ai/aqs) in Honolulu.

Sunscreen is a must and mosquito repellent quite a good idea, just make sure you put them in your check-in baggage. A hat will protect your dome from the sun, and binoculars are key if you plan on whale- or bird-watching. And please don't forget your camera.

TRAVELING WITH CHILDREN

For those traveling with young children, consider leaving all the gear at home to make your luggage lighter and less cumbersome. Car rental companies rent car seats for a small fee, and you can rent all kinds of other products for your stay on O'ahu, like cribs, portable cribs and play yards, strollers, and high chairs, even beach gear. **Paradise Baby** (808/561-1061, www.paradisebabyco.com) rents luxury baby equipment with free islandwide delivery and pickup. **Baby Aboard** (808/393-7612, www.babyaboard.com) serves the entire island, and **Baby's Away** (808/640-6734 or 800/496-6386, https://babysaway.com) rents equipment for Honolulu and Waikiki area visitors.

For family beach days with the little ones just getting their feet wet for the first time, choose beaches with little to no shore break, like **Kaimana Beach** in Waikiki or the **Ko Olina Lagoons.** And don't forget to pick up an umbrella for respite from the sun.

ACCESS FOR TRAVELERS WITH DISABILITIES

For a smooth trip, travelers with disabilities should make as many arrangements ahead of time as possible. Tell the transportation companies and hotels you'll be dealing with the nature of your restrictions in advance so they can make arrangements to accommodate you. Bring your medical records and notify medical establishments of your arrival if you'll need their services. Travel with a friend or make arrangements for an aide on arrival. Bring your own wheelchair if possible and let airlines know if it is battery powered. Boarding interisland carriers sometimes requires steps. They'll board wheelchairs early on special lifts, but they must know you're coming. Most hotels and restaurants accommodate persons with disabilities, but always call ahead just to make sure.

The state Commission on Persons with Disabilities was designed with the express purpose of aiding disabled people. It is a source of invaluable information and distributes self-help booklets, which are published jointly by the Disability and Communication Access Board and the Hawaii Centers for Independent Living. Any person with disabilities heading to Hawai'i should write first or visit the office of the **Hawaii Centers for Independent Living** (414 Kuwili St., #102, Honolulu, HI 96817,

808/522-5400, www.hcil.org). Additional information is available on the Disability and Communication Access Board website: www.hawaii.gov/health/dcab/home.

O'ahu Services

At Honolulu International Airport, parking spaces are on the fourth floor of the parking garage near each pedestrian bridge and on each level near the elevators at the Interisland Terminal. Several of the airport shuttles have lifts for wheelchairs, and there is an on-demand van shuttle service for transportation between locations within the airport facility. O'ahu's public transit system, **TheBus**, operates most buses with lift capability, but most van transportation and taxis have steps.

For getting around, the City of Honolulu offers a curb-to-curb service for disabled persons; call **Handi-Van** (808/456-5555). You must make arrangements at least a day in advance or up to seven days in advance. A private special taxi company operating all over the island is **Handi-Cabs of the Pacific** (808/848-4500); **TheCAB** (808/422-2222) taxi service also has wheelchair-accessible vans. Most of the large rental car companies can put hand controls (right or left) on their cars, but some restrict these controls to a certain size or type of vehicle. They generally require prior arrangements, one or two days at least, preferably when making your advance reservation. Rates are comparable with standard rental cars.

Valid out-of-state **disabled-person parking placards** may be used throughout the state of Hawai'i. Passes for disabled but ambulatory persons using **TheBus** cost $10. Check at **TheBus Pass Office** (811 Middle St., Honolulu, 808/848-4500; 7:30am-3:30pm Mon.-Fri.).

For **medical equipment rental,** see the following establishments for all kinds of apparatus: **Apria Healthcare** (98-720 Kuahao Pl., Pearl City, 808/485-0178, www. apria.com), **C. R. Newton Co.** (1575 S. Beretania St., Ste. 101, Honolulu, 808/949-8389 or 800/545-2078, www.crnewton. com), and **Hawaiian Islands Medical** (841 Pohukaina St., Ste. 8, Honolulu, 808/597-8087 or 866/246-4633, www.himed.cc).

LGBT TRAVELERS

The overall mind-set in Hawai'i, and on O'ahu, has long been acceptance of the LGBT community. In 2011, the state legalized civil unions for same-sex couples. O'ahu has gay and lesbian bars, nightclubs, accommodations, and beaches. **Hula's Bar & Lei Stand** in Waikiki is a well-known hangout, as is **Queen's Beach** and the surrounding area of Kapi'olani Park, just a short walk from Hula's.

The **Travel Alternative Group** (www. tagapproved.com), a resource for accommodations and attractions, has approved **Aqua Hotels & Resorts** (www.aquagaytravel. com), which offers discounts on reservations for LGBT travelers, and **Aston Hotels & Resorts** (www.AstonHotels.com). Another resource for finding accommodations and tours is the **International Gay and Lesbian Travel Association** (954/630-1637, www. iglta.org). They have tapped **Hotel Renew** (www.hotelrenew.com), **Discover Hawaii Tours** (808/690-9050, www.discoverhawaii-tours.com), and **Waikiki Beach Marriott Resort & Spa** (www.marriott.com), among many other establishments, as gay and lesbian friendly.

Health and Safety

With the perfect weather, a multitude of fresh-air activities, soothing negative ionization from the sea, and a generally relaxed and carefree lifestyle, everyone seems to feel better in the islands. There are no cases of malaria, cholera, or yellow fever. Because of a strict quarantine law, rabies is also nonexistent. There is no need for vaccinations when traveling to O'ahu, the water is safe and the air quality is the best in the country.

The most common health risks come from heatstroke, sunburn, intoxication, dehydration, and drowning. If you cut yourself on the reef, make sure to clean the wound periodically and treat it with an antibiotic ointment to avoid infection, as cuts tend to heal slower in the tropical climate.

SUN

The warming yet harmful rays of the sun come through more easily in Hawai'i than on the mainland because of the sun's angle, and you don't feel them as much because there's always a cool breeze. The worst part of the day to be in direct sun is 11am-3pm. O'ahu lies about 21.5 degrees north latitude, not even close to the equator, but it's still more than 1,000 miles south of sunny southern California beaches. Use sunscreen on your face and exposed skin every day, even if you're not at the beach. Hats, sunglasses, beach umbrellas, plenty of water, and a dose of common sense will keep you active outdoors without a sunburn souvenir. And just because it's cloudy doesn't mean you can skip the sunscreen.

Whether out on the beach, hiking in the mountains, or just strolling around town, be aware of dehydration. The sun and wind tend to sap your energy and your store of liquid. Carry bottled water with you at all times. For those choosing to imbibe, make sure to drink even more water than normal to account for the stress on your body under the strong Hawai'i sun.

MOSQUITOES AND COCKROACHES

Mosquitoes were unknown in the Hawaiian Islands until their larvae stowed away in the water barrels of the HMS *Wellington* in 1826 and were introduced at Lahaina in Maui. They bred in the tropical climate and rapidly spread to all the islands. They are a particular nuisance in the rainforests, watersheds, and periodically damp areas like the windward coast and mountains. Be prepared, and bring a natural repellent like citronella oil, available in most health stores on the islands, or a commercial product available in grocery and drugstores. Campers will be happy to have mosquito coils to burn at night as well.

Cockroaches are common in Hawai'i, and there are several different kinds you'll come across. There are the small roaches that live in leaf litter and the larger flying roaches that seek out light at night. One comforting thought is that in Hawai'i they aren't a sign of filth or dirty housekeeping. They love the climate like everyone else, and it's a real problem keeping them under control. Just do your best to handle it. They won't hurt you.

LEPTOSPIROSIS

Present in streams, ponds, and muddy soil, **leptospirosis** is a freshwater-borne bacteria deposited by the urine of infected animals. From 2 to 20 days after the bacteria enter the body, there will be a sudden onset of fever accompanied by chills, sweats, headache, and sometimes vomiting and diarrhea. Preventive measures include staying out of freshwater sources and mud where cattle and other animals wade and drink, not swimming in freshwater if you have an open cut, and not drinking stream water. Although not always the case, leptospirosis may be fatal if left untreated.

Dengue Fever

Dengue Fever, a mosquito-borne tropical disease, is not endemic to Hawaii; however, in 2015 it was brought to the Big Island by an infected traveler. As of early 2016 there were over 200 known cases of dengue fever identified on the Big Island—the majority of cases from residents and not visitors to the island. In early 2016, Waipio Valley was closed to visitors in order to minimize the potential for new cases of Dengue. Typically, infected individuals are asymptomatic but symptoms may include: fever, joint pain, headache, and rash. The best way to avoid Dengue is to avoid being bitten by an infected mosquito. Therefore, public health professionals often urge individuals to stay away from high risk areas. Check the Hawaii Department of Health Website (http://health. hawaii.gov/docd/dengue-outbreak 2015/) for information about what areas are affected or where you may be at higher risk for acquiring the disease. If you are visiting a higher risk area, be sure to cover yourself, especially during sunrise and sunset (the time when mosquitoes are most active) and to use bug spray with DEET. (*Contributed by Bree Kessler, author of* Moon Big Island of Hawaii)

OCEAN SAFETY

More people drown in Hawai'i than anywhere else in the world. In addition, powerful shore breaks are also the cause of severe injuries like broken backs and necks. But don't let these statistics deter you from enjoying the ocean. Instead, educate yourself on the day's and area's ocean conditions and enjoy the water responsibly. Ask lifeguards or beach attendants about conditions and follow their advice. Common sense, good judgment, and respect for the ocean go a long way. And never turn your back on the ocean while enjoying the shoreline. Rogue waves can wash over reef, rock, and beach and pull you out into the water. Obey all warning signs posted on the beach, and if you're swimming, surfing, or snorkeling, return to shore before you get tired. If you engage in an ocean activity by yourself, make sure you tell others in your party your planned whereabouts in the event of an emergency. If you find yourself on the beach psyching yourself up to get in the water, it's probably better to heed the warning, "If in doubt, stay out."

Sharks, Urchins, and Coral

Sharks live in all the oceans of the world. Most mind their own business and stay away from shore. Hawaiian sharks are well fed—on fish—and don't usually bother with unsavory humans. If you encounter a shark, don't panic! Never thrash around because this will trigger a shark's attack instinct.

Portuguese man-of-wars and other **jellyfish** put out long, floating tentacles that sting if they touch you. Jellyfish are blown into shore by winds on the 8th, 9th, and 10th days after the full moon. Don't wash the sting off with freshwater because this will only aggravate it. Locals will use hot saltwater to take away the sting, as well as alcohol (the drinking or rubbing kind), aftershave lotion, or meat tenderizer (MSG), but lifeguards use common household vinegar. After rinsing, soak with a wet towel. An antihistamine may also bring relief. Expect to start to feel better in about a half hour.

Coral can give you a nasty cut, and it's known for causing infections because it's a living organism. Wash the cut immediately and apply an antiseptic. Keep it clean and covered, and watch for infection. With coral cuts, it's best to have a professional look at it to clean it out. Most infection comes from tiny bits of coral that are left deep in the cut. Never stand on or grab coral. It damages the fragile lifeform and can send you to the hospital.

Poisonous **sea urchins**, like the lacquer-black *wana*, are found in shallow tidepools and reefs and will hurt you if you step on them. Their spines will break off, enter your foot, and severely burn. There are cures. Soaking a couple of times in vinegar for half an hour or so should stop the burning. If vinegar is not available, the local cure-all is urine.

Leave the fish, turtles, and seals alone. Fish should never be encouraged to feed from humans. Green sea turtles and seals are endangered species, and stiff fines can be levied on those who knowingly disturb them. Have a great time looking and taking pictures, but give them respect and space.

MEDICAL SERVICES

Full-service hospitals include **The Queen's Medical Center** (1301 Punchbowl St., Honolulu, 808/538-9011, www.queensmedicalcenter.net), **Kapiolani Medical Center for Women and Children** (1319 Punahou St., Honolulu, 808/983-6000, www.hawaiipacifichealth.org/kapiolani), and **Straub Clinic and Hospital** (888 S. King St., Honolulu, 808/522-4000, www.straubhealth.org) in Honolulu; **Castle Medical Center** (640 Ulukahiki St., 808/263-5500, http://castlemed.org) in Kailua; **Wahiawa General Hospital** (128 Lehua St., 808/621-8411, www.wahiawageneral.org) in Wahiawa; and **Kahuku Medical Center** (56-117 Pualalea St., 808/293-9221, www.hhsc.org/oahu/kahuku/index.html) in Kahuku on the North Shore.

Information and Services

TOURIST INFORMATION

The **Hawaii Visitors and Convention Bureau** (HVCB, 2270 Kalakaua Ave., Ste. 801, 808/524-0722 or 800/464-2924, www.gohawaii.com) is the state of Hawai'i's official tourism agency and website. The great thing about the HVCB is that everything it offers is free. The staff is extremely knowledgeable, and the office is packed with excellent brochures on virtually every facet of living in, visiting, or simply enjoying Hawai'i. The website features travel tips, quick facts, regional information, and service providers to help inform your vacation.

There is plenty of free tourist literature available at all major hotels, shopping malls, the airport, and stands along Waikiki's streets. They all contain up-to-the-minute information on what's happening and a treasure trove of free or reduced-price coupons for various attractions and services. Always featured are events, shopping tips, dining and entertainment, and sightseeing. The main ones are *This Week Oahu,* the best and most complete; and *Where Oahu,* with good sections on dining and sightseeing. Heavy on sightseeing attractions and activities, *101*

Things To Do: Oahu also has maps, advertising, and some coupons. *Oahu Drive Guide,* handed out by all the major rental car agencies, has some excellent tips and orientation maps. It is especially useful to get you started from the airport. The major shopping malls also publish their own magazines.

Maps

Aside from the simple maps in the ubiquitous free tourist literature, the **O'ahu Visitors and Conventions Bureau** and other organizations put out folding pocket **maps** of the island that are available free at the airport and tourist brochure racks around the island. Various Honolulu City and County street maps can be found at bookstores around the island. Perhaps the best and most detailed of the island maps is the University of Hawai'i Press reference map, *Map of O'ahu, The Gathering Place.* This map can also be found at gift and sundries shops around the island. Other useful and detailed maps of the island are the Rand McNally *O'ahu, Honolulu* map and the AAA *Honolulu Hawaii* map. If you are looking for detail, the best street map atlas of O'ahu is a spiral-bound publication by Phears

Mapbooks called *The O'ahu Mapbook*, also available at bookshops around the island. The **Waikiki Business Improvement District** (www.waikikibid.org) publishes a free detailed map of Waikiki with an entertainment calendar, important phone numbers, and a TheBus quick reference guide to major attractions. You can pick up a map at the police substation at Kuhio Beach Park or from one of the friendly aloha ambassadors that walk Waikiki's main drags solely to help visitors. They wear fluorescent yellow shirts, blue hats, and blue shorts.

MONEY AND FINANCES
Currency
Hawai'i uses U.S. **currency**. U.S. coinage in use is $0.01 (penny), $0.05 (nickel), $0.10 (dime), $0.25 (quarter), $0.50 (half dollar), and $1 (uncommon); paper currency is $1, $2 (uncommon), $5, $10, $20, $50, and $100. Bills larger than $100 are not in general circulation. Since 1996, new designs have been issued for the $100, $50, $20, $10, and $5 bills. Both the old and new bills are accepted as valid currency.

Banks
Full-service bank hours are generally Monday-Thursday 8:30am-4pm and Friday 8:30am-6pm. A few **banks** offer limited Saturday service, and weekday hours will be a bit longer at counters in grocery stores and other outlets. All main towns on O'ahu have one or more banks. Virtually all branch banks have automated teller machines (ATMs) for 24-hour service, and these can be found at some shopping centers and other venues around the island. ATMs work only when the Hawaiian bank you use is on an affiliate network with your home bank. Of most value to travelers, banks sell and cash traveler's checks, give cash advances on credit cards, and exchange and sell foreign currency (sometimes with a fee). Major banks on O'ahu are American Savings Bank, Bank of Hawaii, Central Pacific Bank, and First Hawaiian Bank; each has numerous branch offices throughout the island.

Traveler's Checks
Traveler's checks are accepted throughout Hawai'i at hotels, restaurants, rental car agencies, and in most stores and shops. However, to be readily acceptable they should be in U.S. currency. Some larger hotels that frequently have Japanese and Canadian guests will accept their currency. Banks accept foreign-currency traveler's checks, but it'll mean an extra trip and inconvenience. It's best to get most of your traveler's checks in $20 or $50 denominations, anything larger will be hard to cash in shops and boutiques, although not in hotels.

Credit Cards
More and more business is transacted in Hawai'i using credit cards. Almost every form of accommodation, shop, restaurant, and amusement accepts them. For renting a car, they're a must. With credit card insurance readily available, they're as safe as traveler's checks and even more convenient. Write down the numbers of your cards in case they're stolen, and keep the numbers separate from the wallet. Don't rely on credit cards completely because some establishments—some bed-and-breakfasts and small local eateries, for example—only accept cash.

Taxes
Hawai'i does not have a state sales tax, but it does have a general excise tax of 4.712 percent, which will be added to sales transactions and services. In addition, there is an accommodations tax of 9.25 percent, so approximately 14 percent will be added to your hotel bill when you check out.

COMMUNICATION AND MEDIA
Post Offices
There are more than a dozen post offices in Honolulu (800/275-8777) and one in each of the major towns on the island. The normal business hours for window service at many of these are Monday-Friday 9am-4:30pm and Saturday 9am-2pm, although some branch offices have slightly different hours.

The main post office in downtown Honolulu (335 Merchant St.), located next to the King Kamehameha statue, has window hours Monday-Friday 9am-4:30pm. The Waikiki branch (330 Saratoga Rd.) has window hours Monday-Friday 9am-4:30pm, Saturday 9am-1pm.

Telephone

The telephone system on Oʻahu is modern and comparable to any system on the mainland. For land lines, any phone call to a number on Oʻahu is a local call; it's long distance when dialing to another island (even though the area code for the entire state of Hawaiʻi is 808) or beyond the state. With standard long-distance service, long-distance rates go down at 5pm and again at 11pm until 8am the next morning. Rates are cheapest from Friday at 5pm until Monday at 8am. Many long-distance companies have moved to a flat rate per minute fee structure, however, so check with your accommodation. Local calls from public telephones cost $0.50. Emergency calls are always free. Public telephones are found at hotels, street booths, restaurants, most public buildings, and some beach parks. It is common to have a phone in most hotel rooms and condominiums, although a service charge is often collected, even on local calls. You can direct dial from Hawaiʻi to the mainland and more than 160 foreign countries. Undersea cables and satellite communications ensure top-quality phone service. Toll-free calls are preceded by 800, 888, 877, or 866; there is no charge to the calling party. Many are listed in this guide.

Cell phone reception is generally very good throughout the state of Hawaiʻi. However, as anywhere, you will find pockets where reception is poor or nonexistent.

For directory assistance, dial: 411 (local), 1-555-1212 (interisland), or 1-800/555-1212 (toll-free).

Newspapers

Besides special-interest Chinese, Japanese, Korean, Filipino, and military newspapers, Oʻahu has one major daily, the *Honolulu Star-Advertiser* (www.staradvertiser.com). It's $0.75 daily or $2 on Sunday. Other weekly or monthly free papers that you might encounter include *MidWeek* and the *North Shore News*.

Libraries

There are 24 public libraries on Oʻahu, and these include the **Hawaii State Library** (478 S. King St., 808/586-3500), located next to ʻIolani Palace in downtown Honolulu, and the **Library for the Blind and Physically Handicapped** (402 Kapahulu, 808/733-8444). Library cards are available for visitors and nonresidents for $25 (valid for five years), and $10 for up to three months. The library system offers numerous services, including Internet access and reference information (808/586-3621) during library hours. Business hours for each library differ, so check with the one you want to visit. Brochures listing hours and other general information are available at all libraries and online. For additional information, see the Hawaii State Public Library System website: www.librarieshawaii.org.

Radio

Oʻahu's radio stations are a true reflection of the culture, whether you're listening to news and talk radio, or local music. Here are a few stations to tune in when you're driving or in your hotel room:

- **KHPR 88.1 FM:** National Public Radio 1
- **KIPO 89.3 FM:** National Public Radio 2
- **KTUH 90.3 FM:** University of Hawaiʻi at Manoa student radio
- **KHCM 97.5:** Country music
- **KDNN 98.5 FM:** Island music (also available on iHeartRadio)
- **KCCN 100.3 FM:** Island music
- **KUCD 101.9 FM:** Modern rock
- **KINE 105.1 FM:** Hawaiian music
- **KPOI 105.9 FM:** Classic rock

LOCAL RESOURCES

Emergencies

For **police, fire, or ambulance** anywhere on O'ahu, dial **911**. For **nonemergency police** assistance and information, call 808/529-3111. In case of a natural disaster such as hurricanes or tsunamis on O'ahu, call the **Civil Defense** at 808/523-4121 or 808/733-4300. The **Coast Guard Search and Rescue** can be reached at 800/552-6458. The **Sex Abuse Treatment Center Hotline** is available at 808/524-7273 for cases involving sexual assault or rape crisis.

Weather, Marine Report, and Time of Day

For recorded information on local island **weather,** call 808/973-4381; for **marine** conditions phone 808/973-4382; and for the **surf report,** call 808/973-4383. For surf information on the Internet, check www.surfnewsnetwork.com or call 808/596-SURF. For time of day, call 808/643-8463.

Consumer Protection and Tourist Complaints

If you encounter problems with accommodations, bad service, or downright rip-offs, try the following: **Chamber of Commerce of Hawaii** (808/545-4300), **Office of Consumer Protection** (808/587-3222, www.hawaii.gov/dcca/ocp), or the **Better Business Bureau** (808/536-6956).

Auto Service

AAA (1130 Nimitz Hwy., Ste. A170, 808/736-2886, www.hawaii.aaa.com, 9am-5pm Mon.-Wed. and Fri., 9am-7pm Thurs., 9am-2pm Sat.) has an O'ahu office in the Nimitz Center, just west of Hilo Hattie. Stop here for maps, Triptik maps, the Hawaii Tourbook, and other AAA information and travel agency services. If you're a AAA member, call 800/222-4357 (808/AAA-HELP) for 24-hour roadside assistance.

Camping Permits

Camping permits for City and County of Honolulu managed campgrounds can be obtained through the Department of Parks and Recreation (DPR). Walk-in permits are available at the Frank Fasi Municipal Building (650 S. King St.) DPR Permits Office, or online at https://camping.honolulu.gov. For state-run campgrounds, reservations and permits are best obtained through the website, www.hawaiistateparks.org.

WEIGHTS AND MEASURES

Hawai'i, like all of the United States, employs the "English method" of measuring weights and distances. Basically, dry weights are in ounces and pounds; liquid measures are in ounces, quarts, and gallons; and distances are measured in inches, feet, yards, and miles. The metric system is known but is not in general use.

Electricity

The same electrical current is in use in Hawai'i as on the U.S. mainland and is uniform throughout the islands. The system functions on 110 volts, 60 cycles of alternating current (AC); type A (two-pin) and type B (three-pin) plugs are used. Appliances from Japan will work, but there is some danger of burnout, whereas those requiring the normal European current of 220 volts, as well as those using other types of plugs, will not work.

Time Zones

There is no daylight saving time in Hawai'i. When daylight saving time is not observed on the mainland, Hawai'i is two hours behind the West Coast, four hours behind the Midwest, five hours behind the East Coast.

Resources

Glossary

The following list provides a basic vocabulary of Hawaiian words in common usage that you are likely to see or hear. Becoming familiar with them is not a strict necessity, but knowing what they mean will definitely enhance your experience and make speaking with local people more congenial. Many islanders spice their speech with certain words. Feel free to use them when you feel comfortable. You might even discover some Hawaiian words that are so perfectly expressive they'll become regular parts of your vocabulary. Many Hawaiian words have been absorbed into the English language and are found in English dictionaries. The definitions given are not exhaustive, but are generally considered the most common.

'a'a: sharp, rough lava

'ae: yes

ahupua'a: pie-shaped land divisions running from mountain to sea

aikane: friend, buddy

'aina: land

akamai: smart, clever, wise

akua: a god, divine

akua lapu: ghost stories

akua li'i: literally, "little spirits"

alahe'e: native Hawaiian shrub

ali'i: a Hawaiian chief or noble

aloha: common greeting or word of parting meaning hello, good-bye, love, and welcome

'amakihi: yellow Hawaiian honeycreeper (type of bird)

ana: cave

anuenue: rainbow

ao: daylight

'a'ole: no

'apapane: native Hawaiian forest bird

'aumakua: a personal or family god, often an ancestral spirit

auwe: alas

'awa: plant found throughout Polynesia; a calming, mildly intoxicating drink is made from the root (also known as kava)

'elepaio: native Hawaiian forest bird

haku: crown lei

hala: leaf

halakahiki: pineapple

halau: longhouse, when used with hula it means school

hale: house or building

hale koa: military hotel in Waikiki

hana: work

hanai: literally means to feed; commonly used as a term for adopted parents or children (not in a formal or legal sense); a close relationship

haole: literally means no breath; used to describe foreigners or Caucasians

hapa: of mixed ethnicity

hapai: pregnant

hapu'u: native Hawaiian fern

he'e nalu: surfing

heiau: a sacred rock structure used as a temple to worship the gods

hili: to braid

holomu'u: an ankle-length dress that is much more fitted than a mu'umu'u, and often worn on formal occasions

hono: bay

honu: sea turtle

ho'oilo: traditional Hawaiian winter that began in November *ho'olaule'a:* a celebration, usually a party or gathering

ho'omalimali: sweet talk, flattery

huhu: angry, irritated

hui: a group of people or a meeting

hukilau: a shoreline fishing gathering where everyone helps to pull (*huki*) fish to shore in a huge net

hula: a native Hawaiian sacred dance

huli: to turn over; chicken on a rotisserie barbecue is called *huli huli* chicken

humuhumunukunukuapua'a: Hawaiian reef triggerfish

i'a: fish

'ie'ie: pandanus (plant) endemic to the Pacific Islands

'i'iwi: a red Hawaiian honeycreeper (type of bird)

'iliahi: native Hawaiian sandalwood tree

'ilima: shrub with yellow and orange blossoms

imu: an earthen oven

'inamona: condiment made from roasted kukui nut

ipo: sweetheart

ipu: gourd

kahako: a macron used to differentiate between short and long vowels in the Hawaiian language

kahili: a tall pole topped with feathers used by an *ali'i* to announce his or her presence

kahuna: priest, sorcerer, or doctor

kahuna 'ana'ana: black magic

kahuna lapa'au: ancient Hawaiian healer

kai: the sea

kala: the sun

kalo lo'i: taro growing in small ponds

kalua: roasted underground in an *imu*

kama 'aina: a child of the land; a longtime island resident of any ethnic background

kanaka: man or commoner; used to distinguish a Hawaiian from other races

kane: man

kapu: forbidden, taboo; keep out, do not touch

kau kau: slang for eating or food

kauwa: war

keiki: child or children

kiawe: algaroba tree from South America covered in long, sharp thorns commonly found in Hawai'i along the shoreline

koa: endemic Hawaiian tree

kokua: help

kolohe: rascal

kona: leeward side of any Hawaiian Island; a wind blowing from the south or west

konane: a traditional Hawaiian game similar to checkers

ko'olau: windward side of the island

ku'auhau: genealogy, lineage

kui: to string

kukui: candlenut tree; the Hawai'i state tree

kuleana: homesite; a person's right

Kumulipo: ancient Hawaiian genealogical chant that records the pantheon of gods, creation, and the beginning of humankind

kupua: demigods in Hawaiian mythology

kupuna: a grandparent or ancestor

lama: small- to medium-sized Hawaiian tree

lanai: veranda or porch

lani: sky or heavens

lau hala: the leaf (*lau*) of the pandanus (hala) tree; used often in mat and sail weaving

lei: a necklace or garland made of flowers, plants, shells, or nuts

limu: seaweed

lolo: crazy

lomi lomi: traditional Hawaiian massage

lua: the bathroom

luakini heiau: native Hawaiian place of worship where human and animal blood sacrifices were made

lu'au: a celebratory party thrown for birthdays, graduations, or other reasons to feast and enjoy music and dance

mahalo: thank you

mahele: division; the Great Mahele of 1848 broke up traditional common lands and enabled private ownership of property

mahina: moon

mahu: traditionally a third gender similar to a transvestite; today it refers to a gay man

maile: a fragrant vine used in lei making

maka'ainana: native Hawaiians that lived off the land

makai: toward the ocean

make: dead, deceased

malo: a traditional native Hawaiian loincloth

mamo: endemic Hawaiian bird that is now extinct

mana: supernatural or divine power, energy

manini: small, or frugal

manuahi: free, extra

mauka: toward the mountains

mauna: mountain

mele: a song or chant

Menehune: the legendary "little people" of Hawai'i said to possess magical powers

moa: chicken, fowl

moana: the ocean

moe: sleep

mo'o ali'i: genealogy of the chiefs; chiefly line of succession

mo'o kahuna: genealogy of succession of priests

mo'olelo: story, tale, myth

mua: man's eating house

mu'umu'u: an ankle-length dress with a high neckline made from aloha print fabric

nani: beautiful

naupaka: native Hawaiian shrub found at the beach and in the mountains

nui: big, large

'ohana: a family

'ohi'a: endemic Hawaiian tree with bottle-brush flowers

'ohi'a 'ahihi: tree with clusters of delicate red flowers

'okina: a unicameral consonant letter used to mark a glottal stop in the Hawaiian language

'okolehau: traditional fermented beverage made from *ti* root

oli: chant

olona: cord

'ono: delicious

'o'o: small Kauaian forest bird

'opihi: a limpet that clings to rocks and traditionally gathered as food

'opu: belly, stomach

pahoa: dagger

pahoehoe: smooth, ropy lava

pakalolo: marijuana

pake: a Chinese person; cheap

pali: a cliff

paniolo: a Hawaiian cowboy

pau: finished, done

pau hana: happy hour

pilau: stinky, a bad smell

pilikia: trouble, bad news

po: night, darkness; obscurity; the realm of the gods

poi: a glutinous paste made from the pounded corm of taro

poke: local Hawaiian dish with cubes of raw fish

pono: peaceful, righteous

pua: flower

pueo: Hawaiian owl

puka: a hole of any size

pupu: appetizer

pu'u: hill

tapa: a traditional paper cloth made from beaten tree bark

ti: a broad-leafed plant with red, green, and variegated leaves used for wrapping food and religious offerings

tutu: grandmother

ukulele: a small, guitar-like instrument with four strings

ulana: woven mats

wahine: woman

wai: water

wana: black spiny sea urchin

wauke: small paper mulberry tree

wela: hot

wiki: fast, quickly

wili: to wind, twist, or screw

wiliwili: native Hawaiian tree

Suggested Reading

O'ahu is the hub of a vibrant regional book publishing industry. Look for these top publishers: the **University of Hawai'I Press** (www.uhpress.hawaii.edu) has the best overall general list of titles on Hawai'i; the **Bishop Museum Press** (www.bishopmuseum.org/press) puts out many scholarly works on Hawaiiana, as does **Kamehameha Schools Press** (http://kspress.ksbe.edu); **Bess Press** (www.besspress.com), **Mutual Publishing** (www.mutualpublishing.com), **Island Heritage** (www.islandheritage.com), and **Watermark Publishing** (http://bookshawaii.net) all have general interest Hawaiiana books. In addition, a website specifically oriented toward books on Hawai'i, Hawaiian music, and other things Hawaiian is **Hawaii Books** (www.hawaiibooks.com).

ASTRONOMY

Rhoads, Samuel. *The Sky Tonight—A Guided Tour of the Stars over Hawaii.* Honolulu: Bishop Museum, 1993. This book has star charts for every month in Hawai'i.

COOKING

Beeman, Judy, and Martin Beeman. *Joys of Hawaiian Cooking.* Hilo, HI: Petroglyph Press, 1977. A collection of favorite recipes from Big Island chefs.

Choy, Sam. *Little Hawaiian Cookbook for Big Appetites.* Honolulu: Mutual Publishing, 2003. A collection of the famous chef's favorite recipes to execute in your kitchen.

Fukuda, Sachi. *Pupus, An Island Tradition.* Honolulu: Bess Press, 1995. A selection of tasty island appetizers.

Tuell, Bonnie. *Island Cooking.* Honolulu: Mutual Publishing, 1996. This cookbook has an array of island recipes including *pupu*, dinner, and desserts.

Wong, Allen. *New Wave Luau.* Berkeley: Ten Speed Press, 1999. Award-winning chef Alan Wong shares his wonderful Hawaiian food recipes.

CULTURE AND HISTORY

Barnes, Phil. *A Concise History of the Hawaiian Islands.* Hilo, HI: Petroglyph Press, 1999. An easy-to-read examination of the main currents of Hawaiian history and its major players, focusing on the important factors in shaping the social, economic, and political trends of the islands.

Buck, Peter. *Arts and Crafts of Hawaii.* Honolulu: Bishop Museum Press, 1957. The most definitive work on traditional Hawaiian crafts from household use to religious significance.

Cordy, Ross. *Exalted Sits the Chief.* Honolulu: Mutual Publishing, 2000. Cordy, a University of Hawai'i professor, offers wonderful insight into the formation of the Hawaiian culture and society up until the pre-contact period.

Daws, Gavan. *Shoal of Time, A History of the Hawaiian Islands.* Honolulu: University of Hawai'i Press, 1974. A highly readable history of Hawai'i dating from its discovery by the Western world to its acceptance as the 50th state.

Fuchs, Lawrence. *Hawaii Pono.* Honolulu: Bess Press, 1961. A detailed, scholarly work presenting an overview of Hawai'i's history based upon ethnic and sociological interpretations. Encompasses most socioethnological groups from native Hawaiians to modern entrepreneurs.

Handy, E. S., and Elizabeth Handy. *Native Planters in Old Hawaii.* Honolulu: Bishop

Museum Press, 1972. A superbly written, easily understood scholarly work on the intimate relationship of pre-contact Hawaiians and the land.

Ii, John Papa. *Fragments of Hawaiian History.* Honolulu: Bishop Museum, 1959. Hawai'i's history under Kamehameha I as told by a Hawaiian who actually experienced it.

Kamehameha Schools Press. *Life in Early Hawai'i: The Ahupua'a.* 3rd ed. Honolulu: Kamehameha Schools Press, 1994. Written for schoolchildren to give them a better understand the basic organization of old Hawaiian land use and its function, this slim volume is a good primer for people of any age who wish to understand this fundamental societal fixture.

Kirch, Patrick V. *Feathered Gods and Fishhooks: An Introduction to Hawaiian Archaeology and Prehistory.* Honolulu: University of Hawai'i Press, 1997. This scholarly, lavishly illustrated, yet very readable book gives new insight into the development of pre-contact Hawaiian civilization. It focuses on the sites and major settlements of old Hawai'i and chronicles the main cultural developments while weaving in the social climate that contributed to change.

Lili'uokalani. *Hawaii's Story by Hawaii's Queen,* reprint. Honolulu: Mutual Publishing, 1990. Originally written in 1898, this moving personal account explains Hawai'i's inevitable move from monarchy to U.S. Territory as witnessed by its last queen, Lili'uokalani.

McBride, L. R. *Practical Folk Medicine of Hawaii.* Hilo, HI: Petroglyph Press, 1975. An illustrated guide to Hawai'i's medicinal plants as used by the *kahuna lapa'au* (medical healers). Includes a thorough section on ailments, diagnosis, and the proper folk remedies. Illustrated by the author, a

renowned botanical researcher and former ranger at Hawai'i Volcanoes National Park.

Tayman, John. *The Colony.* New York: Scribner, 2006. An in-depth look and true story of how the fear of leprosy swept across Hawai'i and exiled many to Moloka'i.

ANIMALS

Fielding, Ann, and Ed Robinson. *An Underwater Guide to Hawai'i.* Honolulu: University of Hawai'i Press, 1987. The amazing array of marine life found throughout the archipelago is captured in glossy photos with accompanying informative text and reference guide.

Hawaiian Audubon Society. *Hawaii's Birds.* 5th ed. Honolulu: Hawaii Audubon Society, 1997. Excellent bird book giving description, range, voice, and habits of the more than 100 species. Slim volume; good for carrying while hiking.

Hobson, Edmund, and E. H. Chave. *Hawaiian Reef Animals.* Honolulu: University of Hawai'i Press, 1987. Colorful photos and descriptions of the fish, invertebrates, turtles, and seals that call Hawaiian reefs their home.

Kay, Alison, and Olive Schoenberg-Dole. *Shells of Hawai'i.* Honolulu: University of Hawai'i Press, 1991. Color photos and tips on where to look.

Mahaney, Casey. *Hawaiian Reef Fish, The Identification Book.* Planet Ocean Publishing, 1993. A spiral-bound reference work featuring many color photos and descriptions of common reef fish found in Hawaiian waters.

Pratt, Douglas. *A Field Guide to the Birds of Hawaii and the Tropical Pacific.* Princeton, NJ: Princeton University Press, 1987. Useful field guide for novice and expert bird-watchers covering Hawai'i as well as other Pacific Island groups.

Pratt, Douglas. *A Pocket Guide to Hawaii's Birds.* Honolulu: Mutual Publishing, 1996. A condensed version of Pratt's larger work with a focus on bird's of the state.

Tomich, P. Quentin. *Mammals in Hawai'i.* Honolulu: Bishop Museum Press, 1986. Quintessential scholarly text on all mammal species in Hawai'i with description of distribution and historical references; lengthy bibliography.

PLANTS

Kepler, Angela. *Hawaiian Heritage Plants.* Honolulu: University of Hawai'i Press, 1998. A treatise on 32 utilitarian plants used by the early Hawaiians.

Miyano, Leland. *A Pocket Guide to Hawai'i's Flowers.* Honolulu: Mutual Publishing, 2001. A small guide to flowers readily seen in the state. Good for the backpack or back pocket.

Pratt, Douglas H. *A Pocket Guide to Hawai'i's Trees and Shrubs.* Honolulu: Mutual Publishing, 1998. A great trailside companion for identifying native and common trees and shrubs.

Sohmer, S. H., and R. Gustafson. *Plants and Flowers of Hawai'i.* Honolulu: University of Hawai'i Press, 1987. The authors cover the vegetation zones of Hawai'i, from mountains to coast, introducing the wide and varied floral biology of the islands with a history of the evolution of Hawaiian plantlife.

Wagner, Warren L., Derral R. Herbst, and H. S. Sohner. *Manual of the Flowering Plants of Hawai'i,* revised edition, vol. 2. Honolulu: University of Hawai'i Press in association with Bishop Museum Press, 1999. Considered the bible of Hawai'i's botanical world.

Whitton, Kevin. *A Pocket Guide to Hawai'i's Botanical Gardens.* Honolulu: Mutual Publishing, 2009. A colorful and informative guide to 35 botanical gardens across the state.

Valier, Kathy. *Ferns of Hawaii.* Honolulu: University of Hawai'i Press, 1995. One of the few books to treat the state's ferns as a single subject.

LANGUAGE

Pukui, Mary Kawena, and Samuel Elbert. *Hawaiian Dictionary.* Honolulu: University of Hawai'i Press, 1986. The best dictionary available on the Hawaiian language. The *Pocket Hawaiian Dictionary* is a less expensive, condensed version of this dictionary and adequate for most travelers with a general interest in the language.

Pukui, Mary Kawena, Samuel Elbert, and Esther T. Mookini. *Place Names of Hawaii.* Honolulu: University of Hawai'i Press, 1974. The most current and comprehensive listing of Hawaiian and foreign place-names in the state, giving pronunciation, spelling, meaning, and location.

Schutz, Albert J. *All About Hawaiian.* Honolulu: University of Hawai'i Press, 1995. A brief primer on Hawaiian pronunciation, grammar, and vocabulary.

MYTHOLOGY, LEGEND, AND LITERATURE

Beckwith, Martha. *Hawaiian Mythology.* reprint. Honolulu: University of Hawai'i Press, 1976. Over 60 years after its original printing in 1940, this work remains the definitive text on Hawaiian mythology. If you are only going to read one book on Hawaii's folklore, this should be it.

Beckwith, Martha. *The Kumulipo.* reprint. Honolulu: University of Hawai'i Press, 1972. Translation of the Hawaiian creation chant, originally published in 1951.

Kalakaua, His Hawaiian Majesty, King David. *The Legends and Myths of Hawaii*. Edited by R. M. Daggett, with a foreword by Glen Grant. Honolulu: Mutual Publishing, 1990. Originally published in 1888, in this volume Hawai'i's own King Kalakaua draws upon his scholarly and formidable knowledge of the classic oral tradition to bring alive ancient tales from pre-contact Hawai'i.

Melville, Leinanai. *Children of the Rainbow.* Wheaton, IL: Theosophical Publishing, 1969. A book on higher spiritual consciousness attuned to nature, which was the basic belief of pre-Christian Hawai'i. The appendix contains illustrations of mystical symbols used by the *kahuna.*

Pukui, Mary Kawena, and Caroline Curtis. *Hawaii Island Legends*. Honolulu: The Kamehameha Schools Press, 1996. Hawaiian tales and legends for preteens.

Pukui, Mary Kawena, and Caroline Curtis. *Tales of the Menehune*. Honolulu: The Kamehameha Schools Press, 1960. Compilation of legends relating to Hawai'i's "little people."

NATURAL SCIENCES AND GEOGRAPHY

Clark, John. *Beaches of O'ahu*. Honolulu: University of Hawai'i Press, 1997. Definitive guide to beaches, including many off the beaten path with maps and black-and-white photos.

Hubbard, Douglass, and Gordon Macdonald. *Volcanoes of the National Parks of Hawaii*. reprint. Volcanoes, HI: Hawaii Natural History Association, 1989. Details the volcanology of Hawai'i by documenting the major lava flows and their geological effect on the state.

Macdonald, Gorden, Agatin Abbott, and Frank Peterson. *Volcanoes in the Sea, The Geology of Hawaii*. Honolulu: University of Hawai'i Press, 1983. The best reference to

Hawaiian geology. Well explained for easy understanding; illustrated.

Ziegler, Alan C., *Hawaiian Natural History, Ecology, and Evolution*. Honolulu: University of Hawai'i Press, 2002. An overview of Hawaiian natural history with a treatment of ecology and evolution in that process.

SPORTS AND RECREATION

Alford, John, D. *Mountain Biking the Hawaiian Islands*. Ohana Publishing, 1997. A good off-road biking guide to the main Hawaiian islands.

Ambrose, Greg. *Surfer's Guide to Hawai'i*. Honolulu: Bess Press, 1991. Island-by-island guide to surfing spots.

Ball, Stuart. *The Hiker's Guide to O'ahu*. Honolulu: University of Hawai'i Press, 2000. This excellent guide includes hikes across O'ahu with topo maps and detailed directions.

Finney, Ben, and James D. Houston. *Surfing, A History of the Ancient Hawaiian Sport*. Los Angeles: Pomegranate, 1996. Features many early etchings and old photos of Hawaiian surfers practicing their native sport.

McMahon, Richard. *Camping Hawai'i: A Complete Guide*. Honolulu: University of Hawai'i Press, 1997. This book has all you need to know about camping in Hawai'i, with descriptions of different campsites.

Morey, Kathy. *Oahu Trails*. Berkeley, CA: Wilderness Press, 2003. Morey's book is complete with useful maps, historical references, official procedures, and plants and animals encountered along the way.

Sutherland, Audrey. *Paddling Hawai'i*, revised edition. Honolulu: University of Hawai'i Press, 1998. All you need to know about sea kayaking in Hawaiian waters.

Internet Resources

GOVERNMENT

City and County of Honolulu
www.honolulu.gov
The official website of the City and County of Honolulu. Includes information on city government, county data access, visitor information, and information on business and economic development.

Department of Park & Recreation
www1.honolulu.gov/parks
Resource for city and county camping information, obtaining permits, park and trail closures, beach access, and park rules and regulations.

Honolulu International Airport
http://hawaii.gov/hnl
The official website has all the information you need to successfully navigate the Honolulu International Airport.

State of Hawai'i
www.hawaii.gov
The official website for the state with comprehensive information covering government organizations, health, business, and many other services.

TOURISM

Alternative Hawaii
www.alternative-hawaii.com
A source for the path less traveled, ecofriendly general information, and links to specific businesses, with some cultural, historical, and events information.

Best Places Hawaii
www.bestplaceshawaii.com
This site has general and specific information about all major Hawaiian islands, a vacation planner, and suggestions for things to do and places to see, eat, and stay.

Hawaii Ecotourism Association
www.hawaiiecotourism.org
Official Hawaii Ecotourism Association website with information on traveling in Hawai'i, activities, and links to member organizations and related ecotourism groups.

Hawai'i State Foundation on Culture and the Arts
www.state.hi.us/sfca
This site features a calendar of arts and cultural events, activities, and programs held throughout the state.

Hawaii Visitor and Convention Bureau
www.gohawaii.com
The official site of the Hawaii Visitors and Convention Bureau, the state-run tourism organization, has information about all the major Hawaiian islands: transportation, accommodations, eating, activities, shopping, Hawaiian products, an events calendar, a travel planner, and a resource guide for a host of topics, as well as information about conventions.

Hawaiian Music Island
www.mele.com
This is one of the largest music websites to focus on Hawaiian music, books, and videos. It features Hawaiian music culture, concert schedules, Hawaiian music awards, and links to music companies and musicians.

Index

List of Maps

Also Available

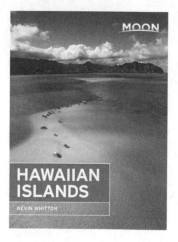

MAP SYMBOLS

Expressway	○	City/Town	✈	Airport	⚓	Golf Course
Primary Road	◉	State Capital	✗	Airfield	P	Parking Area
Secondary Road	⊛	National Capital	▲	Mountain	≜	Archaeological Site
Unpaved Road	★	Point of Interest	✛	Unique Natural Feature	⛪	Church
Feature Trail						Gas Station
Other Trail	●	Accommodation	🌊	Waterfall		Glacier
Ferry	▼	Restaurant/Bar	▲	Park		Mangrove
Pedestrian Walkway	■	Other Location	ⓘ	Trailhead		Reef
Stairs	▲	Campground	🎿	Skiing Area		Swamp

CONVERSION TABLES

°C = (°F - 32) / 1.8
°F = (°C x 1.8) + 32
1 inch = 2.54 centimeters (cm)
1 foot = 0.304 meters (m)
1 yard = 0.914 meters
1 mile = 1.6093 kilometers (km)
1 km = 0.6214 miles
1 fathom = 1.8288 m
1 chain = 20.1168 m
1 furlong = 201.168 m
1 acre = 0.4047 hectares
1 sq km = 100 hectares
1 sq mile = 2.59 square km
1 ounce = 28.35 grams
1 pound = 0.4536 kilograms
1 short ton = 0.90718 metric ton
1 short ton = 2,000 pounds
1 long ton = 1.016 metric tons
1 long ton = 2,240 pounds
1 metric ton = 1,000 kilograms
1 quart = 0.94635 liters
1 US gallon = 3.7854 liters
1 Imperial gallon = 4.5459 liters
1 nautical mile = 1.852 km

°FAHRENHEIT / °CELSIUS

°FAHRENHEIT	°CELSIUS	
230	110	
220		
210	100	WATER BOILS
200		
190	90	
180	80	
170		
160	70	
150		
140	60	
130		
120	50	
110		
100	40	
90		
80	30	
70	20	
60		
50	10	
40		
30	0	WATER FREEZES
20		
10	-10	
0		
-10	-20	
-20	-30	
-30		
-40	-40	

INCH 0   1   2   3   4

CM 0 1 2 3 4 5 6 7 8 9 10

MOON HONOLULU & O'AHU

Avalon Travel
An imprint of Perseus Books
A Hachette Book Group company
1700 Fourth Street
Berkeley, CA 94710, USA
www.moon.com

Editor: Kimberly Ehart
Series Manager: Kathryn Ettinger
Copy Editor: Rosemarie Leenerts
Graphics and Production Coordinator:
  Lucie Ericksen
Cover Design: Faceout Studios, Charles Brock
Interior Design: Domini Dragoone
Moon Logo: Tim McGrath
Map Editor: Mike Morgenfeld
Cartographers: Karin Dahl, Mike Morgenfeld
Indexer: Greg Jewett

ISBN-13: 978-1-63121-387-8
ISSN: 1534-0511

Printing History
1st Edition — 1990
8th Edition — October 2016
5 4 3 2 1